THE SUPREME COURT

AND THE

Judicial Function

T0308971

THE SUPREME COURT

AND THE

Judicial Function

Edited by

PHILIP B. KURLAND

THE UNIVERSITY OF CHICAGO PRESS

CHICAGO AND LONDON

THE UNIVERSITY OF CHICAGO PRESS, CHICAGO 60637
THE UNIVERSITY OF CHICAGO PRESS, LTD., LONDON

ISBN: 0-226-46401-6

To the memory of

ALEXANDER M. BICKEL,

Who will remain, for decades to come,
the primary source of wisdom and tolerance
for those who would evaluate the proper
role of the Supreme Court of the United
States in the American polity. The loss to
the world of scholarship is exceeded only
by the personal loss to his family and
friends, for there are other scholars in
the field, if not so competent, but there
is nothing to replace his
love and affection.

CONTENTS

PREFACE

In 1967, with the exaggeration that was not untypical of him, Adolph Berle announced: "Ultimate legislative power in the United States has come to rest in the Supreme Court of the United States." He was not disturbed or alarmed by this notion. He applauded it. For, to him, the Supreme Court, at least since 1954, had displayed greater wisdom and judgment than the other branches of government and should, therefore, exercise that power which our other institutions of government had eschewed.

Berle failed to take into account certain factors that he chose not to see. The fact was then and is now that the ultimate legislative power in the United States resides not in the judicial branch but in the executive branch of the national government. And the probable cause of this result is that, however grand the authority of the Supreme Court, it has lacked the capacities for administering such laws as it has promulgated. Thus, it was deficient in exactly the same way that the body charged by the American Constitution as the "ultimate legislative power," the Congress, was deficient. And the Court is deficient in still another way in which Congress is deficient. The former by necessity, the latter by choice has lacked the capacity to secure the data on the basis of which well-framed and executed laws are created. The consequence is that both Congress and the courts are left either to very narrow legislation, as where the courts do no more than resolve disputes between individuals, and where Congress passes private bills, or to overbroad and therefore less effective rules, as where Congress grandly defines a problem and simply appropriates money for the executive to solve the problem according to its own standards, or where the Court declares that segregation is unconstitutional and then must await decades before the doctrine is a rule of fact as well as a rule of law.

The limitations on the legislative authority of Congress are manifold. So, too, with the Court. But there is one principal difficulty with assumption by the Court of legislative hegemony and that is the nature and way that it carries on its business.

The Supreme Court of the United States, however political

its nature may be, still operates as a court of law. This means, among other things: (1) that it relies on the adversary process to determine the issues that it will resolve and to secure the information on which to frame its judgments; (2) that the common law process followed by the Court rests heavily on the notion of stare decisis, and (3) that the judicial power was confined by Article III to the resolution of "cases and controversies"; it remained for the Court to broaden that concept far beyond its original meaning, with the acquiescence—nay the encouragement —of the other branches of government.

In the pages of this volume, the authors are concerned with the continued effect of the case and controversy notion—including the role of precedent—on the behavior of the Court. They reveal both the limitations and the strengths that derive from the procedural forms, which may or may not be self-imposed limitations and self-created powers, in the administration of the laws that Berle calls "ultimate legislative power."

Perhaps these articles should be read in the light of Berle's own ruminations. His little book *Three Faces of Power* opened with the hyperbole quoted at the beginning of these remarks. He closed that slim but tantalizing volume with more sober observations about the danger of such accession to power.

> The danger is that they constitute the Supreme Court a variety of benevolent dictator.
>
> Acquiescent acceptance of benevolent dictatorship in time deadens the public to its responsibility for apprehending needs and dangers and demanding that their elected executives and legislators take appropriate measures. As John Stuart Mill observed, it compromises the future. Nonacceptance, on the other hand, piles up political pressures focused against the institution itself. Judicial legislation is not a substitute for political and legislative institutional processes. The will of the most enlightened Court is not the same as the will of the elected representatives of the people, and may cease to be the will of the people itself. Acceptance of its mandates based on respect for the Court is not the same as acceptance of laws commanding popular assent after political debate.

PHILIP B. KURLAND

KENNETH L. KARST

LEGISLATIVE FACTS IN

CONSTITUTIONAL

LITIGATION

Judges make constitutional law as they make other kinds of law, on the basis of facts proved and assumed. They are likely to do a better job when their assumptions rest on information rather than hunch. Such a proposition—itself an assumption beyond proof—is hardly earth-shaking. Recognition of this proposition, however, does offer hope for escaping some of the dilemmas posed by the current multisided debate over the judiciary's role in constitutional development. Whatever a judge's persuasion, he can decide a particular constitutional issue only by appraising the factual basis for governmental action. Today's constitutional litigation demands fact analysis of the most particularized kind, with the most careful identification of the interests that deserve constitutional protection, both for the purpose of deciding cases and for the purpose of explaining them in opinions. The broad generalization[1] and the unconsidered[2] or unexplained[3] deci-

Kenneth L. Karst is Associate Professor of Law, The Ohio State University.

Author's Acknowledgment: A number of my colleagues have read drafts of this article, to my great profit. I am especially indebted to Professor Vaughn C. Ball for his criticisms and his cheerful endurance of many conversations on the subject.

[1] See, *e.g.*, Watkins v. United States, 354 U.S. 178 (1957).

[2] See Brown, *Process of Law* (foreword to *The Supreme Court, 1957 Term*), 72 HARV. L. REV. 77, 93–95 (1958).

[3] See, *e.g.*, Gayle v. Browder, 352 U.S. 903 (1956).

sion tend to substitute judicial fiat not only for the rule of a democratic majority but also for the rule of law.[4]

The urgency of the need for particularization arises out of the rapidity of contemporary social, technological, political, and economic changes which require the courts to uncover and delineate in a short period of time many new interests worthy of constitutional protection. It is not an exaggeration to say that the survival of a system of limited government depends on the continued success of the judiciary in performing this legislative function.

That the function is essentially legislative in character no one now disputes. The experience of eighty years has served to confirm that

> in substance the growth of the law is legislative. And this in a deeper sense than that what the courts declare to have always been the law is in fact new. It is legislative in its grounds. The very considerations which judges most rarely mention, and always with an apology, are the secret root from which the law draws all the juices of life. I mean, of course, considerations of what is expedient for the community concerned.[5]

Holmes was not writing about the Constitution in particular; his concern was with the growth of law generally. Yet the common-law tradition of which he wrote provides the essence of our constitutional development.[6] When protected interests are identified and nourished case by case, there is less need for speculation on the possible impact of the challenged governmental action. Rather the judges can ask, "How has this law operated?" and they can use the experience of the parties before them as a starting point for their inquiry.[7]

Courts are at their best when they deal with such highly particularized questions. Indeed, one principal justification for giving the independent review of legislation to the judiciary lies in the ability of a court to weigh constitutional claims on the basis of experience

---

[4] See Wechsler, *Toward Neutral Principles of Constitutional Law*, 73 HARV. L. REV. 1 (1959).

[5] HOLMES, THE COMMON LAW 35 (1881).

[6] See Stone, *The Common Law in the United States*, 50 HARV. L. REV. 4, 21–25 (1936); LEVI, AN INTRODUCTION TO LEGAL REASONING 41 ff. (1949).

[7] Many of the Supreme Court's rules of self-limitation are traceable to the need to avoid "premature interpretations of statutes in areas where their constitutional application might be cloudy." United States v. Raines, 362 U.S. 17, 22 (1960). See Frankfurter, *A Note on Advisory Opinions*, 37 HARV. L. REV. 1002 (1924); *cf.* Note, *Advisory Opinions on the Constitutionality of Statutes*, 69 HARV. L. REV. 1302 (1956).

which was not available when the legislature acted.[8] Nevertheless, when a court makes law, including constitutional law, it must attempt to decide not only the case before it but also a great many similar "cases" not in court. Uncomfortable as a court may be beyond the area of its special competence, the court's legislative function requires it to be informed on matters far beyond the facts of the particular case. These "legislative facts"[9] of broader application need illumination so that the court[10] can make the best possible prediction of the effects of its decision.

Of course the facts concerning the parties before the court—the "adjudicative facts," as recent fashion would have it—may be important as demonstrations of the general effects of the governmental action. Thus many adjudicative facts are also legislative facts in that they bear on the legislative question of the reasonableness, or constitutionality, of governmental action. The adjudicative facts may even carry a disproportionately heavy weight as legislative facts just because a court is more at home in dealing with facts concerning the immediate parties.[11] Wherever the legislative facts are to be found, a court which examines closely the concrete elements of the factual context of governmental action improves its chances for success in discovering and defining interests of constitutional significance.

I. THE CASE FOR PARTICULARITY: ABSOLUTISTS V. BALANCERS

In a recent case the Supreme Court considered the power of the State of Illinois to require the use of a new kind of contour mudguard by interstate trucks operating on its highways.[12] At the trial, both the challenging truckers and the state produced experts who tes-

---

[8] See HART & WECHSLER, THE FEDERAL COURTS AND THE FEDERAL SYSTEM 77–79, 93 (1953).

[9] The phrase virtually belongs to Professor Kenneth C. Davis, whose valuable thoughts on the subject are now contained in chapter 15 of his ADMINISTRATIVE LAW TREATISE (1958), particularly at § 15.03.

[10] We are here concerned with court-made law rather than that made by administrative agencies. For an exploration of the special problems faced by the agencies, see 2 DAVIS, op. cit. supra note 9, at 377–84, 400–31.

[11] See Brown, *The Open Economy: Justice Frankfurter and the Position of the Judiciary*, 67 YALE L. J. 219, 224 (1957).

[12] Bibb v. Navajo Freight Lines, 359 U.S. 520 (1959).

tified as to the comparative effectiveness of the contour mudguards
and the old-style flap guards, and as to the operational costs of compliance with the regulation. The ultimate question for the trial court
and for the Supreme Court was understood by everyone connected
with the case: How much more effective must the new guard be to
justify a cost of $30 per truck, as well as the attendant operational
inconvenience and loss of business, in light of the fact that other states
permit the use of the old-style guards? There was no protest by counsel or by any of the judges that the ultimate issue could be decided
only by balancing incommensurables. Both courts faced up without a
murmur to a detailed evaluation of a complicated record of legislative
facts. The Supreme Court's solution followed from its agreement
with the lower court's finding that the new mudguard afforded no
greater safety than the old. Thus, with a near-zero quantity on one
side of the balance, the burden on commerce controlled the decision.

Mr. Justice Douglas, writing for the Court, concluded by commenting that "We deal not with absolutes but with questions of degree."[13] Thus he summarized in a single sentence the need for particular identification and careful weighing of the values that compete
for judicial attention. In the commerce cases—those dealing with
state regulation of commerce—just such a balancing process has been
in use for at least 130 years,[14] and has been recognized frankly
throughout our century. Although some of the justices have been reluctant,[15] they now appear to be unanimous in accepting the necessity
of weighing the factual justification of state regulation. The division
in the present Court rather concerns the proper approach to questions
about the fundamental guarantees of liberty and equality. To use Professor Freund's formulation, should we adopt different judicial approaches for the market place of ideas and the market place of goods?[16]

The dispute between the so-called balancers and absolutists only
obscures our understanding of the problems of constitutional litigation: it focuses on an issue which is unreal. The very justices who
assert that the prohibitions in the Bill of Rights are absolute, brooking

---

[13] *Id.* at 530.

[14] At least since Willson v. Black-Bird Creek Marsh Co., 2 Pet. 245 (1829). See
FRANKFURTER, THE COMMERCE CLAUSE 27–34 (1936).

[15] See Mr. Justice Black, concurring, in Morgan v. Virginia, 328 U.S. 373, 386 (1946).

[16] Freund, *Competing Freedoms in American Constitutional Law*, in UNIVERSITY OF CHI-
CAGO LAW SCHOOL, CONFERENCE ON FREEDOM AND THE LAW 26 (1953).

no restriction of the freedoms they protect,[17] have in fact voted to restrict the same freedoms on more than one occasion. A favorite judicial technique in such cases has been to define one's absolute so that its protective scope does not cover the interests before the Court. Thus, "fighting words" are not protected speech;[18] the First Amendment does not protect "business practices condemned by the Sherman Act";[19] commercial leaflets may be restricted where political tracts may not;[20] and public money may be spent on transportation of children to parochial schools.[21] Some absolutes are thus equipped with elastic boundaries. In another class of cases the same justices have upheld the restriction of liberties that are unquestionably protected in the absence of some overriding justification for limiting them. Thus, a religious organization can be required to get a license and pay a fee before it holds a parade that blocks traffic;[22] an aunt may be punished for permitting her nine-year-old niece to endanger her health by selling religious magazines in the streets;[23] peaceful picketing may be enjoined if it is "an integral part of conduct in violation of a valid criminal statute";[24] and, worst of all, perhaps, thousands of devoted citizens may be uprooted from their homes and imprisoned because of military necessity as determined by a military officer if his decision is affirmed by the Commander in Chief.[25] These are absolutes which are absolute only sometimes.

All judges balance competing interests in deciding constitutional questions—even those who most vigorously deny their willingness to

---

[17] *E.g.*, Mr. Justice Black, dissenting, in Barenblatt v. United States, 360 U.S. 109, 134, 141 (1959): "I do not agree that laws directly abridging First Amendment freedoms can be justified by a congressional or judicial balancing process." See also Black, *The Bill of Rights*, 35 N.Y.U.L. REV. 865 (1960).

[18] Chaplinsky v. New Hampshire, 315 U.S. 568 (1942).

[19] Associated Press v. United States, 326 U.S. 1, 7 (1945).

[20] Valentine v. Chrestensen, 316 U.S. 52 (1942). Mr. Justice Douglas has had second thoughts on this question. See his concurrence in Cammarano v. United States, 358 U.S. 498, 513–14 (1959).

[21] "The First Amendment has erected a wall between church and state. That wall must be kept high and impregnable. We could not approve the slightest breach. New Jersey has not breached it here." Everson v. Board of Education, 330 U.S. 1, 18 (1947).

[22] Cox v. New Hampshire, 312 U.S. 569 (1941).

[23] Prince v. Massachusetts, 321 U.S. 158 (1944).

[24] Giboney v. Empire Storage & Ice Co., 336 U.S. 490, 498 (1949).

[25] Korematsu v. United States, 323 U.S. 214 (1944).

do so. But may there be some value in talking about absolute standards in opinions? One argument runs this way: A judge who frequently strikes his balance in favor of individual freedoms may find such talk useful. If he can seem to draw his decisions not from his own evaluation of competing interests but rather from an impersonal absolute, he may be able to resist legislative encroachments on liberty more effectively. In short, a decision that seems more judicial and less legislative may find greater public acceptance.

The difficulty with the argument is that to remove candor from one's description of the decisional process is to strike at the heart of the rule of law. Any tendency to treat constitutional issues on the basis of personal reactions is heightened by a refusal to identify the interests which motivate decisions.[26] Hiding these motivations reduces to a considerable degree the opportunity for the public to evaluate the performance of the judiciary and to participate in the process of mutual education which is so essential to the success of a system of judicial review in a democracy.[27] Like some judges of the Thirties who also pretended to be compelled by absolute standards, the latter-day absolutists risk the independence of the judiciary by denying their basic judicial responsibility, which is to exercise judgment.

A second argument for pretending to rely on absolutes in opinions is that the interests which the balancers would weigh are difficult to measure.[28] "Values and sacrifices are incommensurables. . . . We say that we 'weigh' our joys and sorrows when we choose between them, but that is a metaphor expressing our sense of inner tension, for choice, at least in the universe of desire, is as immediate, absolute and underived as are its component values and sacrifices."[29] Judge Hand's solution, of course, was hardly the adoption of constitutional absolutes. Rather he chose to abandon responsibility at the other extreme by leaving a far greater measure of the ultimate decision-making power to elected legislatures. The Supreme Court will cease to make

---

[26] See Wechsler, *supra* note 4.

[27] See Rostow, *The Democratic Character of Judicial Review*, 66 HARV. L. REV. 193, 208 (1952); FREUND, ON UNDERSTANDING THE SUPREME COURT 73–74 (1949).

[28] "What is the standard by which one can determine when abridgment of speech and press goes 'too far' and when it is slight enough to be constitutionally allowable?" Mr. Justice Black, concurring, in Smith v. California, 361 U.S. 147, 157 (1959).

[29] HAND, THE BILL OF RIGHTS 38 (1958).

such choices based on measurement of incommensurables, however, only when it renounces its historic responsibility.

There is another aspect of this second argument that is more persuasive. Some of the interests to be balanced may be not simply hard to measure but hard to identify. This difficulty has plagued some justices who are quite devoted to the balancing process in most areas. Thus Mr. Justice Frankfurter's opinions have abandoned balancing in favor of rather inarticulate formulas in a number of state taxation cases. Following the dialectical lead of Mr. Justice Brandeis,[30] he has given protection to the free flow of goods within a national economic unit by striking down state taxes characterized as "direct" taxes on interstate commerce.[31] But as Professor Brown has so compellingly shown, even the interests at stake in these recent cases can be made articulate with patient effort.[32] The fact is that there are no interests worthy of constitutional protection which are at the same time beyond description. Of course, as social forces create new problems, new interests will appear at first only indistinctly. But it should be the special task of the courts to make an effort to define those interests so that they can be served effectively. Indeed, the articulation of the interests may be an even more important function for the courts than the balancing process itself. Once the interests are identified, the public has ways of assuring that the proper weights are assigned.

Whatever one's taste in opinions may be, it is plain that a judge cannot successfully balance interests, of constitutional or other dimensions, without information as to the probable effects of his decision. It is equally certain that one who seeks to further the influence of a constitutional absolute needs to know how his absolute relates to the cases before him. There is thus a middle ground. Regardless of the label one assigns to himself, he can agree on the need for close examination of the legislative facts. When all judges make that commitment, the verbal shell of the absolutes-against-balancing dispute should collapse for want of inner substance.

---

[30] See BICKEL, THE UNPUBLISHED OPINIONS OF MR. JUSTICE BRANDEIS 115–18 (1957).

[31] *E.g.*, Freeman v. Hewit, 329 U.S. 249 (1946). See Jaffe, *The Judicial Universe of Mr. Justice Frankfurter*, 62 HARV. L. REV. 357, 390–95 (1949).

[32] Brown, *supra* note 11. See also Barrett, *"Substance" vs. "Form" in the Application of the Commerce Clause to State Taxation*, 101 U. PA. L. REV. 740 (1953).

II. The Issues To Be Illuminated

Nor should the search for particulars be abandoned in civil liberties cases. Suppose, for example, that in a collision between a car and a truck the occupants of the car are killed and the truck driver is knocked unconscious. The police find a nearly empty whiskey bottle in the glove compartment and smell liquor on the truck driver's breath. While he is still unconscious they have a doctor take a sample of his blood by the safest and most modern means. When the truck driver is prosecuted for manslaughter, the state seeks to introduce the results of the blood-alcohol test as evidence of his drunkenness. The judge must rule on the defendant's constitutional argument that the taking of the blood sample was so fundamentally unfair that using the evidence would deprive him of due process of law.

What are the questions of legislative fact? First of all, how serious is the invasion of the accused's person? The test was made in the same manner as other blood tests which have become common features of physical examinations. The test did not endanger the defendant's health, although it now endangers his freedom. But one of the strongest traditions of our law has been the inviolability of a man's person. We should not lightly assume that a government official has the right to take a person's blood.

The next question is: What is the purpose of this invasion of the body? The police were gathering evidence to be used in the possible prosecution of the defendant for the very crime of which he now stands accused. It can hardly be argued that these are not legitimate objectives for men whose public duty it is to enforce the law. But how effectively will the blood test fulfill this purpose? Such tests are almost universally well regarded for their reliability in detecting the percentage of alcohol in the blood stream. Furthermore, there is widespread scientific agreement that, while individuals differ in their tolerance of alcohol, all persons are seriously impaired in their response to outside stimuli and their muscular control after a certain critical blood-alcohol percentage is passed.[33] Thus the test is likely to be effective in achieving its intended purpose.

Still we need to know whether there was available to the police

---

[33] See Slough & Wilson, *Alcohol and the Motorist: Practical and Legal Problems of Chemical Testing*, 44 MINN. L. REV. 673, 675–84 (1960); *cf.* McCoid, *Intoxication and Its Effect upon Civil Responsibility*, 42 IOWA L. REV. 38 (1956).

some alternative way of achieving those same good purposes without causing the same impact on the individual's liberty. To be more specific, was there any other way open to the police to get evidence of the defendant's drunkenness without invading his person in this way? The policemen might have been able to find out how much liquor the defendant had consumed, but that would have required them to gamble on asking him later or finding someone else who could tell them. The policemen might also testify that the defendant smelled of liquor, or that his speech was thick when he awoke, or that he could not walk a straight line; most of this testimony would depend on getting the man to awaken in order to be tested. None of these methods is nearly so effective as taking the blood sample. So the means chosen by the police to achieve their objective do not seem unreasonable in themselves. But suppose it could be shown that the police were equipped—or could have been equipped—with some device like a "drunkometer" balloon which could have been used on an unconscious man. Would that be enough to change the decision?

This hypothetical case is a modified version of a real one, in which the Supreme Court upheld the validity of a New Mexico conviction based on the evidence of such a test.[34] It is discouraging that neither in the New Mexico court's opinion nor in the briefs of counsel were these considerations of legislative fact effectively discussed, and even the Supreme Court gave them the most hurried treatment in the most general terms. There is no need to conclude that the case was decided wrongly, but it should be suggested that on this occasion the legal profession, both on and off the bench, groped its way to a conclusion largely on the basis of hunch.

The legislative facts which should have been (and perhaps were) decisive of the blood test case may look rather different from those which determined the outcome of the Illinois mudguard case, but the ultimate questions are very similar. In the commerce cases we ask:

> How severe is the handicap to out-of-state interests: does the law prohibit, or add to the cost of doing business, or simply inconvenience . . . ? What is the nature of the local interest and how exigent is it: is it protection against pestilence or against cheap goods: What less severe means of protection could be utilized?[35]

---

[34] Breithaupt v. Abram, 352 U.S. 432 (1957).

[35] Freund, *Review and Federalism*, in SUPREME COURT AND SUPREME LAW 86, 99 (Cahn ed. 1954). See also Dunham, *Congress, The States and Commerce*, 8 J. PUB. L. 47 (1959).

Thus every constitutional issue contains important factual elements which control the decision whether they are expressly considered or remain buried in the mental equipment which the judge brings to the decisional process. On the objective (or purpose, or utility) side of the balance, the questions of legislative fact are these:

1. How much will this regulation advance the chosen governmental objective? It is essential to recognize that there are two parts to this question:

a) If the regulation is completely successful, how much more safe, or healthy, or moral will the community be?

b) What is the chance of complete success for the regulation? Of partial success?

2. How much more will this regulation advance the objective than some other regulation which might interfere less with constitutionally protected interests?

On the impact (or cost) side, the questions of legislative fact are exact parallels:

1. How much will freedom (of speech, of commerce, etc.) be restricted by this regulation? This question also divides into two parts:

a) If the regulation operates with its maximum restrictive effect, how, and how much, will freedom be restricted?

b) What is the chance that the regulation will have its maximum restrictive effect? A partial effect?

2. How much more restrictive is this regulation than some other regulation which might achieve the same objective?

All of these are questions of fact; all of them are answered, whether or not the judge recognizes what he is doing. If he does not hear testimony or receive memoranda illuminating these questions, he assumes their answers on the basis of his own experience and education. Thus a judge may make assumptions far beyond the ordinary range of judicial notice, such as that fear of punishment deters conduct which is made punishable; or that increased costs of manufacture of an item tend to be reflected in the item's price, and that increased prices tend to reduce consumer demand for the item. Such assumptions may be correct or incorrect, enlightened or unenlightened, but they are always made.

There is common agreement that a court normally examines legislative facts not to determine their "truth," but to determine whether a reasonable legislative judgment could have been made supporting the statute in its enacted form.[36] In this context, "reasonable" is only a synonym for "constitutional." It means that in view of the countervailing interests, and considering the proper amount of judicial restraint in cases of the kind before the court, the legislative balance of values does not differ sufficiently from the judicial balance for the court to intervene. The reasonableness of governmental action thus resembles other "ultimate" facts such as monopoly, or insanity, or negligence, in that it is only partly determined by a factual inquiry. The other aspects of the issue are questions of values—or, in more familiar terms, questions of law: How important to the community is the objective which the regulation seeks to forward? How important is the interest which is invaded by the regulation? Questions such as these are at the heart of all judicial legislation. They are easily stated, but they defy further analysis. The ultimate balance always reduces to a question which is answerable only on the basis of precedent[37] or the individual judge's ranking of social values or a combination of the two.

The uncertainty inherent in this process of evaluation has pained Professor Wormuth enough to cause him to assert that

> Under the prevailing rules, no effective scrutiny of legislative facts—no appraisal of the relation of the [legislative] program to the [constitutional] goal—is possible. It would be better not to pretend to undertake it. Currently the principal effect of judicial review is to mislead the people by persuading them that a statute has undergone some sort of test and has demonstrated its validity in terms of constitutional goals, which is plainly untrue. If judicial review is to have any meaning, questions of legislative fact which are susceptible to solution should be solved; those not susceptible to solution should be relegated to the category of political questions.[38]

The assumption seems to be that since ultimate questions of reasonableness are not "susceptible to solution" wholly on the basis of findings of fact, courts are somehow disqualified from deciding them.

---

[36] In cases of abuse of police power, no legislative balance has been made before the judicial balance. Perhaps courts should be more concerned with the truth of the underlying facts in these cases. Professor Freund has suggested a similar approach "to the extent that the legislature particularizes" and "approaches the judicial arena." Freund, *Review of Facts in Constitutional Cases*, in SUPREME COURT AND SUPREME LAW 47, 48 (Cahn ed. 1954).

[37] See text *infra*, at notes 125–28.

[38] Wormuth, *The Impact of Economic Legislation upon the Supreme Court*, 6 J. PUB. L. 296, 318 (1957). One of the "prevailing rules" which Professor Wormuth takes far too seriously is the presumption of constitutionality. See text *infra*, at notes 40–67.

The assumption ignores centuries of judicial lawmaking when it denies the competency of courts to weigh competing social interests.
Although the "solution" of the ultimate question of constitutionality
cannot be determined entirely by findings of fact, we need not abandon hope for "effective scrutiny" of whatever factual elements there
are in the question. As we have seen, the judge necessarily decides
these questions of legislative fact whether or not he subjects them to
scrutiny, effective or not. The alternative to the educated judicial
guess, as Professor Wormuth correctly notes, is relegation of the
issue "to the category of political questions." To put it less euphemis-
tically, the alternative is the renunciation of judicial review itself, and
acceptance of the intolerable principle that each level or branch of
government is the judge of its own powers.[39]

III. THE PRESUMPTIONS OF CONSTITUTIONALITY

It has been remarked that emphasis on the legislative facts may
raise concern for the survival of the presumption of constitutionality.[40] The fear is that an invitation to examine the factual basis for
legislation may cause a court to make an independent judgment as if
the legislature's view were entitled to little or no weight. Yet in modern experience judicial activism has accompanied not the close scrutiny of legislative facts but its exact opposite. While one who is
unfamiliar with recent judicial history might expect the possessors of
an ultimate weapon such as a constitutional absolute to be sparing in
its use, it has been the absolutists who have most deserved the label of
"libertarian judicial activists."[41] We have come to expect the greatest
measure of self-restraint from judges who have insisted most strongly
on analysis of the factual setting for governmental action. This answer, however, makes the dubious assumption that current fashions

---

[39] See HAND, *op. cit. supra* note 29, at 27–30 (1958). The British success with parliamentary supremacy is usually explained as resting on geographical and racial unity. If a
new federation, including Eire, were organized, would parliamentary supremacy work?
See Kilmuir, *Individual Freedom under an Unwritten Constitution*, 45 VA. L. REV. 629
(1959); JACKSON, THE SUPREME COURT IN THE AMERICAN SYSTEM OF GOVERNMENT
81–82 (1955).

[40] FREUND, *op. cit. supra* note 27, at 87–88; Freund, *supra* note 36, at 49.

[41] JACKSON, *op. cit. supra* note 39, at 57. See the discussion of Talley v. California in the
text *infra*, at notes 54–73.

in judicial technique will continue to prevail. We shall probably find more lasting answers if we investigate the meaning of the presumption of constitutionality.

There is not just one presumption of constitutionality; there are several, of varying vigor and applicability. Thus the Supreme Court typically pays less deference to the legislative judgment underlying state economic regulations when they are challenged on commerce grounds than when they are challenged as violations of due process.[42] So also, the Court tends to give a greater presumption of validity to congressional legislation than it does to that of the states.[43] Some degree of "preferred position" for First Amendment freedoms over other constitutional values is firmly established, even though the Court has now repudiated earlier suggestions that legislation restricting speech is presumed to be invalid.[44] Finally, when there is no judgment by a legislature at all, as in cases of abuse of power by law enforcement officials, there is little justification for any presumption of constitutionality. The existence of a presumption of constitutionality has been used by the Court on many occasions to soften the impact of legislation by interpreting it to avoid possible constitutional difficulties.[45]

There is no denying that in many cases judges uphold the constitutionality of legislation which is obviously distasteful to them.[46] Judicial self-restraint is itself one of the factors to be added to the balancing process, carrying more or less weight as the circumstances seem to require. Nonetheless, it is not surprising that many judges have

---

[42] Bibb v. Navajo Freight Lines, 359 U.S. 520, 529 (1959).

[43] See Thayer, *The Origin and Scope of the American Doctrine of Constitutional Law*, 7 HARV. L. REV. 129, 154–55 (1893); *cf.* Holmes, *Law and the Court*, in COLLECTED LEGAL PAPERS 295–96 (1920).

[44] See Freund, *The Supreme Court and Civil Liberties*, 4 VAND. L. REV. 533, 545–51 (1951); Mr. Justice Frankfurter, concurring, in Kovacs v. Cooper, 336 U.S. 77, 89 (1949). Professor Pollak evidently would invert the presumption in race cases. Pollak, *Racial Discrimination and Judicial Integrity: A Reply to Professor Wechsler*, 108 U. PA. L. REV. 1, 27–30 (1959).

[45] *E.g.*, Yates v. United States, 354 U.S. 298 (1957); *cf.* Mr. Justice Frankfurter, concurring, in United States v. Raines, 362 U.S. 17, 28 (1960); Greene v. McElroy, 360 U.S. 474 (1959). See STRONG, AMERICAN CONSTITUTIONAL LAW 35–36, 493–94, 496 (1950).

[46] Perhaps the most celebrated recent example is the position of Mr. Justice Frankfurter in the flag-salute cases. Minersville School District v. Gobitis, 310 U.S. 586 (1940); West Virginia State Board of Educ. v. Barnette, 319 U.S. 624, 646 (1943) (dissenting).

found it useful to refer in their opinions to the presumption of constitutionality rather than acknowledge their own self-limitation. A judge gives the appearance of keeping his own evaluations out of the case when he states that he must uphold legislation because there is a sufficient minimum body of opinion supporting its reasonableness. In this fashion the presumption can serve the judge much as would a constitutional absolute, as a shield from hostile reactions to his decision.

Formulas for the presumption of constitutionality vary. It is sometimes said that a statute is presumed valid if its supporters produce evidence of facts supporting the view that it is appropriate legislation, even though the statute's opponents produce countervailing evidence.[47] Another version which seems less formidable for the opponents presumes the statute valid unless contrary evidence is produced "showing that the evil did not exist or that the remedy was inappropriate."[48] The most sweeping formula would make the opponents' task nearly impossible; the statute is presumed valid "if any state of facts reasonably can be conceived" which would make the legislation appropriate.[49]

All of these statements betray one vital difference from the ordinary evidentiary presumption: While each formula gives the impression of relating to the establishment of facts, the facts to be established are those bearing on the appropriateness of the legislation. To give application to the presumption in any form, a court must determine what state of facts does make the legislation appropriate, and in doing so it cannot avoid evaluating competing interests. The presumption of constitutionality is thus revealed as nothing more than an expression of those restraints which properly attend the weighing of legislative values by judges—restraints which are felt more or less strongly, according to the source of the governmental action and the nature and strength of the competing constitutionally protected interests. It may be conceded that the Supreme Court is retreating from a double standard of judicial review toward a unified principle of "bal-

---

[47] *E.g.*, Laurel Hill Cemetery v. San Francisco, 216 U.S. 358, 365–66 (1910).

[48] Hamilton, *The Jurist's Art*, 31 COLUM. L. REV. 1073, 1074 (1931). The more famous statement of Brandeis is that the presumption "must prevail in the absence of some factual foundation of record for overthrowing the statute." O'Gorman & Young v. Hartford Ins. Co., 282 U.S. 251, 258 (1931).

[49] Lindsley v. Natural Carbonic Gas Co., 220 U.S. 61, 78 (1911). See BLACK, THE PEOPLE AND THE COURT 215 ff. (1960).

anced interpretation."[50] Even so, the forces which drive in that direction also demand that each balance be struck not on the basis of dogma but in response to the demonstrated interests involved. Whatever the weight of the presumption of constitutionality in a particular case, the legislative facts must make up the rest of the balance.

The Illinois mudguard case raised questions in an area in which the presumption of constitutionality has seldom been given controlling weight in modern cases. Yet Mr. Justice Douglas found it necessary to say that "These safety measures carry a strong presumption of validity when challenged in court. . . . Policy decisions are for the state legislature, absent federal entry into the field."[51] It is plain that he does not want today's Commerce Clause to replace the Due Process Clause of a generation ago. Nonetheless, the Court felt compelled to make its factual inquiry, and most will agree that "effective scrutiny" of the legislative facts guided the Court to the proper result. But is the same kind of scrutiny desirable when the presumption of constitutionality is at its lowest strength? The cases of *Bates v. Little Rock*[52] and *Talley v. California*[53] offer such contrasting judicial attitudes as to give us a clear view of the contours of the problem.

The *Bates* case is one more chapter in the struggle for racial equality which so insistently claims the attention of our courts. Mrs. Bates was an officer and custodian of the records of the Little Rock branch of the National Association for the Advancement of Colored People, and as such she was prosecuted and fined $25 in an Arkansas court for violating a Little Rock ordinance. Some say that the ordinance, passed in 1957, was aimed directly at the NAACP. Whatever its motive, its command was that any organization operating in the city furnish, on request, a list of all persons who made any contribution to the organization, including dues. Thus, if the ordinance were upheld, the NAACP would have to give the city a list of its members, and the ordinance provided that such lists should be open to public inspection. Mrs. Bates refused to give the city the required lists.

The *Talley* case involved a 1932 Los Angeles ordinance which pro-

---

[50] Strong, *Trends in Supreme Court Interpretation of Constitution and Statute*, 6 WAYNE L. REV. 285, 304–9 (1960).

[51] 359 U.S. at 524; *cf.* Huron Portland Cement Co. v. Detroit, 362 U.S. 440 (1960); Dunham, *supra* note 35.

[52] 361 U.S. 516 (1960).

[53] 362 U.S. 60 (1960).

hibited the distribution of handbills in the city unless the handbills had printed on them the names and addresses of the persons who published and distributed them. Talley violated the ordinance by circulating anonymous[54] handbills which urged a boycott of certain named businesses because they discriminated against various minority groups in their hiring practices. He was fined $10 for his violation.

In opinions handed down thirteen days apart, the Supreme Court reversed both convictions on First Amendment grounds. In expanding constitutional protection for what is coming to be called "political privacy," the decisions are entirely consistent, and even complementary, so that the contrast in the opinions is heightened.

In his *Bates* opinion, Mr. Justice Stewart starts by inquiring into the impact of the ordinance on freedom of association, both in the immediate context of the instant case and in a larger view. He quotes from testimony at the trial which established first that some former members of the NAACP had failed to renew their membership because of "fear of community hostility and economic reprisals,"[55] and secondly that members of the NAACP who were known in the community were in fact subjected to harassment and threats. Then, moving to a more generalized consideration of the relation of exposure of membership to the freedom to associate, and quoting from the earlier case of *NAACP v. Alabama*,[56] he notes that in many cases the retention of anonymity of membership may be essential to preserve the freedom to associate with dissident groups.

Then what was the purpose of the ordinance? Mr. Justice Stewart takes the city at its word, that it was designed to inform tax officials whether the organizations in question were entitled to be exempt from the Little Rock occupational license tax. But a worthy objective is not enough. Mr. Justice Stewart goes on to examine the relation between the city's announced objective and the requirements of the ordinance. For one thing, the tax exemption is not based on an organization's earnings or income but on the nature of its activities. In general, businesses are taxed and nonprofit organizations are not. The NAACP had in fact given the city a rather full statement of its aims and activi-

---

[54] The handbills were identified as the product of the "National Consumers Mobilization." The ordinance required publication of the true names of the sponsors in addition to any fictitious name.

[55] 361 U.S. at 524.

[56] 357 U.S. 449 (1958).

ties. There was no suggestion by anyone that the NAACP's activities made it taxable. Finally, the NAACP had not even made a claim for tax exemption so far as the record showed. It was easy for Mr. Justice Stewart to conclude that there was "no relevant correlation" between the power to tax and forcing the NAACP to disclose the names of its members.[57] The presumption of constitutionality was thus overcome by the combination of a forceful showing of the impact of the ordinance on free speech and the weakest kind of justification by the city; in the face of such evidence of legislative fact even a strong presumption could not have survived.

The *Talley* opinion of Mr. Justice Black is markedly different. There is no nonsense about balancing interests. The ordinance—not its application—is invalid, because exposure (in general) has a restrictive effect on speech (in general). The opinion asserts that exposure restricts freedom to speak; recounts the history of praiseworthy anonymous pamphleteering; cites the *Bates* case and the case of *NAACP v. Alabama;* and holds the Los Angeles ordinance void on its face. Nowhere in the opinion or in the record is there any statement that Talley himself would be hurt in any way if the publisher's name and address were printed on his handbills.[58]

Still, one paragraph of the opinion does take notice of the purpose of the ordinance: to identify persons responsible for publishing fraudulent advertising or libelous matter. Mr. Justice Black's response is that the ordinance goes beyond such objectionable literature to include all handbills. "Therefore," he says, "we do not pass on the validity of an ordinance limited to prevent these or any other supposed evils."[59] This is as close as the opinion comes to examining the operation of the ordinance, and even this analysis makes no reference to the content of the handbills in the case before the Court.

Perhaps the opinion of the Court would have grappled more effectively with the issues of legislative fact if those issues had been explored more fully by counsel and the lower courts. In contrast with its position in the *Bates* case, the Court was here faced with a record almost entirely devoid of consideration of the legislative facts, and with briefs of counsel which only partly filled the void.

---

[57] 361 U.S. at 525.

[58] *Cf.* Smith v. Oldham 15 C.L.R. 355 (Aust. 1912), discussed in Professor Sawer's comment on Holmes, *Evidence in Constitutional Cases*, 23 AUST. L. J. 235, 241 (1949).

[59] 362 U.S. at 64.

It would have helped the Court to know a great deal more about facts on both sides of the constitutional balance. On the objective side, these questions are pertinent, and unanswered: If the city's objective is to prevent fraud, or obscenity, or libel, or invasion of privacy, how many occurrences of such evils have there been in Los Angeles which have involved the use of anonymous handbills? How many prosecutions? How many complaints to the police, or the Better Business Bureau, or other agencies? How many civil actions for fraud, etc., involving anonymous handbills? Is there any way to determine the ratio of the number of such occurrences to the number of complaints received?

Still on the objective side of the balance, and assuming the existence of some level of incidence of such occurrences, another question remains: How much of this evil can be prevented by enforcement of this ordinance? Here we might consider the problem of fraud separately; the cheat must leave a trail for his victims to follow so that money can change hands, even if he uses only the identification of a post-office box number. He cannot remain completely hidden, or he will be unable to carry out his plan. As to libel and the like, is it not true that enforcement of this ordinance is likely to catch more people like Talley who are engaging in legitimate speech than people who are guilty of criminal libel? Will not a man knowingly guilty of criminal libel remain anonymous despite the ordinance requiring data of the kind demanded in Los Angeles? Would the statistics suggested before throw any light on this question?

Now for the opposite side, the impact on freedom: Does it hurt Talley to expose himself?[60] Would he fear to circulate the same handbill if it carried his name and address? Perhaps he would. There were recitals in his briefs in the Supreme Court that there recently had been a number of incidents of racial conflict in the Los Angeles area,[61] enough to cause advocates of social (racial) reform to be cautious about publicizing their names and addresses. The main support for the assertion came from a report by the Los Angeles County Commission on Human Relations, and consisted principally of a list of such incidents, only one of which involved employment of Negroes

---

[60] The city's brief pointed out that there was no evidence that Talley himself had printed or published the handbill. Respondent's Brief, pp. 17–18.

[61] Petitioner's Opening Brief, pp. 21–25; Petitioner's Reply Brief, pp. 12–23

and the rest of which apparently involved housing of Negroes in previously white neighborhoods. The assertion would have been more persuasive if it had been made and supported at the trial or intermediate appellate level at a time when its implications could be explored.[62]

Assuming that Talley would not have distributed handbills which identified him, would the enforcement of the ordinance deter speech which is protected by the First Amendment? Certainly it is clear that his handbills were not libelous, obscene, or fraudulent. Furthermore, even if Talley could not show that he would be hurt by exposure, the very existence of the ordinance may be a deterrent to protected speech on the part of others, as in the case of an excessively vague statute restricting speech.[63] Even an ordinance which struck only at anonymous handbills that were libelous or fraudulent would have the potential effect of deterring speech which was unobjectionable as well as that which was punishable, because some persons might refrain from publishing innocent anonymous handbills for fear of being close to the line of criminality. Perhaps this was what Mr. Justice Black had in mind. Perhaps this was also what Mr. Justice Harlan meant when he referred in his concurring opinion to "the deterrent effect on free speech which this all-embracing ordinance is likely to have."[64]

Finally, the appeal to history made by the briefs for Talley[65] and for the *amicus curiae*[66] is largely a makeweight, useful to dramatize what the Court had already accepted in *NAACP v. Alabama*:[67] that the espousal of an unpopular cause is more readily undertaken when anonymity is assured.

All in all, it was a meager record of legislative fact, meager enough so that each side properly accused the other of failure to substantiate its position. A believing man might have expected the presumption of constitutionality to dispose of the case. Of course it did not. Mr. Jus-

[62] The report most strongly relied on was issued after the petition for certiorari had been granted. At the trial, Talley could have used earlier reports of the same body.

[63] See, *e.g.*, Winters v. New York, 333 U.S. 507 (1948).

[64] 362 U.S. at 67.

[65] Petitioner's Opening Brief, pp. 17–21.

[66] Brief of the American Jewish Congress, *Amicus Curiae*, pp. 8–10. The *amicus* brief also used text references about consumer research polls and employee suggestion plans to show that anonymity encouraged expression. Pp. 10–12.

[67] 357 U.S. 449 (1958).

tice Clark's dissent relied on the presumption, arguing that the purpose of the ordinance was legitimate and that the means adopted to achieve the purpose must be approved as reasonable in "the absence of any showing to the contrary by Talley."[68] In his concurring opinion, Mr. Justice Harlan reached the conclusion that the ordinance was unduly restrictive of speech "[i]n the absence of a more substantial showing as to Los Angeles' actual experience with the distribution of obnoxious handbills . . . ."[69] Thus he put the onus on the city to justify such a broad restriction on liberty. By so doing Mr. Justice Harlan has neither abandoned the presumption nor joined those who would invert it in free-speech cases. His opinion may be understood to say that the serious restriction on lawful speech as well as on unlawful speech imposed by this ordinance overcame the presumption of constitutionality, standing alone and unsupported by any basis in legislative fact presented to the Court. Thus the justices who struck down the ordinance on its face did so without emphasis on the factual underpinning of the legislation, while the other two opinions, both of which gave weight to the presumption of constitutionality, underscored the need to examine the legislative facts. Reasoning backward from the refusal of Mr. Justice Harlan and Mr. Justice Clark to change position in the absence of proof of additional legislative facts, we can see that they have started by assigning different weights to the competing interests. Responses in accord with a priori persuasions are to be expected when the record of legislative fact is inadequate.[70]

It probably is desirable to give some special constitutional consideration to freedom of expression, and, whether they speak the language of "preferred position" or not, all or nearly all of the present members of the Court do give some preference to these values. But a preference can be expressed within the weighing process, as Mr. Justice Harlan shows in his *Talley* concurrence.[71] It is quite another thing to abandon the weighing process altogether, and to say, as Mr. Justice Douglas once did, that "even a reasonable regulation of the right to free speech is not compatible with the First Amendment."[72] Whether

[68] 362 U.S. at 69–70.

[69] 362 U.S. at 66.

[70] See text *infra*, at notes 74–83.

[71] 362 U.S. at 66.

[72] Dissenting, in Poulos v. New Hampshire, 345 U.S. 395, 425 (1953).

the question be one of political freedom or economic freedom, "We deal not with absolutes but with questions of degree."[73] And regardless of the weight one attaches to the presumption of constitutionality, the same questions—the objectives of the regulation, the means of achieving them, and the impact on the protected interest—remain to be illuminated by the legislative facts.

IV. Inadequate Records in the Supreme Court

The Supreme Court can avoid deciding a case on an inadequate record of legislative fact by denying certiorari or dismissing the appeal. The same result may be achieved even after the case has been argued.[74] But the Court may prefer not to terminate the litigation, leaving the constitutional issues unresolved. In that event, the alternatives are distinctly limited. The Court may remand for further consideration of the legislative facts in the lower courts; or it may retain the case, ordering augmentation of the record, or further briefing or argument; or it may proceed to decide the case on the record, briefs, and argument before it and on the basis of its own research.

The last procedure is unhappily typical. If a justice prefers to decide without further exploration of the legislative facts, we have seen that reliance on the presumption of constitutionality or on a constitutional absolute may serve his purpose. When a majority's inclination to decide is added to the natural momentum of the case toward resolution of the parties' dispute, a form of institutional inertia makes it difficult to delay a decision, even though more digging into the legislative facts may be quite desirable.

In the *Talley* case the Court neither remanded nor ordered further briefing or argument, despite the fact that its attention had been called to the inadequacies in the development of the legislative facts. We can only guess the reasons. Was the Court persuaded that the record of legislative facts really was adequate? Perhaps the majority was so persuaded, but the opinions of Justices Harlan and Clark showed dissatisfaction.

The Court's reluctance to remand may be traceable to a doubt that further efforts in the lower courts would produce enough additional light on the legislative facts to be worth the very considerable extra

---

[73] Mr. Justice Douglas, in Bibb v. Navajo Freight Lines, 359 U.S. 520, 530 (1959).

[74] See Stern & Gressman, Supreme Court Practice 158 (rev. ed. 1954).

expense and delay which would inevitably result for the parties. Is it fair to an individual criminal defendant to put him through the judicial wringer a second time? It may be appropriate to do just that when large interests are represented as parties or sponsors of the litigation.

The additional value obtainable by remanding depends in part on the complexity of the issues to be examined and the need for time to sort out the issues of fact. More importantly, it may depend on the adaptability of the issues of fact to presentation by memoranda to the Supreme Court, or, conversely, on the desirability of a trial. Some of the Court's hesitancy to remand may stem from an assumption that the trial of legislative facts will be hedged in by restrictive rules of evidence and procedure which would not hamper its own investigation. As hereinafter shown,[75] such an assumption is unfounded. Trial procedure for legislative fact-finding is considerably more flexible than that of the Supreme Court. In the *Talley* case, a trial of the issues of legislative fact would have helped the Court to write a more meaningful opinion, but the ordinance was so broadly drawn that the result of the case probably would have been unchanged. Still the failure to order further exploration of the legislative facts by way of memoranda to the Supreme Court seems unfortunate. The extra expense to the City of Los Angeles and to the American Civil Liberties Union, which assisted Talley's defense, and the delay in settling Talley's obligation to pay a $10 fine are not enough to justify a decision on so skimpy a record.

Although documentation is impossible, it does seem that most of the justices feel more confident of their own unaided evaluations of the legislative facts when they are dealing with civil liberties than when the issues are economic in nature. Such a feeling may result from doubts about the ability of experts to improve on the justices' own efforts to measure the severity of restrictions on personal freedom, and in that respect the feeling may not be unwarranted. It nevertheless comes as a surprise that the Court is willing to decide an important economic question on the basis of a record little better than that in the *Talley* case. That is just what the Court did at the last term in the case of *Huron Portland Cement Co. v. Detroit*.[76]

---

[75] See text *infra*, at notes 84–132. The Court may simply believe that further investigation would be unproductive. See Elkins v. United States, 364 U.S. 206, 218 (1960): ". . . it is hardly likely that conclusive factual data could ever be assembled."

[76] 362 U.S. 440 (1960).

When the City of Detroit began to enforce the criminal provisions of its anti-smoke ordinance against the ships which Huron operated in interstate commerce, Huron sought an injunction. Its grounds were that (*a*) compliance with federal inspection and licensing requirements immunized the ships from state regulation, since Congress had "occupied the field" with its regulation scheme; and (*b*) enforcement of the ordinance unconstitutionally burdened interstate commerce. The Michigan courts decided against Huron,[77] and the Supreme Court affirmed.

At least since *In re Rahrer*[78] it has been accepted that "Congress has undoubted power to redefine the distribution of power over interstate commerce."[79] Although the question of federal pre-emption is a question of statutory interpretation, in cases of economic regulation it does not differ in its essential analytical elements from the Commerce Clause question: What is the meaning of congressional silence, or, less artificially, is there justification for state regulation of this incident or transaction which Congress has not specifically regulated?

In the *Huron* case it was noted that Congress had declared that the states were primarily responsible for smog control, and the decision probably rests principally on that ground. The two dissenters argued that the true congressional policy was contained in the detailed inspection and licensing provisions of the federal law governing steam vessels, and that the Detroit ordinance conflicted with the federal license by excluding from commerce the very boilers which had Coast Guard approval.[80]

With these two federal policies before the Court, the controversy would seem to be governed by the facts of Detroit's need for the regulation and the degree of interference with Huron's interstate operation; both the majority and the dissenting opinions, however, speak generally about congressional policy and only in passing about specifics. Is it entirely an accident that the Court was unanimous in the Illinois mudguard case, when it had a detailed factual record before it, and that the Court divided in this case when it decided on an inadequate record?

---

[77] 355 Mich. 227 (1959).

[78] 140 U.S. 545 (1891).

[79] Mr. Chief Justice Stone, in Southern Pacific Co. v. Arizona, 325 U.S. 761, 769 (1945); *cf.* Parker v. Brown, 317 U.S. 341 (1943).

[80] Mr. Justice Douglas, with Mr. Justice Frankfurter, 362 U.S. at 449–55.

What is the danger to the inhabitants of Detroit from air pollution? What losses of health or property have resulted, before and after the adoption and enforcement of the ordinance? What dangers would result if Detroit were to exempt from the ordinance those sources of smoke which are impossible to eliminate without adding substantially to the cost of interstate commerce? Is other equipment available which would permit Huron to comply with the ordinance?[81] How much would it cost for Huron to comply?[82] How many other federally licensed vessels which operate in Detroit are equipped with the same kind of boiler?[83]

All that the record contains on these questions are the bare findings of the trial court, unsupported and apparently uncontested by the parties, and limited to the burden on Huron's operations. The record contains no exploration of the justification of the ordinance, but does include two pages of testimony that other equipment could be installed in Huron's ships that would comply with the ordinance. In effect, the parties stipulated to the findings of legislative fact, and the Supreme Court seemed content to accept them. At the very least the Court should have ordered that more of the evidence on questions of legislative fact be added to the record. If the available additional evidence would not have illuminated the issues of legislative fact any better than the record before the Court, the case should have been remanded. The inferences which were deduced from the various acts of Congress were not outrageous, but they needed support in the form of concrete experience.

Part of the Supreme Court's problem is created by the unwillingness of lower court judges to complicate their proceedings with factual inquiries that go beyond the facts about the parties. Part of the Supreme Court's task is to train lower court judges to do just that. Occasional exhortations in opinions may help, but remanding a few cases may turn out to be more effective.

---

[81] The trial court agreed that such equipment was available. Record, p. 20.

[82] The trial court found that it would cost from $70,000 to $100,000 per ship. Record, p. 22.

[83] At the trial, only the activities of Huron's ships were discussed; the court found that the two ships chiefly involved in the case docked in Detroit 22 and 25 times in a year, for average stays of about 24 and 16 hours, respectively, and that it was not possible for them to use their boilers in Detroit without violating the ordinance. Record, pp. 18–19.

V. Educating the Judges

It is easy enough to accept these views, which after all are no more than an elaboration of Holmes's observation that "General propositions do not decide concrete cases."[84] But putting them into effective practice requires more from counsel than many members of the bar seem to realize. Professor Hurst has reminded us that ". . . there is probably no type of lawsuit in which lawyers more miserably fail in their supposed functions as officers of the Court"[85] than constitutional litigation. Some responsibility for this failure must also be laid to judges who do not demand that counsel fulfill their obligations.

A judge's background in legislative fact always consists principally of his own prior education and experience. No doubt most of our constitutional stability is produced by the common fund of experience and attitudes shared by the whole community, including the judges. It is only such a broad consensus that permits judicial review to work at all. But our present concern is narrower; it is with the education of judges which takes place during the litigation, the enlightenment which comes from testimony, from standard texts, from specially prepared memoranda, and from the "findings" of legislative fact in other cases.

1. *The facts to be proved.* It is hard to imagine any fact, however "raw" or isolated, which is incapable of being used as a legislative fact. If it be proved that the U.S. Weather Bureau reported a high temperature of 93 degrees for Chicago on July 21, 1960, such a fact might be important in determining the constitutionality of a local ordinance regulating the refrigeration of perishable food. But ordinarily the legislative facts are more complex, for reasons which inhere in the nature of legislation. Charles Curtis has remarked that these are facts which look to the future.[86] They tend to be facts which relate to other "cases" which may never be decided. When we evaluate the chance that a regulation will have a certain restrictive effect, or that it will achieve its objectives, we enter the realm of prediction and probability.[87] When we ask, "What is the probability

---

[84] Dissenting, in Lochner v. New York, 198 U.S. 45, 76 (1905).

[85] Comment on Freund, *supra* note 36, at 51.

[86] Comment on Freund, *supra* note 36, at 52.

[87] The answers to such questions of fact are not the facts themselves, but propositions of fact which are (in the incompleteness of knowledge) probable, while the facts them-

that this regulation will cause X dollars of burden on interstate commerce, or that it will prevent X number of potential speakers from speaking?"[88] we are asking about the facts of other cases.[89] The isolated case is unlikely to reach the Supreme Court, since the Court's policy ordinarily excludes from consideration the case of isolated significance.[90] Thus most legislative facts are of a complex nature, built on an intricate structure of data and inferences. Inevitably, judicial competence to evaluate the legislative facts varies inversely with their distance from the facts concerning the parties. When the judge must make a decision "about scientific or social processes"[91] he needs expert help.

2. *Expert opinion: form.* The Brandeis brief[92] was devised to acquaint appellate judges with legislative facts. "It drew on reports of public investigating committees, books and articles by medical authorities and social workers, and the practice of legislatures here and abroad."[93] For its limited purpose—supplying factual support for the presumption of constitutionality—this technique has enjoyed considerable success and popularity. But the obvious limitations on this textual method of proof have caused counsel to turn more frequently to the trial process for their presentation of legislative facts. The Supreme Court has given this practice its blessing.[94] From time to

selves either exist or do not. See MICHAEL & ADLER, THE NATURE OF JUDICIAL PROOF 8 (1931).

[88] The two may be combined in a single case, as in Breard v. Alexandria, 341 U.S. 622 (1951).

[89] Thus it is misleading to say that a court "is concerned with [legislative] facts only to the extent necessary to formulate a just ground for the decision of the controversy before it," without the qualification that a just ground requires the consideration of all like cases. See Hart & McNaughton, *Evidence and Inference in the Law,* in EVIDENCE AND INFERENCE 48, 63 (Lerner ed. 1958).

[90] See, *e.g.,* Rice v. Sioux City Memorial Park Cemetery, 349 U.S. 70 (1955); Dorsey v. Stuyvesant Town Corp., 299 N.Y. 512 (1949), cert. denied, 339 U.S. 981 (1950).

[91] Wormuth, *supra* note 38, at 304.

[92] The brief filed by Brandeis as counsel in Muller v. Oregon, 208 U.S. 412 (1908), and widely imitated thereafter, was not the first to include such materials, but they were used more extensively and dramatically there than had been the practice.

[93] FREUND, *op. cit. supra* note 27, at 86–87.

[94] *E.g.,* Borden's Farm Products Co. v. Baldwin, 293 U.S. 194 (1934); Chastleton Corp. v. Sinclair, 264 U.S. 543 (1924). See FREUND, *op. cit. supra* note 27, at 89–90. See also Biklé, *Judicial Determination of Questions of Fact Affecting the Constitutional Validity of Legislative Action,* 38 HARV. L. REV. 6 (1924); Denman, *Comment on Trials of Fact in*

time it has expressed its reluctance to decide constitutional issues on the basis of the pleadings, without the illumination of those issues which can come from a trial in which adjudicative facts can carry important legislative-fact implications.[95] In large part the decision to proceed with a trial of the issues of legislative fact of a broader scope rests on the desirability of proving such facts by testimony rather than by memoranda. But even when memoranda seem more appropriate, they should be presented for the consideration of the trial court. Although an appeal may seem certain, a lower court judge can make an important contribution to the development of the law by giving the appellate court the benefit of his sorting and evaluation of a complex record of legislative fact,[96] no less when that record consists of technical memoranda than when it consists of technical testimony.

In general, testimony tends to be more costly to the parties than the proof of facts by memoranda, but it does permit cross-examination. Thus, in general, the expected value of cross-examination is central to any decision to proceed with testimony on a particular issue. There is little justification for repeating the testimony taken in legislative hearings,[97] or requiring that the parties authenticate the statements of authors of standard texts.[98] Judge Wyzanski goes further, suggesting that whenever the expert opinion "has primarily an argumentative character," testimony is inappropriate, and an offer of the opinion through briefs or statements of counsel is preferable.[99] It is true that

---

Constitutional Cases, 21 A.B.A.J. 805 (1935); Note, *The Presentation of Facts Underlying the Constitutionality of Statutes*, 49 HARV. L. REV. 631 (1936); Note, *Social and Economic Facts— Appraisal of Suggested Techniques for Presenting Them to the Courts*, 61 HARV. L. REV. 692 (1948).

[95] One of the most eloquent statements of this position is to be found in Mr. Justice Frankfurter's dissent in Adler v. Board of Education, 342 U.S. 485, 497 (1952). The opinion of the Court solved this problem by ignoring it. See also Holmes, *supra* note 58, at 238.

[96] See Wyzanski, *A Trial Judge's Freedom and Responsibility*, 65 HARV. L. REV. 1281, 1296 (1952).

[97] Although there is typically no right to cross-examine witnesses in legislative hearings, the questions of legislators will frequently represent the contesting interests. Where they do not, the court ought to permit amplification by new testimony, but repetition of the testimony for the purpose of allowing cross-examination will not normally be worth the cost.

[98] Rule 63(31) of the Uniform Rules of Evidence excepts "a published treatise" of "a reliable authority" from the hearsay rule. See McCORMICK, EVIDENCE 620–21 (1954).

[99] Wyzanski, *supra* note 96, at 1296.

testimony about broad social or economic processes, followed by cross-examination, is not ordinarily calculated to produce an educational effect comparable to that which is attainable through the detached study of memoranda and counter-memoranda.[100] But when the facts concerning the litigants are also important as legislative facts, and when the expert's opinion is based on such adjudicative-legislative facts, then the obvious value of cross-examination makes live testimony by the expert more appropriate, even though it may be "argumentative" in the sense that it rests on a chain of debatable inferences based on standards of the expert's own selection.[101]

Testimony will frequently be more appropriate to develop the facts which relate to the impact of the governmental action on the constitutionally protected interest than to support the action's validity. Thus the cost of the contour mudguards to the regulated truckers[102] and the restriction on free association caused by exposure of members of the NAACP[103] are questions particularly suited for illumination through testimony and cross-examination, while the need for exposure of publishers of libelous or fraudulent handbills seems more suited for discussion in memoranda or briefs of counsel.[104]

The expert need not be confined to one or the other of these techniques. In many cases it may be wise to have him prepare a memorandum of his views and then submit to cross-examination on such matters as his statistical methods, his reasons for drawing inferences as he does, and the like.[105] In such cases it is essential for the offering party to make the memorandum available to the opponent well before the trial, and to give the opponent a chance to examine any available raw data on which the expert's conclusions are based. Such a practice has been used with success in some large anti-trust cases,[106] and seems

---

[100] See 2 DAVIS, *op. cit. supra* note 9, at 402 n. 4.

[101] See 2 *id.* § 15.10.

[102] See the detailed findings in Navajo Freight Lines v. Bibb, 159 F. Supp. 385 (S.D. Ill. 1958).

[103] In the *Bates* case, counsel for Mrs. Bates made a persuasive record on this question. Record, pp. 11–19, 54–65.

[104] See Respondent's Brief in *Talley*, pp. 14–17.

[105] *Cf.* § 2 of the Uniform Business Records as Evidence Act, discussed in McCORMICK, *op. cit. supra* note 98, at 607–9 (1954).

[106] See McGlothlin, *Some Practical Problems in Proof of Economic, Scientific and Technical Facts*, 23 F.R.D. 467, 471–73 (1959).

adaptable to constitutional litigation. Many an anti-trust decree, after all, performs the function of legislating for a whole industry.

3. *Expert opinion: content.* When a court inquires into the legislative facts, there is only limited need for the usual exclusionary rules of evidence. Even in testifying as to adjudicative facts, expert witnesses are permitted to draw inferences from experience which includes their special training.[107] There is all the more reason to ignore the opinion-evidence rule when experts testify as to legislative facts; since the judge will decide such issues with or without enlightenment, he should have the benefit of whatever assistance is available.

Of course no witness is ever asked whether in his expert opinion a statute is constitutional. The ultimate question of reasonableness would not properly be put to a witness, any more than would ultimate questions of negligence and the like, since in part it calls for a conclusion of law. But a rather similar result may be achieved when the legal test is spelled out for a witness at the next lower level of abstraction, and he is permitted to give his opinion on that question.[108] Thus the key issue of legislative fact, as the courts approached the school segregation cases, was whether racial segregation of itself created a measure of inequality for the Negro school children. All the lower courts approached the cases as if the answer to this question would determine the equal-protection issue, although some of them felt that the issue had been settled by the precedent of *Plessy v. Ferguson.*[109] Yet various experts who testified at the trials[110] and the social science brief filed with the Supreme Court[111] asserted that segregation interfered with the Negro children's education, and none of the courts excluded such testimony for fear of having their function as triers of legislative fact usurped. Such a judicial attitude is fortunately typical. A verbal distinction may serve some purpose in protecting a lay jury from being overwhelmed by an expert, but judges know that constitutional decisions speak principally to the future, so that legislative facts often must be in the nature of predictive opinions. When such

---

[107] See McCormick, *op. cit. supra* note 98, at 28–29.

[108] Thus medical testimony in criminal cases frequently responds to the question whether the accused knew the nature and quality of his act, or knew that his act was wrong, in order to determine the issue of insanity—an issue of law, not of medicine.

[109] 163 U.S. 537 (1896). See text *infra*, at notes 125–28.

[110] See Greenberg, *Social Scientists Take the Stand,* 54 MICH. L. REV. 953, 962–64 (1956).

[111] Reprinted in 37 MINN. L. REV. 427 (1953).

opinions are expressed more abstractly, they are less persuasive but not devoid of value.

The hearsay rule similarly carries less force when it is applied to the proof of legislative facts. Obviously a great deal of the most useful expert opinion is based on data not proved in court, whether the expert opinion concerns the issues of adjudicative fact or issues of legislative fact. The very qualities which make a man an expert—his training and experience—are "likely to be honeycombed with hearsay, including hearsay about hearsay, and the opinions of others."[112] So no one suggests that all expert opinion be limited to factual premises proved to the trier's satisfaction.[113] Still there lingers some suspicion of the expert from an inexact science who expresses opinions not premised on data in evidence.

Professor Dession has said that the latitude to be given to the expert

> depends on the multiple factors of (a) the scope of his expertness, (b) the apparent validity of such hearsay information as he may profess to take into account, and (c) the extent to which the premises for his inferences are based on his own study, experience, and observation, rather than on specific information supplied by other witnesses or evidence in the case.[114]

Parts (a) and (b) of this analysis relate to the qualification of the expert, including the respect which is properly owing to his branch of learning. To make the expert stick to the evidence before the court in selecting his premises unless he represents "a recognized and trusted discipline or science"[115] would invite judges to exclude much social science testimony. When a court is trying to determine issues of adjudicative fact, Professor Dession's limitation is a good one. It is not proper, however, when the issue is one of legislative fact. Inexact as the social sciences are, they are the best we have. If this kind of evidence is excluded, the decision will be based on the hearsay and opinion which have formed the judge's attitudes before the litigation began.

The third part of Professor Dession's analysis is the most persua-

---

[112] MORGAN, MAGUIRE, & WEINSTEIN, CASES AND MATERIALS ON EVIDENCE 232 (4th ed. 1957).

[113] See note 98 supra.

[114] Dession, The Trial of Economic and Technological Issues of Facts: II, 58 YALE L. J. 1242, 1263 (1949).

[115] Ibid. The statement is echoed in Maguire & Hahesy, Requisite Proof of Basis for Expert Opinion, 5 VAND. L. REV. 432, 443 (1952).

sive in our context. What sets the expert apart from the trier of fact, legislative or adjudicative, is the special experience which permits him to draw inferences from premises beyond the trier's ability to evaluate. But when the expert bases his opinion on premises which are available to the trier for his scrutiny, then those premises should be stated expressly, so that the trier can discredit the expert's conclusions if his premises should be rejected.

4. *Expert opinion: evaluation.* The really difficult problems posed by the use of expert assistance in interpreting raw data concern not the admissibility of expert opinion but its evaluation. A judge without special training finds it hard to criticize an expert's methods of gathering data or the inferences he draws from them. Yet experts are fallible. Worse, they have axes to grind—at least professional axes.[116] Anyone familiar with recent contributions of scientists to political decisions knows that scientific and political preferences have a way of coinciding, whether the question be the effects of a heart attack on a presidential candidate or the dangers inherent in continued testing of nuclear weapons. When experts help the courts make policy, they are not likely to shed their attitudes on the ultimate policy issues. This is one reason for misgivings about social science testimony and memoranda in the school segregation cases. Unfortunately, the scientific method employed in a substantial portion of the social science effort in those cases does little to dispel suspicion that the conclusions expressed, however we laymen may approve of them, were more social than scientific.[117]

Is the answer to be found in the adversary system? Do we dare to rely on counter-experts, hoping that judges can reach wise decisions when the experts differ? Such a solution has been typical in the disposition of conflicting expert testimony as to adjudicative facts, such as medical testimony in personal injury litigation. But one great beauty of that system is that the effects of such a lay decision ordinarily are confined to a single case.[118] The same cannot be said of the decision of a constitutional issue. The fact that the decision does

---

[116] See McGlothlin, *supra* note 106, at 480.

[117] The criticisms leveled by Professor Cahn show that there are some kinds of leaps of logic that a lay critic can evaluate. See Cahn, *Jurisprudence*, 30 N.Y.U.L. Rev. 150, 157–68 (1955). Professor Pollak's apparent solution is the reversal of the presumption of constitutionality, requiring supporters of racial distinctions to produce factual justification or have their distinctions invalidated. See note 44 *supra*.

[118] See Hart & Sacks, The Legal Process: Basic Problems in the Making and Application of Law 384 (mimeographed 1958).

affect the interests of many who are not in court causes some concern lest the immediate parties fail to represent the interested absentees.[119]

The Supreme Court has from time to time recognized the need for outside aid, encouraging the filing of briefs and memoranda by *amici curiae*.[120] This practice is adequate in many classes of cases because many large interest groups regularly follow—even stimulate—the progress of constitutional litigation for the purpose of influencing constitutional development. The result is a form of judicial lobbying, which helps the courts to act as "decision brokers"[121] when they enter the political arena in deciding constitutional questions. The obvious danger is that the interests which get left out because they are not represented by judicial lobbies are likely to be the same ones which are denied consideration in the legislative halls.

To some extent the courts can make an attempt to serve a truly national interest, perhaps with some greater chance of success than legislators have. The insulation of the judiciary from party politics contributes to this end. Some aid may be obtained by inviting government agencies to participate as *amici curiae*. But ultimately there is no way for the conscientious judge to escape making a determined effort to learn enough about the subject matter of the litigation to formulate his own views with the assistance—not the domination—of the experts.[122]

---

[119] See Hart & McNaughton, *supra* note 89, at 62; Note, 61 HARV. L. REV. 692, 700 (1948).

[120] One notable recent effort of this kind resulted in the very able and persuasive *amicus* brief filed at the Court's invitation, 354 U.S. 936 (1957), in Lambert v. California, 355 U.S. 225 (1958). It is still true, as Mr. Justice Black notes, that the Court's Rule 42 is too restrictive on the filing of *amicus* briefs. See On Lee v. United States, 343 U.S. 924 (1952). Might there not also be room for some limited participation of *amici* at the trial level?

[121] See Miller, *The Constitutional Law of the "Security State,"* 10 STAN. L. REV. 620, 645–53 (1958); Vose, *Litigation as a Form of Pressure Group Activity,* 319 ANNALS 20 (1958).

[122] The goal is not unattainable. At the trial of United States v. United Shoe Mach. Corp., 110 F. Supp. 295 (D. Mass. 1953), *aff'd*, 347 U.S. 521 (1954), Judge Wyzanski appointed an economist as an assistant over a period of two years. For the economist's views of the case, see KAYSEN, UNITED STATES V. UNITED SHOE MACHINERY CORPORATION (1956). Judge Wyzanski was following a practice which has long been recognized in England. See Beuscher, *The Use of Experts by the Courts,* 54 HARV. L. REV. 1105, 1118 (1941). The appointment of the expert as a master, although limited in the federal courts to cases which are "the exception and not the rule," FED. R. CIV. P. 53(b), is another solution. See Borden's Farm Products Co. v. Ten Eyck, 11 F. Supp. 599 (S.D.N.Y. 1935), *aff'd*, 297 U.S. 251 (1936).

When the presumption of constitutionality is strong, the judge may be rescued from the need to second-guess the experts. Perhaps it is no accident that the presumption of constitutionality is weakest in those areas in which there is the least difference between the competence of lay judgment and that of expert judgment.[123] In the expansive areas of human freedom and equality, social science experts have not yet devised methods of measurement which are precise enough to give them a significant advantage over the judge's own ability to measure. A court which paid great deference to the legislative judgment in the school segregation cases would be just as deserving of criticism as one which paid great deference to the social science brief which dealt with the probable effects of immediate desegregation.[124] Still the courts should not ignore such offerings. They should accept them with the skepticism which properly attends activity on scientific frontiers.

5. *Stare decisis: the findings of other judges.* It is beyond dispute that findings of legislative fact have influence beyond the cases in which they are made; the law reports are thus an important source of legislative fact. Professor Davis has ably described the process by which questions of legislative fact are first debated, then decided, then embedded in propositions of law, then gradually abandoned as they are shown to be mistaken or obsolete.[125] In this fashion, such "factual propositions of law"[126] develop and wither through the ordinary process of *stare decisis.* Thus findings of legislative fact are more readily transferable from one case to another when they have been thoroughly considered. The necessity of the finding to the decision, the volume and quality of evidence produced on the subject, the opportunity given·to opponents to challenge the proposed finding, the quality of analysis and interpretation by the court—all are relevant, in the usual common-law manner. So also the weight of a previous finding of legislative fact diminishes to the extent that the ultimate question of law to

---

[123] The rules of evidence traditionally exclude evidence which is too "speculative." See Dession, *supra* note 114, at 1261.

[124] Reprinted in 9 J. Soc. Issues No. 4 (1953). This brief draws several generalized conclusions from statements in magazine articles, individual events not shown to be representative, press releases, and the like. Far more persuasive was the main social science brief, note 111 *supra*, which demonstrated at least a substantial unanimity among social scientists on the issues in question.

[125] Davis, *op. cit. supra* note 9, at § 15.04.

[126] *Ibid.*

be decided differs from the question which called the finding into being, again in the best common-law tradition.

The impression is too easily gained, however, that findings of legislative fact are accorded the same weight as ordinary propositions of law. Much of the law's vitality comes from the willingness of courts to re-examine findings of legislative fact to a far greater extent than they re-examine other propositions of law. Abstractly, we might say that no rule of law should outlive its basis in legislative fact. But the need for apparent stability,[127] coupled with traditional judicial reluctance to make law, properly gives legal precedent—including constitutional precedent—a force of its own. There is no corresponding need to preserve the underlying findings of legislative fact beyond the time when they cease to reflect judicially determined reality. In other words, outmoded assumptions of legislative fact need not be extended to new cases, and the obvious corollary is that counsel must be given the opportunity to show that earlier findings fail to describe present fact.

Yet it is true that some kinds of legislative-fact findings tend to be more acceptable in new cases than do others. The broader the application of a finding of fact, the more likely it is to be transferable in this sense. Thus when a court makes a finding as to the relative success of a statutory regulation in achieving its announced objectives, that finding will carry greater weight in another case than a finding on the other side of the constitutional balance. A court's evaluation of the impact of the same statute on some constitutionally protected interest may depend largely on the showing made of the impact on the litigants before the court. Where the legislative facts of the earlier case concerned only the immediate parties, generalized findings are entitled to less respect in later cases. Perhaps this is just a complicated way of saying that normally[128] legislation is invalid (or valid) only in its application and not in the abstract.

6. *Opportunity to challenge; statement of findings.* Wholly apart from the court's legislative functions, there are sufficient reasons for allowing the litigants to present their arguments as to the legal standards

---

[127] Ralph Gabriel has engagingly discussed the symbolism of the Constitution in THE COURSE OF AMERICAN DEMOCRATIC THOUGHT 396–407 (1940); *cf.* Powell, *The Logic and Rhetoric of Constitutional Law*, 15 J. PHIL., PSYCH. & SCI. METHOD 654 (1918), reprinted in 1 SEL. ESSAYS ON CONST. LAW 474 (1938).

[128] The *Talley* case typifies a narrow class of exceptions in the free speech area.

which should govern their case. Some such reasons relate to the quality of the decision: the parties may, by their partisan presentations, help the judge to reach a decision which gives the optimum protection to their contesting interests. Other reasons are mainly political: a loser is less likely to take his grievance into the streets if he feels that his case has been given proper attention by the tribunal.[129]

When the court makes law, however, it does so, if not for "generations of litigants yet unborn,"[130] at least for a great many others who are not in court. A minimum requirement is some statement of the legislative facts (other than those facts on which everyone plainly agrees) that affect the decision. Furthermore, our forced reliance on the litigants to help represent broad social interests demands that the parties be given a chance to contest such assertions of legislative fact. This opportunity to challenge should be given whenever the determination of an issue of legislative fact affects the ultimate decision, even though the legislative fact be a "background fact,"[131] and even though it may be necessary to reopen the trial for this purpose.

It will be observed that this proposal envisages judges who take a more aggressive role than that which is customary, judges who do not leave to the parties the determination of the issues to be litigated but who actively promote the exploration of issues which the parties might be content to leave untouched. Such an incursion into the adversary system is justified precisely because assumptions of legislative fact do become legal precedents. Stipulations are permitted to determine issues of adjudicative fact because only the immediate parties are affected by such determinations, but the acceptance of stipulations of legislative fact as final would permit the litigants to make the law to an unacceptable extent.[132]

---

[129] See Wechsler, *supra* note 4.

[130] Mr. Justice Walter V. Schaefer has recently cautioned against overconsideration of such litigants' interests. See 1959 PROCEEDINGS, ASS'N AMER. LAW SCHOOLS 12, 19 (1960).

[131] Professor Davis's suggested factors unfortunately imply that such facts may affect the decision and be disputed by the parties, and yet be appropriately withheld from the trial. See 2 DAVIS, *op. cit. supra* note 9, at 393, 403–4.

[132] See ROBERTSON & KIRKHAM, JURISDICTION OF THE UNITED STATES SUPREME COURT § 111 (Wolfson & Kurland eds. 1951). A court might accept as binding a stipulation as to adjudicative fact, but refuse to be bound by the same stipulation in its legislative-fact implications.

In any case, it adds little to say that the trial court should have "discretion" whether to notify the parties of his assumptions of legislative fact. McCORMICK, *op. cit. supra* note

VI. The Case for Particularity: "Neutral Principles" v. The Third Legislative Chamber

Recently the Supreme Court was called on to decide constitutional questions on the basis of "neutral principles."[133] Such principles would "transcend any immediate result that is involved"[134] and appeal in their generality to both sides of an argument, presumably so that today's loser might find comfort in the knowledge that the same principles may work to his advantage in tomorrow's case. Since Professor Wechsler issued his call partly in response to Judge Hand's characterizatio⌐ of much of the Court's work as that of a third legislative chamber,[135] perhaps all that was intended was the necessary qualification that the Court properly acted under restrictions which do not bind legislators. But it has been noted that the search for neutrality of principle may be intended as more than a caution against judicial activism. It may represent an effort to avoid the application by judges of their own value choices and to substitute the application of reason to principles which are universally accepted.[136]

Since this broader interpretation of the call for neutrality states a position which is untenable, it would do no credit to Professor Wechsler to hang it around his neck.[137] Such a retreat from choice among values is obviously impossible, for when two or more great principles collide a judge cannot reason to his decision on the basis of one of them without sacrificing another. However neutral the opposing principles may be when stated singly or abstractly, one cannot neutrally choose between them. Thus an argument for such pure

---

98, at 708; 2 Davis, *op. cit. supra* note 9, at 393–94, 404. If the court fails to notify them, and either the loser or the appellate court doubts an assumption's validity, memoranda can be presented to contradict it, or the appellate court can remand for more testimony. If the assumption is unstated and also unsuspected by the appellate court, there is no danger that the decision will be affirmed on that ground.

[133] Wechsler, *supra* note 4.

[134] *Id.* at 19.

[135] Hand, *op. cit. supra* note 29, at chap. 2.

[136] Pollak, *supra* note 44, at 33.

[137] Professor Pollak does not go this far. See *id.* at 32–34. So broad an interpretation of the Wechsler statement provides a vulnerable target. See Mueller & Schwartz, *The Principle of Neutral Principles*, 7 U.C.L.A. L. Rev. 571 (1960).

neutrality in decision-making would partake of the same vice that inheres in the position of the constitutional absolutists: both would seek an unattainable escape from the exercise of judgment.[138]

Emphasis on the legislative facts points a way out of the difficulties—presumed or real—raised by the call for neutrality. If such neutral principles do exist, and if we are to derive our decisions from them, then it takes no argument to show that a court will do a better job of deciding if it has been adequately informed as to the factual links between the challenged governmental action and the neutral principles involved. If the Equal Protection Clause expresses such a principle, then a court which decides on the constitutionality of racial segregation on public busses ought to know whether the segregation puts the challenging Negroes at a disadvantage. And we ought to have an opinion which explains how the Court concludes that it does put them at a disadvantage.[139]

Assuming, however, that there is room for "the disciplined exercise by a Supreme Court justice of that justice's individual and strongly held philosophy,"[140] we should not give up our inquiry into the concrete facts which underlie legislation. One justification for the inquiry is political: Since each case decided by the Supreme Court makes law for thousands of similar transactions for the future, the Court needs information about those other transactions so that the decision of the case before it can reflect the Court's chosen values— whatever they may be—in as many transactions as possible. Since the principle of *stare decisis* limits the Court's ability to maneuver in future cases, the Court must, in effect, consider those cases as it decides the case at hand.

Politics aside, there may be another justification. While we cannot be sure that exposure of the judge to information will produce a decision based on information, we can hope that the development of the

---

[138] Professor Wechsler is plainly no absolutist. In speaking of the "preferred position" of First Amendment freedoms, he says, ". . . the concept is pernicious if it implies that there is any simple, mechanistic basis for determining priorities of values having constitutional dimension . . . [yet] some ordering of social values is essential. . . ." Wechsler, *supra* note 4, at 25.

[139] But see Gayle v. Browder, *supra* note 3. This is one of Professor Wechsler's most compelling examples. Wechsler, *supra* note 4, at 22–23.

[140] Pollak, *supra* note 44, at 33.

legislative facts will produce something of that effect. If we cannot be certain of informed decisions, we can hope that informed judges will give us better decisions. Such a position requires no apology. After all, much of our constitutional law rests on propositions which cannot be proved. When we hold a truth to be self-evident, we mean we believe it on faith. The traditional American faith in the value of education seems no less justified when applied to judges who make choices of community policy than when applied to the community itself.

ROBERT G. McCLOSKEY

ECONOMIC DUE PROCESS

AND THE SUPREME COURT:

AN EXHUMATION AND REBURIAL

I. The Problem

American political life has often been marked by a tendency
to adopt policies today and to think about them in some remote
tomorrow, if at all. This national habit of mind is presumably rooted
in our famous pragmatic temperament. Much can be—and has been
—said for it. But the attribute, like most attributes, has the defects of
its merits. If Jack builds a house without thinking the plan through
in advance, he may then justly congratulate himself that he is at
least sheltered from the elements while his more deliberative neigh-
bor still shivers. But he should not be surprised if it turns out that
the corners are a little awry or that the second bedroom impinges
on what he hoped would be an ample living room. He must accommodate himself to the fact that the *ad hoc* decisions of the past may
set unforeseen limits on his way of life in the future.

These general reflections about American propensities and their
consequences are also applicable to the modern history of America's
peculiar institution, the Supreme Court of the United States. Since
about 1937, the Court has been rebuilding its constitutional dwell-
ing place, knocking down a wall here, constructing a new corridor

Robert G. McCloskey is Professor of Government, Harvard University.

there, in response to a bewildering succession of conflicting impulses. If these impulses are united by some commonly shared understanding about the form and extent of the ultimate structure, the Justices have been remarkably taciturn about revealing it. Vast new areas of constitutional supervision have been opened in such decisions as *Palko v. Connecticut*,[1] *Burstyn v. Wilson*,[2] and *Brown v. Board of Education*,[3] to name only three among many. Other regions, once significant, have been closed off to judicial intervention: the fields of the national commerce power and of economic due process are the standard examples.[4] Still others have been temporarily opened, then more or less firmly shut again—or vice versa. One thinks of picketing as free speech,[5] on the one hand, and the flag-salute issue, on the other.[6] Each of these developments has been accompanied by one or more Court opinions offering a particularized justification: it would be nice to have that extra living room; or, no house really needs a separate dining room these days. But little attempt has been made to reckon with their effect on each other or on the over-all structure that was taking shape.

The purpose of this paper is to trace one such development in the disorderly constitutional flux of the past twenty-five years: the decline and virtual demise of "economic due process." Such a survey might seem to be mere bootless antiquarianism. But the story of the senescence of this once-robust doctrine may provide us with hints about several live questions that concern students of the Supreme Court. What is the character of the process which the Court goes through when it reaches a radical turning point in its doctrinal history? Why does this process take the form it does? More specifically, why did the Court abandon the cause of economic rights, and why so completely? Can the abandonment be fully justified in the light of any consistent view of the rights themselves or of the

---

[1] 302 U.S. 319 (1937).

[2] 343 U.S. 495 (1952).   [3] 347 U.S. 483 (1954).

[4] See Stern, *The Problems of Yesteryear—Commerce and Due Process*, 4 VAND. L. REV. 446 (1951).

[5] See Cox, *Strikes, Picketing and the Constitution*, 4 VAND. L. REV. 574 (1951).

[6] Minersville School Dist. v. Gobitis, 310 U.S. 586 (1940); West Virginia Bd. of Educ. v. Barnette, 319 U.S. 624 (1943); see MANWARING, RENDER UNTO CAESAR (1962); KURLAND, RELIGION AND THE LAW 41–47 (1962).

Court's role in our political system? If not, is it either likely or desirable that the law should retrace its steps in this field, or has the possibility of a second guess been foreclosed by the general drift of judicial history?

II. The Demise of a Doctrine: The Method

The judicial reaction against economic due process after 1937 is unique in the history of the Supreme Court. There have been gradual shifts from negativism to permissiveness, as in the antitrust field during the decades after *E. C. Knight*;[7] there have been abrupt departures from salient negative doctrines as in *Nebbia*[8] or in *Graves v. New York*.[9] But it is hard to think of another instance when the Court so thoroughly and quickly demolished a constitutional doctrine of such far-reaching significance. The concomitant destruction of "dual federalism" in the commerce field is doubtless the closest analogue. But there the negative standard had rested in fact on a comparatively scanty handful of precedents, and the Court in *United States v. Darby*[10] could draw on a line of contrary pronouncements beginning with Marshall. On the other hand, the judicial power to strike down an economic statute on the ground that it was "arbitrary, capricious, or unreasonable" had been frequently exercised and seemed to stand on a solid base. Most of the Court's critics and some of its friends might have hoped in the early 1930's that the "rational basis" standard would be applied more leniently. But only a singularly prescient observer could have dreamed that the Court would soon abandon the concept altogether.

Yet that is what happened. There is no need to retell the familiar story in detail,[11] but a few high points are worth repeating. *West Coast Hotel v. Parrish*[12] is commonly and rightly thought of as the

---

[7] United States v. E. C. Knight Co., 156 U.S. 1 (1895).

[8] Nebbia v. New York, 291 U.S. 502 (1934).

[9] Graves v. New York ex rel. O'Keefe, 306 U.S. 466 (1939).

[10] 312 U.S. 100 (1941).

[11] See Stern, *supra* note 4; Rodes, *Due Process and Social Legislation in the Supreme Court—a Post Mortem*, 33 Notre Dame Law. 5 (1957); Hetherington, *State Economic Regulation and Substantive Due Process of Law*, 53 Nw. U. L. Rev. 13, 226 (1958); Wood, Due Process of Law 1932–1949 (1951).

[12] 300 U.S. 379 (1937), overruling Adkins v. Children's Hospital, 261 U.S. 525 (1923).

watershed case. We know that it was because of what occurred thereafter. But the actual words of Chief Justice Hughes in that case did not suggest very plainly that the whole doctrine of substantive due process was scheduled for destruction. He spoke of the wage regulation as "reasonable," citing a 1911 decision,[13] and he even invoked in defense of the present law the distinction made in 1908 between men and women as parties to a labor contract.[14] It was still possible to believe, then, that the Court was merely overruling *Adkins*, but maintaining its power to strike down other economic legislation that might fail the reasonableness test. *Senn v. Tile Layers Protective Union*,[15] a little later in the Term, suggested that the range of allowable legislative judgment was growing but not that it was unlimited. In *United States v. Carolene Products*,[16] a year later, Justice Stone for the majority went a little further, declaring that regulatory legislation is valid unless the facts "*preclude* the assumption that it rests upon some rational basis." But he still assumed "for present purposes" that an economic statute could be attacked by disproving the facts that were supposed to provide the law with its rational base, and his approval of the law seemed to rest in part on his judicial knowledge that there were facts to support a legislative ukase against "filled milk."

But by 1941, in *Olsen v. Nebraska*,[17] the Court was ready to take another long stride away from the pre–1937 doctrine. The subject matter of this case evoked fond memories of those bygone days, for it concerned regulation of employment-agency rates, and such regulation had been roundly condemned by the old Court in *Ribnik v. McBride*.[18] But now Mr. Justice Douglas, for a unanimous Court, not only repudiated *Ribnik* and its famous doctrine of "business affected with a public interest," but came close to announcing that the issue of economic regulation was no longer of judicial concern. There is no requirement, he said, that the State make out a case for the needfulness or appropriateness of the law. "Differences of opinion on that score suggest a choice which 'should be left where

---

[13] Chicago, B. & Q. R.R. v. McGuire, 219 U.S. 549 (1911), cited 300 U.S. at 392.

[14] Muller v. Oregon, 208 U.S. 412 (1908), cited 300 U.S. at 394.

[15] 301 U.S. 468 (1937).

[16] 304 U.S. 144, 152 (1938). (Emphasis added.)

[17] 313 U.S. 236.   [18] 277 U.S. 350 (1928).

... it was left by the Constitution—to the states and to Congress.' "[19] There was no suggestion here, as there was in *West Coast Hotel* and *Carolene Products*, that the State must point to facts which might reasonably justify the regulation. The presumption of constitutionality was no longer debatable. *Olsen* suggested, as a contemporary comment put it, that there was then "a complete lack of constitutional foundation for the assertion of private right under the due process clause where contractual or proprietary interests are involved."[20]

In case the business community and its legal minions might have missed the point in 1941, the Court made it pellucid in later decisions. Everyone has his favorites among these, but a reference to *Day-Brite Lighting v. Missouri*[21] and *Williamson v. Lee Optical Co.*[22] should suffice. In the first, the Court, again via Mr. Justice Douglas, declared that it was not the business of the Court to decide whether legislation "offends the public welfare"[23] and that "debatable issues as respects business, economic, and social affairs" were for legislative decision.[24] In the second, the same Justice upheld a law requiring a prescription from an optometrist or ophthalmologist before an optician could even fit old lenses into a new frame. Though the law may exact a "needless, wasteful requirement in many cases," the legislature "might have concluded" that the waste was justified in order to achieve the objective of protecting health.[25] When these cases were taken together with a companion series in which the Equal Protection Clause was given a similarly permissive scope,[26] there could be little doubt as to the practical result: no claim of substantive economic rights would now be sustained by the Supreme Court. The judiciary had abdicated the field.

This was the result. But it is of some interest to note how the result had been achieved. Obviously two paths lay open. One was that which seemed to be suggested by Mr. Justice Black's dissent in

---

[19] 313 U.S. at 246.

[20] 40 MICH. L. REV. 743, 745–46 (1942).

[21] 342 U.S. 421 (1952).

[22] 348 U.S. 483 (1955).

[23] 342 U.S. at 423.

[24] *Id.* at 425.

[25] 348 U.S. at 487.

[26] See, *e.g.*, Railway Express Agency, Inc. v. New York, 336 U.S. 106 (1949); Queenside Hills Realty Co. v. Saxl, 328 U.S. 80 (1946).

Connecticut General Life Insurance Co. v. Johnson,[27] *i.e.,* to repudi-
ate in explicit and unmistakable terms the very bases for the Court's
jurisdiction over economic questions. Such a course was at least
imaginable. The Justices might have reconsidered not only the
corporation-as-person doctrine, as Black proposed, but the very
idea of substantive due process in the economic field. They might,
that is, have held in so many words that economic legislation was no
longer subject to judicial review on the question whether it had a
"rational basis." This possibility may have been in Stone's mind
(though never, one suspects, in his plans) when in *Carolene Products* he only assumed "for present purposes" that the rational basis
test was still relevant; it may partly explain Black's disavowal of
that portion of Stone's opinion.[28] Certainly Douglas came close to it
in *Olsen.* A few years later, in the *Lincoln Union* case,[29] Black came
even closer when he implied that the only constitutional limits in
the economic field were the specific prohibitions of the Constitution.

The other possibility was to retain the rhetoric of the rational
basis standard, but to apply it so tolerantly that no law was ever
likely to violate it. This was the course ultimately chosen, one more
consonant with Stone's view that such issues were better dealt with
"gradually and by intimation."[30] Even Douglas seems to have accepted the rational basis concept for these rhetorical purposes.[31]

This was perhaps the "judicial" way to bring the result about. It
preserved some shreds of the idea of continuity, and that idea,
myth or not, is important to the constitutional tradition. It enabled
the Justices to feel their way along toward a policy whose contours
were probably not yet clear in their own minds. It may have helped
to maintain unanimity: it is hard enough to understand how Justice
Roberts could have accepted the *Olsen* opinion; it is even harder to
envision him concurring in an explicit renunciation of all judicial
authority to protect property holders.

[27] 303 U.S. 77, 83 (1938).   [28] 304 U.S. at 155.

[29] Lincoln Federal Labor Union v. Northwestern Iron & Metal Co., 335 U.S. 525
(1949).

[30] MASON, HARLAN FISKE STONE: PILLAR OF THE LAW 469 (1956); see also Dunham,
Mr. Chief Justice Stone, in DUNHAM & KURLAND, MR. JUSTICE 47 (1956).

[31] See DOUGLAS, WE THE JUDGES (1956).

So much at least can be said for the approach chosen, leaving aside for the moment the question whether the result itself was desirable. But the matter has another aspect. When policies are established "gradually and by intimation," when the question of their existence is partially obscured by preservation of the old rhetoric, there is always a chance that the destruction of those policies will not be recognized. A flat decision to discard substantive due process root-and-branch would have compelled the Justices to explain themselves, to examine the basis for their abnegation. In the actual event they have never fully done so, at least in public, and this leaves, to say the least, a large gap in the rationale that underlies the structure of modern constitutional law.

The reticence of the Court does, however, provide the non-judicial observer with an opportunity. It leaves him free to speculate about the explanations and justifications that the Justices have neglected to provide. And the speculation at least seems desirable: one of the cardinal doctrines of American constitutional history should not be denied the modest rite of a funeral oration.

III. Action and Reaction

What then was the explanation of this extraordinary shift in judicial values? It must be emphasized that this is not merely the question why the Court took leave of the unyielding negativism represented by such judgments as *Adair v. United States*[32] or *Coppage v. Kansas*[33] or by the anti–New Deal dogmatics of 1934–1936. That question may not be an easy one, for historical questions seldom are, but its mysteries are not unfathomable. An answer would have to begin with the specific enigma of Justice Roberts; after that the road is comparatively clear. His shift in 1937 created a majority opposed to the extreme version of constitutional laissez faire, and it was to be expected that that majority would be strengthened as new appointments were made in the following years. The shift from *Morehead v. New York ex rel. Tipaldo*[34] to *West Coast Hotel*, startling though it was as a specific event, was not beyond prediction: the basis for it had been well laid in the recent past by both judges and scholars.

The harder question is: Why did the Court move all the way from

---

[32] 208 U.S. 161 (1908).   [33] 236 U.S. 1 (1915).   [34] 298 U.S. 587 (1936).

the inflexible negativism of the old majority to the all-out tolerance of the new? Why did it not establish a halfway house between the extremes, retaining a measure of control over economic legislation but exercising that control with discrimination and self-restraint?

Precisely such a halfway house had frequently been described in judicial opinions of the past, so there is little chance that the post-1937 Justices had overlooked its conceptual existence. Justice Brandeis in *New State Ice Co. v. Liebmann*[35] had admonished the Court against erecting its prejudices into legal principles but had still conceded that "the reasonableness of every regulation is dependent on the relevant facts."[36] Indeed, he conducted an exhaustive examination of those facts in his opinion. Justice Stone had himself carefully adumbrated such a position, saying in *Ribnik* that price regulation is within the States' power when "any combination of circumstances seriously curtails the regulative force of competition, so that buyers or sellers are placed at such a disadvantage in the bargaining struggle that a legislature might reasonably anticipate serious consequences to the community as a whole."[37] To be sure, Justice Holmes had, in *Tyson & Brother v. Banton*,[38] laid down a standard comparable in its permissiveness to the *Olsen* doctrine:[39] "The truth seems to me to be that, subject to compensation when compensation is due, the legislature may forbid or restrict any business when it has a sufficient force of public opinion behind it." This is the *de facto* policy of the modern Court. But Stone, as has been said, filed a separate dissent in *Tyson*, and even Holmes in other opinions had conceded that the supposed rational basis of economic statutes is subject to judicial scrutiny.[40] As a result of such scrutiny, the Court would not strike down an arguably rational law, but it would require some showing by the State that there was a basis for believing it to be rational and would consider evidence to the contrary presented by the affected business. Laws like those involved in the *Lee Optical* case[41] and in *Daniel v. Family Security Life Ins.*

35 285 U.S. 262, 311 (1932).   36 *Id.* at 301–02.

37 277 U.S. at 360 (dissenting opinion).

38 273 U.S. 418, 445 (1927) (dissenting opinion).   39 *Id.* at 446.

40 See, *e.g.*, Adkins v. Children's Hospital, 261 U.S. 525, 567 (1923) (dissenting opinion).

41 Note 22 *supra*.

Co.[42] might be invalidated, or at any rate more sharply queried.

Assuming then that this standard—this modest residue of the old economic supervision—was consciously and purposefully rejected, what explains the rejection? And, to make the difficulty a little more acute, what accounts for the fact that such survivors of the old Court as Stone and Roberts concurred in the choice, that the *Olsen* opinion was unanimous? A couple of "behavioral" or psychological explanations come to mind as possibilities. They are put forward diffidently, for motive is hard to ascertain with respect to only one man; when a group of nine highly sophisticated individuals is involved, the complexities become awesome.

For one thing, it may be that Stone and Roberts joined in the movement so as to preserve the rhetoric of supervision and thus some faint shadow of doctrinal continuity. Black, as his biographer says, wanted to "reject utterly and completely the doctrine . . . that the due-process clause gives to courts the power to determine the reasonableness of regulations."[43] Considering his well-known enthusiasm for calling a spade a spade,[44] we can well believe that Black would have liked to spell this out in an explicit abdication speech. We cannot tell how many of his brethren would have joined him then. But by the spring of 1941, there were, besides himself, four Roosevelt appointees on the Court, and further appointments were obviously pending. The veterans may have felt that the most they could hope for was the fictional survival of the rational basis test.

A second possible explanation may be more fruitful, since it relates, not only to the question why the veterans were willing to retreat so far, but also why the newer Justices seemed resolved to do so. It is that extremism had bred extremism in thinking about the role of the Supreme Court. Between 1923 and 1937, a conservative majority had, from time to time, embraced a policy of adamant resistance to economic experiment, and this obstructionist spirit had reached its zenith in the judicial reaction against the New Deal.

---

[42] 336 U.S. 220 (1949). The statute prohibited life insurance companies and their employees from operating undertaking businesses, and undertakers from serving as agents for life insurance companies.

[43] FRANK, MR. JUSTICE BLACK: THE MAN AND HIS OPINIONS 111 (1949).

[44] See MENDELSON, JUSTICES BLACK AND FRANKFURTER: CONFLICT IN THE COURT (1961).

What the Chief Justice himself had said in the *Railroad Retirement* case[45] was true of the conservative majority in most of the great anti–New Deal decisions. That majority had raised a barrier, not only against particular features of the law, but "against all legislative action of this nature by declaring that the subject matter itself lies beyond the reach" of governmental authority.[46] This intransigence had tended to discredit the whole concept of judicial supervision in the minds of those who felt that government must have reasonable leeway to experiment with the economic order. The result was that the two wings of the Court (and of the country) had almost ceased to communicate with each other. The dissenting opinions of Stone in *United States v. Butler*[47] and Sutherland in *West Coast Hotel*[48] are not a dialogue between men who share a common ground but disagree about its implications. The opinions represent wholly different realms of discourse. If the position of the conservatives had been less extreme, there might have been in 1937 the basis for a viable, moderate doctrine of economic supervision. It is almost touching to observe Sutherland, in *Carmichael v. Southern Coal & Coke Co.*,[49] after the "revolution" of 1937, urging that the State law could be cured of its constitutional infirmities and that, if it were, the objective of relieving unemployment could be attained despite the Due Process Clause. This language of sweet reason had not been conspicuous in the negative decisions of previous years. Now it came too late. The extreme of the past had generated the extreme of the present. The Court which had claimed the full loaf was winding up without even the half. Such a result is not surprising when dogmatism has been substituted for discussion.

Factors like these may help to explain the impulse to discard the old due process doctrine, bag and baggage. Yet one would like to think that a more thoughtful process was going on somewhere below the surface, that the policy of virtual abdication was not merely a reflex against the excesses of the past but a considered and justified decision about the proper scope of judicial review. The written

[45] Railroad Retirement Board v. Alton R.R., 295 U.S. 330, 374 (1935) (dissenting opinion).

[46] *Id.* at 375.

[47] 297 U.S. 1, 78 (1936).

[48] 300 U.S. at 401.   [49] 301 U.S. 495, 527 (1937) (dissenting opinion).

record to support such a supposition is not, alas, very convincing.[50] Scattered remarks in decisions cited above, and in others, assailed the dead horse of "the Allgeyer-Lochner-Adair-Coppage" doctrine,[51] *i.e.*, the Justices argued against "social dogma" and for "increased deference to the legislative judgment"[52] in the economic field. But they did not explain why the abuses of power in those earlier decisions justified abandonment of the power itself, nor why the deference to the legislature should be carried to the point of complete submission. The nearest thing to an explanation is perhaps to be found in Mr. Justice Frankfurter's concurrence in *American Federation of Labor v. American Sash & Door Co.*, where he argued that "the judiciary is prone to misconceive the public good" and that matters of policy, depending as they do on imponderable value issues, are best left to the people and their representatives.[53] This is a coherent and not unconvincing viewpoint, but the trouble with it has always been that it implied similar judicial withdrawal, not only from the economic field, but from other areas that pose questions of policy, such as freedom of expression. Well aware of this difficulty, Frankfurter tried to meet it in this opinion by declaring that matters like press censorship and separation of church and state are different, because "history, through the Constitution, speaks so decisively as to forbid legislative experimentation" with them.[54] Scholarship has since provided reason to doubt that history speaks so plainly after all, even on these subjects,[55] and without a strong historical rationale the argument falters badly, for the arguments against judicial intervention in economic affairs become arguments against intervention in the policy sphere generally. Learned

---

[50] FREUND, ON UNDERSTANDING THE SUPREME COURT 11 (1949); Learned Hand said in 1946: "Just why property itself was not a 'personal right' nobody took the time to explain." HAND, THE SPIRIT OF LIBERTY 206 (1960). Nobody, so far as I am aware, has yet taken that time.

[51] Lincoln Federal Labor Union v. Northwestern Iron & Metal Co., 335 U.S. 525, 535 (1949).

[52] A. F. of L. v. American Sash & Door Co., 335 U.S. 538, 544 (1949) (concurring opinion).

[53] *Id.* at 556.

[54] *Id.* at 550.

[55] LEVY, LEGACY OF SUPPRESSION (1960); Brief for Appellees, McCollum v. Board of Educ., 333 U.S. 203 (1948).

Hand of course was ready to accept this implication[56] and Frank-furter himself has come very near to it. But it is certainly not the dominant doctrine of the modern Court, which has fairly con-sistently held to the "dual standard" enunciated by Stone in the *Carolene Products* case.[57] So we are left with a judicial policy which rejects supervision over economic matters and asserts supervision over "personal rights"; and with a rationale, so far as the written opinions go, that might support withdrawal from both fields but does not adequately justify the discrimination between them.

IV. The Doubtful Distinction between Economic and Civil Rights

Although no such rationale can be detected in the written opinions, however, the possibility of its existence cannot be entire-ly dismissed. The Supreme Court has sometimes preferred to leave ultimate arguments unexpressed, to let justification for a course of conduct, as well as the course itself, emerge "gradually and by inti-mation." And this may be the case with the great retreat from eco-nomic supervision. Perhaps there is a coherent apologia for that retreat; perhaps this apologia was in the Justices' minds when they shaped the modern constitutional policy. The second "perhaps" can never be transmuted into certainty unless the art of judicial psycho-analysis reaches unforeseen heights. But its plausibility may increase if it appears that there is a rationale which *might* have formed the basis of the policy.

The arguments for demoting economic rights to their modern lowly constitutional status—lowly when compared wtih "personal rights"—fall into two categories. First, there is a group of arguments based on judgments about the nature and relative importance of the rights concerned. For example, it is sometimes argued that laws limiting freedom of expression impinge on the human personality more grievously than do laws curbing mere economic liberty, and that the Court is therefore justified in protecting the former more zealously than the latter.[58] The individual has, *qua* individual, "the

---

[56] Hand, The Bill of Rights (1958).

[57] Freund, *op. cit. supra* note 50.

[58] Hastie, *Judicial Method in Due Process Inquiry*, in Government under Law 326 (Sutherland ed. 1956). He makes an exception of subsistence.

right to be let alone."[59] The right to free choice in the intellectual
and spiritual realm is particularly precious to him. A major difficulty with this formulation is that there is the smell of the lamp
about it: it may reflect the tastes of the judges and dons who advance it, rather than the real preferences of the commonality of mor-
tals. Judges and professors are talkers both by profession and avoca-
tion. It is not surprising that they would view freedom of expression
as primary to the free play of their personalities. But most men
would probably feel that an economic right, such as freedom of
occupation, was at least as vital to them as the right to speak their
minds. Mark Twain would surely have felt constrained in the most
fundamental sense, if his youthful aspiration to be a river-boat pilot
had been frustrated by a State-ordained system of nepotism.[60] Needless to say, no disparagement of freedom of expression is here intended. But its inarguable importance to the human spirit, on the
one hand, does not furnish an adequate ground for downgrading all
economic rights, on the other.

So much for a purely individual-centered justification for the dis-
parity between economic rights and other civil liberties. Another
suggested rationale looks toward the community rather than the
separate individuals within it. Progress, it is said, "is to a considerable extent the displacement of error which once held sway as
official truth by beliefs which in turn have yielded to other beliefs."[61] To encourage societal progress, it is important then to protect "those liberties of the individual which history has attested as
the indispensable conditions of an open as against a closed society,"[62]
e.g., freedom of expression.

Presumably this "open society" argument would be relevant no
matter how the political system was organized—even a benevolent
autocracy must tolerate freedom of expression or risk stagnation.
But Alexander Meiklejohn has contended that the point takes on an
extra dimension when applied to popular government, to democracy
as the West understands that term. In any political system, so the
argument runs, the ruler must be fully informed if he is to govern

[59] Brandeis, J., dissenting, in Olmstead v. United States, 277 U.S. 438, 478 (1928).
[60] Kotch v. Pilot Commissioners, 330 U.S. 552 (1947).
[61] Frankfurter, J., concurring, in Kovacs v. Cooper, 336 U.S. 77 at 95.
[62] *Ibid.*

well, and he cannot be fully informed when someone else is deciding what ideas he shall be allowed to hear. In a democracy the
people are sovereign, and it follows that they and no one else must
decide what and whom they will listen to. And it further follows
that the Constitution must protect any freedoms that help the
people to acquire "the intelligence, integrity, sensitivity, and gen-
erous devotion to the general welfare that, in theory, casting a
ballot is assumed to express."[63] In short, the special importance of
certain civil rights derives from their special relationship to the
process of self-government. Other rights, including the economic,
can be abridged when the legislature deems abridgment desirable.

Some such reasoning probably underlies the related point implied
by Mr. Justice Stone in the first paragraph of his famous "footnote
four"[64] and by Mr. Justice Frankfurter in the concluding words of
the first flag-salute opinion[65] (though neither would of course have
followed Professor Meiklejohn in the absolutist conclusions he
drew). Stone suggested that judicial scrutiny would be especially
exacting when legislation restricted "those political processes which
can ordinarily be expected to bring about repeal of undesirable legislation,"[66] and Frankfurter intimated that the crucial question is
whether "all the effective means of inducing political changes are
left free from interference."[67] These pronouncements may rest
partly on Professor Meiklejohn's point that the governors must be
fully informed; but they also seem to involve a separable idea: that
a majoritarian system must, in the name of both justice and progress,
preserve the right of a present minority to make its views the views
of the majority. A businessman's price may be controlled by the
mandate of a popularly elected legislature, but, if his right to work
politically for repeal of the control law is untrammeled, the funda-
mentals of a just democratic polity are still maintained and so is the
fluidity of the sociopolitical order.

The whole "open society" line of argument in its various forms
is convincing enough as a justification for protecting the free trade

---

[63] Meiklejohn, *The First Amendment Is an Absolute*, [1961] SUPREME COURT RE-
VIEW 245, 255.

[64] United States v. Carolene Products Co., 304 U.S. 144, 152 (1938).

[65] Minersville School Dist. v. Gobitis, 310 U.S. 586, 600 (1940).

[66] 304 U.S. at 152.   [67] 310 U.S. at 600.

in ideas. If one feels the need to explain why the free speech guarantees are important, these explanations will do pretty well for a start. But they are rather less satisfactory as the basis for a policy of *not* protecting economic freedom, of regarding it as unimportant in a democratic system. For one thing, it is not entirely clear why liberty of economic choice is less indispensable to the "openness" of a society than freedom of expression. Few historians would deny that the growth of entrepreneurial and occupational freedom helped to promote material progress in England in the eighteenth and nineteenth centuries and in America after the Civil War (although they might of course argue that the price paid for this progress was unconscionably high). It is one thing to argue that economic liberty must be subject to rational control in the "public interest"; it is quite another to say in effect that it is not liberty at all and that the proponent of the "open society" can therefore regard it as irrelevant to progress.

As for the "political process" subthemes of the open-society argument—the Meiklejohn-Stone-Frankfurter rationales just described—they too must be queried insofar as they purport to justify a downgrading of economic rights. In fact, their basic difficulty is that, in exalting the freedoms bearing on the political process, they bypass the question of other freedoms altogether. Meiklejohn's arguments for protecting liberty of expression are cogent, but they do not on their face explain why other, "private," rights should be neglected. A decision to protect Peter does not necessarily involve the decision to abandon Paul. In Meiklejohn's own formulation there is indeed a hint that the political is primary, that a right associated with the governing process somehow, because of that association, matters more than any other. This might be so in some imaginary democratic city-state where the political and the social were identical, but it is more dubious when applied to the United States where the sphere of private value can make high claims of its own. One may agree that it is necessary for popular government to protect the political process. But it does not follow that all concern for rights comes to an end when that protection has been provided. Moreover, there is some evidence that Meiklejohn's categories refuse to stand still, even in his own mind. He is not content to define the governing-process freedoms narrowly. He rightly says that "voting is merely the external expression of a wide and diverse number of activities by means of which citizens attempt to meet the responsibilities of making judgments";[68] and this enables him to bring literature and the arts within the concept, since they "lead the way toward sensitive and informed appreciation and response to the values out of which the riches of the general welfare are created."[69] We can refuse to swallow whole the dogmas of nineteenth-century rugged individualism and can still believe that some freedom of occupation and economic choice is also instrumental to the development of this self-determining and sensitive citizen-governor.

If Meiklejohn's argument contains the unexamined assumption that the political is primary and almost exclusive, the "Stone-Frankfurter"[70] point described above contains this and an assumption of its own as well: the majoritarian idea in a peculiarly unqualified form. The notion seems to be that the citizen can have nothing really fundamental to complain about in a law if a free majority has enacted it and if he is protected in his right to agitate for its repeal. But this view ascribes a preponderance to the majority will that has certainly not been acknowledged by the American political tradition. In that tradition, it is not assumed that an unjust law becomes just by virtue of majority approval, not even if the victim has the theoretical right to persuade the majority to change its mind. The denial of that right would aggravate the injustice, but the granting of the right does not dispel it. As Justice Jackson said in the flag-salute dialogue,[71] the very purpose of a Bill of Rights was to place certain fundamental rights beyond the reach of majorities.[72] Of course, it may be argued that economic freedom in its various forms can never be so fundamental a right, but that shifts the discussion to a quite different level.

Furthermore this argument overlooks a difficulty partly recognized by Stone himself in the *Carolene Products* footnote[73] and in-

---

[68] Meiklejohn, *supra* note 63.

[69] *Id.* at 257.

[70] This term is used only for the purposes of expositional convenience. It does not imply that the particular point referred to represents the full position of either of the two Justices on this question or that their views on the question were identical.

[71] West Virginia Bd. of Educ. v. Barnette, 319 U.S. 624 (1943).

[72] *Id.* at 638.   [73] 304 U.S. at 152, n. 4.

voked by him in the first flag-salute case, the problem of "discrete and insular minorities,"[74] *i.e.*, those who have no realistic chance of influencing the majority to rescind the law that does them harm. Stone was speaking specifically of religious, national, or racial minorities, and his suggestion was that prejudice against them might curtail the political processes that would ordinarily be expected to protect their rights. Prejudice against Jehovah's Witnesses for their "queerness" makes repressive governmental action more probable, and precisely because of their queerness they are not likely to be numerous enough or influential enough in any given community so that their weight will be felt in the city council. To speak of their power to defend themselves through political action is to sacrifice their civil rights in the name of an amiable fiction. Yet it is not clear why the thrust of this point should be restricted to ethnic and religious minorities. Perhaps it is true that a prosperous corporation can effectively plead its case at the bar of legislative judgment by resort to publicity and direct lobbying. Economic power may be an adequate surrogate for numerical power; no tears need be shed for helpless General Electric. But the scattered individuals who are denied access to an occupation by State-enforced barriers are about as impotent a minority as can be imagined. The would-be barmaids of Michigan[75] or the would-be plumbers of Illinois[76] have no more chance against the entrenched influence of the established bartenders and master plumbers than the Jehovah's Witnesses had against the prejudices of Minersville School District. In fact the Witnesses may enjoy an advantage, for they are at least cohesive; and other "discrete" minorities, such as racial groups, have occasionally displayed respectable capacities to exert political leverage by virtue of their very discreteness. Not so the isolated economic man who belongs to no identifiable group at all.

V. JUDICIAL CAPACITY IN THE REALM OF ECONOMIC REGULATION

For one reason or another then, none of these justifications of the Court's modern hands-off policy in the economic field quite

---

[74] Stone, J., dissenting, 310 U.S. at 606.

[75] Goesaert v. Cleary, 335 U.S. 464 (1948).

[76] People v. Brown, 407 Ill. 565 (1951). See GELLHORN, INDIVIDUAL FREEDOM AND GOVERNMENTAL RESTRAINTS 123–24 (1956).

stands up. The distinctions they rely on, between economic rights on the one hand and personal rights on the other, tend to blur when we examine them. And, even if it were thought that the distinctions were tenable, the case would remain incomplete. It might, squeezing it hard, justify a difference in the kind and degree of protection afforded economic rights; but it would not warrant a policy of no protection at all.

Although the policy of abdication cannot be justified in terms of an analysis of the nature and relative unimportance of the rights concerned, there is a second line of thought that merits consideration. Perhaps the decision to leave economic rights to the tender mercy of the legislative power is based on the idea that the Supreme Court is peculiarly ill-equipped to deal with this subject. No one would argue that the right enshrined in Article IV, the guarantee of a republican form of government, is unimportant. Yet the Court has refused to protect it, because of well-founded doubts about judicial competence to make effective judgments in this field. It may be that similar doubts underlie the policy of abdication in the area of economic affairs.

At first blush, this argument seems highly persuasive, at least in broad terms. Anyone familiar with the entanglements resulting from *Smyth v. Ames*[77] will be alive to its merits. Probably no court was really equipped to make the intricate and imponderable economic judgments that the doctrine of that case entailed. And those who remember the Court's crusades against the rise of the welfare state may be dubious about judicial competence on somewhat different grounds. They may feel that economic policy is not only beyond the reach of the Court's expertise, but beyond the reach of its practical power. Whether the nation shall have a minimum-wage law; whether the government shall control prices; whether social security shall be publicly guaranteed—these are questions so "high"[78] and so basic that no court could determine them even if it should. They involve in a word the momentous issue of the welfare state itself, and that issue will be determined by "dominant opinion" with or without judicial approval.

There are, of course, economic subjects so recondite that judicial surveillance of them would be anomalous. The choice between

---

[77] 169 U.S. 466 (1898).

[78] Finkelstein, *Judicial Self-Limitation*, 37 HARV. L. REV. 338, 345 (1924).

"historical cost" and "replacement cost" as a basis for rate making must be made by the legislature, not because it will always choose well, but because the judiciary lacks the knowledge and expertise for distinguishing good from bad in this area. But this point will carry only as far as its logic will bring it, and there are fields of economic regulation less intricate than the problem of public utility rates. To be sure, even the problems raised in these fields may not be simple. A fair evaluation of Oklahoma's need for its anti-optician law would require the Court to make judgments about a complex matter. But this can be said about most questions that reach the Supreme Court in any field. Our problem is not to identify the issues that present difficulties and then to discard them as improper subjects for judicial review. That would be to abandon judicial review in most of the fields where it is now exercised. Our problem is to determine whether economic statutes always or usually involve such extraordinary difficulties that a modest judiciary must eschew them, even though that same judiciary does claim the competence to judge other, more difficult, issues.

Is it easier for example for the Court to appraise a law empowering a board of censors to ban an "immoral" movie[79] than a law empowering a real estate licensing board to deny a license unless the applicant is of "good moral character"?[80] The two standards would seem to be equally vague and the possibility of arbitrary administrative action would seem to be as menacing in one situation as in the other. Is it plainly easier to balance New Hampshire's need to get information against Paul Sweezy's right to withhold it,[81] than it is to balance South Carolina's need to stamp out the funeral insurance business against the right of an agent of the Family Security Life Insurance Company to make a living selling such insurance?[82] The "public need" in both cases was all but invisible. Is it easier to see that the State corporate registration law in *N.A.A.C.P. v. Alabama*[83] was being used to facilitate private reprisals against Association members than it is to see that State boards of plumbers, barbers, and morticians sometimes use their publicly granted powers to pro-

---

[79] Kingsley International Pictures Corp. v. Regents, 360 U.S. 684 (1959).

[80] GELLHORN, *op. cit. supra* note 76, at 121.

[81] Sweezy v. New Hampshire, 354 U.S. 234 (1957).

[82] Daniel v. Family Security Life Ins. Co., 336 U.S. 220 (1949).

[83] 357 U.S. 449 (1958).

tect the private financial interests of present guild members to the disadvantage of non-members?[84]

The point is not that the cited cases should necessarily have been decided differently, but rather that the issues they present stand on a common level of difficulty and that judicial scrutiny seems as feasible (or unfeasible) for one issue as for the other. And the further, related, point is that there are kinds and kinds of economic subjects and that it is difficult to fashion a generalization that applies to all. Some subjects may be so inscrutable that judicial review cannot fruitfully cope with them; but this is not a justification for avoiding other economic subjects which are no more opaque than the "personal rights" issues that are the standard coinage of judicial discourse these days.

This point likewise applies to the suggestion that the Court, as the relatively weak and non-political branch, simply lacks the power to dictate the economic order, however otherwise competent its members may be. No doubt the Court was presumptuous to imagine, before 1937, that it could hold back such waves as the wage-control movement or the demand for social security. The tide of the welfare state was flowing, and no court could have reversed it. But neither does the judiciary have the practical power to halt any major social developments backed by insistent popular demand. And this would be so whether the development involved economic questions or questions of "personal rights." It was the dimension of the issues in the anti–New Deal cases that made them incongruous for judicial decision, not the mere fact that they were economic in character. No such judicial delusions of grandeur would be implied by enforcement of the requirement that an occupational qualification must be rationally based, or by similar modest applications of substantive due process. The awful will of the sovereign people is not likely to be aroused because the Court has told the morticians of Winnemac that they cannot use State power to maintain a monopoly—or at least no more than it is aroused by other constitutional decisions that issue almost weekly during each Term. In short, while doubts about judicial expertise and power may warrant withdrawal from some economic questions, they cannot justify withdrawal from all such questions, unless the doubter is willing to go

---

[84] See Grant, *The Gild Returns to America,* 4 J. Pol. 303 (1942).

the full distance with Learned Hand and give up most of the residue of modern judicial review.

VI. The Disappearing Double Standard

In the light of the inadequacies that seem to afflict all of the arguments for judicial abdication of the field of economic rights, we are perhaps justified in concluding that the policy of abstention was never really thought through. It seems to have been a kind of reflex, arising out of indignation against the excesses of the Old Court, and resting on the vague, uncritical idea that "personal rights" are "O.K." but economic rights are "Not O.K." Thus are fashioned the decisions about the shape of our constitutional polity.

This conclusion gains strength when we note from time to time certain signs of uneasiness with the "double standard." The most familiar such manifestation appears in the judicial and extra-judicial remarks of jurists like Learned Hand, Robert Jackson,[85] and Felix Frankfurter. Their misgivings center around the problem of justifying judicial activism in any field where the Court's only guideposts are the inexplicit "moral adjurations"[86] of the Bill of Rights. They have doubts about a judge's capacity to enforce such adjurations in the economic realm, and their modesty is not altogether dissipated when they turn to the field of personal rights; for they are unsatisfied by easy phrases like "preferred position." Hand, as has been said, carried his doubts somewhat further than the others, perhaps because he was speaking *non ex cathedra* in semiretirement. Jackson and Frankfurter have expressed themselves more restrainedly and therefore less clearly, but the broad drift of their qualms has been plain enough. They would partly resolve the dilemma of the double standard by adopting a modest approach to both economic rights and personal rights, though still retaining perhaps some distinction between them.

The other possibility of course would be, not to protect both kinds of rights less, but to protect both equally, *i.e.*, to reassert the Court's power to disallow economic legislation that lacks a rational basis. It would be too much to say that such a development is por-

---

[85] Jackson, The Supreme Court in the American System of Government 57–58 (1955).

[86] Hand, *op. cit. supra* note 50, at 163.

tended by a few sporadic judicial pronouncements in recent years, but they may indicate a measure of disquiet with the prevailing dichotomy. From the first the modern Court has been troubled by a recurring problem: how does the dichotomy stand up when economic matters and personal rights are involved in a single governmental action? Examples abound: statutes that strike at picketing, which may be both free speech and an economic activity;[87] State-supported professional dues-paying requirements, such as that involved in *Lathrop v. Donohue;*[88] labor regulations that impinge on freedom of religion;[89] license requirements, and other restrictions with a secular purpose, that nevertheless impose burdens on religious practice,[90] to name only a few. It is no help to the judge faced by these hybrid problems to tell him that the economic order is Caesar's affair while personal rights are the Constitution's affair, for the twain have met and he must decide between one or the other. One solution is to hold that a law primarily "secular" in purpose must stand even if it operates incidentally to infringe personal rights; that the law or an application of it will fall only if it was aimed at or discriminates against personal rights as such.[91] Leaving aside the very real difficulty of determining what a law's primary purpose is, the trouble with this formula is that it does permit the state to impose *de facto* burdens on the exercise of personal rights, and this has disturbed some of the Justices. A Court that has resolved to protect personal rights because of their indispensability to democracy is not likely to be content with a doctrine that allows them to be frittered away, even though an otherwise legitimate secular purpose can be descried. Another imaginable solution is to filter out the personal-rights elements in the law and insist on their protection; the economic-rights residue being left, as usual, to the chance of legislative judgment. But this can involve very nettling problems of discrimination and remedy, as is demonstrated by the

---

[87] Thornhill v. Alabama, 310 U.S. 88 (1940).

[88] 367 U.S. 820 (1961).

[89] Prince v. Massachusetts, 321 U.S. 158 (1944).

[90] Murdock v. Pennsylvania, 319 U.S. 105 (1943); and cases cited in note 91 *infra*.

[91] Braunfeld v. Brown, 366 U.S. 599 (1961); Gallagher v. Crown Kosher Super Market, 366 U.S. 617 (1961); McGowan v. Maryland 366 U.S. 420 (1961); Two Guys from Harrison-Allentown, Inc. v. McGinley, 366 U.S. 582 (1961).

arguments in such recent decisions as *Lathrop v. Donohue*[92] and the Sunday Law cases.[93]

Moreover this last solution is likely to strain the logic of the Court's position more than it can perhaps bear. In the situation presented by the *Lathrop* case, for example, the Court would have to say that a lawyer has a "right" to practice his profession free from the kinds of restrictions to which the First Amendment refers, that he has under these circumstances a constitutional "right to work," but that the right somehow vanishes when the statute is cured of its First Amendment defects. The State can be as arbitrary as it likes in regulating my occupational freedom just so long as the regulations do not touch on my speech (or religion, or race, or perhaps national origin[94]). The logical strain inherent in such a position has been suggested above. The Court's dilemma is reminiscent of the 1920's, when constitutional history was moving in the opposite direction. A Court that had enshrined economic liberty in the Constitution under the due-process rubric found it increasingly difficult to maintain that the Due Process Clause did not protect other liberties that men might deem important. In spite of the flat statement to the contrary in 1922,[95] within three years thereafter freedom of expression was acknowledged as a constitutional right enforceable against State action.[96]

Perhaps an analogous restlessness helps account for hints about economic freedom, especially the right to work, that have turned up here and there in recent years. In *Barsky v. Board of Regents*[97] in 1954, the Court sustained the suspension of a physician's license against a charge of unreasonableness. The majority was willing to allow the license-revoking authority virtually unlimited discretion and would not conclude that whim and caprice had guided the authority's decision even though the evidence to that effect seemed fairly strong. This is the standard, extreme presumption of validity, that has effectively barred judicial review in the economic field. But the dissenters used language that may point in a rather different

---

[92] Note 88 *supra*.   [93] Note 91 *supra*.

[94] But see State of Ohio ex rel. Clarke v. Deckebach, 274 U.S. 392 (1927).

[95] Prudential Insurance Co. v. Cheek, 259 U.S. 530 (1922).

[96] Gitlow v. New York, 268 U.S. 652 (1925).   [97] 347 U.S. 442.

direction. Mr. Justice Frankfurter, while conceding that the Court must presume the validity of the State agency's action in the absence of evidence to the contrary, nevertheless argued that such evidence should be considered if it does appear on the record. And, in considering it, the Court should ask whether the revocation has "some rational relation to the qualifications required of a practitioner" in the profession. "If a State licensing agency lays bare its arbitrary action, or if the State law explicitly allows it to act arbitrarily, that is precisely the kind of State action which the Due Process Clause forbids."[98] True, the case involved the possibility that the agency here had been influenced by the appellant's supposed left-wing connections, so that this might be regarded as merely another example of special judicial sensitivity when personal rights and economic rights are mixed. But Frankfurter's words do not suggest that he would be any less hostile to an irrelevant standard because it lacked First Amendment undertones. And Douglas, also dissenting, described the right to work in terms that hardly suggest a niggardly interpretation of its range:[99]

> The right to work, I had assumed, was the most precious liberty that man possesses. Man has indeed as much right to work as he has to live, to be free, to own property. . . . To work means to eat. It also means to live. For many it would be better to work in jail, than to sit idle on the curb. The great values of freedom are in the opportunities afforded man to press to new horizons, to pit his strength against the forces of nature, to match skills with his fellow man.

It would be a little hard to laud a right so fully in one breath and in the next to say that judicial review has no concern with it except insofar as another right like freedom of speech is also involved.

In view of such pronouncements it is not surprising that the Court a few years later struck down such a restraint on occupational freedom. In *Schware v. Board of Bar Examiners*,[100] petitioner had been refused permission to take the State bar examination on the ground that he lacked "good moral character." Again First Amendment problems were mingled with the right-to-work issue, but again the language of the Justices suggested a standard that

---

[98] *Id*. at 470 (dissenting opinion).

[99] *Id*. at 472.   [100] 353 U.S. 232 (1957).

would forbid arbitrary determinations in general. Mr. Justice Black for the Court declared that State-imposed qualifications "must have a rational connection with the applicant's fitness or capacity" to practice the occupation, and continued: "Even in applying permissible standards, officers of a State cannot exclude an applicant when there is no basis for their finding that he fails to meet these standards, or when their action is invidiously discriminatory."[101] This language is potentially far-reaching, for its suggests (as does the body of the opinion) that the Court is prepared to review and evaluate the administration of licensing requirements in the professions and trades in general. If its potentiality were realized, it would mean that licensing boards were now constitutionally required to show that their findings had a basis in evidence, and that would go far to bring economic rights back under the shelter of the Constitution.

This is probably too much to wring from the decision, although it is easy to believe that Black would be quite prepared to carry it thus far. Mr. Justice Frankfurter's concurring opinion for himself and two others was much more careful. He would, as in his *Barsky* opinion, allow the Board wide discretion in judging "moral character" and would not question individual determinations simply because they involve intuitions, impressions, and other "subjective factors," rather than hard, objective evidence. But even he would overthrow a determination based on "*avowed* considerations" that were inadmissible under appropriate doctrines of due process.[102] This in itself would establish a modest but significant degree of judicial surveillance in the economic field. Nor is there anything in a trio of 1961 "right-to-work" decisions[103] to suggest that the Court was backtracking on this point. To be sure the majority found in each case that the State restriction was rationally justified. But Mr. Justice Harlan, who spoke for the Court in all three, went to considerable lengths to find and evaluate that rational basis. However unsatisfactory his conclusions were to the dissenters, the process of reaching them did not have the perfunctory quality of cases like

---

[101] *Id*. at 239.   [102] *Id*. at 249. (Emphasis added.)

[103] Cohen v. Hurley, 366 U.S. 117; In re Anastaplo, 366 U.S. 82; Konigsberg v. State Bar, 366 U.S. 36.

Olsen[104] and *Queenside Realty*,[105] where the rational-basis terminology seemed to be recited for rhetorical purposes only. Here, on the contrary, a real inquiry was being made.

VII. REQUIESCAT IN PACE

It appears then that the Court has at least taken the preliminary steps for re-establishing judicial review of laws infringing occupational freedom. Whether the operative doctrine should be the rather strict one suggested by Mr. Justice Black in *Schware*[106] or the more tolerant one implied in Mr. Justice Frankfurter's concurrence,[107] the fact is that some genuine review of laws in this field does seem plausible. The doctrinal road is open. Of course, the opening of that road with respect to the right to work does not necessarily clear the way for review of other governmental inroads on economic freedom. As has been intimated, there may be special reasons for protecting the right to work: the primacy of the right to the affected individual, the difficulty of protecting it through ordinary political processes. Indeed, there is no assurance that the apparently new attitude toward occupational freedom will itself be translated into the actuality of constitutional limitation. The Court's present position is somewhat similar to the position of 1925–1930 when a doctrinal basis had been laid for protecting speech against State action, but no State law had actually been struck down. Only the Justices themselves could tell us whether the guilds are going to have their comfortable world disturbed by the *deus ex machina* of the Constitution. And perhaps even they could not enlighten us, for there is little in the preceding survey to suggest that they are prone to think a course of action out before embarking on it.

Nevertheless it is legitimate, and perhaps timely, for an observer of the Court's work to ask whether constitutional law *should* move down that road again, whether the Court should reassert its claim to examine the reasonableness of economic legislation. To reiterate a point that has perhaps already been sufficiently made, this is not a question whether the Justices should return to the dogmatics

---

[104] Olsen v. Nebraska, 313 U.S. 236 (1941).

[105] Queenside Hills Realty Co. v. Saxl, 328 U.S. 80 (1946).

[106] Note 100 *supra*.   [107] *Id*. at 247.

of *Adkins*[108] and *Ribnik*,[109] or to the delusions of grandeur that prompted the judicial crusade against the New Deal, or to the tangled thickets of *Smyth v. Ames*.[110] The Court could not re-establish "laissez faire" even if it wanted to; some economic matters are too big for the Court to handle and some are too intricate. The question is simply whether the Court should begin to apply a modest but real version of the rational-basis standard in economic fields that are not intrinsically inaccessible to the judicial power.

As has been argued earlier, none of the usual justifications for saying "no" to this question will quite do. Some of the rights involved, such as occupational freedom, are not unimportant, nor are they necessarily any more beyond the reach of judicial capacity than other rights which the Justices have chosen to protect. If this were 1937, if the Court were poised on the brink of the modern constitutional era, the case for retaining some constitutional limits in the economic field might be strong. Those who planned the course of future events might well feel that the objective of a just society would be best served by a judicial policy in which economic rights held a respected place. But the year is not 1937, it is 1962; and modern constitutional policy has developed, not by plan but by impulse, not as a coherent body of doctrine but as a congeries of *ad hoc* responses. These circumstances raise a point that takes us back to the opening paragraphs of this essay. They may constitute in themselves a compelling reason for leaving economic due process in repose.

The reason has to do with what might be called judicial economy. The Court's personal-rights decisions in the past twenty-five years have involved constitutional law in some of the most difficult and emotion-charged issues that modern American government faces. The problem of defining and defending the legal rights of Negroes, in a society that has long shamefully neglected their rights, is alone formidable enough to tax the intellectual and power resources of a single tribunal. Yet this is only the beginning of the lofty assignments the Justices have set for themselves. They have undertaken to evaluate governmental encroachments on political and artistic expression, to supervise, in increasing degree, State administration of criminal law. And each of these major personal-

---

108 Adkins v. Children's Hospital, 261 U.S. 525 (1923).

109 Ribnik v. McBride, 277 U.S. 350 (1928).   110 169 U.S. 466 (1898).

rights categories is replete with subcategories, each of which poses ample problems of its own. Nor is there any sign that the rate of accretion is slowing down. In 1962, the Court, in one opinion, brought the jungle of electoral apportionment under judicial scrutiny[111] and, in another, reasserted its willingness to act as a national school board in the field of church-state relationships.[112]

Even if there were no practical, political limitations on the range of Court power, this multitude of self-imposed tasks would be intimidating. The lines between liberty and authority, between justice and injustice, between the necessary and the intolerable, are not easy to draw in a single field: to lay them down in such a variety of fields requires a whole series of painstaking evaluations in which not only intuition, but hard, searching analysis must play its part. It is a common and just complaint that the modern Court has so far failed to develop reasoned formulations for many of its judgments in the personal-rights area.[113] This means that important work is left undone each time the Court gathers to itself a new subject for review. Having spent the last twenty-five years assuming new tasks, the Justices could easily spend the next twenty-five working out the problem of how those tasks should be done. These considerations in themselves might argue against taking on any further assignments for the time being, leaving the question of practical power out of account.

In the long run, however, that issue cannot be left out of account. The Supreme Court is an agency of government and, like other agencies of government, must work within the limits of political possibility. It has been suggested above that a revival of economic due process in connection with a subject like occupational freedom would not by itself overstrain the Court's power. But when the prospect of such a development is considered against the background of other recent assumptions of authority, the calculus may be very different. Various personal-rights decisions during that period have taxed not only the "time-chart"[114] and the reasoning

111 Baker v. Carr, 369 U.S. 186 (1962). See Neal, *Baker v. Carr: Politics in Search of Law*, [1962] SUPREME COURT REVIEW, *infra*.

112 Engel v. Vitale, 370 U.S. 421 (1962). See Kurland, *The Regents' Prayer Case: "Full of Sound and Fury, Signifying . . ."* [1962] SUPREME COURT REVIEW 1, *supra*.

113 See Wechsler, *Toward Neutral Principles of Constitutional Law*, 73 HARV. L. REV. 1 (1959); KURLAND, *op. cit. supra* note 6.

114 See Hart, *Foreword: The Time Chart of the Justices*, 73 HARV. L. REV. 84 (1959).

power of the Justices but their effective prestige as well. In the summer of 1958, an accumulation of political resentment led to one of the most serious—and most nearly successful—congressional counterattacks in judicial history.[115] No one yet knows whether *Baker v. Carr* will make more friends for the Court than it makes enemies, but there seems at this writing to be little question about *Engel v. Vitale* on this score.[116] Doubtless it is regrettable that factors like these must be brought into an assessment of judicial capacities. A world in which the ethical-legal mandates of the Court were accepted without question by those affected would be a comfortable world for the Justices and perhaps not a bad one for the United States as a whole. But it is not, and never has been, the world the Court lives in; and in the real world a friend of the Court quails at the thought of seeing it assume still another politically delicate task.

All things considered, then, it seems best that the cause of economic rights be left by the Supreme Court to lie in its uneasy grave. This need not mean that the legislatures of the nation are warranted in ignoring them, nor that the State courts, applying their own constitutions, should be indifferent to plausible due-process claims.[117] These rights, or some of them, do have a bearing on the justness of a society and on the happiness and well-being of the people who live in it. If the Supreme Court of today had a free hand in choosing the subjects of judicial review, there might well be an argument for choosing the right to work over some of the other subjects that engage Court attention. But it does not have a free hand; its liberty of choice has been considerably foreclosed by the episodic course of constitutional law since 1937. The Supreme Court, like the American political system of which it is a part, proceeds by impulse rather than by design, pragmatically rather than foresightedly. Like the United States, the Court derives advantages from this approach; but like the United States, the Court, too, is bound by its limitations.

---

[115] See MURPHY, CONGRESS AND THE COURT (1962).

[116] See Lewis, *Supreme Court's Term Viewed As One of Most Significant in Its History,* N.Y. Times, July 2, 1962, p. 12; *The Court Decision—and the School Prayer Furor,* 60 NEWSWEEK 43 (July 9, 1962); Kurland, *supra* note 112.

[117] But see Hoskins & Katz, *Substantive Due Process in the States Revisited,* 18 OHIO ST. L. J. 384 (1952).

FELIX FRANKFURTER
NATHANIEL L. NATHANSON

FORBIDDEN DIALOGUE: STANDARDS
OF JUDICIAL REVIEW OF
ADMINISTRATIVE ACTION

F.F.:[1] [A] *"Apart from the text and texture[2] of a particular law in relation to which judicial review is sought, 'judicial review' is a mischievous abstraction. There is no such thing as a common law of judicial review in the federal courts."*

N.L.N.: "I have always regarded this as good law, but I must confess that it is honored more in the breach than in observance.

Felix Frankfurter is Associate Justice of the Supreme Court of the United States (retired).

Nathaniel L. Nathanson is Professor of Law, Northwestern University.

This dialogue, unlike some recent expressions in which the author is talking to himself, actually occurred. But it took the form of exchange of letters, as the language would indicate, rather than the conversation that the title would suggest. The actual exchange was opened, typically, by a letter from the Justice commenting on the content of Nathanson, American Administrative Law, 6 J. Soc. Teachers Pub. Law 39 (1961).—Editor.

[1] From Stark v. Wickard, 321 U.S. 288, 312 (1944).

[2] F.F.: "The preceding sentence gives the scope of 'texture.'" That sentence reads: "Recognition of the claim turns on the provisions dealing with judicial review in a particular statute and on the setting of such provisions in that statute as part of a scheme for accomplishing the purposes expressed by that statute." *Ibid.*

The language of the commentators and judicial opinions, including those of Mr. Justice Frankfurter, abound with [B] *statements of general principle purporting to define,* apart from particular statutes, *the appropriate relationships between administrative agencies and the courts."*

F.F.: ". . . what I want is what I have just indicated, indulgence in enunciating such principles and not utilizing [C] *what might be called 'general principles' for purposes of construing any specific statute.* Surely there is a difference between [A] and [C] on the one hand and [B] on the other!"

N.L.N.: "Certainly there is a difference between [B] and [C]. But are [A] and [B] different? That depends on whether you mean to limit [A] solely to the question whether there is any review at all, excluding all questions of scope, timing, interim relief, etc.

"But you stray from the terms of the indictment. Of course you are not accused of enunciating general principles without utilizing them for purpose of construing specific statutes. How much federal administrative law could possibly be divorced from construction of specific statutes? The soft impeachment was the use of general principles which themselves purport to define, apart from particular statutes, the appropriate relationships between administrative agencies and the courts. For example: 'The court thus applied a principle, now firmly established, that in cases raising issues of fact not within the conventional experience of judges or cases requiring the exercise of administrative discretion, agencies created by Congress for regulating the subject matter should not be passed over.' From your opinion in *Far East Conference v. United States.*[3] And again: 'Thus, this Court has recognized that bodies like the Interstate Commerce Commission, into whose mould Congress has cast more recent administrative agencies, 'should not be too narrowly constrained by technical rules as to admissibility of proof . . . should be free to fashion their own rules of procedure and to pursue methods of inquiry capable of permitting them to discharge their multitudinous duties.' This is from *FCC v. Broadcasting Co.*[4] But on the other hand: 'Just as a judge cannot be subjected to such scrutiny . . . so the integrity of the administrative process must be

---

[3] 342 U.S. 570, 574 (1952).   [4] 309 U.S. 134, 143 (1940).

equally respected.' That comes from *United States v. Morgan*.[5]
And finally: 'An historic procedure for preserving rights during
the pendency of an appeal is no less appropriate—unless Congress
has chosen to withdraw it—because the rights to be vindicated are
those of the public and not of the private litigants.' *Scripps-Howard
Radio, Inc. v. FCC*.[6] All these and doubtless many more are statements of general principle purporting to define, apart from particular statutes, the appropriate relationships between administrative
agencies and the courts."

F.F.: "The statement about reviewing findings of fact is equally
true about juries, masters in chancery, Trinity Brethren in English
admiralty cases—nothing peculiar to administrative agencies. Again,
what is quoted in *Far East*, *Morgan*, and *Scripps-Howard* did not
remotely make the decisive difference between the Court's principle of judicial review and my denial of it, because for me there is
'no such thing as a common law of judicial review in federal
court.' "

N.L.N.: "As I already indicated, you may confine your statement in *Stark v. Wickard* to the 'decisive question' whether there
is judicial review. But why the decisive difference? Even in determining whether there is to be any review, statutes must be construed—both the Agricultural Marketing Agreements Act and the
general statutory basis for the equity jurisdiction of the federal
courts."

F.F.: "My heavens, if that's all you meant, what else do you
expect to find in judicial opinions? Can one give reasons without
stating or assuming general principles? Can one interpret statutes
without being guided by assumptions drawn from experience and
refined by rationalization and articulation? Is every statute to be
approached as if it were something naked, unique and entirely un-
anticipated, with no guides to judgment but the words of the
particular statute and its own peculiar history? Is that the sterility
to which you would condemn one of the most delicate of the
lawyer's arts? And is that what you find suggested in the simple
almost incontrovertible statement: 'There is no such thing as a
common law of judicial review in the federal courts'?"

N.L.N.: "Incontrovertible—yes indeed—if also interpreted so as

---

[5] 313 U.S. 409, 422 (1941).   [6] 316 U.S. 4, 15 (1942).

to deprive it of all genuine significance.[7] The federal courts are courts of statutory jurisdiction. In any problem of judicial review of administrative action in the federal courts, the ultimate reference, apart from the Constitution, must be either a statute establishing the administrative agency or a statute establishing the jurisdiction of the court or both. But that very statutory jurisdiction includes the principles of equity jurisdiction which have frequently been invoked both to grant and to deny relief against unlawful administrative action. Consider for example the passage in the opinion in *Rochester* which reads:[8] 'In this type of situation a complainant seeking judicial review under the Urgent Deficiencies Act of adverse action by the Commission must clear three hurdles: (a) "case" or "controversy" under Article III; (b) the conventional requisites of equity jurisdiction; (c) the specific terms of the statute granting to the district courts jurisdiction in suits challenging "any order" of the Commission.' But there was nothing in the statute about the conventional requisites of equity jurisdiction. Are they to be implied from Article III itself—'all cases in law and equity'—and if so does the implication operate only as a hurdle and never as an aid to jurisdiction? Suppose, for example, there had been no special statutory provision for judicial review of ICC orders. Would the equity jurisdiction of the federal courts have been powerless to provide a remedy to review any orders of the Commission—even when their enforcement threatened irreparable injury? Indeed, I might even be tempted to suggest that the second hurdle mentioned in the *Rochester* opinion—the conventional requisites of equity jurisdiction—was itself a slip of the judicial pen. My theory would be that one of the most significant effects of the Urgent Deficiencies Act provision for judicial review of ICC orders was to dispense with the requisites of equity jurisdiction which would otherwise have been applicable to suits to enjoin the enforcement of such orders."

F.F.: "Of course in any judicial proceeding in the federal courts is the presupposition of its historic lineage as a Court. But *Stark v. Wickard* required a closer analysis of the court's function in a

[7] F.F.: "No, and in saying 'no,' I am not, in deep conviction, indulging implicitly in semantics—the favorite word of half-educated scholars."

[8] Rochester Tel. Corp. v. United States, 307 U.S. 125, 132 (1939).

particular area, namely, court relief from an order of Secretary of Agriculture *because* he was Secretary of Agriculture, *i.e.*, an 'administrative agency.' "

N.L.N.: "Isn't this the nub of the matter? How can we interpret the 'equity jurisdiction' of the federal courts without becoming involved in common-law principles? Compare for example your own opinion in *Joint Anti-Fascist Refugee Comm. v. McGrath*,[9] especially Part II. True you say the issue is 'justiciability' but how do you decide 'justiciability'? By analogy to common-law principles. How else could you decide in the absence of explicit statutory provision, whether there is a 'legal interest'? Note well, however, that I never attacked your conclusion in *Stark v. Wickard*. In all candor, I agree with it. But I venture to suggest that basic difference between the majority and dissent lay in conceptions of 'legal interest' apart from any specific statutory provisions for judicial review. The positions would, I expect, have been the same had there been no statutory provisions at all for judicial review. If I am wrong in this, then I am wrong throughout. But if I'm right in this assumption, then how explain the fundamental difference of opinion? Is it statutory reading, logic, sense of history, conceptions of public policy, or a combination of all of these. Can all of these be divorced from the common law of judicial review?"

F.F.: "Now I begin to catch the drift of your complaint. Whenever I refer to the general principles of equity jurisdiction, you would have me refer to the particular statute, and vice versa. But the basis of your preference escapes me as much as mine escapes you. But what beats me most of all is how, with the views you now express, you could quote from the dissenting opinion in *Stark v. Wickard*—'There is no such thing as a common law of judicial review in the federal courts'—and then you say you have always regarded this as good law."

N.L.N.: "That's the easiest of all to answer. I was influenced by my teachers at such an early age that I cannot entirely escape the influence, even when they do not practice everything they preach."

---

[9] 341 U.S. 123, 157–60 (1951).

JEROLD H. ISRAEL

GIDEON v. WAINWRIGHT:

THE "ART" OF OVERRULING

During the 1962 Term, the Supreme Court, on a single Monday, announced six decisions concerned with constitutional limitations upon state criminal procedure.[1] The most publicized of these,[2] though probably not the most important in terms of legal theory or practical effect, was *Gideon v. Wainwright.*[3] In an era of constantly expanding federal restrictions on state criminal processes,[4]

Jerold H. Israel is Assistant Professor of Law, University of Michigan.

[1] Four of the decisions dealt directly with the procedure in state criminal cases. See Draper v. Washington, 372 U.S. 487 (1963) (concerning the nature of the record that must be furnished an indigent to afford him an equal opportunity to utilize the state appellate process); Lane v. Brown, 372 U.S. 477 (1963) (rejecting an Indiana law requiring a public defender's approval before an indigent defendant can obtain a free transcript of his trial record which is a prerequisite to an appeal from a denial of a writ of error *coram nobis*); Douglas v. California, 372 U.S. 353 (1963) (requiring the appointment of counsel to assist an indigent in prosecuting a nondiscretionary appeal); and Gideon v. Wainwright, 372 U.S. 335 (1963) (requiring the appointment of counsel for indigent defendants in state noncapital criminal cases). The other two decisions concerned federal habeas corpus for state prisoners. Fay v. Noia, 372 U.S. 391 (1963); Townsend v. Sain, 372 U.S. 293 (1963).

[2] See, *e.g.,* TIME 17–18 (March 29, 1963); Editorial, Washington Post, March 21, 1963, p. A-22, col. 1.

[3] 372 U.S. 335 (1963).

[4] See Allen, *The Supreme Court and State Criminal Justice,* 4 WAYNE L. REV. 191, 192–96 (1958); Allen, *The Supreme Court, Federalism, and State Systems of Criminal Justice,* 8 DE PAUL L. REV. 213 (1959); Morris, *The End of an Experiment in Federalism—A Note on Mapp v. Ohio,* 36 WASH. L. REV. 407 (1961).

the holding of *Gideon*—that an indigent defendant in a state criminal prosecution has an unqualified right to the appointment of counsel[5]—was hardly startling.[6] And while *Gideon* will obviously have an important effect in the handful of states that still fail to appoint counsel at the trial level,[7] it has probably caused far less alarm among prosecutors than its sister decisions that relaxed the

---

[5] Although the Court had before it only the case of an indigent accused of a felony, there are indications that this holding is designed to extend to "all criminal cases" as does the Sixth Amendment. See note 337 *infra*. The suggestion has been made, however, that the "petty offense" exception that the Court has found applicable to the Sixth Amendment right to jury trial may be applied here. Kamisar, *Betts v. Brady Twenty Years Later: The Right to Counsel and Due Process Values*, 61 MICH. L. REV. 219, 268–70 (1962). But the right to appointed counsel would seem more analogous to other Sixth Amendment rights, such as the right of confrontation, that surely are applicable to all criminal cases. In any event, whether *Gideon* is applied to all misdemeanors or only some, it will require a major extension of the appointment practice in the vast majority of states. See Note, 48 CALIF. L. REV. 501 (1960). See note 7 *infra*.

[6] See Kamisar, note 5 *supra*, at 219–60; Kamisar, *The Right to Counsel and the Fourteenth Amendment: A Dialogue on "The Most Pervasive Right" of an Accused*, 30 U. CHI. L. REV. 1, 2–42 (1962); *cf., e.g.,* Mapp v. Ohio, 367 U.S. 643 (1961); Ker v. California, 374 U.S. 23 (1963); Douglas v. California, 372 U.S. 353 (1963); Alcorta v. Texas, 355 U.S. 28 (1957). The impending overruling was so obvious that it was predicted by computers (with only two mistakes as to the position of individual Justices). See Lawlor, *What Computors Can Do: Analysis and Prediction of Judicial Decisions*, 49 A.B.A.J. 337, 343 (1963). See also Pollock, *Equal Justice in Practice*, 45 MINN. L. REV. 737 (1961); Boskey, *The Right to Counsel in Appellate Proceedings*, 45 MINN. L. REV. 783, 787 (1961); *The Supreme Court, 1961 Term*, 76 HARV. L. REV. 54, 116 (1962); and Note, 14 W. RES. L. REV. 370 (1963).

[7] See Ann Arbor News, Aug. 6, 1963, p. 18, col. 4 (4,000 Florida convicts have petitioned for release on the basis of *Gideon*). Kamisar, *supra* note 6, at 17–20, lists Alabama, Florida, Mississippi, and North and South Carolina as the only states in which appointment of counsel in felony cases is neither a legal requirement nor an "almost invariable" court practice. Of course, *Gideon* will affect many more states if it is extended to misdemeanor as well as felony cases. See note 5 *supra*. The retrospective application of *Gideon*—which seems likely, *cf.* Eskridge v. Washington, 357 U.S. 214 (1958)—would also increase the decision's practical significance, although here the impact would be substantially muted by the fact that at least thirty states regularly appointed counsel in felony cases as far back as 1942. See Kamisar, *supra* note 6, at 17. Despite both of these possibilities, twenty-two states presented an *amicus curiae* brief in *Gideon* urging the overruling of Betts v. Brady, 316 U.S. 455 (1942). See 372 U.S. at 336. Included in this group were a few states that had only recently adopted provisions requiring the appointment of counsel. See, *e.g.,* Massachusetts (1958), Colorado (1961).

prerequisites for obtaining a federal writ of habeas corpus[8] and imposed a requirement that states also provide counsel on appeals.[9] What distinguished *Gideon*—and what attracted the attention of the press—was that the result there reached overruled an important prior decision of the Court.[10] *Betts v. Brady*,[11] decided in 1942, had held that the Due Process Clause of the Fourteenth Amendment did not impose upon the states, as the Sixth Amendment imposed upon the federal government, an absolute requirement to appoint counsel for all indigent defendants in criminal cases. It required the states to provide an attorney only where the particular circumstances of a case indicated that the absence of counsel would result in a trial lacking "fundamental fairness."[12] In *Gideon,* the Court explicitly rejected the *Betts* rule and held that the "Sixth Amendment's [unqualified] guarantee of counsel for all indigent defendants" is a "fundamental right . . . made obligatory upon the States by the Fourteenth Amendment."[13] *Gideon* thus joined the ranks of a rather select group of cases. For, despite its widespread reputation as a Court most ready to "disregard precedent and overrule its own earlier decisions,"[14] the Supreme Court in fact has directly overruled prior decisions on no more than a hundred occasions in over

[8] See Fay v. Noia, 372 U.S. 391 (1963); see generally the authorities cited in Reitz, *Federal Habeas Corpus: Impact of an Abortive State Proceeding,* 74 HARV. L. REV. 1315 n.1, 1350 n.120 (1961).

[9] Douglas v. California, 372 U.S. 353 (1963). Only a handful of states, if that many, follow a practice that meets the requirements of *Douglas.* See People v. Brown, 55 Cal.2d 64, 69 n.1, (1960) (concurring opinion of Justice Traynor citing the various state practices). See ASSOCIATION OF THE BAR OF THE CITY OF NEW YORK and NATIONAL LEGAL AID AND DEFENDER ASSOCIATION, EQUAL JUSTICE FOR THE ACCUSED 97–111 (1959). Of course, the retrospective application of *Douglas* will require only that the state grant the indigent a new appeal, not a new trial as in *Gideon.*

[10] In Fay v. Noia, 372 U.S. 391 (1963), the Court also overruled a prior decision but not one nearly so renowned.

[11] 316 U.S. 455 (1942).   [12] *Id.* at 473.   [13] 372 U.S. at 340, 342.

[14] Bernhardt, *Supreme Court Reversals on Constitutional Issues,* 34 CORNELL L.Q. 55 (1948). See also AUERBACH, GARRISON, HURST & MERMIN, THE LEGAL PROCESS 172 (1961); Catlett, *Development of the Doctrine of Stare Decisis and the Extent to Which It Should Be Applied,* 21 WASH. L. REV. 158, 163 (1946); Jackson, *The Task of Maintaining Our Liberties: The Role of the Judiciary,* 39 A.B.A.J. 961, 962 (1953); 103 CONG. REC. 2935 (1957).

a century and a half of judicial review.[15] And only about half of these instances involved cases, like *Gideon,* in which the Court was dealing with a constitutional question.[16]

Gideon v. Wainwright, moreover, is unique even among this small group of "constitutional" overruling decisions. Division among the Justices has not been uncommon in such cases, but the

---

[15] "Direct overruling," as used here, refers only to these instances where (1) the Court's opinion has expressly overruled a prior decision, or (2) subsequent opinions have expressly recognized that the particular decision overruled a prior case, or (3) the occasional case in which the Court has made no effort effectively to distinguish a prior decision and commentators have universally recognized the case as overruling that decision. *E.g.,* Brown v. Board of Education, 347 U.S. 483 (1954), overruling Plessy v. Ferguson, 163 U.S. 537 (1896). A case is not considered directly overruled where its applicability has been sharply limited by subsequent "distinguishing" decisions. See, *e.g.,* Nelson v. County of Los Angeles, 362 U.S. 1 (1960), distinguishing Slochower v. Board of Education, 350 U.S. 551 (1956); and Rutkin v. United States, 343 U.S. 130 (1952), limiting to its facts Commissioner v. Wilcox, 327 U.S. 404 (1946).

Various compilations of overruling opinions are listed in Ulmer, *An Empirical Analyses of Selected Aspects of Lawmaking of the United States Supreme Court,* 8 J. Pub. L. 414 n.1 (1959). The most thorough list, that in Blaustein & Field, *"Overruling" Opinions in the Supreme Court,* 57 Mich. L. Rev. 151, 184–94 (1958), cites eighty-one overruling decisions (excluding rehearings) in the period from 1803 to 1958. Seven cases, cited in Ulmer, *supra,* should, perhaps, be added to this list. Darr v. Burford, 339 U.S. 200 (1950); Graves v. Schmidlapp, 315 U.S. 657 (1942); United States v. Hastings, 296 U.S. 188 (1935); Eisner v. Macomber, 252 U.S. 189 (1920); Thompson v. Whitman, 18 Wall. 457 (1873), Mason v. Eldred, 6 Wall. 231 (1867); United States v. Percheman, 7 Pet. 51 (1833). In addition, there are at least eight overruling cases decided since 1958: Fay v. Noia, 372 U.S. 391 (1963), overruling Darr v. Burford, 339 U.S. 200 (1950); Gideon v. Wainwright, 372 U.S. 335 (1963), overruling Betts v. Brady, 316 U.S. 455 (1942); Ferguson v. Skrupa, 372 U.S. 726 (1963), overruling Adams v. Tanner, 244 U.S. 590 (1917); AFL-CIO v. Curry, 371 U.S. 542 (1963), overruling Montgomery Bldg. & Constr. Trades Council v. Ledbetter Erection Co., 344 U.S. 178 (1952); Smith v. Evening News Assn., 371 U.S. 195 (1962), overruling Assn. of Westinghouse Salaried Employees v. Westinghouse Corp., 348 U.S. 437 (1955); Mapp v. Ohio, 367 U.S. 643 (1961), overruling Wolf v. Colorado, 338 U.S. 25 (1949); James v. United States, 366 U.S. 213 (1961), overruling Comm'r v. Wilcox, 327 U.S. 404 (1946); United States v. Raines, 362 U.S. 17 (1960), overruling United States v. Reese, 92 U.S. 214 (1875), and Barney v. City of New York, 193 U.S. 430 (1904). This makes a grand total of 96 "direct overrulings."

[16] Approximately fifty-two of the overruling cases fit this category. Bernhardt, *supra* note 14, at 56–59, cites twenty-nine such decisions (excluding those that either involved rehearings or were based on non-constitutional grounds). To this group should be added twenty-three decisions either in Blaustein & Field, *supra* note 15 or in note 15.

argument in the past always has centered on whether a decision should be overruled.[17] In *Gideon* the Court divided simply over what should be said in overturning a prior decision that every Justice agreed should be rejected. Though Justice Black's opinion for the Court was concurred in by six of his brethren, both Justices Clark and Harlan found it necessary to write separate opinions concurring only in the Court's judgment. Justice Clark did not mention the Court's opinion, but Justice Harlan's objection to that opinion was clearly stated in the first sentence of his concurrence. "I agree," he said, "that *Betts* should be overruled, but consider it entitled to a more respectful burial than has been accorded [by the Court]."[18]

This unique expression of concern over the Court's manner of overruling a past decision raises some basic questions concerning judicial craftsmanship in overruling opinions. What special functions, if any, should the Court seek to accomplish with an overruling opinion? What techniques of opinion writing have been used in the past to fulfill these functions? Did the majority opinion in *Gideon* fail to perform the proper function of an overruling opinion? Would it have done so by giving *Betts* a "more respectful burial"? These are, of course, questions concerning method, not result. Admittedly, as Dean Rostow recently pointed out in answering current criticisms of the Court's craftsmanship, "opinion writing is only one phase of the judicial craft . . . not the whole of it nor even its most important feature."[19] Yet, as even the Dean acknowledged, opinion writing remains a "vital phase" of the judicial process.[20] It is, moreover, a phase which, if the frequency of separate opinions are any indication, causes great concern within the Court itself.

I. The "Art" of Overruling

A. THE TASK OF THE OVERRULING OPINION

The Supreme Court long has recognized that the doctrine of *stare decisis* has only "a limited application in the field of constitu-

---

[17] The Court has been divided in approximately one-half of the "constitutional" overruling decisions. See Blaustein & Field, *supra* note 15, at 184–94; Bernhardt, *supra* note 14, at 56–59.

[18] 372 U.S. at 349.   [19] Rostow, The Sovereign Prerogative 36 (1962).

[20] *Ibid.* See also Llewellyn, The Common Law Tradition 288–309 (1960).

tional law."[21] The classic explanation of this position was presented by Justice Brandeis in one of his oft-quoted dissents:[22]

> Stare decisis is usually the wise policy, because in most matters it is more important that the applicable rule of law be settled than that it be settled right. . . . This is commonly true even where the error is a matter of serious concern, provided correction can be had by legislation. But in cases involving the Federal Constitution, where correction through legislative action is practically impossible, this Court has often overruled its earlier decisions.

Although persuasive, this explanation speaks only to part of the problem that the Court encounters in overruling constitutional decisions. For the very factor that Brandeis advances to justify abandoning constitutional precedents—the impracticality of "correction through legislative action"—creates certain difficulties of its own, that make the task of overruling a particularly delicate one.

In a nation that prides itself on being a democracy, the absence of any practical legislative process for correcting the Court's constitutional decisions always presents a potential barrier to the complete acceptance of judicial review.[23] To overcome this obstacle, the Court must operate within a framework that maintains

---

21 St. Joseph Stock Yards Co. v. United States, 298 U.S. 38, 94 (1936) (concurring opinion of Justices Cardozo and Stone). See also Glidden Co. v. Zdanok, 370 U.S. 530, 543 (1962); Passenger Cases, 7 How. 282, 470 (1849) (dissenting opinion of Chief Justice Taney); Jackson, *supra* note 14, at 693. Some commentators have suggested that the principles of *stare decisis* should not be given any consideration in constitutional adjudication. See Boudin, *The Problem of Stare Decisis in Our Constitutional Theory*, 8 N.Y.U.L.Q. 589, 601–02 (1931); *cf.* Chamberlin, *Doctrine of Stare Decisis as Applied to Decisions of Constitutional Questions*, 3 HARV. L. REV. 125 (1890).

22 Burnet v. Coronado Oil & Gas Co., 285 U.S. 393, 406–07 (1932). In referring to the practical impossibility of correction through legislative action, Brandeis noted that on only two occasions had "the process of constitutional amendment been successfully resorted to, to nullify decisions of this Court." Moreover, even there, it had taken eighteen years to procure one of the amendments. *Id.* at 409 n.5. See also Commissioner v. Estate of Church, 335 U.S. 632, 677 (1949) (dissenting opinion of Justice Frankfurter). But *cf.* Shapiro, *Judicial Modesty, Political Reality, and Preferred Position*, 47 CORNELL L. Q. 175, 193 (1962).

23 See BICKEL, THE LEAST DANGEROUS BRANCH 16–23 (1962); Dahl, *Decision-making in a Democracy: The Supreme Court as a National Policy-Maker*, 6 J. PUB. L. 279, 283 (1957). Of course, whether the judicial review is actually characterized as a "democratic institution" will depend to a large degree upon one's definition of democracy. *Compare* ROSTOW, *supra* note 19, at 117–21, 148–56, *with* Dahl, *supra*, at 6.

its image as a disinterested decision-maker applying those fundamental values reflected in the Constitution.[24] A general willingness to adhere to precedent has always been an important aspect of this framework. Certainly, the Court could not have maintained its role as the interpreter of a document that symbolizes continuity if its decisions had, as Justice Jackson once claimed, "a mortality rate almost as high as their authors."[25] Decisions can hardly gain acceptance as based upon the enduring principles of the Constitution without the prospect that they will live an "indefinite while," at least beyond the life expectancy of the Justices deciding them.[26] So too, the view of the Court as an impersonal adjudicator has depended to some degree on the assumption that the judge, unlike the legislator, is sharply restricted in relying upon his personal predilections by the necessity of following the decisions of his predecessors.[27]

The importance of *stare decisis* in promoting an acceptable image of judicial review thus imposes a special burden upon the Court in overruling its prior decision. On one hand, constitutional law, even more than other areas of the law, must be subject to judicial change.[28] And while this often can be achieved by distinguishing or even ignoring inconsistent precedents, there are times when intellectual honesty and proper application of the new rule by the

---

[24] See McCloskey, *Foreword, The Reapportionment Case*, 76 HARV. L. REV. 54, 67 (1962); Bickel, *supra* note 23, at 23–29. This, of course, attempts to justify judicial review, not as a majoritarian institution, but rather as an institution performing an essential governmental function which other institutions cannot perform. *Cf.* HART & WECHSLER, THE FEDERAL COURTS AND THE FEDERAL SYSTEM 92–93 (1953).

[25] Jackson, *The Task of Maintaining Our Liberties: The Role of The Judiciary*, 39 A.B.A.J. 961, 962 (1953). In one sense Jackson was accurate. There have been fewer Justices than there have been opinions overruled. See also Douglas, *Stare Decisis*, 49 COLUM. L. REV. 735, 736 (1949). For a discussion of the symbolism of the Constitution, see GABRIEL, THE COURSE OF AMERICAN DEMOCRATIC THOUGHT 396–407 (1940); Bickel, note 23 *supra*, at 29–31.

[26] See Henkin, *Some Reflections on Current Constitutional Controversy*, 109 U. PA. L. REV. 637, 660 (1961).

[27] See WASSERSTROM, THE JUDICIAL DECISION 75–79 (1961); *cf.* Henkin, note 26 *supra*, at 656.

[28] See FREUND, THE SUPREME COURT OF THE UNITED STATES 26 (1961); LEVI, AN INTRODUCTION TO LEGAL REASONING 41–44 (1949).

lower courts require that a prior decision be directly overruled.[29] On the other hand, the overruling decision represents a source of danger to both professional and popular acceptance of the Court as the disinterested interpreter of the Constitution. Even where the end result in a particular case meets with general approval, the rejection of *stare decisis* may well raise doubts both as to the Court's impersonality and as to the principled foundations of its decisions, as evidenced by their lack of "staying power."[30] The overruling decision generally will tend to emphasize the subjective elements in judicial review by focusing attention on the background and personal philosophies of the various justices. This is especially true when the change in the law has occurred over a comparatively short period of time marked by a significant alteration in the Court's personnel.[31] Of course, not every overruling decision will have this effect. And even those that do will not cause the Court to lose overnight the "public faith in its objectivity and detachment" that is the ultimate basis of its authority.[32] Nevertheless, some danger is inherent in almost every overruling decision, and each case that does emphasize the personal and temporary

[29] See generally Traynor, *Comment on Courts and Lawmaking*, in LEGAL INSTITUTIONS TODAY AND TOMORROW 48, 54–55 (Paulsen ed. 1959); LLEWELLYN, THE COMMON LAW TRADITION 257 (1960). In many instances, the Court has been forced to overrule cases explicitly because lower courts had refused to recognize that the case had lost all its vitality. See, *e.g.*, California v. Thompson, 313 U.S. 109 (1941); and Olsen v. Nebraska, 313 U.S. 236 (1941). The technique of direct overruling may also be preferred because it generally insures that a "dead" case will stay buried. *Cf.* Adkins v. Children's Hospital, 261 U.S. 525, 562, 564, 570 (1923) (dissenting opinions of Chief Justice Taft and Justice Holmes commenting upon the revival of *Lochner v. New York*).

[30] See HART & SACHS, THE LEGAL PROCESS 612, 613 (mimeo. 1958); The Legal Tender Cases, 12 Wall. 457 (1870); Boudin, *supra* note 21, at 613–15; note 93 *infra*.

[31] Approximately three-quarters of all overruling cases have reversed cases decided within the previous twenty-five years, Bernhardt, *supra* note 14, at 56–59, and have occurred within a five-year period after significant changes (3 to 6 Justices) in the Court's composition. Ulmer, *supra* note 15 at 434. See also Kadish, *Judicial Review in the United States Supreme Court and the High Court of Australia*, 37 TEXAS L. REV. 133, 154–55. Douglas, *supra* note 25, at 736.

[32] Kurland, *The Supreme Court and Its Judicial Critics*, 6 UTAH L. REV. 457, 466 (1959). In this regard, it is the confidence of the bar that is particularly important. See Shapiro, *The Supreme Court and Constitutional Adjudication of Politics and Neutral Principles*, 31 GEO. WASH. L. REV. 587, 605 (1963). Yet it is the bar that most frequently has been critical of departures from precedent.

quality of a judicial rule further tarnishes the image that is necessary to maintain judicial review in a democracy.

Although only occasional opinions by individual Justices have expressly recognized this special problem of the overruling case,[33] an examination of the opinions for the Court in these cases suggests that it has not been overlooked. The Court over the years has employed certain "techniques" in overruling opinions that, as a general pattern, tend to preserve the impersonal qualities of the judicial process by emphasizing factors other than the vicissitudes of changing personnel.

B. THE TECHNIQUES OF OVERRULING

1. *Changing conditions.*—Even those Justices most opposed to overruling constitutional decisions have acknowledged that the "law may grow to meet changing conditions" and that the doctrine of *stare decisis* should not require a "slavish adherence to authority where new conditions require new rules of conduct."[34] It is not surprising therefore that overruling opinions in several cases have emphasized the changed circumstances brought about by the passage of time.[35] Indeed, this technique was employed in one of the earliest overruling decisions, *The Genesee Chief*,[36] which rejected a unanimous holding of the Court decided only twenty-four years earlier in *The Thomas Jefferson*.[37] Chief Justice Taney's opinion for the Court in *The Genesee Chief* refused to follow the prior ruling that the national admiralty jurisdiction was limited, in accord with English common law, to waters that "ebbed and flowed."[38] After stressing that the "great and growing commerce"

---

[33] See Pollock v. Farmers' Loan & Trust Co. 157 U.S. 429, 652 (1895) (dissenting opinion); Brown v. Allen, 344 U.S. 443, 535 (1953) (concurring opinion of Justice Jackson); Graves v. New York *ex rel.* O'Keefe, 306 U.S. 466, 487 (1939) (concurring opinion of Justice Frankfurter).

[34] Roberts, J., dissenting, in Mahnich v. Southern S.S. Co., 321 U.S. 96, 113 (1944).

[35] See, *e.g.,* Brown v. Board of Education, 347 U.S. 483, 493–94 (1954); Burstyn v. Wilson, 343 U.S. 495, 502 n.12 (1952); Tigner v. Texas, 310 U.S. 141, 145–46 (1940); West Coast Hotel Co. v. Parrish, 300 U.S. 379, 399 (1937). This approach has also been employed in non-constitutional cases. See, *e.g.,* United States v. Percheman, 7 Pet. 50, 88–89 (1833).

[36] 12 How. 443 (1851).

[37] 10 Wheat. 428 (1825).   [38] 12 How. at 459.

on inland waters had made the extension of admiralty jurisdiction to non-tidewater areas a practical necessity, he noted that *The Thomas Jefferson* had been decided "when the great importance of the question as it now presents itself could not be foreseen."[39] The earlier decision had been rendered in 1825, "when the commerce on the rivers of the west and on the lakes was in its infancy, and, of little importance, and but little regarded compared with that of the present day."[40] Accordingly, while the Court was "sensible of the great weight" to which its prior decision was entitled, it nevertheless could rightfully overrule *The Thomas Jefferson*, since the reasoning there was clearly inapplicable to the contemporary situation.[41]

Subsequent overruling opinions relying upon changed conditions have emphasized new developments in areas far less pragmatic than the commercial traffic involved in *The Genesee Chief*. In *Brown v. Board of Education*,[42] for example, the Court cited the change in the status of public schools since *Plessy v. Ferguson*, as well as the present state of scientific knowledge about psychological developments of children.[43] Indeed, the growth of knowledge concerning various aspects of economic and social development has been a fairly common point of emphasis in those opinions that have rejected prior precedent on the ground that "time and circumstances had drained [the overruled] case of vitality."[44]

Reliance upon the "changed conditions" argument logically should permit an overruling opinion both to reject a precedent and at the same time acknowledge its correctness when originally decided.[45] The Court has never gone quite this far, however, al-

---

[39] *Id.* at 453. Taney also noted that the English common law, on which *The Thomas Jefferson* was based, had developed before the advent of the steamboat.

[40] *Id.* at 456.   [41] *Ibid.*   [42] 347 U.S. 483 (1954).

[43] *Id.* at 492–94. The Court did not make a specific reference to a change in scientific knowledge since *Plessy*, but did state that "whatever may have been the extent of psychological knowledge at the time of *Plessy v. Ferguson*," the present findings were "amply supported by modern authority."

[44] Tigner v. Texas, 310 U.S. 141, 144 (1940). See also, *e.g.*, West Coast Hotel Co. v. Parrish, 300 U.S. 379, 399 (1937); *cf.* Edwards v. California, 314 U.S. 160, 177 (1941).

[45] "In refusing to follow a precedent a court must not always assert that its predecessor erred. Yesterday's wise decisions were commands for yesterday, but only

though at least one opinion intimated that the writer might have accepted the overruled case under the circumstances applying at the time of its decision.[46] More often, the Court simply has taken no position as to the validity of the rejected case.[47] But even where the Court does suggest that the overruled decision was incorrect, an opinion emphasizing the changed circumstances naturally will contain the countersuggestion that, in any event, the former Court might well have decided differently if confronted with today's conditions.[48] Thus, with the change-in-circumstances rationale, the Court may obtain the best of both worlds. Not only is the prior decision overruled, but the adverse emphasis upon differences in the Court's personnel that normally attends such action is eliminated, or at least diluted, by relying upon grounds consistent with that concept of impersonal decision-making ordinarily supported by *stare decisis*.

2. *The lessons of experience.*—Closely related to the change-in-circumstances rationale is the argument that a prior precedent may be rejected when it has failed to pass the "test of experience."[49] The Court has frequently acknowledged that "the process of trial and error, so fruitful in the physical sciences is appropriate also in the judicial function."[50] This willingness to make adjustments in the light of the "lesson of experience"[51] has been cited as at least a partial ground for overruling precedent on several occasions.[52] In

---

instructions for today." Moore & Oglebay, *The Supreme Court, Stare Decisis, and Law of the Case,* 21 TEX. L. REV. 514, 523 (1943).

[46] See Glidden Co. v. Zdanock, 370 U.S. 530, 543 (1962).

[47] See, *e.g.,* Brown v. Board of Education, 347 U.S. 483 (1954); Edwards v. California, 314 U.S. 160 (1941); Tigner v. Texas, 310 U.S. 141 (1940).

[48] See, *e.g., The Genesee Chief,* 12 How. 443 (1851).

[49] Barden v. Northern Pacific Railroad, 154 U.S. 288, 322 (1894).

[50] Burnet v. Coronado Oil & Gas Co., 285 U.S. 393, 407 (1932) (dissenting opinion). See also Helvering v. Hallock, 309 U.S. 106, 122 (1940); Sweezy v. New Hampshire, 354 U.S. 234, 266 (1957) (concurring opinion); Green v. United States, 356 U.S. 165, 195 (1958) (dissenting opinion); Jackson, *The Task of Maintaining Our Liberties: The Role of the Judiciary,* 39 A.B.A.J. 961, 962 (1953): ". . . the years [have] brought about a doctrine that [constitutional] decisions must be tentative and subject to judicial cancellation if experience fails to verify them."

[51] Burnet v. Coronado Oil & Gas Co., 285 U.S. 393, 407 (1932) (dissenting opinion).

[52] See, *e.g.,* Helvering v. Producers Corp., 303 U.S. 376, 384–85 (1938); Farmers Loan & Trust Co. v. Minnesota, 280 U.S. 204, 209 (1930); National Ins. Co. v. Tide-

most cases, the overruling opinion based the rejection of the earlier decision upon the administrative difficulties and uneven results revealed by its application.[53] In other instances, however, experience in the application of a rule has been used to show the erroneous nature of the factual or policy assumption upon which it was based. In *Mapp v. Ohio*,[54] for example, the Court noted that the experience of various states had revealed the error in the supposition that remedies other than the exclusionary rule could effectively deter unreasonable searches and seizures.

In relying upon the "lesson of experience," the Court has once again tended to depreciate changes in its personnel as the cause of the change in the law by either the outright suggestion or, at least, the insinuation that the present result was one that its predecessors might well have reached if they had had the same information, derived from experience under the rule first promulgated.[55] This role of the "experience" rationale may be accentuated by the reminder that "courts are not omniscient"[56] and that "judicial opinions must yield to facts unforeseen."[57] On occasion, it may be further implemented by the conclusion that the result of applying a particular doctrine has been exactly the opposite of that intended by the earlier Court and that the achievement of this original objective can in fact be accomplished only through reversal of the original deci-

---

water Co., 337 U.S. 582, 618 (1949) (concurring opinion of Justice Rutledge); and Washington v. W. C. Dawson & Co., 264 U.S. 219, 237 (1924) (dissenting opinion of Justice Brandeis). *Cf.* Helvering v. Hallock, 309 U.S. 106, 110 (1940) (overruling on non-constitutional grounds). See also Douglas, *Stare Decisis*, 49 COLUM. L. REV. 735, 747 (1949); and Green, *Stare Decisis and the Supreme Court of the United States*, 4 NAT'L B.J. 191, 201 (1946), discussing United States v. Darby, 312 U.S. 100 (1941), which overruled Hammer v. Dagenhart, 247 U.S. 251 (1918).

[53] See, *e.g.*, Erie R.R. v. Tompkins, 304 U.S. 64, 74 (1938); Farmers Loan & Trust Co. v. Minnesota, 280 U.S. 204, 209 (1930); Helvering v. Producers Corp., 303 U.S. 376, 384–85 (1938). See also the non-constitutional overrulings in New England R.R. v. Conroy, 175 U.S. 323, 341 (1899); Helvering v. Hallock, 309 U.S. 106, 110 (1940).

[54] 367 U.S. 643, 651–52, (1961), overruling Wolf v. Colorado, 338 U.S. 25 (1949); *cf.* Erie R.R. v. Tompkins, 304 U.S. 64, 74 (1938).

[55] See Washington v. W. C. Dawson & Co., 264 U.S. 219, 237 (1924) (dissenting opinion of Justice Brandeis).

[56] Green v. United States, 356 U.S. 165, 195 (1958) (dissenting opinion).

[57] Jaybird Mining Co. v. Weir, 271 U.S. 609, 619 (1926) (Justice Brandeis dissenting).

sion itself.[58] Of course, reliance upon difficulties experienced in the application of the overruled case will lose much of its effectiveness in de-emphasizing shifts in the Court's composition when such difficulties were readily foreseeable at the time the problem was first decided. Yet, even here, there remains the remote possibility that problems that may not have seemed very serious when contemplated in the abstract might well have caused a reversal of position when faced as a matter of practical reality.

3. *The requirements of later precedent.*—In the majority of overrulings, the opinions have been based upon neither changing conditions nor the lessons of experience. They have relied simply upon the "error" of the earlier decision.[59] Only a small number of these opinions, however, have relied solely upon the force of reasoning now considered superior to the rationale of the overruled case.[60] The Court generally has attempted to buttress its position by showing that the rejection of the overruled case was required, or at least suggested, by other, later decisions basically inconsistent with its earlier ruling.[61] Examples of the use of this technique in overruling opinions are extremely varied. While most of the "inconsistent precedent" has been found in cases dealing with the same problem as the overruled decision, the Court occasionally has relied upon rulings in related areas that, while not directly questioning the overruled case, could be treated as having "impaired its authority."[62] In *Mapp v. Ohio*, for example, the majority opinion pointed to the basic inconsistency between the Court's refusal to exclude unconstitutionally seized evidence and the required exclusion of

[58] See Fay v. Noia, 372 U.S. 391, 437 (1963) (non-constitutional overruling).

[59] See, *e.g.,* United States v. Raines, 362 U.S. 17, 25–26 (1960); State Tax Comm'n v. Aldrich, 316 U.S. 174 (1942); West Coast Hotel Co. v. Parrish, 300 U.S. 379, 397 (1937).

[60] The Court has based its decision solely on the ground that the overruled case was wrong in only about a half-dozen cases. See United States v. Rabinowitz, 339 U.S. 56, 64–66 (1950); Board of Education v. Barnette, 319 U.S. 624 (1943); Madden v. Kentucky, 309 U.S. 83, 93 (1940); O'Malley v. Woodrough, 307 U.S. 277, 281 (1939); Fox Film Corp. v. Doyal, 286 U.S. 123, 131 (1932); The Legal Tender Cases, 12 Wall. 457 (1870).

[61] See, *e.g.,* cases cited note 59 *supra.*

[62] Gore v. United States, 357 U.S. 386, 388 (1958). See Smith v. Allwright, 321 U.S. 649, 659–62 (1944); Mapp v. Ohio, 367 U.S. 643, 656 (1961).

all coerced confessions, irrespective of their reliability.[63] Similarly, in *Smith v. Allwright*,[64] the Court found that its decision in *United States v. Classic*[65] holding that a party primary could be an integral part of the election machinery subject to congressional regulation under Article I, §4 "call[ed] for a re-examination" of its holding in *Grovey v. Townsend*[66] that the action of a political party convention in excluding Negroes from a primary election did not constitute state action.[67]

Overruling opinions also have differed in their treatment of the inconsistency between the earlier ruling and the later precedent. In some cases the Court has acknowledged that the decisions could be reconciled, but found it necessary to overrule the earlier decision because the basis of distinction between the cases was not justifiable in terms of the function of the legal principle involved.[68] More often, the Court has maintained, sometimes in the face of obvious distinctions,[69] that it has no choice but to overrule the earlier decision, since that ruling is totally irreconcilable with subsequent cases.[70] A variation of this approach has been employed in those opinions overruling a principle that had been sharply limited by a long series of cases creating numerous exceptions to its application.[71] In such instances, the overruling opinions, after noting that the later decisions already had "stricken the foundation" from the original case,[72] have asserted the result as merely "a

---

[63] 367 U.S. 643 (1961).

[64] 321 U.S. 649 (1944).   [66] 295 U.S. 45 (1935).

[65] 313 U.S. 299 (1941).   [67] 321 U.S. at 661.

[68] See, *e.g.*, State Tax Comm'n v. Aldrich, 316 U.S. 174, 179 (1942); Sherrer v. Sherrer, 334 U.S. 343, 353 (1948); Helvering v. Mountain Producers Corp., 303 U.S. 376, 383 (1940).

[69] See, *e.g.*, United States v. Chicago, M., St. P. & P. R.R., 312 U.S. 592 (1941); California v. Thompson, 313 U.S. 109 (1941).

[70] See, *e.g.*, the cases cited note 69 *supra;* Graves v. Schmidlapp, 315 U.S. 657, 665 (1942); West Coast Hotel Co. v. Parrish, 300 U.S. 379, 398 (1937).

[71] See, *e.g.*, Graves v. Schmidlapp, 315 U.S. 657 (1942); Graves v. N.Y. *ex rel.* O'Keefe, 306 U.S. 466 (1939); Pennsylvania R.R. v. Towers, 245 U.S. 6 (1917). See also Gordon v. Ogden, 3 Pet. 33 (1830).

[72] Oklahoma Tax Comm'n v. Texas Co., 336 U.S. 342, 352 (1949).

logical culmination of a gradual process of erosion."[73] On occasion, the Court has even gone so far as to declare that its previous decision already had been overruled *sub silentio* by the "tide" of later cases.[74]

No matter which of these variations is utilized, the mere presence of these previous decisions indicates that the Court's ruling is not the result of a sudden shift. On the contrary, particularly where the authority of the overruled case was gradually undermined by a series of decisions, the Court may properly emphasize that the downfall of the overruled case was not the product of a "little coterie of like minded justices" recently appointed to the bench,[75] but of a long line of judges who, over the years, participated in the various undermining decisions.[76] This quality of borrowing support from the past also provides what is probably the primary value of the "inconsistent precedent" rationale: a court can overrule a decision while purporting to follow the principles of *stare decisis*. In pointing to subsequent decisions basically at odds with the case to be overruled, the Court places itself in a position where it must choose between two lines of authority. It must either overrule a precedent or "disregard a contrary philosophy expressed in a later case."[77] Moreover, where the inconsistent precedent consists of a group of later cases showing a continuous trend away from the original decision, the Court has suggested that it really has no choice but to follow the path of subsequent decisions and overrule

[73] Kadish, *Judicial Review in the United States Supreme Court and the High Court of Australia*, 37 TEX. L. REV. 133, 155 (1958).

[74] See, *e.g.*, Ferguson v. Skrupa, 372 U.S. 726 (1963); Phelps Dodge Corp. v. N.L.R.B., 313 U.S. 177, 187 (1941); Leisy v. Hardin, 135 U.S. 100, 118 (1890).

[75] Allen, *The Supreme Court and State Criminal Justice*, 4 WAYNE L. REV. 191, 192 (1958).

[76] An interesting variation of this approach was employed in Louisville R.R. v. Letson, 2 How. 497, 555 (1844). The opinion there noted: "By no one was the correctness [of the overruled decisions] more questioned than by the late chief justice who gave them. It is within the knowledge of several of us, that he repeatedly expressed regret that those decisions had been made. . . ." See also United States v. Raines, 362 U.S. 17, 25–26 (1960); Graves v. N.Y. *ex rel.* O'Keefe, 306 U.S. 466, 480–85 (1939); *In re* Ayers, 123 U.S. 443, 487–89 (1887).

[77] Blaustein & Field, *"Overruling" Opinions in the Supreme Court*, 57 MICH. L. REV. 151, 174 (1958).

the original case.[78] As one opinion put it: "No interest which could be served by . . . rigid adherence to *stare decisis* is superior to the demands of a system based on a consistent application of the Constitution."[79] In fact, carried to its limits, the argument based upon the force of subsequent decisions has permitted the Court to disclaim the responsibility for anything more than the formalistic burial of a case already dead.[80]

4. *The place of the overruling art.*—Changing conditions, lessons of experience, and inconsistent later cases clearly have been the basic grounds of overruling decisions. There are very few such cases in which the Court has not employed one or the other.[81] A description of the rationale of overruling opinions would not be complete, however, without mentioning certain other factors commonly emphasized by the Court. Overruling opinions, particularly those relying upon the inconsistency of later decisions, frequently have attempted to depreciate the precedent value of the overruled case even as of the time it was decided.[82] Thus, the opinions often have noted, and sometimes stressed, that the overruled case was decided by a divided Court.[83] Similarly, attention has been focused on the fact that the particular context in which an issue was originally presented had prevented the Court from giving to it the "deliberate consideration" normally afforded significant constitutional issues.[84] Still another point emphasized in overruling opinions

---

[78] See, *e.g.*, Scherrer v. Scherrer, 334 U.S. 343 (1948); State Tax Comm'n v. Aldrich, 316 U.S. 174 (1942); Graves v. Schmidlapp, 315 U.S. 657 (1942).

[79] Graves v. Schmidlapp, 315 U.S. 657, 665 (1942). See also Burnet v. Coronado Oil & Gas Co., 285 U.S. 393, 405 (1932) (Justice Brandeis dissenting).

[80] See, *e.g.*, Leisy v. Hardin, 135 U.S. 100, 118 (1890); Olsen v. Nebraska, 313 U.S. 236, 244 (1941); Ferguson v. Skrupa, 373 U.S. 726 (1963).

[81] See note 60 *supra*.

[82] See, *e.g.*, East Ohio Gas Co. v. Tax Comm'n, 283 U.S. 465, 471–72 (1931); California v. Thompson, 313 U.S. 109, 116 (1941); Thompson v. Whitman, 18 Wall. 457, 464 (1873); see also O'Malley v. Woodrough, 307 U.S. 277, 298 (1939) (noting academic criticism and professional opinion in opposition to the overruled decision).

[83] See, *e.g.*, United States v. Darby, 312 U.S. 100, 115 (1941); United States v. Chicago, M., St. P. & P. R.R., 312 U.S. 592, 578 (1941); Gordon v. Ogden, 3 Pet. 33, 34 (1830).

[84] See, *e.g.*, Wabash, St. L. & P. Ry. Co. v. Illinois, 118 U.S. 557, 568 (1886); Mercoid Corp. v. Mid-Continent Co., 320 U.S. 661, 668, n.1 (1944); and Graves v. New York *ex rel.* O'Keefe, 306 U.S. 466, 480–85 (1939); *cf.* Monroe v. Pape, 365 U.S. 167, 218 (1961) (Frankfurter, J., dissenting).

—with two very notable exceptions[85]—has been the unavailability
of a lesser ground that would permit the Court to reach the correct
result without overruling its prior decision.[86] Although these factors do not themselves furnish an independent ground for reversing
prior decisions, they may effectively supplement the primary arguments based upon changed conditions, experience, or the effect of
later cases. The image of the overruling process presented in the
Court's opinion still rests, however, essentially upon the use of these
basic rationales.

In this regard it should be emphasized that while these arguments obviously improve that image by minimizing the importance
of alterations in the Court's composition, they are not mere façades
put forth as a matter of good public relations.[87] Differences in
viewpoints between present and past members of the Court obviously are important,[88] but changed conditions, the lesson of experience, and the course of later decisions are relevant factors that
do and should have considerable bearing upon the Court's determination to overrule a prior decision.[89] As the Court has frequently
recognized, the principles of *stare decisis* still have some applicability in the area of constitutional law.[90] There remains, at the least, a

[85] Mapp v. Ohio, 367 U.S. 643 (1961); Erie R.R. v. Tompkins, 304 U.S. 64 (1938).

[86] See West Coast Hotel Co. v. Parrish, 300 U.S. 379, 387–88 (1937); Chicago
& E. Ill. R.R. v. Industrial Comm'n, 284 U.S. 296, 298 (1932); Williams v. North
Carolina, 317 U.S. 287, 292 (1942).

[87] But *cf.* Kadish, *supra* note 73, at 153, suggesting that various attacks upon the
"Court's free and easy ways with stare decisis . . . center principally upon the politi-
cal consideration of adverse public reaction to a too slight regard by the court for
its own pronouncements, rather than upon the integrity of the legal principle";
Douglas, *Stare Decisis*, 49 COLUM. L. REV. 735, 740 (1949); see also Arnold, *Professor
Hart's Theology*, 73 HARV. L. REV. 1298, 1310 (1960).

[88] See FRANKFURTER, LAW AND POLITICS 113 (1939); and ROSTOW, THE SOVEREIGN
PREROGATIVE 37 (1962). See also Douglas, *supra* note 87, at 736–37.

[89] *Cf.* Henkin, *Some Reflections on Current Constitutional Controversy*, 109
U. PA. L. REV. 637, 654–55 (1961); JACKSON, THE SUPREME COURT IN THE AMERICAN
SYSTEM 79–80 (1955).

[90] See, *e.g.*, Green v. United States, 355 U.S. 184, 192 (1957); Di Santo v. Pennsylvania, 273 U.S. 34, 42 (1927) (dissenting opinion of Brandeis, J.): "It is usually
more important that a rule of law be settled, than that it be settled right. . . . Often
this is true although the question is a constitutional one."
Several examples of constitutional cases in which Justices voted against the position they would ordinarily have taken because of the weight of *stare decisis* are

presumption of validity that attaches to the conclusions expressed in prior opinions.[91] Of course, this may be overcome by a finding that the opposite result is clearly the correct one, but the assumption that the later Court thus has obtained "a knowledge and wisdom . . . denied to its predecessors"[92] naturally carries with it a certain uneasiness. Any doubts of this sort, however, may be substantially lessened if, in addition to the arguments supporting its position, the Court can depreciate the views of its predecessor by showing either that they concerned conditions far different from those of today, that they were made without the information gained through experience in their application, or even that they stand against the tide of the views expressed by other courts over the years. Thus, in relying upon these factors, the Court has merely followed the standard policy of attempting to present the strongest case for the result it has reached, which, in this instance, involves showing not only the reasonableness of its own views but also the inappropriateness of following the contrary views expressed by its predecessor.

The basic patterns of reasoning traditionally employed in overruling cases, therefore, are consistent in all respects with the proper objectives of the judicial opinion. Of course, this is not to suggest that these rationales are suited to every case. There have been overruling decisions, like *The Legal Tender Cases*[93] and *Rabinowitz v. United States*,[94] so patently based on the changes in personnel that no explanation for the overruling other than the difference in the

---

cited in Reed, *Stare Decisis and Constitutional Law*, 35 PA. B.A.Q. 131, 137 (1938). *But see* Kadish, *supra* note 73, at 153 n.84.

[91] See cases cited *supra* note 90; *but see* Douglas, *supra* note 87, at 736. This is particularly true where a ruling has been adhered to in a number of subsequent decisions. See, *e.g.*, Green v. United States, 355 U.S. 184, 192 (1957); Gore v. United States, 357 U.S. 386, 392 (1958); Galvan v. Press, 347 U.S. 522, 531–32 (1954); Ullman v. United States, 350 U.S. 422, 437–38 (1956); see also United States v. Rabinowitz, 339 U.S. 56, 85 (1950) (dissenting opinion); Pollock v. Farmers Loan & Trust Co., 157 U.S. 429, 630–33 (1895).

[92] Smith v. Allwright, 321 U.S. 649, 667 (1944) (dissenting opinion); see also Pollock v. Farmers Loan & Trust Co., 157 U.S. 429, 519–20 (argument of James C. Carter).

[93] 12 Wall. 457 (1870). See Boudin, *Stare Decisis in Our Constitutional Theory*, 8 N.Y.U.L.Q. 588, 612 (1931).

[94] 339 U.S. 56 (1950).

views of the Justices originally in the majority and their successors could reasonably be offered.[95] (It might be noted in passing that neither of these sudden shifts in position did much to enhance the Court's reputation among the bar,[96] and *The Legal Tender Cases* actually "shook popular respect for the Court."[97]) But where these justifications for disregarding precedent are applicable, they should be employed in the interests of both the logical persuasiveness of the Court's position and the maintenance of the profession's confidence—and through it the public's confidence—in the impersonal and principled qualities of the judicial process. It is with this standard in mind that the Court's opinion in *Gideon v. Wainwright* will be analyzed.

II. The Overruling Technique of Gideon v. Wainwright

A. THE TWO OPINIONS

An analysis of the overruling technique employed in *Gideon* must properly begin with the opinion in *Betts v. Brady*.[98] Smith Betts, charged with robbery in a Maryland court, had requested the appointment of counsel to represent him. When the trial court denied the request, Betts pleaded not guilty, waived his right to a jury, and conducted his own defense. Found guilty and sentenced to prison, Betts filed a habeas corpus petition with Chief Judge Bond of the Maryland Court of Appeals alleging that the trial judge's failure to appoint counsel violated the federal Constitution. Judge Bond rejected this claim, and the Supreme Court, on writ of certiorari, affirmed by a vote of six to three. The majority opinion, written by Justice Roberts and concurred in by Chief Justice Stone, and Justices Reed, Frankfurter, Byrnes, and Jackson, was modeled to a large extent upon the opinion of Judge Bond below.[99] The Court's opinion noted at the outset that since the Sixth Amendment applied only to federal courts, Betts's rights would be

---

[95] See also Jones v. Opelika, 319 U.S. 103 (1943). For a discussion of that case see Kadish, *supra* note 73, at 154 n.97.

[96] On *The Legal Tender Cases*, see 5 Am. L. Rev. 366 (1870). On *Rabinowitz*, see Note, 49 Mich. L. Rev. 128 (1950).

[97] Hughes, The Supreme Court of the United States 52 (1928).

[98] 316 U.S. 455 (1942).

[99] Record, pp. 29–30 (opinion of Judge Bond).

determined under the Due Process Clause of the Fourteenth Amendment, which was "less rigid and more fluid" than the specific provisions of the Bill of Rights.[100] The question posed by petitioner's argument accordingly was viewed as "whether due process of law demands that in every case, whatever the circumstances, a State must furnish counsel to an indigent defendant."[101] Justice Roberts found that this precise question had never been "squarely adjudicated," though language in some clearly distinguishable opinions did "lend color" to petitioner's contentions.[102]

Turning to the merits of the question, he noted that the Due Process Clause encompassed only those rights that were "fundamental and essential to a fair trial." Whether the absolute right to appointed counsel fell within this category would be determined in the light of the "common understanding of those who lived under Anglo-American system of law."[103] After examining past and present state practices in appointing counsel, Roberts found that, in most states, the "considered judgment" of the people, their representatives and the courts was that "appointment of counsel [was] not a fundamental right . . . essential to a fair trial" but merely a matter of "legislative policy."[104] This judgment, he noted, was sustained by the practice in Maryland. For example, Judge Bond, in his opinion below, had stated that his experience presiding over more than 2,000 cases "had demonstrated . . . that there are fair trials without counsel employed for prisoners."[105] Justice Roberts concluded that "while want of counsel in a particular case may result in a conviction lacking in . . . fundamental fairness," the Court could not "say that the Amendment embodies an inexorable command that no trial for any offense, or in any court, can be fairly conducted and justice accorded a defendant who is not represented by counsel."[106] Due process only requires that counsel be

---

[100] 316 U.S. at 462.   [101] Id. at 464; see also id. at 462.

[102] Id. at 462–63.   [103] Id. at 464, 465.   [104] Id. at 471.

[105] Id. at 472 n.31. This statement was cited to supplement the Court's argument, also advanced by Judge Bond below, that non-jury trials in Maryland were conducted on a more informal basis and the trial judge was "in a better position to see impartial justice done than when the formalities of a jury trial are involved." Id. at 472.

[106] Id. at 473. The Court also stressed that acceptance of such a position would require appointment of counsel in all types of cases, including small crimes tried

provided where the special circumstances of the individual case indicate that the absence of legal representation would deprive the defendant of a fair trial. Justice Roberts found no evidence that the case before him fell within this category. His opinion emphasized that Betts had had a non-jury trial, which left the judge more leeway to "see impartial justice done," and that the case had presented only the "simple issue" of veracity of conflicting testimony that an adult with Betts's background could adequately handle himself.[107]

Justice Black wrote a dissenting opinion in *Betts* that was joined by Justices Murphy and Douglas. He argued that the Fourteenth Amendment automatically made the Sixth Amendment "applicable to the States,"[108] but that the right to appointment of counsel was constitutionally protected even under the majority's view of the Due Process Clause, since it was a "fundamental right." In support of this conclusion the dissent quoted from various cases recognizing the importance of counsel, including Justice Sutherland's opinion for the Court in *Powell v. Alabama*.[109] Justice Black also emphasized that most of the states, thirty-five by his count, had recognized the fundamental nature of the right to counsel by "constitutional provisions, statutes, or established practice judicially approved, which assure that no man shall be deprived of counsel merely because of his poverty."[110] The dissent also mentioned that Betts was "a farm hand . . . out of a job and on relief," and that he had "little education," but no attempt was made to cite specific instances at the trial where Betts might have been prejudiced by the absence of counsel.[111]

Justice Black wrote again in *Gideon v. Wainwright*,[112] but this time it was an opinion for the Court joined by Justice Douglas, a fellow dissenter in *Betts*, and five Justices appointed in the twenty-

---

before justices of the peace and "presumably" even offenses tried in traffic court. In fact, the Court argued, "the logic of the petitioners' position would even require appointment of counsel in civil cases." *Ibid*.

[107] *Id*. at 472, 473.

[108] *Id*. at 474. This was the position he later developed more fully in Adamson v. California, 332 U.S. 46, 71–72 (1947).

[109] 287 U.S. 45 (1932).　　　　[111] *Id*. at 474.

[110] *Id*. at 477. See note 318 *infra*.　　[112] 372 U.S. 335.

two-year interim since *Betts*.[113] Clarence Gideon, like Smith Betts, was an indigent convicted of a felony (breaking and entering with intent to commit a misdemeanor) in a state (Florida) court. Like Betts he had made a request for the assignment of counsel that had been rejected. Again like Betts, Gideon had pleaded not guilty and had conducted his own defense; but his trial was before a jury. Found guilty and sentenced to five years' imprisonment, he filed a writ of habeas corpus in the Florida Supreme Court that was rejected. The United States Supreme Court then granted certiorari, its order directing counsel "to discuss in their briefs and oral arguments the following: Should this Court's holding in *Betts* v. *Brady* . . . be reconsidered."[114]

Justice Black's opinion in *Gideon* started out by employing one of the common techniques of overruling opinions. Noting the various similarities in the fact situations of *Betts* and *Gideon*, he found the two cases "so nearly indistinguishable" that "the *Betts* v. *Brady* holding if left standing would require [the Court] . . . to reject Gideon's claim."[115] Accordingly, the Court was compelled to reconsider the validity of the *Betts* decision. On this score, the opinion accepted "the *Betts* v. *Brady* assumption, based as it was on . . . prior cases, that a provision of the Bill of Rights which is 'fundamental and essential to a fair trial' is made obligatory upon States by the Fourteenth Amendment."[116] It disagreed, however, with the conclusion "that the Sixth Amendment's guarantee of counsel is not one of these fundamental rights." Support for this disagreement was found primarily in pre-*Betts* precedents. Justice Black pointed out that, ten years before *Betts*, in *Powell* v. *Alabama*, "[the] Court, after full consideration of all the historical data examined in *Betts*, had unequivocally declared that the 'right to the aid of counsel is of this fundamental character.' "[117] He also noted that seven years later in *Grosjean* v. *American Press Co.*,[118] the "right of the accused to the aid of counsel in a criminal prosecution" had been

---

[113] Chief Justice Warren, and Justices Brennan, Stewart, White, and Goldberg.

[114] 370 U.S. 908. *Cf.* Mapp v. Ohio, 367 U.S. 643 (1961).

[115] 372 U.S. at 339. The Court did not mention the difference between the jury trial in *Gideon* and the non-jury trial in *Betts*, although the *Betts* Court had stressed that factor. See 316 U.S. at 474.

[116] 372 U.S. at 342.   [117] *Id.* at 342–43.   [118] 297 U.S. 233 (1936).

listed as one of those fundamental rights of the first eight Amendments that were "safeguarded against state actions by the due process clause of the Fourteenth Amendment."[119] Similar support was found in *Johnson v. Zerbst*,[120] *Avery v. Alabama*,[121] and *Smith v. O'Grady*,[122] other cases decided before *Betts.* The opinion concluded that "the Court in *Betts* v. *Brady* [had] made an abrupt break with its own well considered precedents." "In returning to these old precedents" the present Court was merely "restor[ing] constitutional principles established to achieve a fair system of justice."[123]

Justice Black's opinion went on to find that the rejection of the *Betts* rule was supported "not only" by these pre-*Betts* precedents but also by "reason and reflection." The absolute necessity of the assistance of counsel in order to obtain a fair trial was, he stated, "an obvious truth," evidenced by the fact "that government hires lawyers to prosecute and defendants who have money hire lawyers to defend."[124] As a further illustration of this absolute need for counsel, Justice Black quoted with approval the following passage from Justice Sutherland's opinion in *Powell* (which had also been cited in his *Betts* dissent):[125]

> The right to be heard would be, in many cases, of little avail if it did not comprehend the right to be heard by counsel. Even the intelligent and educated layman has small and sometimes no skill in the science of law. If charged with crime, he is incapable, generally, of determining for himself whether the indictment is good or bad. He is unfamiliar with the rules of evidence. Left without the aid of counsel he may be put on trial without a proper charge, and convicted upon incompetent evidence, or evidence irrelevant to the issue or otherwise inadmissible. He lacks both the skill and knowledge adequately to prepare his defense, even though he have a perfect one. He requires the guiding hand of counsel at every step in the proceedings against him. Without it, though he be not guilty, he faces the danger of conviction because he does not know how to establish his innocence.

---

119 372 U.S. at 343, quoting from 297 U.S. 233, 243–44.

120 304 U.S. 458 (1938).

121 308 U.S. 444 (1940).

122 312 U.S. 329 (1941).

123 372 U.S. at 344.

124 *Id*. at 344.

125 *Id*. at 344–45, quoting 287 U.S. at 68–69.

Justice Black concluded by noting that *Betts v. Brady*, having "departed from the sound wisdom" of *Powell*, had been "an anachronism when handed down"[126] and was now properly overruled.

Although the decision to overrule *Betts* was unanimous, there were three separate opinions by individual Justices. A short concurring opinion by Justice Douglas was concerned solely with the general relationship of the Bill of Rights and the Fourteenth Amendment.[127] The opinions of the other two Justices, however, dealt with the indigent's right to counsel and the overruling of *Betts*. Justice Clark concurred in the final judgment on the grounds that the Court should no longer distinguish between defendants in non-capital cases like *Gideon* and those in capital cases, where the right to appointment of counsel was absolute.[128] Justice Harlan's concurrence, as previously mentioned, was critical of the Court's treatment of the *Betts* decision, particularly the charge that it had departed from prior precedent. Justice Harlan would have overruled *Betts* on the ground that the rule of that case "was no longer a reality," having been eaten away by exceptions, and that its formal rejection was necessary to clarify lower court appreciation of the actual state of the law.[129]

B. BETTS AS A DEPARTURE FROM PRECEDENT

Justice Black's opinion in *Gideon* relied essentially on two points: Betts was clearly erroneous as a matter of reason and *Betts* itself had been an "abrupt" departure from well-established prior decisions. The first point represents, of course, the basic argument of most overruling cases.[130] It could, perhaps, have been stated more persuasively,[131] but, in any event, it expresses no more than the dis-

---

126 372 U.S. at 345. Justice Black noted that this characterization of *Betts* was suggested by the twenty-two states that argued *amicus curiae* for the overrule of that case. The language was used in the states' brief in describing the relation of *Betts* to the state practices at the time that case was decided.

127 *Id.* at 345.   129 *Id.* at 350–52.

128 *Id.* at 347–49.   130 See text at note 39 *supra*.

131 In particular, the state's customary employment of a lawyer as prosecutor hardly seems the most compelling argument for the proposition that "the accused cannot be assured a fair trial unless counsel is provided for him." *But see* Green, *The Bill of Rights, the Fourteenth Amendment and the Supreme Court*, 46 MICH. L. REV. 869, 883 (1948).

agreement of the present members of the Court with the logic of their predecessors. The dominant characteristic of overruling opinions has been, however, the Court's consistent reliance upon more than just the alleged superiority of the views of its present membership as the basis for rejecting a precedent. In *Gideon*, this supplementary support for overruling obviously must come, if at all, from the second point of the Court's opinion.

The contention that "the Court in *Betts* v. *Brady* made an abrupt break with its own well considered precedents"[132] represents another form of the common practice of depreciating the original significance of the rejected case. It has been used infrequently before.[133] Overruled cases have been characterized previously as a "sport in the law,"[134] an "arbitrary break with the past,"[135] and simply as a "departure" from well-accepted principles.[136] The objective of this emphasis upon inconsistency with earlier decisions is much the same as that rationale based upon inconsistency with later decisions. The Court is placed in a position to reject a precedent and at the same time claim adherence to *stare decisis*. As one opinion put it, "*stare decisis* is a principle of policy and not a mechanical formula of adherence to the latest decision, however recent and questionable, when such adherence involves collision with a prior doctrine more embracing in its scope, intrinsically sounder, and verified by experience."[137] Accordingly, though the tactic of emphasizing the abrupt departure of the overruled decision from prior precedent may not provide the "more respectful

---

[132] 372 U.S. at 344.

[133] See United States v. Darby, 312 U.S. 100 (1941); California v. Thompson, 313 U.S. 109, 115–16 (1941); State Tax Comm'n v. Aldrich, 316 U.S. 174, 179 (1942); see also Helvering v. Hallock, 309 U.S. 106, 114–15 (1940) (non-constitutional overruling); *cf.* United States v. Rabinowitz, 339 U.S. 56, 64–65 (1950). The criticism on this level is likely to be much more severe in a concurring opinion than in the Court's opinion. *Compare* Williams v. North Carolina, 317 U.S. 287, 297 (1942), *with id.* at 307 (Frankfurter, J., concurring), and State Tax Comm'n v. Aldrich, 316 U.S. 174, 179 *with id.* at 183 (1942) (Frankfurter, J., concurring).

[134] Screws v. United States, 325 U.S. 91, 112–13 (1945).

[135] Williams v. North Carolina, 317 U.S. at 307 (concurring opinion).

[136] California v. Thompson, 313 U.S. at 116.

[137] Helvering v. Hallock, 309 U.S. at 119; see State Tax Comm'n v. Aldrich, 316 U.S. at 183.

burial" that Justice Harlan requested,[188] it serves to characterize the Court's decision as an automatic correction of a rare judicial freak independently of any change in the Court's personnel.

While the "departure-from-precedent" rationale employed in *Gideon* is thus an effective overruling technique, its applicability to the *Gideon* situation is highly questionable. *Betts v. Brady*, whatever its other defects, is not a very likely candidate for the role of an eccentric among precedents. The Court's opinion in *Gideon* stressed particularly the inconsistency between *Betts* and *Powell v. Alabama*, but a close reading of *Powell* seems to support Justice Harlan's view that *Betts* fell well within the basic pattern cut by the *Powell* opinion.[189] Justice Black's analysis seems to ignore the fact that *Powell* dealt primarily with the historically separate right of the individual to employ his own counsel,[140] and it was only in the last few pages of Justice Sutherland's lengthy opinion that he considered the state's duty to appoint counsel.[141] Thus, Justice Black stresses that *Powell*, after examining the same history as *Betts*, had declared that the right to counsel was "fundamental,"[142] but both the historical analysis and the cited declaration were made concerning the right to employ counsel.[148] When the *Powell* opinion turned to the state's duty to appoint counsel, it carefully restricted its ruling to the type of situation presented by the case before the Court: "a capital case . . . where the defendant . . . is incapable adequately of making his own defense because of ignorance, feeble mindedness, illiteracy or the like."[144] Justice Black

---

188 372 U.S. at 349. See text at note 18 *supra*.

189 *Id.* at 341–43, 349–50.

140 Allen, *The Supreme Court, Federalism, and State Criminal Justice,* 8 DE PAUL L. REV. 213, 224 (1959); *cf.* FREUND, THE UNITED STATES SUPREME COURT 50–58 (1961).

141 287 U.S. at 71–73.   142 372 U.S. at 343, citing 287 U.S. at 68.

143 287 U.S. at 60–68. See Kadish, *Methodology and Criteria in Due Process Adjudication—A Survey and Criticism,* 66 YALE L. J. 319, 329 (1957). *But cf.* Green, *supra* note 131, at 879. It should be noted that several of the state cases cited by Justice Sutherland as "recogniz[ing] the right to the aid of counsel as fundamental" did involve appointed counsel, although the issue usually concerned matters such as failure to grant counsel sufficient time to prepare his case. See, *e.g.,* State v. Ferris, 16 La. Ann. 424 (1862); Sheppard v. State, 165 Ga. 460, 464 (1928); and State v. Moore, 61 Kan. 732, 734 (1900). The Court later described the right to appointment of counsel under the particular facts of the *Powell* case as fundamental. 287 U.S. at 73.

144 287 U.S. at 71.

discounted this restriction as an example of the Court's customary practice of formally limiting its holdings,[145] a factor that did not detract from the opinion's conclusion concerning the fundamental nature of the right to counsel. Leaving aside the question how readily such a standardized restriction should be disregarded,[146] the fact is that the discussion of the state's duty to appoint counsel in *Powell* was not limited merely by the usual incidental remark at the end of the opinion concerning the scope of Court's ruling (as was the case with respect to the Court's discussion of the right to employ counsel). The restriction of the duty to appoint counsel to circumstances involving illiterate or otherwise incapable defendants was repeated throughout the Court's discussion.[147] Surely, the Court in *Powell* would not have so continuously emphasized these factors if a broader rule had been intended.[148]

This reading of *Powell* is supported by the context in which that case arose as well as by the language of the opinion. *Powell* was, after all, one of the first, if not the first, of the "modern" procedural due process cases.[149] The duty to appoint counsel involved a previously unconsidered area, unmentioned in petitioners' excellent brief,[150] and obviously containing various unforeseen possibilities as to scope and application. Under these circumstances, it would have been unusual for the Court even to suggest establishing a flat rule requiring appointment in all cases.[151] In keeping with the traditional appellate function in a case of first impression,[152] Justice Sutherland obviously sought to decide the particular question be-

---

[145] 372 U.S. at 343.

[146] *Cf.* Allen, *supra* note 140, at 224, on the importance of such limitation to "the operation of the judicial process in a Fourteenth Amendment case."

[147] 287 U.S. at 71–73. Within the space of a few pages, the Court made over a half-dozen references to the special circumstances that entitled defendants to appointed counsel.

[148] *Cf., e.g.,* Johnson v. Zerbst, 304 U.S. 458 (1937).

[149] Allen, *supra* note 140, at 223.

[150] Brief for Petitioners, pp. 48–60. The brief relied on many grounds in addition to the counsel problem.

[151] This is particularly true when one considers that Sutherland was author of the opinion. See Fellman, *The Federal Right to Counsel in State Courts,* 31 NEB. L. REV. 15, 19 (1951).

[152] LLEWELLYN, THE COMMON LAW TRADITION 306–10 (1960).

fore him while at the same time allowing for such future growth as
the Court might later find desirable.[153] Thus, the emphasis upon the
right to a fair hearing rather than the specific terms of the Sixth
Amendment provided for the possibility of a flexible expansion of
the right to appointed counsel in keeping with the Court's view of
due process.[154] This cautious approach was taken even in the opinion's eloquent description of the defendant's need for counsel that
Justice Black quoted at length in *Gideon*.[155] Justice Sutherland's
statement was carefully limited by its first sentence:[156] "the right to
be heard would be, *in many cases,* of little avail if it did not com-
prehend the right to be heard by counsel." *Powell v. Alabama* provided a steppingstone to either a *Betts* or a *Gideon,* depending
upon how far and how fast the Court utilized the opinion's potential for expansion.[157] Certainly, neither would have been an "abrupt
break" from the precedent, or even the "wisdom," of the *Powell*
decision.[158]

The other pre-*Betts* cases cited in *Gideon* scarcely furnish any
more support for the Court's characterization of *Betts* as an "abrupt break" from precedent. Admittedly, the portion of the *Grosjean* opinion quoted by Justice Black did describe *Powell* as holding

[153] Thus, the *Powell* opinion has been described as a "model" of the traditional
due process approach of deciding the case at hand while providing for expansion.
Allen, *The Supreme Court and State Criminal Justice,* 4 WAYNE L. REV. 191, 192
(1958). See also Fellman, *supra* note 151; BEANEY, THE RIGHT TO COUNSEL IN AMERI-
CAN COURTS 155 (1955).

[154] See Allen, *supra* note 153, and Fellman, *supra* note 151.

[155] See BEANEY, *op. cit. supra* note 153, at 155. This section of Justice Sutherland's
opinion has been quoted often in later opinions. See, *e.g.,* Williams v. Kaiser, 323 U.S.
471, 475 (1945); Johnson v. Zerbst, 304 U.S. 458, 463 (1938); Bute v. Illinois, 333
U.S. 640, 680 (1948) (Douglas, J., dissenting).

[156] 287 U.S. at 68–69. (Emphasis added.)   [157] Allen, *supra* note 140, at 225.

[158] "Commentators were rather cautious in estimating (Powell's) effect." BEANEY,
op. cit. supra note 153, at 156. The possible extension of the *Powell* reasoning to all
felony cases was not always recognized. See Ireton, *Due Process in Criminal Trials,*
67 U.S.L. REV. 83 (1933); Nutting, *The Supreme Court, the Fourteenth Amendment
and State Capital Cases,* 3 U. CHI. L. REV. 244 (1936). Where it was anticipated,
such an extension was usually treated as something less than a foregone conclusion.
Comment, *Constitutional Law–Due Process and Equal Protection–The Right to
Counsel,* 31 MICH. L. REV. 245 (1932); Note, 17 MINN. L. REV. 415 (1933); Note,
22 VA. L. REV. 957 (1936); 18 IA. L. REV. 383 (1933); 81 U. PA. L. REV. 337 (1933);
18 ST. LOUIS L. REV. 161 (1933).

that "the right of an accused to the aid of counsel" was "funda-mental,"[159] but here again the reference was probably to the right to employ counsel.[160] In any event, a short statement in a free-speech case attempting to illustrate the relationship between the Bill of Rights and the Fourteenth Amendment can hardly be taken as a significant authority on the scope of the indigent's right to appointed counsel.[161] The ambiguous nature of the *Grosjean* type of statement is well illustrated by a similar discussion of the scope of the Fourteenth Amendment in *Palko v. Connecticut*,[162] a pre-*Betts* decision which Justice Black did not cite. In *Palko*, Justice Cardozo described *Powell* in almost the same terms as *Grosjean* when he listed the various rights protected by the Fourteenth Amendment,[163] but, at another point, he recognized, and indeed stressed, that *Powell* "had turned upon the fact that in the particular situation laid before us in the evidence the benefit of counsel was essential to the substance of a hearing."[164] *Smith v. O'Grady*[165] and *Avery v. Alabama*,[166] other cases cited in *Gideon*, have essentially the same weakness in terms of their precedential significance as does *Grosjean*.[167] In *Avery* there was an ambiguous suggestion that the refusal to appoint counsel would have been a denial of due

---

159 "We concluded that certain fundamental rights, safeguarded by the first eight amendments against federal action, were also safeguarded against state action by the due process of law clause of the Fourteenth Amendment, and among them the funda-mental right of the accused to the aid of counsel in a criminal prosecution." Grosjean v. American Press Co., 297 U.S. 233, 243–44 (1936).

160 *But see* Note, *Betts v. Brady*, 21 CHI.–KENT L. REV. 107 (1942). It is interesting to note that Justice Roberts, who wrote *Betts*, described *Powell* in approximately the same terms in his dissent in Snyder v. Massachusetts, 291 U.S. 97, 133 (1934).

161 The Court there held that a privilege tax levied on a publisher violated the freedom of the press protected under the Due Process Clause of the Fourteenth Amendment. 297 U.S. at 244–45.

162 302 U.S. 319, 324 (1937).   163 *Id.* at 324–25.

164 *Id.* at 327. See Green, *The Bill of Rights, the Fourteenth Amendment and the Supreme Court*, 46 MICH. L. REV. 869, 873 n.24 (1948), suggesting that this difference in description was "apparently intended to distinguish between the right to represen-tation by counsel, with its corollaries, and the right of appointment of counsel for the indigent accused."

165 312 U.S. 329 (1941).   166 308 U.S. 444 (1940).

167 "[*Smith and Avery*] did not significantly expand or clarify the law as it had been left by the decision of *Powell*." Allen, *supra* note 140, at 225.

process, but this was only an offhand remark of an opinion concerned solely with the denial of appointed counsel's request for a continuance.[168] Similarly, in *Smith*, the failure to appoint counsel was only one of numerous allegations held to add up to a denial of due process in a fact situation similar to that in *Powell*.[169]

The remaining case cited by Justice Black, *Johnson v. Zerbst*,[170] provides his strongest support, but hardly goes so far as to make *Betts* an aberration. The Court in *Johnson* specifically characterized the indigent's right to appointment of counsel as a "fundamental human right" based upon the "obvious truth that the average defendant does not have the professional legal skill to protect himself."[171] *Johnson*, however, dealt with the federal courts, and the Court there spoke solely in terms of the right to appointment under the Sixth Amendment.[172] *Powell*, and later cases like *Palko*, on the other hand, repeatedly had emphasized the limited relevance of the specific terms of the Bill of Rights in determining standards applicable to state courts under the Fourteenth Amendment.[173] So, while *Johnson* might have had the force of a persuasive analogy, it was hardly a binding precedent insofar as the right to appointed counsel under the Due Process Clause was concerned.[174]

---

168 Although counsel had been appointed, the opinion (by Justice Black) noted that "[h]ad petitioner been denied any representation of counsel at all, such a clear violation of the Fourteenth Amendment's guarantee of assistance of counsel would have required a reversal of his conviction." 308 U.S. at 445. The Court cited *Powell v. Alabama* as direct authority for this statement. *Avery* like *Powell* was a capital case, but the opinion did not recite any special disabilities of the defendants as found in *Powell*.

169 The petitioner there charged that "he had been denied any real notice of the true nature of the charge against him . . . that because of deception by the state's representatives he had pleaded guilty to a charge punishable by twenty years life imprisonment; that his request for the benefit and advice of counsel had been denied by the court and that he had been rushed to the penitentiary where his ignorance, confinement and poverty had precluded the possibility of his securing counsel. . . ." 312 U.S. at 334.

170 304 U.S. 458 (1938).   171 *Id.* at 462–63.

172 *Ibid. But cf.* Kamisar, *Betts v. Brady Twenty Years Later: The Right to Counsel and Due Process Values,* 61 MICH. L. REV. 219, 245 (1962).

173 See Palko v. Connecticut, 302 U.S. 319, 323–28 (1937); Brown v. Mississippi, 297 U.S. 278, 285 (1936); Powell v. Alabama, 287 U.S. 45, 66–68 (1932); see also Snyder v. Massachusetts, 291 U.S. 97, 105–06 (1934).

174 Justice Black also referred to "many other prior decisions," but did not mention which ones he had in mind. There were only a few other decisions that

In sum, even with *Johnson*, Justice Roberts' description of the pre-*Betts* decisions as only "lend[ing] color" to the argument for an unqualified constitutional right to appointed counsel would seem more accurate than Justice Black's position that these decisions logically and as precedents compelled enunciation of such a right in *Betts*.[175] Certainly, one might well have predicted, as some commentators did,[176] that the Court would impose the same requirement for the appointment of counsel upon the states as it had imposed upon the federal government. On the other hand, the great significance which the Court had attached to the *Palko* doctrine constituted a clear warning that any such assumption was highly speculative.[177] This uncertainty in the law prior to *Betts* was perhaps best reflected by the split in the several lower court decisions dealing with the right to appointed counsel during the period between *Johnson* and *Betts*.[178] If there was a clear precedent from which *Betts* could depart, it certainly was not recognized by these decisions, most of which adopted the *Betts* analysis.[179]

Finally, even if *Betts* had been an aberration when decided, Justice Black's emphasis upon this "abrupt break" with precedent could hardly achieve the usual objective of that overruling technique in the context of the *Gideon* situation. The effectiveness of this argument in depicting the overruling decision as part of a natural process of eliminating occasional "sports" in the law necessarily requires that the overruled decision fit within the concept of

cited *Powell* and they added nothing. See, *e.g.*, Brown v. Mississippi, 297 U.S. 278 (1936); Glasser v. United States, 315 U.S. 60, 70 (1942). Other cases like Walker v. Johnson, 312 U.S. 275 (1940), dealt solely with the Sixth Amendment.

175 *Cf.* Allen, *supra* note 140; Comment, 23 TEXAS L. REV. 66 (1944); Note, 31 ILL. B.J. 139 (1942). *But see* Note, 21 CHI.–KENT L. REV. 107 (1942).

176 See BEANEY, THE RIGHT TO COUNSEL IN AMERICAN COURTS 170 (1955); Note, *The Indigents Right to Counsel and the Rule of Prejudicial Error*, 97 U. PA. L. REV. 855 (1949); ROTTSCHAEFER, HANDBOOK OF AMERICAN CONSTITUTIONAL LAW 811 (1939).

177 Consider also Adamson v. California, 332 U.S. 46 (1947), and Ward v. Texas, 316 U.S. 547 (1942).

178 *Compare* Commonwealth *ex rel.* Shaw v. Smith, 147 Pa. Super. 423 (1942); Wilson v. Lanagan, 99 F.2d 544 (1st Cir. 1938), affirming 19 F. Supp. 870 (D. Mass. 1937), *cert. denied*, 306 U.S. 634 (1939); Gall v. Brady, 39 F. Supp. 504 (D. Md. 1941); and Coates v. State, 180 Md. 502 (1942), *with* Boyd v. O'Grady, 121 F.2d 146 (8th Cir. 1941), and Carey v. Brady, 125 F.2d 253 (4th Cir. 1942).

179 See the first group of cases cited *supra* note 178; see also Lyons v. State, 77 Okla. Cr. 197 (1943); House v. State, 130 Fla. 400 (1937).

a judicial oddity. The development of the law since *Betts* was decided, however, made it impossible in 1963 to treat *Betts* as an "isolated deviation from the strong current of precedents."[180] During the twenty-two years of its existence, the *Betts* rule had frequently been acknowledged by the Court, once after a "full scale re-examination"[181] and often over vigorous dissents.[182] It was hardly the "derelict on the waters of the law"[183] that customarily has been the subject of the "departure-from-precedent" reasoning. Thus, if Justice Black had desired to offer some support for rejecting *Betts* beyond the alleged superiority of the Court's present reasoning, he would have best looked to the traditional overruling rationale based upon changed circumstances, the lessons of experience, or the requirements of later precedent.

III. The Alternatives Available in Gideon

A. THE FORCE OF SUBSEQUENT DECISIONS

The overruling rationale most clearly applicable in *Gideon* was that based upon the force of inconsistent later decisions. There were abundant instances where *Betts* had been undermined by subsequent decisions dealing either with the right to appointed counsel itself or with related problems.

1. *The unqualified right to hire counsel.*—In a series of post-*Betts* decisions, most notably *Chandler v. Fretag*,[184] the Court had clearly established prior to *Gideon* an "unqualified" right of the individual to retain counsel at his own expense.[185] Unlike the right

---

180 Lambert v. California, 355 U.S. 225, 232 (1957).

181 Allen, *supra* note 140, at 227, referring to Bute v. Illinois, 333 U.S. 640 (1948), which affirmed the *Betts* doctrine.

182 See, *e.g.*, Foster v. Illinois, 332 U.S. 134 (1947); Bute v. Illinois, *supra* note 181; Gryger v. Burke, 334 U.S. 736 (1947); see also Gayes v. New York, 332 U.S. 145 (1947). The failure of the Court to "squarely cite *Betts* as a constitutional precedent" for the first few years of its life had suggested that it might indeed become a "sport in the law." See Allen, *supra* note 140, at 227; see also Mayo v. Wade, 158 F.2d 614 (5th Cir. 1946). But this possibility was eliminated by a series of later decisions, including *Bute*. See Allen, *id.* at 226–32; see also Carter v. Illinois, 329 U.S. 173 (1946).

183 Lambert v. California, 355 U.S. at 232.

184 348 U.S. 3 (1954); see also Ferguson v. Georgia, 365 U.S. 570 (1960); Reynolds v. Cochran, 365 U.S. 525 (1961); Hawk v. Olson, 326 U.S 271 (1945); House v. Mayo, 324 U.S. 42 (1945).

185 348 U.S. at 9–10.

to appointed counsel under *Betts*, the defendant's right here did not depend on his showing that the lack of legal assistance would deprive him of a fair trial. Three years before *Gideon*, two members of the Court had already suggested that the decisions establishing this uniqualified right to employ counsel had removed any logical basis for the qualified right to the appointment of counsel under *Betts*.[186] The potential difficulty with this argument, however, lies in its assumption that both rights are based on the same policy.

Any rule governing the right to appointed counsel will necessarily be aimed at achieving that objective of procedural due process that Professor Kadish has characterized as "insuring the reliability of the guilt-determining process" by "reducing to a minimum the possibility that an innocent individual will be punished."[187] *Betts* accepted this goal, but assumed that counsel was not always needed to achieve the "fair trial" that it demands. The right to retain counsel obviously is designed to achieve this same objective,[188] and, if that were its only function, then the unqualified nature of this right clearly would be inconsistent with the premise of *Betts*. For, if the use of one's own counsel is always necessary to insure a fair trial, then certainly the use of appointed counsel must fall in the same category—a defendant's need for counsel does not vary directly with his ability to afford one.[189]

The right to employ one's own counsel, however, is also based upon an additional value quite different from insuring reliability of the guilt-determining process and not involved in the right to appointed counsel. In cases like *Chandler* the Court is dealing not merely with the state's duty to insure the fairness of the trial but also with the state's interference with the individual's desire to defend himself in whatever manner he deems best, using any legiti-

---

186 McNeal v. Culver, 365 U.S. 109, 117 (1960); see also Kamisar, *Betts v. Brady Twenty Years Later: The Right to Counsel and Due Process Values*, 61 MICH. L. REV. 219, 244 (1962); *cf. The Supreme Court, 1961 Term*, 76 HARV. L. REV. 115 (1962).

187 Kadish, *Methodology and Criteria in Due Process Adjudication—A Survey and Criticism*, 66 YALE L.J. 319, 346 (1957); see also Carter v. Illinois, 329 U.S. 173, 174 (1946); and Kamisar, *supra* note 186, at 219, 230.

188 Kamisar, *supra* note 186, at 228–30. See Ferguson v. Georgia, 365 U.S. 570 (1960); Reynolds v. Cochran, 365 U.S. 525 (1961).

189 In fact, it may be argued that the indigent has a greater need for counsel. See Kamisar, *supra* note 186, at 227.

mate means within his resources.[190] In other words, what is involved
here is a principle that fits within that category of procedural due
process rights designed to insure "respect for the dignity of the
individual."[191] The presence of this separate interest as a basis for
the defendant's right to retain counsel is suggested in some of the
earlier state constitutional guarantees that are phrased in terms of
the individual's right to represent himself.[192] It is more clearly illustrated by the situation in which an accused refuses either to hire
counsel or accept an appointed counsel and insists upon conducting
his own defense.[193] The Court here must consider not only the
need for a lawyer in order to preserve the reliability of the guilt-
determining process but also the possibly conflicting interest of the
individual in determining the means of his own defense.

This dual basis for the individual's right to retain counsel could
completely undermine the argument for rejecting *Betts* as inconsistent with later cases like *Chandler*. If the unqualified nature of
the right were founded upon this second due process value rather
than upon the objective of insuring a reliable guilt-determining
process, then the different rules for the right to employ counsel
and the right to appointed counsel could be easily reconciled.
Language in the cases following *Chandler*, however, indicates that
the absolute nature of the right to retain counsel probably has been
grounded solely upon the need to insure a reliable guilt-determining process.[194] The opinions in these cases particularly have stressed
the importance of counsel to assure the defendant a fair trial. In
the light of this emphasis, the decisions establishing an absolute
right to retain counsel certainly provided as strong a basis for re-
considering and overruling *Betts* as *Classic* provided with respect

190 *Cf. id.* at 228.

191 Kadish, *supra* note 187, at 347. As to the "hybrid" quality of the values served
by many procedural rights, see Kamisar, *supra* note 186, at 238–39.

192 BEANEY, THE RIGHT TO COUNSEL IN AMERICAN COURTS 18–22 (1955).

193 People v. Mattson, 51 Cal.2d 777 (1959); Linden v. Dickson, 278 F.2d 755 (9th
Cir. 1960); Reynolds v. United States, 267 F.2d 235 (9th Cir. 1959); *cf.* Cannon v.
Gladden, 203 F. Supp. 504 (D. Ore. 1962).

194 See, *e.g.*, Reynolds v. Cochran, 365 U.S. 525, 532–33 (1961); Ferguson v.
Georgia, 365 U.S. 570, 594–95 (1961); see also Chandler v. Fretag, 348 U.S. 3, 9–10
(1954).

to *Grovey v. Townsend,* or the coerced confession cases with respect to *Wolf v. Colorado.*[195]

2. *Betts and Equal Protection.*—If *Chandler v. Fretag* and its progeny had not "removed the underpinnings" from the *Betts* rule by themselves, they certainly did so when added to *Griffin v. Illinois,*[196] and its offspring.[197] Briefly stated, *Griffin* held that where state law conditioned appellate review upon the availability of a stenographic transcript or report of the trial proceedings, the Equal Protection Clause of the Fourteenth Amendment demanded that the state make the same review available to defendants who were financially unable to submit the transcript or report. Various commentators,[198] including two of our most distinguished judges,[199] have suggested that the general philosophy underlying *Griffin* may well make the appointment of counsel to represent indigents an essential requirement of equal protection. Certainly, Justice Black's opinion for four members of the *Griffin* majority went beyond the limited problem of providing transcripts when it stressed the broad objective of affording equal opportunity to the indigent and pecunious defendant. In particular, the opinion contained the sweeping statement that "there can be no equal justice where the kind of trial a man gets depends on the amount of money he has."[200] The relationship between this central theme of the *Griffin* case and *Betts v. Brady* has been succinctly stated by Justice Walter V. Schaefer:[201]

---

[195] Here, also, there had been a valid ground for distinction until the Court indicated that the exclusion of confessions was not aimed merely at elimination of unreliable evidence but also at deterring illegal police practices. See Allen, *Due Process and State Criminal Procedures: Another Look,* 48 Nw. L. Rev. 16, 17–21, 25–28 (1953).

[196] 351 U.S. 12, 18 (1956).

[197] See Douglas v. California, 372 U.S. 353 (1963); see also Burns v. Ohio, 360 U.S. 252 (1959); Eskridge v. Washington, 357 U.S. 214 (1958); Smith v. Bennett, 365 U.S. 708 (1961); Douglas v. Greene, 363 U.S. 192 (1960). See Allen, *Griffin v. Illinois: Antecedents and Aftermath,* 25 U. Chi. L. Rev. 151 (1957).

[198] See articles cited in Holly v. Smyth, 280 F.2d 536, 541–42 n.8 (4th Cir. 1960). See also Comment, *Appointment of Counsel for Indigent Defendants in Criminal Appeals,* [1959] Duke L. J. 484, 488; Allen, *supra* note 197, at 156–57.

[199] Schaefer, *Federalism and State Criminal Procedure,* 70 Harv. L. Rev. 1, 10 (1956); Traynor, J., in People v. Brown, 55 Cal. 2d 64 (1960); *cf.* People v. Breslin, 4 N.Y. 2d 73 (1958).

[200] 351 U.S. at 19.   [201] Schaefer, *supra* note 199, at 10.

The analogy to the right to counsel is close indeed: if a
state allows one who can afford to retain a lawyer to be represented by counsel, and so to obtain a different kind of trial,
it must furnish the same opportunity to those who are unable
to hire a lawyer. Since indigence is constitutionally an irrele-
vance, it would seem that a successful argument might be
based upon the proposition that the defendant by reason of his
poverty is deprived of a right available to those who can
afford to exercise it.

Though the analogy described by Justice Schaefer is indeed
"close," it is far from perfect. Some significant criticisms have been
leveled against the position that the decision in *Griffin* required the
overruling of *Betts*.[202] When the broad language of Justice Black's
opinion is limited to the context of the *Griffin* fact situation,[203]
various grounds can be advanced for distinguishing between the
problem of appointing counsel and that of providing a trial transcript. One factor frequently stressed is the difference in the nature
of the state action in the two situations.[204] In *Griffin*, the appeal
was an integral part of the state's process for determining criminal
liability.[205] In making a transcript or report the prerequisite for
appeal, the state effectively denied the indigent access to a major
portion of this process. In *Betts*, on the other hand, the Court dealt
not with the defendant's access to the criminal process but with
the separate problem of insuring the efficacy of the process—a
problem that is more properly analyzed in terms of fairness than
equality.[206] *Betts* could only be compared to *Griffin*, so the argument goes, if a state conditioned the right to a criminal trial upon
the presence of counsel.

This criticism of the *Griffin* analogy is supplemented by the
contention that a view of equal protection that necessitates over-

---

202 See Comment, *Post-Conviction Due Process—Right of Indigent to Review of
Nonconstitutional Trial Errors*, 55 MICH. L. REV. 413 (1957); Qua, *Griffin v. Illinois*,
25 U. CHI. L. REV. 143, 150 (1957); and Kamisar, *supra* note 186, at 244–45.

203 See Comment, *The Effect of Griffin v. Illinois on the State's Administration
of Criminal Law*, 25 U. CHI. L. REV. 161, 170 (1957); Kamisar, *supra* note 186, at
244–45.

204 See Comment, *supra* note 202; Comment, *supra* note 198.

205 Allen, *The Supreme Court and State Criminal Justice*, 4 WAYNE L. REV. 191,
194 (1958).

206 Kamisar, *supra* note 186, at 247–48.

ruling *Betts* would lack any "limiting principles."[207] If constitutionally required equality of treatment includes the appointment of counsel, then it may also include the provision of funds for psychiatrists, investigators, reimbursement of witnesses' expenses, and more.[208] The accused may insist that equal protection requires not just those resources that are ordinarily necessary to insure the accuracy of the guilt-determining process but the same resources that may offer the more affluent individual a better chance of gaining acquittal even when guilty. Furthermore, this view of equal protection could easily be extended beyond the criminal proceeding to encompass habeas corpus and even ordinary civil proceedings[209] (although a distinction between the civil and criminal process might be based on the ground that the latter is initiated by the government for the achievement of a governmental purpose and entails the imposition of severe sanctions). Such an almost unrestricted scope of applicability, it is argued, reveals the fundamental weakness in a concept of equal protection that ignores the basic distinctions between the *Griffin* and *Betts* situations.

In view of the substantial nature of these criticisms, the refusal of a Court to employ the *Griffin* analogy in overruling *Betts* ordinarily would be both justified and understandable. In the particular circumstances surrounding *Gideon,* however, the Court's failure to rely on this ground was merely puzzling. For, on the very same day that *Gideon* was decided, the Court necessarily faced and rejected each of these criticisms in reaching its decision in a companion case, *Douglas v. California.*[210] The Court there held invalid on equal protection grounds the California practice of refusing to appoint counsel on an appeal by an indigent when the appellate court, after reviewing the trial record, concluded that "no good whatever could be served" by the appointment.[211] Justice Douglas' opinion for a six-member majority[212] found no difference between

---

[207] Allen, *supra* note 205, at 198.

[208] See United States *ex rel.* Smith v. Bald, 192 F.2d 540 (3d Cir. 1951); see also Kamisar, *supra* note 186, at 250–51.

[209] *Cf.* Jacoby, *Legal Aid to the Poor,* 53 HARV. L. REV. 940, 942–44 (1940).

[210] 372 U.S. 353 (1963).   [211] *Id.* at 355.

[212] Justices Clark, Harlan, and Stewart dissented. Of these only Justice Stewart joined the Court's opinion in *Gideon.*

the state's refusal to give the indigent a transcript in *Griffin* and its refusal to provide counsel on appeal. In either case, the opinion noted, there was "discrimination against the indigent . . . for there can be no equal justice where the kind of an appeal a man enjoys depends on the amount of money he has."[213] This conclusion seems clearly to deny the relevance of those factors that might have distinguished *Betts* from *Griffin*. Once the Court has found that *Griffin* requires equality in the *quality* as well as the right of appeal, it necessarily follows that the same type of equality is required at the trial level.[214] As one of the dissenting opinions in *Douglas* noted, the Court's decision in that case made the *Gideon* analysis of the right to appointed counsel under the Due Process Clause "wholly unnecessary."[215] The decision in *Douglas* on equal protection grounds provided the Court with an *a fortiori* basis for overruling *Betts*. It presented a far stronger example of the subsequent development of a principle in a related area that had undermined the overruled case than those situations in which the Court previously had used that line of reasoning.[216] Nevertheless, the Court carefully avoided any mention of the Equal Protection Clause in *Gideon*. In fact, there is some indication that the *Douglas* case, originally argued during the 1961 Term, was set over for reargument during the 1962 Term so as to avoid an earlier decision that would have effectively foreclosed the full-scale re-examination of *Betts* on due process grounds.[217]

---

[213] 372 U.S. 355 (1963), quoting 351 U.S. 12, at 19.

[214] See Hamley, *The Impact of Griffin v. Illinois on State Court–Federal Court Relationships*, 24 F.R.D. 75, 79 (1959); Comment, *supra* note 203, at 171.

[215] 372 U.S. at 363 (Harlan, J., dissenting). There had been indications in a prior opinion that the Court might consider the question of counsel on appeal primarily in terms of the Due Process Clause. In Newsom v. Smyth, 365 U.S. 604 (1961), the Court dismissed its writ of certiorari on the ground that the defendant's right of counsel on appeal had not been properly presented below. The *per curiam* opinion stated that certiorari had been granted to consider the problem under the Due Process Clause. 365 U.S. 604 (1961). A dissent arguing against dismissal, however, referred to the question as one involving the Equal Protection Clause. 365 U.S. 604, 607 (Douglas, J., dissenting).

[216] *Cf.* the cases cited note 62 *supra*.

[217] *Douglas* was originally argued in April, 1962, before five members of the subsequent six-member majority. On June 4, 1962, certiorari in *Gideon* was granted with counsel directed to the question whether *Betts* should be overruled. 370 U.S.

3. *The capital offense exception.*—Prior to the *Douglas* decision, the most obvious ground for the argument that *Betts* had been undermined by a contrary principle adopted in later cases was that suggested in Justice Clark's concurring opinion in *Gideon*[218]—the development of a special exception to the *Betts* "fair trial" rule in cases involving crimes punishable by death. In the capital case, the Court had held that the Due Process Clause imposed an automatic requirement that counsel be appointed; there was no need to show that, under the particular facts of the case, the absence of counsel would result in a trial lacking in fundamental fairness. This departure from the case-by-case analysis of the *Betts* rule was gradual. While Justice Sutherland's opinion in *Powell* emphasized that the defendants there "stood in deadly peril of their lives," it also stressed various other factors including "the ignorance and illiteracy of the defendants, their youth," and "the circumstances of public hostility."[219] One of the pre-*Betts* cases following *Powell* possibly could be read as suggesting an unqualified right to appointed counsel in capital cases, but there was no explicit statement to that effect.[220] It was not until 1948, in *Bute v. Illinois*,[221] that the capital offense exception was explicitly acknowledged, and then only in dictum. This dictum was repeated in later decisions,[222] but it was only in

---

908 (1962). On June 25, 1962, reargument was ordered in *Douglas*, 370 U.S. 930. The Court did not direct counsel's attention on reargument to any special question, as is often done. If the decision in *Douglas* had been handed down in June, 1962, the Court would have found itself in the awkward position of having already answered the question to which counsel in *Gideon* were directed. The Court might well have felt that the question of overruling *Betts* should be faced "head on" rather than in a case involving counsel on appeal. This is all, of course, in the realm of speculation, and various other explanations of the juxtaposition of the two cases are equally plausible. It should be noted, moreover, that the Court had indicated a willingness to consider the question of counsel on appeal a full two years before *Gideon* was decided. See Newsom v. Smyth, *certiorari granted*, 363 U.S. 802 (1960), *dismissed for failure to present a federal question*, 365 U.S. 604 (1961).

[218] 372 U.S. at 348.

[219] 287 U.S. at 71; see also Williams v. Kaiser, 323 U.S. 471 (1944).

[220] Avery v. Alabama, 308 U.S. 444 (1940). *But see* Williams v. Kaiser, 323 U.S. 471 (1945), a post-*Betts* case dealing with a capital crime and emphasizing special circumstances that required the appointment of counsel. *Id.* at 474–75; see also Tompkins v. Missouri, 323 U.S. 485 (1944).

[221] 333 U.S. 640, 674 (1948).

[222] See, *e.g.*, Uveges v. Pennsylvania, 335 U.S. 437, 441 (1948).

Hamilton v. Alabama,[223] decided two years before *Gideon,* that the Court for the first time squarely based its decision on the ground that the case before it involved a capital crime and its reversal therefore did not require a showing of prejudice resulting from the absence of counsel.

The special rule for capital cases has been continuously criticized by commentators as basically inconsistent with the thesis of the *Betts* rule.[224] It frequently has been noted that the need for skilled representation may be as great in non-capital cases as in capital cases, that non-capital offenses in fact are often more complex and more difficult to defend than various offenses classified as capital in different states.[225] Certainly, there is no greater likelihood that a defendant on a first-degree murder charge will be more capable of adequately conducting his own defense in Michigan, which long ago abolished capital punishment, than in Ohio, where the death penalty still prevails.[226] The Court has never answered directly this claim of inconsistency inherent in the capital-noncapital distinction. Opinions of individual Justices, however, have suggested that the special exception for capital cases was justified by the awesome finality of the death penalty.[227] In light of this factor, it was explained, the Court had been "especially sensitive of the demands . . . for procedural fairness" by taking the extra precaution of imposing an absolute requirement of counsel.[228]

Aside from its logical difficulties, in terms of both the text of the Fourteenth Amendment[229] and its implicit admission of the likely

---

[223] 368 U.S. 52 (1961).

[224] See, *e.g.,* the articles cited in notes 225, 226, 229, and 233, *infra.*

[225] Allen, *The Supreme Court, Federalism, and State Criminal Justice,* 8 DE PAUL L. REV. 213, 230–31 (1959).

[226] Kamisar, *supra* note 186, at 256.

[227] See Kinsella v. Singleton, 361 U.S. 234, 255–56 (1960) (Harlan, J., dissenting); Reid v. Covert, 354 U.S. 1, 45–46 (1957) (Frankfurter, J., concurring); see also Williams v. Georgia, 349 U.S. 375, 391 (1955). *But see* Note, 97 U. PA. L. REV. 865 (1949).

[228] 354 U.S. at 65, 77; 361 U.S. at 255. The opinions have not attempted to support the capital-noncapital distinction on the grounds that it "finds support in history." See Kamisar, *supra* note 186, at 258–59.

[229] Commentators have frequently noted that "The Fourteenth Amendment speaks equally of life [and] liberty." Comment, 12 DE PAUL L. REV. 115, 118 (1962).

inaccuracy of the fair trial rule, this position had been thoroughly undermined by recent Court decisions rejecting a capital-noncapital distinction in related areas of constitutional law. In *Kinsella v. Singleton*[230] the Court refused to distinguish between noncapital and capital offenses as regards the application of various constitutional rights under the Fifth and Sixth Amendments to civilian dependents of military personnel stationed overseas.[231] Later in *Ferguson v. Georgia*,[232] the Court rejected the suggestion that this distinction be made applicable to the right to retain counsel. Yet, after both of these decisions, the Court adhered to an unqualified requirement for appointment of counsel in *Hamilton*. This would seem to add up to a "ready-made" situation for the traditional argument that the overruled case must be rejected in order to maintain consistency with a contrary position adopted in a subsequent decision. Admittedly, there is a certain air of unreality in relying only now on an inconsistency that has been apparent over the years,[233] but then again, as Justice Clark noted, it was not until *Hamilton* that the capital-offense exception was squarely upheld.[234]

4. *The special circumstances rule.*—There remains what may have been the best ground, at least in terms of the function of an overruling opinion, for arguing that the rejection of *Betts* was necessitated by the course of subsequent decisions. In his concurring opinion, Justice Harlan suggested that the *Betts* rule had been so "substantially . . . eroded" by decisions requiring the appointment of counsel in noncapital cases that it was "no longer a reality."[235] The reference here was to a steady stream of cases since *Betts* that had attempted to determine under what circumstances the failure to appoint counsel would result in a trial lacking in "fundamental fairness."[236] The "special circumstances" found in

---

[230] 361 U.S. 234 (1960).

[231] *Id.* at 246.   [232] 365 U.S. 570, 596 (1960).

[233] See, *e.g.*, Note, 95 U. PA. L. REV. 793 (1947); Allen, *supra* note 225, at 230; Note, 10 PITT. L. REV. 232 (1948).

[234] See particularly Justice Clark's attitude toward this exception in Crooker v. California, 357 U.S. 433, 441 n.6 (1958).

[235] 372 U.S. at 350–51.

[236] During the period between *Betts* and *Gideon*, the Court considered more than thirty cases involving claims based upon the lack of counsel in state trials. In most

these cases to require the appointment of counsel generally fell
into three categories: (1) the personal characteristics of the defendant, such as youth or mental incapacity; (2) "the complicated
nature of the offense charged and the possible defenses thereto";[237]
and (3) events during the trial that raised difficult legal problems.
Although many indigent defendants have the characteristics found
in the first category,[238] the primary erosion of the Betts rule came
through the decisions relying upon circumstances falling within the
second and third categories.[239] In fact, even prior to Gideon, two
fairly recent decisions from this group—Hudson v. North Carolina[240] and Chewning v. Cunningham[241]—had been recognized as
effectively abrogating the Betts rule.[242]

In Hudson, decided in 1960, the petitioner and two companions
had been tried before a jury in a North Carolina court on a charge

---

of these, the Court's decision dealt with the Betts rule. See Schilke, The Right to
Counsel—An Unrecognized Right, 2 WM. & MARY L. REV. 318, 321 (1960) ("right
to counsel [had] been principally decided . . . twenty-three times" between 1942 and
1960).

[237] Uveges v. Pennsylvania, 335 U.S. 437, 441 (1948); see Note, 109 U. PA. L. REV.
623, 625 (1961).

[238] This takes into consideration such factors as age, experience in court, literacy,
and mental ability or retardation. See, e.g., Palmer v. Ashe, 342 U.S. 134 (1951);
Wade v. Mayo, 334 U.S. 672 (1948); see also Note, 109 U. PA. L. REV. 623, 625–26
(1961) (collecting cases that relied upon such factors to find that counsel was required). Most of the special circumstances cases have fallen within this category.
The Supreme Court, 1961 Term, 76 HARV. L. REV. 54, 114 (1962).

[239] The limitations of the personal characteristics of the defendant as a basis for
requiring counsel are graphically demonstrated in Hudson v. North Carolina, 363
U.S. 697 (1960). Although reversing on other grounds, the Court did state that
Hudson was "not a case where it can be said the failure to appoint counsel for the
defendant resulted in a constitutionally unfair trial because . . . of the defendant's
chronological age." Id. at 701–02. The defendant there "was only eighteen and had
been only to the sixth grade in school." Id. at 701. However, the hearing examiner
had stated that the defendant was "intelligent, well-informed, and was familiar with
and experienced in court procedure and criminal trials." Ibid. See also the dissenting
opinion, 363 U.S. 704, 705, emphasizing the defendant's familiarity with courts as a
result of having been "tried on different occasions for careless and reckless driving
while under the influence of intoxicating liquor and for assault and robbery. . . ."
Id. at 707.

[240] 363 U.S. 697 (1960).   [241] 368 U.S. 443 (1962).

[242] See Kamisar, Betts v. Brady Twenty Years Later: The Right to Counsel and
Due Process Values, 61 MICH. L. REV. 219, 280 (1962); The Supreme Court, 1961
Term, supra note 238, at 115; Note, 14 W. RES. L. REV. 370 (1963); see also Pollock,
Equal Justice in Practice, 45 MINN. L. REV. 737, 741 (1961).

of robbery. Petitioner's request for the appointment of counsel was denied, the trial judge stating that he would "try to see that [petitioner's] rights [were] protected throughout the case."[248] During the trial, a lawyer representing one of the other defendants tendered a plea of guilty to the lesser offense of petit larceny. The guilty plea, made in the presence of the jury, was accepted by the judge without any special comment. The trial of petitioner and his co-defendant then proceeded to its conclusion with the jury finding both defendants guilty of larceny from the person. On review of a habeas corpus proceeding, the Court found that the particular circumstances of the case had required the appointment of counsel. It noted that for most of the trial, the petitioner, who had been described by a lower court as "familiar with and experienced in court procedure,"[244] had been adequately represented through the efforts of his co-defendant's attorney. The attorney's action in entering his client's plea of guilty in the presence of the jury, however, had raised problems "requiring professional knowledge and experience beyond a layman's ken."[245] Although North Carolina law had definitely recognized the potential prejudice of such an occurrence, the "precise course to be followed by a North Carolina trial court in order to cure the prejudice" was not "entirely clear." At the least, the North Carolina decisions had established that "when request therefor is made, it is the duty of the trial judge to instruct the jury that a co-defendant's plea of guilty is not to be considered as evidence bearing upon the guilt of the defendant then on trial."[246] No such request had been made by Hudson, who, as a layman, could hardly be expected to know that he was even entitled to any "protection" against the prejudicial effect of the co-defendant's plea, not to mention an obvious unawareness as to the "proper course to follow to invoke such protection." The Court concluded that Hudson therefore clearly needed a lawyer and the failure to appoint one had resulted in a denial of due process.[247]

---

[248] 363 U.S. at 698.

[244] *Id.* at 701. The findings of the lower court on the post-conviction hearing were accepted by the Supreme Court. *Ibid.*

[245] *Id.* at 704–05.   [246] *Id.* at 702–03.

[247] Justices Clark and Whittaker dissented on the ground that the petitioner had not been prejudiced by his co-defendant's guilty plea. 363 U.S. at 704.

In *Chewning*, decided two years later, the indigent petitioner was charged under the Virginia recidivist statute with having been three times convicted and sentenced for a felony.[248] The trial judge refused a request for the appointment of counsel, though he did attempt to advise the petitioner of all his rights. The petitioner acknowledged that he had been the person mentioned in the prior conviction, and the court sentenced him to ten years of imprisonment. On appeal, the Supreme Court found that the failure to appoint counsel was a denial of due process because the complex "nature of the charge" required the assistance of an attorney. "In trials of this kind," the Court noted, "the labyrinth of the law is, or may be, too intricate for the layman to master."[249] The issue of "identity," for one, could have presented "difficult local law issues." The Court also mentioned that an attorney might have searched for defects in prior convictions that would have precluded their admission in the multiple-offender proceeding. This could have raised a whole host of issues including the jurisdiction of the courts rendering the prior judgments, the validity of the prior sentences, and the fairness of the previous trials. "Double jeopardy and ex post facto application of the law" were other "questions which . . . [might] well be considered by an imaginative lawyer, who looks critically at the layer of prior convictions on which the recidivist charge rests."[250] The Court was careful to note that it "intimated no opinion on whether any of the problems mentioned would arise on petitioner's trial or, if so, whether any would have merit."[251] It "only conclud[ed]" that the "issues presented under Virginia's statute [were] so complex," and "the potential prejudice from the absence of counsel so great," that due process required the appointment of counsel to represent the accused.[252]

---

[248] The charge was brought in connection with the last conviction on which the petitioner was still serving his sentence. 368 U.S. at 443–44.

[249] *Id.* at 446. The opinion heavily relied upon Reynolds v. Cochran, 365 U.S. 525 (1961), which dealt with an individual's right to be represented by his own counsel on a recidivist charge.

[250] 368 U.S. at 446–47.   [251] *Id.* at 447.

[252] *Ibid.* In a concurring opinion, Justice Harlan argued that "the bare possibility that any of these improbable claims could have been asserted does not amount to the 'exceptional circumstances' which, under *Betts* v. *Brady* . . . must be present before the Fourteenth Amendment impresses on the state a duty to provide

Taken together, the *Hudson* and *Chewning* decisions would seem to have expanded the special circumstances concept to the point where, as Justice Harlan put it, "the mere existence of a serious criminal charge constituted in itself special circumstances requiring the services of counsel. . . ."[253] Even narrowly read, *Hudson* required the reversal of any conviction where the record contained a prejudicial occurrence that, under state law, might have been prevented, or at least modified, by appointed counsel.[254] Moreover, a subsequent case suggested that this principle might even carry so far as to encompass every trial where the unrepresented defendant failed to use some advantageous procedure or tactic that counsel might have employed.[255] The *Chewning* decision had an even broader scope, since it was not limited to those situations in which there was a trial. Surely research would almost always reveal, as it did in *Chewning*, that the defendant was charged with a crime to which an imaginative lawyer might, under some circumstances, raise a complex legal defense beyond a layman's grasp.[256] Combined with *Hudson*, the *Chewning* decision would find a denial of due process in practically every situation where "the defendant may have made a poorer showing than he would have if he had had counsel." It would be a rare case that failed this test.[257]

---

counsel. . . ." *Id.* at 459. Justice Harlan found that the defendant, nevertheless, had been denied due process because he was forced to plead immediately after the recidivist charge was made known to him. *Id.* at 457–58.

[253] 372 U.S. at 351.

[254] See generally *The Supreme Court, 1959 Term*, 74 HARV. L. REV. 81, 137 (1960); Note, 109 U. PA. L. REV. 623, 629 (1961).

[255] Carnley v. Cochran, 369 U.S. 506 (1962). The Court here held that the petitioner had been denied due process by the state's failure to appoint counsel to represent him in defending against a charge of incest with his minor daughter. The opinion cited, *inter alia*, certain tactics that counsel might have employed that were not related to any potentially prejudicial occurrence during the trial such as was involved in *Hudson*. Thus, the Court noted that counsel might have filed for a psychiatric or psychological examination of the accused. *Id.* at 509–10. Similarly, he might have requested that the sentencing judge commit the petitioner to a hospital for treatment rather than to prison. The Court also noted that the illiterate defendant had hardly cross-examined his daughter and son, the state's primary witnesses, although there were possible grounds for impeachment.

[256] Kamisar, *supra* note 242, at 280; *The Supreme Court, 1961 Term, supra* note 238, at 115.

[257] *The Supreme Court, 1959 Term, supra* note 254, at 137.

The full impact of the *Chewning* and *Hudson* decisions upon the *Betts* "fair trial" rule is probably best illustrated by the fact that they would have required reversal in the *Betts* case itself. Certainly there are complex legal defenses that the imaginative lawyer might raise, even to the everyday charge of robbery. As Professor Kamisar's analysis of the *Betts* record has shown,[258] an appointed counsel in that case might well have defended on the ground that Betts had been so intoxicated as to lack the requisite intent.[259] With respect to the trial, the *Betts* record is replete with prejudicial occurrences that, as in *Hudson*, raised problems "requiring professional training beyond a layman's ken." For example, counsel representing Betts might well have forced the exclusion of crucial testimony on the grounds of hearsay, violation of the privilege against self-incrimination, and patent unreliability.[260] This illustration of the impact of *Chewning* and *Hudson* on the *Betts* case is reinforced by consideration of the fact situation in *Gideon*, that the Court described as a "nearly indistinguishable" from *Betts*.[261] As in *Betts*, the defendant in *Gideon* failed to raise both defenses and objections that counsel might have employed.[262] For example, no objection was made either to the admission of opinion testimony or to the trial judge's rulings which improperly restricted the scope of cross-examination.[263]

As exemplified by their application to the *Betts* and *Gideon* fact situations, the *Chewning* and *Hudson* decisions might well have

---

[258] Kamisar, *The Right to Counsel and the Fourteenth Amendment: A Dialogue on "the Most Pervasive Right" of an Accused*, 30 U. CHI. L. REV. 1, 42–57 (1962).

[259] There was testimony at the trial that Betts appeared to have been "drinking." *Id*. at 56.

[260] *Id*. at 45, 50–51, 46–48.

[261] 372 U.S. at 339. It should be noted that the trial record and transcript were not before the Florida Supreme Court. Brief for the Respondent, p. 3. They were added to the record on review before the United States Supreme Court, Brief for the Petitioners, p. 4, but they could not properly be considered as a basis for the Court's judgment. See Hedgbeth v. North Carolina, 334 U.S. 806 (1948).

[262] Coincidentally, there was testimony in the *Gideon* record, like that in *Betts*, that might have suggested a defense based upon defendant's intoxication. Gideon was acquitted after a retrial in which he was represented by counsel. New York Times, Aug. 7, 1963, p. 56, col. 1.

[263] *Id*. at 15; see Brief for Petitioner, p. 50; Adkinson v. State, 48 Fla. 1 (1904).

served as the basis for the argument in *Gideon* that, as a practical matter, *Betts* had already been overruled. Moreover, here, as opposed to the use of a similar argument based upon *Griffin* and *Douglas,* the abrogation of the rule was the product not of a sudden expansion of a previous ruling but rather of a gradual process of erosion involving a long line of cases. Though commentators have characterized *Chewning* and *Hudson* as "departure[s] from prior holdings,"[264] these decisions actually did little more than provide the final, logical extension of well-established principles.

The string of decisions leading up to *Chewning,* for example, started with the very first right-to-counsel case decided after *Betts.* In *Williams v. Kaiser,*[265] the Court found that the defendant, who pleaded guilty to the offense of robbery by means of a dangerous weapon, had been constitutionally entitled to appointment of counsel because the various degrees of that offense raised legal questions far too technical for a layman to appreciate. Three months later, in *Rice v. Olson,*[266] the Court found a denial of due process where the unrepresented defendant could have raised a defense involving questions of federal jurisdiction that were "obviously beyond the capacity of even an intelligent and educated layman."[267] Similarly, in *Moore v. Michigan,*[268] the Court concluded that the various "technical" defenses to murder, such as insanity and mistaken identity, had required the appointment of counsel to represent a defendant who had pleaded guilty.[269] The same line of reasoning was also employed to require reversals in

---

[264] *The Supreme Court, 1961 Term, supra* note 238, at 114; see also *The Supreme Court, 1959 Term, supra* note 254, at 136–37; Kamisar, *supra* note 242, at 236; Note, 109 U. Pa. L. Rev. 623, 627–29 (1961).

[265] 323 U.S. 471 (1945). *Accord,* Tompkins v. Missouri, 323 U.S. 485 (1945). Although these were capital cases, the Court emphasized the special complexity of the legal problems as a basis for finding a denial of due process.

[266] 324 U.S. 786 (1945).

[267] *Id.* at 789. The jurisdictional defense arose out of the fact that the petitioner was an Indian and the crime was allegedly committed on an Indian reservation.

[268] 355 U.S. 155 (1957).

[269] *Id.* at 159–61. Although primary emphasis was on this ground, the opinion also cited the petitioner's youth and lack of education.

Pennsylvania ex rel. Herman v. Claudy[270] and *McNeal v. Culver*.[271] Thus, by the time the Court reached *Chewning*, the possible complexity of even some fairly routine legal problems had been recognized as requiring the appointment of counsel. Admittedly, in most of these cases, unlike *Chewning*, the Court's opinions had relied upon "complex" defenses that the fact situation showed to be available to the defendants.[272] In at least *Williams*, however, the likelihood that the defendant might have taken advantage of the difference in degrees of the crime was only slightly less speculative than the possibility that Chewning might have attacked his prior convictions on the grounds mentioned in the Court's opinion.[273]

As with *Chewning*, the antecedents of *Hudson* had established a firm foundation for the concept of "special" circumstances advanced in that case. The Court recognized fairly soon after *Betts* that the failure to appoint counsel denied the defendant due process where his trial had been marred by "a deliberate overreaching by

---

270 350 U.S. 116 (1956). Here the Court cited, *inter alia*, both the number and the complexity of the charges against the petitioner. He was charged with thirty offenses, eight each of burglary and forgery, two of false pretenses, and twelve of larceny.

271 365 U.S. 109 (1960). The Court here noted complex legal problems arising out of various degrees of assault under Florida law and the differences in the intent required for each offense. It also relied upon petitioner's lack of education and his mental state as a separate ground for requiring appointment of counsel.

272 This was the factor emphasized in *The Supreme Court, 1961 Term, supra* note 238, in characterizing *Chewning* as a "genuine departure from prior holdings." See also Kamisar, *supra* note 186, at 279, 280.

Although some cases had spoken in terms of the "active operation" of unfairness, see Foster v. Illinois, 332 U.S. 134 (1947), this did not require a showing of an actual trial error as the only basis for reversal. In those cases, like *Chewning*, which emphasized the nature of the crime, it had always been sufficient that fundamental unfairness was apt to result from the failure to appoint counsel. See 97 U. PA. L. REV. 855, 857 (1949); *cf. The Supreme Court, 1948 Term*, 63 HARV. L. REV. 119, 135 (1949); BEANEY, THE RIGHT TO COUNSEL IN AMERICAN COURTS 163 (1955).

273 See 323 U.S. at 475–76: "If we assume that petitioner committed a crime we cannot know the degree of prejudice which the denial of counsel caused. . . . only counsel could discern from the facts whether a plea of not guilty to the offense charged or a plea of guilty to a lesser offense would be appropriate." The opinion gave no indication of the facts upon which counsel might make such a determination. In Moore v. Michigan, 355 U.S. 155 (1957), the only indication that the defendant might have relied upon the defense of mistaken identity was the fact "that the evidence pointing to him as perpetrator of the crime was entirely circumstantial." *Id.* at 160.

Court or prosecutor" that an attorney might have prevented.[274] In *Gibbs v. Burke*[275] this approach was extended to a situation involving only normal trial errors, such as the admission of hearsay evidence, the exclusion of relevant evidence, and the improper designation of a prosecution witness as defendant's witness. *Cash v. Culver*[276] went even further in holding that the state's mere introduction of accomplice testimony created problems "beyond a layman's ken" that required the appointment of counsel. Although the *Cash* opinion did note that there had been a "serious question" as to the admissibility of portions of the accomplice's testimony, much of its emphasis was upon missed opportunities rather than actual trial errors. The Court particularly stressed the defendant's failure to minimize the effect of the accomplice's testimony by such tactics as requesting a jury instruction cautioning against reliance on such testimony, cross-examining the accomplice as to whether he testified under an "agreement for leniency," and using the witness' testimony at a previous trial as a basis for impeachment.[277] Thus, from *Cash*, the step to *Hudson* was not a very large one.[278] Of course, *Cash* involved more omissions by the defendant that were clearly prejudicial, but its basic thesis seemed applicable so long as there were any occurrences at trial on which a lawyer's advice might have proved helpful.[279] Also, while the

---

[274] Hudson v. North Carolina, 363 U.S. 697, 701–02 (1960). See Townsend v. Burke, 334 U.S. 736 (1948); DeMeerleer v. Michigan, 329 U.S. 633 (1947) (based in part on this ground); see also Williams v. Kaiser, 323 U.S. 471, 476 (1945) (dictum); Marino v. Ragen, 332 U.S. 561 (1947).

[275] 337 U.S. 773 (1949); see also Palmer v. Ashe, 342 U.S. 134 (1951).

[276] 358 U.S. 633 (1959).

[277] *Id.* at 637–38. While the Court also mentioned petitioner's youth and inexperience, the decision expressly was grounded on the "complexity of the proceedings." *Ibid.*

[278] See also McNeal v. Culver, 365 U.S. 109 (1961).

[279] Some commentators had suggested that the Court found a denial of due process only when a particular trial error was thought to be especially prejudicial. See, *e.g.*, Fellman, *The Federal Right to Counsel in State Courts*, 31 NEB. L. REV. 15, 26 (1951); *The Supreme Court, 1948 Term, supra* note 272, at 135. The Court, however, had never acknowledged the commission of an error in a case where a denial of due process was not found, and the language in various opinions, particularly in the later cases, seemed to reject any such analysis. See cases cited notes 283, *infra*, 268–71 *supra*.

legal problem that arose in *Hudson*, perhaps unlike those in *Cash*, would not have been assessable before the trial began,[280] the same had been true in cases like *Gibbs v. Burke*.

As this history of the "special circumstances" cases shows, the Court had consistently whittled away at the *Betts* rule until with *Chewning* and *Hudson* it was almost completely eroded. Admittedly, though this development started almost immediately after *Betts*, not every case during the twenty-two-year period required the appointment of counsel. Most of the cases that seemingly "reinforced" the *Betts* rule, however, actually were based on independent grounds such as the waiver of counsel.[281] In others, like *Bute v. Illinois*,[282] the Court was restricted by the limited scope of the common-law record.[283] So despite occasional setbacks, all of which occurred within six years after *Betts*, the over-all view of the counsel cases represents a fairly steady stream of development over twenty-two years in which eighteen different Justices had participated, including most of those who joined Justice Roberts in *Betts*. The eventual outcome of this progression had been recognized even before *Hudson* and *Chewning*.[284] In fact, it was so clear by the time of *Chewning* that counsel there was able to argue that, in effect, *Betts* had already been overruled.[285] Surely after the *Chewning* decision, the Court in *Gideon* could well have maintained that *Betts* indeed had been overruled *sub silentio* by the subsequent course of decisions, so that all that remained to be done was to publish its obituary—a task unfortunately necessitated by

---

280 See Note, 109 U. PA. L. REV. 623, 627–28 (1961), distinguishing *Hudson* on this point.

281 See, *e.g.*, Quicksal v. Michigan, 339 U.S. 660 (1950) (waiver); Carter v. Illinois, 329 U.S. 173 (1946) (waiver); Gayes v. New York, 332 U.S. 145· (1947) (issue of right to counsel not properly open to attack); see also Foster v. Illinois, 332 U.S. 134 (1947) (seeming to rely at least in part on waiver).

282 333 U.S. 640 (1948).

283 See *id*. at 668, 673–74. In Gryger v. Burke, 334 U.S. 728 (1948), another case in which the Court sustained the conviction, the Court stressed that the only issue open under the recidivist charge against the defendant was whether he was in fact the person named in the prior convictions. Also, the Court refused to accept the contention advanced in the dissent that the trial judge had sentenced the defendant on the basis of an erroneous assumption.

284 See, *e.g.*, Note, 26 TEXAS. L. REV. 665 (1948); Note, 1 U. FLA. L. REV. 450 (1948).

285 Brief for the Petitioner, pp. 35–37.

the refusal of some state courts, like the Florida court in *Gideon*, to recognize the true state of the law.[286]

B. BETTS AND THE LESSONS OF EXPERIENCE

The Court in *Gideon* could also have argued that the rejection of the *Betts* rule was supported by knowledge derived from experience in applying that rule, which, had it been available originally, would have presented the *Betts* case in an entirely different light. In fact, the Court might even have suggested that, considering the limited experience of the *Betts* Court in this area, the fundamental approach it adopted in *Betts* was entirely proper, though misapplied to the particular facts of that case. While the broad reach of plaintiff's argument and the dissenting opinion may have led the majority to pass over the *Betts* record too casually,[287] the basic approach of a case-by-case analysis of the need for appointment of counsel arguably was well suited to the context of the problem at that time.[288] The Court in *Betts* lacked the sense of sureness needed to adopt a firm rule that defendants in state courts had to be represented by counsel in order to insure the fair hearing guaranteed by the Due Process Clause.[289] There were various matters that had to be determined before such a position could be taken: *e.g.*, what were the various offenses that might be involved, what types of procedures did the states employ when the defendant represented himself, and how did state judges conduct trials in such cases?[290] Lacking the general background that comes with

---

[286] See 372 U.S. 349, 351 (Harlan, J., concurring); see also Kamisar, *supra* note 242, at 281.

[287] Neither counsel for Betts nor the dissenting opinion attempted to cite any incidents where Betts might have been prejudiced by the absence of counsel. See Brief for the Petitioner, pp. 16–24; 316 U.S. at 474–80; see also Kamisar, *supra* note 258, at 52.

[288] Other cases decided at the time also emphasized this approach. See Palko v. Connecticut, 302 U.S. 319 (1937); Snyder v. Massachusetts, 291 U.S. 97 (1934); see also Adamson v. California, 332 U.S. 46 (1947).

[289] The emphasis here must, of course, be on the diverse nature of state courts, since the Court had already been convinced that this was the case in federal courts. See Johnson v. Zerbst, 304 U.S. 458, 462–63 (1938).

[290] The states have sometimes maintained that the informality of such trials gives the defendant great latitude in presenting defenses, examining witnesses, etc. See, *e.g.*, Brief for the States of Alabama and North Carolina as *amicus curiae* in *Gideon v. Wainwright* at pp. 9–10. See also 316 U.S. at 472.

consistent review of decisions in a particular area,[291] the Court had not fully developed what Llewellyn described as an appreciation of the total "situation-pattern" with all its "detailed variants."[292] Under these circumstances, the formulation of a narrow rule, a case-by-case approach, was consistent with the normal process of appellate decision-making.[293] It was particularly understandable when one considers that the use of the Due Process Clause as an effective device for the regulation of the state criminal process was then still a fairly recent innovation,[294] and that Judge Bond, a highly respected jurist, had observed that in his state "there [were] fair trials without counsel employed for the prisoners."[295]

The experience of twenty-two years, however, had provided a basis for re-examining the crucial assumptions upon which *Betts* was based. For one thing, the presumption that a lawyerless defendant would usually, or even frequently be able to defend himself adequately had been largely disproved by the constant expansion of the special circumstances concept. Certainly, the routine nature of many of the cases in which "special" circumstances were found suggests that the instances in which an indigent layman could appreciate all his legal defenses and rights are, to say the

---

[291] See Allen, *supra* note 205, at 193–95, discussing the Court's rather limited consideration of the criminal process in the states prior to *Powell*. While the Court had considered some cases involving state criminal procedure (including two right-to-counsel cases) during the period between *Betts* and *Powell*, it still lacked the familiarity with the practices and problems in this area that has come with the constantly expanding scope of due process. See note 294 *infra*.

[292] LLEWELLYN, THE COMMON LAW TRADITION 268–70, 426–27 (1960).

[293] *Id.* at 427–29.

[294] See generally Allen, *supra* note 205. Some of the most important restrictions upon the states had not yet been considered by the Court. See, *e.g.*, Wolf v. Colorado, 338 U.S. 25 (1949). In other areas where initial action had already been undertaken, the Court had considered only the relatively "easy" cases where the abusive aspects of the state's action were most glaringly presented. *Compare, e.g.,* Chambers v. Florida, 309 U.S. 227 (1940), *with* Turner v. Pennsylvania, 338 U.S. 62 (1949), or Colombe v. Connecticut, 367 U.S. 568 (1961); Mooney v. Hollohan, 294 U.S. 103 (1935), *with* Alcorta v. Texas, 355 U.S. 28 (1957).

[295] 316 U.S. at 472 n.31. See also FREUND, THE SUPREME COURT OF THE UNITED STATES 146 (1961), where the author speculates as to "whether the decision in *Betts* v. *Brady* . . . would have been the same had the opinion of the court below been written by someone less highly esteemed than Chief Judge Bond of Maryland, who is referred to by name in Mr. Justice Roberts's opinion no fewer than fifteen times." The Court had taken special note of Judge Bond's scholarship even before *Betts*. See O'Malley v. Woodrough, 307 U.S. 277, 281 n.8 (1939).

least, exceedingly rare[296]—probably too rare in fact even to bother considering in framing a constitutional rule governing appointment of counsel.[297]

Furthermore, even if such instances were far more common, experience in applying the *Betts* rule had shown the frequent impossibility of determining which defendants would be deprived of a fair hearing without a lawyer. As cases like *Hudson* illustrate, the legal difficulties that defendant will face are frequently unassessable at the start of the proceedings. The judge can hardly be expected to predict accurately the course of the trial or the indigent's response to the problems that might arise. *Betts*, of course, assumed that the trial judge would help the defendant over any such unexpected hurdles,[298] but, as *Hudson* again exemplifies, even where the trial judge is making every effort to do this,[299] he cannot, consistent with his judicial function, truly place himself in the position of defendant's advocate.[300] Also, as cases like *Chewning* show, even if problems concerning the trial are avoided because the defendant pleads guilty, one can never be sure that a lawyer's investigation and analysis might not have produced a defense, unknown to the defendant, that could have resulted in a different plea.[301]

---

[296] Even the most severe critics of the *Betts* rule have recognized that there may be instances in which the absence of counsel did not deprive the defendant of a fair hearing. See, *e.g.*, Kamisar, *supra* note 258, at 42. *But see* Schilke, *supra* note 236, at 342.

[297] *Cf.* Mapp v. Ohio, 367 U.S. 643 (1961).

[298] See 316 U.S. at 472 (referring particularly to a judge in non-jury trial); see also Gibbs v. Burke, 337 U.S. 773, 781 (1949). It should be noted that *Betts* did not reinstate Coke's argument, rejected in *Powell*, that the judge could perform all of the functions of counsel. See 287 U.S. at 61. The *Betts* opinion apparently accepted the same assumption that was made in *Powell* that the judge would "see to it that in the proceedings before the Court the accused shall be dealt with fairly and justly," presumably by advising him of all of his rights. *Compare* Betts, 316 U.S. at 472, and Gibbs, 337 U.S. at 781, *with* Powell, 287 U.S. at 61.

[299] See 363 U.S. at 698, 700–01; *cf.* Carnley v. Cochran, 369 U.S. 506 (1962).

[300] Thus, in *Hudson*, the judge can hardly inform the defendant of a jury instruction that was not required, but might be to his advantage. See also Pollock, *Equal Justice in Practice*, 45 MINN. L. REV. 737, 741–42 (1961).

[301] This defect in the *Betts* rule is reinforced by the paradox that the more the accused needs counsel, the less likely it is that he will be capable of proving this need to the court. BEANEY, THE RIGHT TO COUNSEL IN AMERICAN COURTS 185 (1955).

Finally, even if a judge following the *Betts* rule could recognize all the instances in which counsel were needed, the difficulties revealed in the administration of the rule might outweigh any advantages it would have over a flat requirement that counsel be appointed. The necessary vagueness of the special circumstances concept left the *Betts* rule open to extreme manipulation by the lower courts. In some states, the courts had twisted the rule to the point where the right to appointed counsel was almost non-existent no matter what the nature of the case.[302] And while the time-consuming process of constant review of counsel cases by the Court might have corrected these tendencies,[303] experience had revealed that the very nature of *Betts* rule made it inevitable that lower court application would always be uncertain and uneven.[304]

On the other side, the lessons of experience had revealed the myth in what the Court had considered a major advantage of the *Betts* rule—that it was more consistent with the "obligations of federalism" than an absolute requirement of counsel, since it kept to a

---

[302] See, *e.g.*, Butler v. Culver, 111 So. 2d. 35 (Fla. 1959); Commonwealth *ex rel.* Simon v. Maroney, 405 Pa. 562 (1961); Shaffer v. Warden, 211 Md. 635 (1956). All the post-*Betts* state cases listed in the state reports are collected in the brief *amicus* of the American Civil Liberties Union in *Gideon* at pp. 50–51. They show, for example, that the Florida court has found a denial of due process in only one of fourteen reported cases involving the refusal to appoint counsel. (One other was remanded for a hearing.) Maryland reversed three out of thirty-nine cases, two out of the three being cases reviewed on direct appeal. The ratio for cases decided since 1949 are about the same, even though the Supreme Court has reversed over a dozen state cases during that period without one affirmance.

[303] Full appreciation of the *Betts* rule seemed to improve in certain states following Supreme Court reversals of their state court decisions finding no need for counsel. See, *e.g.*, People v. Whitsitt, 359 Mich. 656 (1960); People v. Coates, 347 Mich. 626 (1957).

[304] See generally Allen, *The Supreme Court, Federalism, and State Criminal Justice.* 8 DE PAUL L. REV. 213, 228–29 (1959). For one thing, the lower court results often will vary, according to the willingness of the trial judge to undertake the heavy burden placed upon him both in advising defendants of their rights and in attempting to learn enough about defendant's view of the facts so as to know whether any "complex" defenses might be considered by a lawyer. The scope of this task is illustrated by the lengthy list of inquiries that one judge has suggested as absolutely necessary to be able properly to apply the *Betts* rule. See Sloan, *The Jail House Lawyer versus Court and Counsel: Some Ideas for Self-Protection,* 1 WASHBURN L.J. 517, 524, 526 (1962). Past cases indicate that many state judges would be reluctant to go so far as Justice Sloan suggests.

minimum the federal restriction upon the "historic power of the states to prescribe their own local court procedures."[305] Experience with the *Betts* rule had shown that it probably engendered as much friction between federal and state courts as an absolute requirement would have produced. *Betts* was in large part responsible for proliferation of the vexing habeas corpus cases in federal courts.[306] Probably more state prisoners were released by federal courts for the failure of the state to appoint counsel than on any other ground.[307] In other cases, reversals were based on obvious errors that presumably would have been prevented had defendant been represented by counsel.[308] Moreover, the reaction to these reversals of state convictions was probably intensified by the type of analysis the federal courts were required to make under *Betts*. The special circumstances concept, particularly in the light of cases like *Hudson* and *Cash*, required the reviewing court to make an extensive examination of state law in order to find errors or unconsidered issues that showed the need for counsel. State court judges were told not only that they had failed to give "adequate judicial guidance or protection" to the defendant,[309] but that their error had been in the misapplication of their own state law.[310] In the light of this experience, a strong argument could be made that the obligations of federalism would be more adequately served by

---

[305] Bute v. Illinois, 333 U.S. 640, 668, 652–54 (1948); see also Foster v. Illinois 332 U.S. 134, 136–38 (1947); Carter v. Illinois, 329 U.S. 173, 175 (1946).

[306] See Reitz, *Federal Habeas Corpus: Post-Conviction Remedy for State Prisoners*, 108 U Pa. L. Rev. 461, 465, 483–85 (1960); Note, 15 U. Chi. L. Rev. 107, 119–20 (1947); see also the Brief for the American Civil Liberties Union in Gideon v. Wainwright, p. 29.

[307] See Reitz, *supra* note 306, at 483.

[308] See Brief for the State of Oregon as *amicus curiae* in Gideon v. Wainwright, pp. 4–6, citing statistics on the cases reversed under the Oregon Post Conviction Act.

[309] Gibbs v. Burke, 337 U.S. 773, 781 (1949).

[310] See, *e.g.*, McNeal v. Culver, 365 U.S. 109, 116 (1961), where the Court found both that the admission of certain evidence had been a "patent violation" of state law and that defendant had been convicted of a crime that probably did not exist under state law. See also Cash v. Culver, 358 U.S. 633 (1959); Gibbs v. Burke, *supra* note 309. In Hudson v. North Carolina, 363 U.S. 697, 705 (1960), the Court *sua sponte* found a problem that the trial court, the post-conviction court, and counsel on both sides had overlooked.

a simple, unqualified requirement for the appointment of counsel than the inevitable reversals (and subsequent retrials) under the special circumstances doctrine of *Betts*.[311] Thus, the Court in *Gideon* could have suggested, as it did in another recent case, that experience under the overruled case had shown that at least one of the earlier Court's basic objectives could best be achieved through reversal of its original decision.[312]

C. BETTS AND CHANGING CONDITIONS

There remains for consideration the possibility of employing in *Gideon* the argument that "changed conditions" had "completely sapped [*Betts*] of [its] authority."[313] Based as it was on due process, "the least frozen concept of our law—the least confined to history and the most absorptive of powerful standards of a progressive society,"[314] the *Betts* decision naturally lends itself to the rationale of the changed conditions. This is particularly true in the light of the Court's opinion. Mr. Justice Roberts relied heavily upon "the common understanding of those who have lived under the Anglo-American system of law" to sustain the Court's conclusion that appointment of counsel was not invariably essential to a fair trial and therefore was not "fundamental."[315] This consensus of Anglo-American opinion was found in the "constitutional and statutory provisions subsisting in the colonies and the states prior to the [adoption] of the Bill of Rights . . . and in the constitutional, legislative, and judicial history of the states to the present date."[316] Such "material demonstrates," said Justice Roberts, "that, in the great majority of the States, it has been the considered judgment of the people, their representatives and their courts that appointment of counsel is not a fundamental right, essential to a fair trial. On the contrary, the matter has generally been deemed one of legislative policy."[317]

---

[311] Indeed, the practical difficulties of relitigating years after the crime occurred will often make a retrial unlikely.

[312] *Cf.* Fay v. Noia, 372 U.S. 391, 437–38 (1963); Kamisar, *supra* note 251, at 36.

[313] Phelps Dodge Corp. v. Labor Board, 313 U.S. 177, 187 (1941).

[314] Griffin v. Illinois, 351 U.S. 12, 20–21 (1956) (concurring opinion).

[315] 316 U.S. at 464.   [316] *Id.* at 465.

[317] *Id.* at 471. The same conclusion was reached, after a similar analysis of both state and pre-1938 federal practices, in Bute v. Illinois, 333 U.S. 640, 660–68 (1948).

Obviously, one basis for the Court's conclusion—the original colonial and state provisions—has not and will not change. It might be urged, nevertheless, that developments within the pattern of current state practices over the past twenty-two years had reached the point where Justice Roberts' judgment as to the "common understanding" of the community was no longer accurate. When *Betts* was decided, thirty-one states had "some clear legal requirement or an established practice that indigent defendants in serious non-capital . . . cases be . . . provided with counsel."[318] Today, thirty-eight states have legal provisions requiring the appointment of counsel in such cases,[319] and seven more almost invariably follow that procedure as a matter of practice.[320] There also have been increased indications that these state requirements are viewed as "fundamental" laws rather than matters of "legislative policy" subject to modification "from time to time as [the legislature] deemed necessary."[321] Since *Betts*, at least seven additional states, making ten in all, have held that a statutory requirement merely restated a constitutional guarantee of the defendant's right to appointed counsel.[322]

---

[318] 316 U.S. at 477 n.2 (dissenting opinion). The appendix to Justice Black's dissent listed thirty-five states in this category. But four states were "misclassified." See Kamisar, *supra* note 258, at 17 n.74. Of the remaining thirty-one states, all required counsel in at least every felony case except New Hampshire, which furnishes counsel only where the defendant is charged with an offense punishable by at least three years' imprisonment.

[319] Kamisar, *supra* note 258, at 17–18. One of the new additions to this group, however, Maryland, only provides counsel in cases where the maximum sentence is at least five years' imprisonment.

[320] Kamisar, *supra* note 258, at 18–20.

[321] See Betts v. Brady, 316 U.S. 455, 471 (1942).

[322] Justice Roberts' opinion cited three state courts that had held that appointment of counsel was constitutionally required. *Id.* at 469 (listing Georgia, Kentucky, and Wisconsin). See also Therman v. State 205 Ark. 376, (1943); People v. Mattson, 51 Cal. 2d 777, (1959); State *ex rel.* Grecco v. Allen Circuit Court, 238 Ind. 571 (1958); Wiley v. Hudspeth, 162 Kan. 516 (1947); State v. Johnson, 63 N.J. Super 16 (1960); State v. Garcia, 47 N. Mex. 319 (1943) (dictum); *In re* Motz, 100 Ohio App. 296 (1955); Hunter v. State, 288 P. 2d 425 (Okla. Cr. 1955); *cf.* People v. Waterman, 9 N.Y. 2d 561 (1961). There are many states, however, that have held that appointment of counsel is not constitutionally required. See Brief for the American Civil Liberties Union in *Gideon*, pp. 51–55. See, *e.g.*, Kelley v. People, 206 P. 2d 337 (Colo. 1949); Sneed v. Mayo, 66 So. 2d 865 (Fla. 1953); Marvin v. Warden, 212 Md. 634 (1957); People v. Haddad, 306 Mich. 561 (1943); State v. Delaney, 332 P. 2d 71 (Ore. 1958).

Moreover, with the passage of an additional twenty-two years, many of these statutory provisions have become so firmly embedded in a state's law that they have practically achieved the "sanctity" of a constitutional provision.[323]

While similar developments in state practices have been cited in past opinions,[324] the nature and degree of these changes since *Betts* do not provide a strong case for arguing that contemporary views on appointment of counsel have so changed in twenty-two years that they now represent a "permanent and pervasive feeling" "rooted in our traditions and conscience."[325] This is not to suggest, however, that such changes have no bearing on the argument for overruling *Betts*. The positions taken in statutes, court decisions, and state constitutions over the years may be valid criteria for determining whether a particular value or principle is "fundamental" to our society, but that was not the issue before the Court in *Betts*. Justice Roberts' analysis began with the acceptance of the fundamental principle of a fair hearing, which requires *inter alia* a process insuring the reliability of the final determination of

---

[323] The trend toward the mandatory appointment of counsel has been primarily a post-Civil War development, so most of the state provisions will be less than a century old. Bute v. Illinois, 333 U.S. 640, 665 (1948). But a provision in existence for even half that period might be considered almost on a par with state constitutions, which do not usually last much longer than that without major modifications. This is particularly true in those states where constitutional amendments are fairly easily adopted. See, *e.g.*, MINN. CONST., art. 14, § 1 (1898).

It should also be noted that the passage of time has lessened the practical consequences of applying the *Gideon* decision retrospectively. Those states that had only recently adopted appointment provisions in 1942 are unlikely to have many prisoners in jail today, as they would have had then, who will be entitled to release on the basis of *Gideon*. The Court had previously suggested that its rejection of an absolute requirement of appointment of counsel was reinforced by the fact that "such an abrupt innovation . . . would furnish opportunities hitherto uncontemplated for opening wide the prison doors of the land." Foster v. Illinois, 332 U.S. 134, 139 (1947).

[324] See Kadish, *Methodology and Criteria in Due Process Adjudication—A Survey and Criticism,* 66 YALE L.J. 319, 331–32 (1959) (collecting cases); *cf.* Elkins v. United States, 364 U.S. 206 (1960). As Professor Kadish notes, the "use of a commonly followed state practice as evidence that a contrary practice violates due process has found favor primarily in dissenting opinions."

[325] Solesbee v. Balkcom, 339 U.S. 9, 16 (1950) (dissenting opinion); Snyder v. Massachusetts, 291 U.S. 97, 105 (1934); see also *The Supreme Court, 1961 Term, supra* note 256, at 114.

guilt.[326] The issue in *Betts* was whether a lawyer was needed to achieve that objective, *i.e.*, whether the innocent but lawyerless defendant may be convicted "because he does not know how to establish his innocence."[327] This is largely a question of fact, not of values, to which state practices serve as no more than evidence of how others have approached this same problem. In this respect, the increase in the number of states affording counsel to indigents might well have been used to support the *Gideon* result in the same manner that the *Mapp* opinion employed the states' shift to the exclusionary rule.[328]

IV. CONCLUSION

It seems fair to say that the Court in *Gideon* could easily have relied upon at least two of those rationales that have traditionally been employed in overruling opinions. Not only were arguments based upon the "lessons of experience" and the requirements of later precedent relevant and persuasive, but they had been urged upon the Court both by petitioner's brief and by the separate opinions of Justices Douglas and Black in two recent cases.[329] Moreover, the application of these "techniques" of overruling was particularly appropriate under the circumstances surrounding the *Gideon* decision. During a Term in which so many of the Court's rulings had been attributed to recent changes in personnel,[330] it would have been especially advantageous to emphasize those factors other than the different outlook of the present Court that contributed to the rejection of a renowned decison of its predecessor. It was, perhaps, inevitable, no matter what the Court wrote, that the *Time* article on *Gideon* would observe that the "flow of U.S. law . . . often reverses its course according to the personalities and

[326] See Kadish, *supra* note 324, at 346.

[327] Powell v. Alabama, 287 U.S. 45, 69 (1932); see Kadish, *supra* note 324, at 333–34.

[328] 367 U.S. at 651–53; see text at note 54 *supra*.

[329] See Petitioner's Brief, pp. 20–33, 36–43, 50–53; McNeal v. Culver, 365 U.S. 109, 117–22 (1961) (Douglas, J., concurring); Carnley v. Cochran, 369 U.S. 506, 517–20 (1962) (Black, J., concurring).

[330] See, *e.g.*, Lewis, *Focus on High Court*, New York Times, April 7, 1963, § 4, p. 13, col. 1; U.S. News and World Report 19 (March 4, 1963).

politics of reigning justices," and, with obvious innuendo, would pose the question "what do all those earlier decisions mean?"[331] Still, and perhaps particularly for that reason, the Court might have framed an opinion that provided its supporters with a foundation for answering that question consistent with the accepted image of judicial review.

One further thought might be added. In keeping with Justice Frankfurter's admonition that a true evaluation of an opinion must take into account the "considerations that lead a court to write an opinion one way rather than another,"[332] the question should be asked why the *Gideon* opinion followed the path that it did. Many speculations might be offered, but the thesis that seems the most convincing, though hardly a complete explanation, is simply that the failure of the *Gideon* opinion to utilize the usual overruling rationale is attributable primarily to its authorship by Justice Black. As the writer of the dissent in *Betts*, Justice Black would have a natural interest in vindicating his original opinion (which might well be reflected in *Gideon's* emphasis upon the argument that *Betts* represented "an abrupt break with its own well-considered precedents").[333] But to explain the *Gideon* opinion solely or even primarily in terms of this interest hardly does justice to the depth of the Justice's views. One of the cornerstones of Justice Black's constitutional philosophy[334] has been his belief, most clearly articulated in his *Adamson* dissent,[335] that the Fourteenth Amendment "incorporates" all of the guarantees of the Bill of Rights. Of

[331] These comments were also directed at Fay v. Noia, 372 U.S. 391 (1963), see note 1 *supra*, and Gray v. Sanders, 372 U.S. 368 (1963) (holding invalid the Georgia County Unit system as applied to statewide elections), two cases decided on the same day as *Gideon* that were also classified as overruling decisions. The article also noted, as might be expected, that Justice Black had dissented in *Betts* while all of the members of the majority in that case were either deceased or retired.

[332] PHILLIPS, FELIX FRANKFURTER REMINISCES 296 (1960).

[333] See text at notes 136–83. Although Justices who dissented in the original case have frequently joined subsequent overruling opinions, they have only infrequently been assigned the Court's opinion in the overruling case. See Blaustein & Field, *"Overruling" Opinions in the Supreme Court*, 57 MICH. L. REV. 151, 184–94 (1958).

[334] See generally, Reich, *Mr. Justice Black and the Living Constitution*, 76 HARV. L. REV. 673 (1963); Cahn, *Justice Black and the First Amendment "Absolutes": A Public Interview*, 37 N.Y.U.L. REV. 549, 559 (1962).

[335] Adamson v. California, 332 U.S. 46, 68, 71–72 (1947).

course, his opinion for the Court in *Gideon* did accept the prevailing "fundamental rights" interpretation of the Fourteenth Amendments,[336] but that "acceptance" was carefully based only on the force of prior precedent and even then seemingly was limited to a view of the "fundamental rights" test that requires "complete absorption" of each such right.[337] Moreover, the Court's opinion was

---

[336] 372 U.S. at 342: "We accept *Betts v. Brady*'s assumption, *based as it was on our prior cases*, that a provision of the Bill of Rights which is 'fundamental and essential to a fair trial' is made obligatory upon the States by the Fourteenth Amendment." (Emphasis added.) Justice Black ordinarily has been most willing to disregard precedents in constitutional cases. See Reich, *supra* note 334, at 681; Green v. United States, 356 U.S. 165, 193 (1958) (dissenting opinion). *But cf.* United States v. Rabinowitz, 339 U.S. 56, 66 (1950) (dissenting opinion).

[337] Under the traditional view of the "fundamental rights" approach, the Fourteenth Amendment may encompass only a portion of a right protected against the federal government under one of the first eight Amendments. See Palko v. Connecticut, 302 U.S. 319 (1937); Adamson v. California, 332 U.S. 46, 66 (1947) (concurring opinion). See also Henkin, *Some Reflections on Current Constitutional Controversy*, 109 U. PA. L. REV. 637, 641 (1961).

Justice Brennan recently has advanced the view that individual rights within the Bill of Rights that are ranked as fundamental must be "absorbed" by the Fourteenth Amendment "in toto," *i.e.*, these individual rights must have the same scope in their application to the states as they do to the federal government. See Ohio *ex rel.* Eaton v. Price, 364 U.S. 263 (1960) (dissent from the judgment of an equally divided Court); Cohen v. Hurley, 366 U.S. 117, 154 (1961) (dissenting opinion). Justice Black apparently has accepted this view as the best alternative to the total "incorporation" position of *Adamson*. See Ohio *ex rel.* Eaton v. Price, *supra*. There are various indications that the *Gideon* opinion was written with this view in mind. First, the opinion consistently refers to the "Sixth Amendment right to counsel" that is made applicable to the states. See, *e.g.*, 372 U.S. at 340, 342. In the same vein, the opinion notes that "those guarantees of the Bill of Rights which are fundamental safeguards of liberty immune from federal abridgment are *equally* protected against state invasion by the Due Process Clause. . . ." *Id*. at 341. (Emphasis added.)

It is also interesting to note that the opinion describes *Palko* simply as a case that refused to make the "double jeopardy provision of the Fifth Amendment" obligatory in the states. There is no reference to Justice Cardozo's careful restriction of the *Palko* opinion to the particular aspect of double jeopardy involved there, including a suggestion that other aspects of double jeopardy may apply to the states *via* the Fourteenth Amendment. See 302 U.S. at 328. It was apparently these features of the *Gideon* opinion that made Justice Harlan feel it necessary to express his "understanding" that the Court was not embracing the concept that the Fourteenth Amendment "incorporates" the Sixth Amendment as such. See 372 U.S. at 352. Justice Douglas argued in reply that total incorporation of each federal guarantee was clearly the present constitutional standard. *Id*. at 346. Even if Justice Douglas' views on this score are not accepted by a majority, certainly the *Gideon* opinion is consistent with the later adoption of this concept of the

accompanied by a separate statement of Justice Black's co-dissenter in *Adamson*, Justice Douglas, that the *Gideon* decision "happily" would not prevent the Court from adopting the "total incorporation" view sometime in the future.[338] In the light of this position, Justice Black certainly could not be expected to adopt any rationale that even hinted at the original validity of *Betts*, a decision that exemplifies for him all the evils of the "fundamental rights" approach.[339] Neither could he adopt any argument, such as the gradual erosion of *Betts* under the "special circumstances" cases, that might seemingly accept the basic premise of that approach. In any event, all such arguments are superfluous to one who believes that the Fourteenth Amendment automatically includes the right to appointment of counsel because the same guarantee is contained in the Sixth Amendment.

The contents of the *Gideon* opinion thus were almost preordained by the deeply set views of its author. With all due respect to Justice Black, one might suggest that so long as his philosophy is not accepted by a majority, the interests of the Court would have been better served if the Court's opinion had been written by a Justice whose views permitted him to employ the traditional arts of overruling.[840]

Fourteenth Amendment. At the least, the opinion indicates that so far as the right to counsel is concerned, the standards under the Sixth and Fourteenth Amendments will be the same. *Cf.* Ker v. California, 374 U.S. 23 (1963), where the Court took this same approach in the more complex area of search and seizure.

[338] 372 U.S. at 346; see note 336 *supra*.

[339] See, *e.g.*, his comments upon *Betts* in the following separate opinions: International Shoe Co. v. Washington, 326 U.S. 310, 326 (1945); Adamson v. California, 332 U.S. 46, 83, 84, 90 (1947).

[840] *Cf.* Kauper, *Prayer, Public Schools and the Supreme Court*, 61 MICH. L. REV. 1031 (1963).

TERRANCE SANDALOW

HENRY v. MISSISSIPPI AND THE ADEQUATE STATE GROUND: PROPOSALS FOR A REVISED DOCTRINE

More than a century ago, the then former Justice Curtis reminded the Bar that "questions of jurisdiction were questions of power as between the United States and the several States."[1] Accordingly, any expansion of the jurisdiction of federal courts is an occasion for alarm for those to whom the slogan of "state's rights" is a substitute for analysis. Justice Curtis was aware, however, that Scylla and Charybdis were both to be avoided. Failure to extend the jurisdiction of federal courts to appropriate cases may be as great a disservice to the federal system as an undue expansion of that jurisdiction.[2] The charting of a course between these hazards would be difficult enough if, as in the legend, the location of the hazards were stationary. The difficulty is compounded, however, by the necessity of giving due consideration to changes in federal-state relationships.

Terrance Sandalow is Professor of Law, University of Minnesota.

Author's Acknowledgment: I wish to express my gratitude to my colleagues Professors Jesse H. Choper and John J. Cound for their valuable suggestions in the preparation of this article.

[1] 2 THE LIFE AND WRITINGS OF B. R. CURTIS 341 (Curtis ed. 1879).

[2] *Ibid.*

Jurisdictional rules formulated in 1789 or in the aftermath of the Civil War are not necessarily adequate to the problems of 1965.

These considerations suggest both the difficulty and the delicacy of the task which the Court appears to have set itself last Term in *Henry v. Mississippi*.[3] That decision, if I read it correctly, strongly intimates that at least five Justices are prepared to undertake—perhaps have already undertaken—a major reassessment of the Court's jurisdiction to review judgments of state courts, the first such reassessment since the decision in *Murdock v. City of Memphis*[4] exactly ninety years earlier.[5]

Murdock established that the presence in a case of a federal question adequate to permit the exercise of jurisdiction did not confer upon the Court a general power to decide all of the questions presented. We need not pause for extended inquiry into whether that result was constitutionally compelled;[6] the decision has not been

---

[3] 379 U.S. 443 (1965).

[4] 20 Wall. 590 (1875).

[5] Major modifications of the Court's jurisdiction did, of course, occur during this period through legislation. The Judiciary Act of 1914, 38 Stat. 790, for the first time extended the Court's jurisdiction to cases in which a state court upheld a claim of federal right. And the Judiciary Act of 1916, 39 Stat. 726, together with the Judges' Bill in 1925, 43 Stat. 936, conferred discretionary jurisdiction over a wide category of cases which theretofore had been within the mandatory jurisdiction of the Court. See generally, FRANKFURTER & LANDIS, THE BUSINESS OF THE SUPREME COURT 211–16, 265–66 (1928).

[6] Mr. Justice Bradley, dissenting in *Murdock*, argued that it was not a constitutional requirement because Article III "declares that the judicial power shall extend to all *cases*, in law and equity, arising under this Constitution, the laws of the United States, and treaties made under their authority—not to all *questions*, but to all *cases*." 20 Wall. at 641. The argument finds some support in the familiar doctrine that federal courts in the exercise of original jurisdiction under the "arising under" clause may decide both federal and non-federal questions. Hurn v. Oursler, 289 U.S. 238 (1933); Osborn v. Bank of the United States, 9 Wheat. 738 (1824); Note, 62 COLUM. L. REV. 1018 (1962).

More recently, Mr. Justice Harlan, dissenting in Fay v. Noia, 372 U.S. 391, 466–67 (1963), urged the contrary view as implicit in the division of state and federal power marked out by the Constitution, a position strongly supported by the doctrine of Erie R.R. v. Tompkins, 304 U.S. 64 (1938). A general power in the Supreme Court to review questions of state law in the face of an authoritative declaration by the state courts would plainly be incompatible with the constitutional overtones of that doctrine. On this view, the power of federal courts exercising original jurisdiction to decide questions of state law provides no support for the exercise of a similar power by the Supreme Court on review of state decisions because in the latter situation, unlike the former, there has been an authoritative declaration of local law by the state court in the particular case.

seriously questioned for nearly a century[7] and the premises upon which it rests are so deeply imbedded in our law that it may fairly be deemed a part of our "working constitution."[8]

In the years since *Murdock* the Court has been concerned only with the problem of defining what questions, other than those which confer jurisdiction, are open to its review. The product of these labors is the familiar rule that in a case raising a question within its jurisdiction the Court will examine any non-federal grounds upon which the decision below may have rested to determine whether they independently and adequately support the state court judgment.[9] If the Court did not to that extent encroach upon the function of state courts to declare state law, vindication of federal rights would be subject to impermissible interference by a decision upon state grounds, for it is an obvious corollary of *Murdock* that a state ground of decision which is adequate insulates the judgment from reversal by the Court.[10]

The significance of *Henry v. Mississippi* is in its intimation that a majority of the Court apparently are prepared to redefine the adequate state ground doctrine with a view toward substantial restriction of the situations in which a non-federal ground of decision will be adequate to preclude review of the federal questions presented. Although *Henry* is directly concerned only with the effect of state procedural rules on the vindication of federal rights, an appreciation of that problem requires an examination of the adequate state ground doctrine in the varied contexts in which it is relevant. After a statement of *Henry*, therefore, I shall proceed to a general analysis

---

[7] But *cf*. CROSSKEY, POLITICS AND THE CONSTITUTION 711–937 (1953).

[8] See Hart, *Foreword: The Time Chart of the Justices*, 73 HARV. L. REV. 84, 111 n. 80 (1959).

[9] The rule is usually stated negatively: "Where the decision of the state court is deemed to rest upon a non-federal ground which independently and adequately supports the state court judgment, the Supreme Court will not exercise jurisdiction to review notwithstanding the raising of federal questions upon the state court record or the decision of these questions by the state court." ROBERTSON & KIRKHAM, JURISDICTION OF THE SUPREME COURT OF THE UNITED STATES § 89, at 163 (Wolfson & Kurland ed. 1951).

[10] In *Murdock* the Court indicated that a judgment resting on an adequate non-federal ground ought to be affirmed. The Court's general practice, however, has been to treat the adequate non-federal ground as a bar to the exercise of its jurisdiction. See Note, 74 HARV. L. REV. 1375, 1376–77 (1961).

of the doctrine and to proposals for its modification based upon that
analysis.

I. HENRY V. MISSISSIPPI

Of all the problems raised by *Henry*, none is more troublesome than that of determining the material facts. Almost the first
lesson taught in law school is that "facts of person, time, [and] place
. . . are presumably immaterial unless stated [by the court] to be
material. As a rule the law is the same for all persons, at all times,
and at all places within the jurisdiction of the court."[11] Yet, even
though not mentioned by the Court, is it really immaterial that the
petitioner was not merely a man charged with disturbing the peace,
but Aaron Henry, a Negro resident of Clarksdale, Mississippi, and
president of both the Coahoma County Branch of the National
Association for the Advancement of Colored People and of its State
Conference of Branches?[12] Is it, moreover, immaterial that the prosecution was commenced in 1962 in Mississippi[13] and not at another
time and in another place? The traditional answer to these questions,
one suspects, is neither entirely realistic nor necessarily desirable.
Yet more than a lawyer's conservatism argues for caution in accepting a conclusion that the Court was or ought to have been influenced
by such factors, particularly in a case which touches what historically has been one of the more sensitive areas of federal-state relationships.

A. THE PROCEEDINGS IN THE STATE COURTS

Aaron Henry was tried and convicted on a charge of disturbing
the peace by making indecent proposals to and an assault upon a
hitchhiker to whom he allegedly had given a ride. He was sentenced

---

[11] Goodhart, *Determining the Ratio Decidendi of a Case*, 40 YALE L.J. 161, 169–
70 (1930).

[12] Petition for Certiorari, p. 19.

[13] On the use (or abuse) of the legal machinery of certain states to interfere
with the civil rights movement, see *id.* at 19–24; UNITED STATES COMMISSION ON
CIVIL RIGHTS, THE 50 STATES REPORT 6–15 (1961); MARSHALL, FEDERALISM AND CIVIL
RIGHTS (1964); Amsterdam, *Criminal Prosecutions Affecting Federally Guaranteed
Civil Rights: Federal Removal and Habeas Corpus Jurisdiction To Abort State
Court Trial*, 113 U. OF PA. L. REV. 793 (1965); Gellhorn, *A Decade of Desegregation—Retrospect and Prospect*, 9 UTAH L. REV. 3 (1964); Lusky, *Racial Discrimination and the Federal Law: A Problem in Nullification*, 63 COLUM. L. REV. 1163
(1963).

to sixty days in jail and a fine of $250, both well below the maximum permitted by law.[14] At the trial, the evidence against Henry consisted primarily of the testimony of the alleged victim. In an attempt to corroborate this testimony, the state introduced the testimony of a police officer who had searched Henry's car shortly after his arrest, which, in turn, had taken place within a few hours of the alleged crime. The latter testimony tended to corroborate that of the complaining witness by substantiating its accuracy concerning details of the interior of Henry's car that could have been observed only by one who had been inside the car.[15]

No objection was made to the officer's testimony at the time it was offered or, indeed, until the close of the state's case, at which time counsel for Henry, in the course of a motion for a directed verdict, urged that the testimony was the product of an unlawful search. Although the basis for this claim was not then stated by counsel, it rested upon the fact that, as the officer had testified, the search was not authorized by a warrant or incident to an arrest, but was justified, if at all, solely upon the basis of permission given by Henry's wife. The motion was summarily denied. Upon completion of the defense, the motion was renewed, without further specification, and again summarily denied.

On appeal,[16] the Misisssippi Supreme Court initially reversed the conviction without reference to Henry's claim under the Fourteenth Amendment.[17] It held the search unlawful under the state constitution and, therefore, that evidence resulting from it was inadmissible under a state exclusionary rule long antedating *Mapp v. Ohio*.[18]

---

[14] Miss. Code 1942 § 2089.5 (Supp. 1964), under which Henry was charged, authorizes a sentence not to exceed six months in jail and fine of $500. The justice of the peace before whom the case was originally tried gave Henry the maximum sentence. Petition for Certiorari, p. 4. A trial de novo in the County Court apparently resulted in the lighter sentence. See Henry v. State, 154 So.2d 289, 290 (Miss. 1963).

[15] Both the complaining witness and police officer testified that an ashtray in the car was filled with Dentyne chewing gum wrappers and that a cigarette lighter was not properly functioning. *Id.* at 294.

[16] The Circuit Court of Bolivia County, apparently an intermediate appellate court, had affirmed the conviction. *Id.* at 290.

[17] With respect to the merits of the issue under the Fourteenth Amendment, *compare* Roberts v. United States, 332 F.2d 892 (8th Cir. 1964), *with* Cofer v. United States, 37 F.2d 677 (5th Cir. 1930).

[18] 367 U.S. 643 (1961). See Tucker v. State, 128 Miss. 211 (1922).

Reversal was required, notwithstanding the customary rule that an appeal will not lie from the introduction of evidence to which contemporaneous objection has not been made, for two reasons. First, the court apparently assumed that Henry had been represented only by out-of-state counsel unfamiliar with local procedure.[19] Second, it found that the case came within the "narrow rule" established by an earlier decision, that "[e]rrors affecting fundamental rights are exceptions to the rule that questions not raised in the trial court cannot be raised for the first time on appeal."[20]

After the opinion was handed down, a "Suggestion of Error" was filed by the state pointing out that Henry had been represented at the trial by local as well as nonresident counsel.[21] The court thereupon withdrew its first opinion and affirmed the conviction in a new opinion identical with the first except for differences concerning the effect of failure to make timely objections. The court now concluded that that omission resulted in a "waiver" of the right to object. Moreover, the "narrow rule" excepting errors affecting fundamental rights from the prohibition upon raising issues to which

---

[19] That assumption is not explicitly stated in the Court's opinion. However, in explaining the reason for departing from its customary practice, the Court did say: "It appears from the records reaching this Court that numerous cases have been tried recently in this state by nonresident attorneys who have traveled great distance to appear in defense of persons charged with misdemeanor and minor offenses, but who are not adept in the technique of jury trials in criminal court in Mississippi." Petition for Certiorari, p. 11a. The statement, obviously, was relevant only on the assumption that Henry had been represented by a nonresident attorney.

[20] Brooks v. State, 209 Miss. 150, 155 (1950). The court relied on Brown v. Mississippi, 297 U.S. 278 (1936), for a similar proposition, although seemingly only as persuasive authority and not because it considered itself bound by that decision.

[21] The Suggestion of Error also informed the court that one of Henry's out-of-state attorneys was "regular full time counsel for the NAACP in New York City and, since the appointment of Thurgood Marshall to Federal Judiciary, has been general counsel for that organization." See Brief in Support of Suggestion of Error, reprinted as Appendix 4 in Answer to Petition for Certiorari, p. A40. Inclusion of that information in the Suggestion of Error may be given a sinister interpretation as suggested by Henry's counsel, see Petition for Certiorari, pp. 22–23, or it may be deemed justified by the wholly proper purpose of bringing to the court's attention the experience of Henry's lead counsel and the consequent probability of his familiarity with the necessity for timely objection to inadmissible evidence. See Brief for Respondent, p. 12.

Similarly conflicting inferences may be drawn from the information provided the court that "[t]he writer is not alone in his feeling with respect to the opinion of the court in this case. It has been discussed with numerous lawyers and judges and each has urged the filing of this suggestion of error that the Court might reconsider its decision." Brief in Support of Suggestion of Error, supra, at A37.

timely objection had not been made was now found to be even narrower: the earlier decision establishing that rule was now construed
to depend upon the incompetence of counsel. Henry had been
represented by three experienced trial lawyers of his own selection,
one of whom was from Mississippi. "In such circumstances, even if
honest mistakes of counsel in respect to policy or strategy or otherwise occur, they are binding upon the client as a part of the hazards
of courtroom battle."[22]

B. THE OPINIONS IN THE SUPREME COURT

On certiorari, the Supreme Court divided three ways, a majority
concluding that the state court judgment should be vacated and the
case remanded to determine whether the failure of Henry's counsel
to object to the police officer's testimony at the time it was introduced resulted from a deliberate waiver of Henry's federal claim.[23]
The majority thus avoided, at least temporarily, the necessity of deciding whether the Mississippi judgment affirming the conviction
rested on a state ground adequate to preclude the assertion of jurisdiction by the Supreme Court. Avoidance of decision did not, however, deter the majority from an interesting and perhaps far-reaching discussion of the adequate state ground doctrine.

Mr. Justice Brennan, writing for the majority, opened the discussion by stating that although the doctrine applies both to substantive
and procedural grounds, it is important nonetheless to distinguish
between the two. "Where the ground involved is substantive, the
determination of the federal question cannot affect the disposition if
the state court decision on the state law question is allowed to
stand."[24] Since, under the decision in *Murdock* the Court has no
power to revise state court judgments on questions of state law, "the
adequate nonfederal ground doctrine is necessary to avoid advisory
opinions."[25]

These considerations, the opinion continues, are inapplicable
where the state ground is purely procedural. "A procedural default
which is held to bar challenge to a conviction in state courts, even on

---

[22] 154 So.2d at 296.

[23] Although the Mississippi Supreme Court stated that Henry had "waived his
right to object" to the testimony, it seems plain that it had not found an intentional
abandonment of the claim. The "waiver," more precisely, was a forfeiture resulting
from the failure to comply with state procedure.

[24] 379 U.S. at 446.   [25] *Id.* at 447.

federal constitutional grounds, prevents implementation of the federal right."[26] Accordingly, prior decisions establish, as a matter of federal law, that "unless the state's insistence on compliance with its procedural rule serves a legitimate state interest,"[27] consideration of federal claims by the Court is not precluded.

The majority opinion recognizes "a legitimate state interest" in the state's requirement of a contemporaneous objection to the introduction of evidence, but goes on to suggest that on the record that interest "may have been substantially served" by the motion for a directed verdict. If the evidence were inadmissible, the trial judge might have stricken it from the record, and if there were other competent evidence sufficient to sustain a conviction, the case could have been submitted to the jury with appropriate cautionary instructions to ignore the illegally obtained evidence.

A decision on whether the availability of this alternative negated the state's interest in enforcing its contemporaneous objection rule was, however, viewed as unnecessary because the record before the Court suggested the possibility that the failure of Henry's counsel to object when the evidence was introduced may have been attributable to a conscious waiver of the objection.[28] That question could not be determined without a hearing, and a remand to permit such a hearing, the Court said, would be particularly appropriate since, even if the writ of certiorari were dismissed on the basis of an adequate state ground, the doctrine of *Fay v. Noia*[29] would permit Henry to assert his federal claim in a federal habeas corpus proceeding unless it could be shown that he had deliberately bypassed state procedure. Permitting the state courts to make an initial determina-

---

[26] *Ibid.*   [27] *Ibid.*

[28] Several facts were cited in support of this possibility. (1) The state's Brief in Support of its Suggestion of Error stipulated that the reversal of the conviction should stand if any one of Henry's defense counsel would file an affidavit "that he did not know that at some point in a trial in criminal court in Mississippi that an objection to such testimony must have been made." (As thus stated, however, the state's offer was irrelevant on the question whether defense counsel knew of the contemporaneous objection rule.) (2) An affidavit filed by the state in the Supreme Court asserted that when the officer's testimony was introduced one of Henry's attorneys stood up as if to object and was pulled down by co-counsel. (3) The record suggests that the failure to object might have been based on trial strategy. Both the complaining witness and the officer testified that a cigarette lighter in the car did not work. The defense called a mechanic who testified that he had repaired the lighter. Hence, counsel may, by not objecting to the officer's testimony, have intended to discredit both of the state's witnesses. *Id.* at 450–52.

[29] 372 U.S. 391, 439 (1963). *Fay* is discussed in text *infra*, at notes 179–94.

tion of waiver would not only decrease the burden on federal courts; it would serve the cause of "harmonious federal-state judicial relations,"[30] perhaps ameliorating the irritation created by federal habeas corpus jurisdiction.

Mr. Justice Black dissented. Without considering the state's interest in enforcement of its contemporaneous objection rule, he concluded that the forfeiture under state law was inadequate to preclude review because previous state decisions established that the Mississippi court had power to consider Henry's federal claim and had at times exercised its discretion to hear similar claims notwithstanding failure to make a contemporaneous objection. Under *Williams v. Georgia*,[31] therefore, the state ground was inadequate.

Mr. Justice Harlan (joined by Justices Clark and Stewart) also dissented but on quite different grounds. Although apparently not in disagreement with Mr. Justice Brennan's formulation of the test for determining the adequacy of state procedural grounds, he found the state's interest in the integrity of its procedure plainly adequate to bar review of Henry's federal claim by the Court.[32] Mr. Justice Harlan saw more in the majority's opinion, however, than a simple failure to assess properly the state's interest in its contemporaneous objection rule. That opinion, as he read it, "portends a severe dilution, if not complete abolition of the concept of 'adequacy' as pertaining to state procedural grounds," in effect "an early step towards extending in one way or another the doctrine of *Fay v. Noia* to direct review."[33]

C. THE SIGNIFICANCE OF THE DECISION

The initial question raised by the Court's decision in *Henry* is whether it does, as suggested by Mr. Justice Harlan, look toward a substantial revision of the adequate state ground doctrine or whether

[30] 379 U.S. at 452.

[31] 349 U.S. 375 (1955). See discussion in text *infra*, at notes 158–62.

[32] The majority's suggestion that the purpose of the contemporaneous objection rule might have been substantially served by the motion for a directed verdict was, in Mr. Justice Harlan's view, "fanciful." 379 U.S. at 458. The reference to the assertedly unlawful search consisted of a single sentence, in the middle of a motion directed to other matters, which failed even to specify the basis upon which the search was claimed to be unlawful. "It is simply unrealistic in this context to have expected the trial judge to pick out the single vague sentence from the directed verdict motion and to have acted upon it with the refined imagination the Court would require of him." *Id.* at 461.

[33] *Id.* at 457.

it has a more limited significance. Several factors point toward the latter reading. Nothing in Mr. Justice Brennan's discussion of the adequate state ground doctrine explicitly suggests an intention to apply other than "settled principles."[34] The only attempt to state a general standard for determining the adequacy of state procedural grounds is, as one commentator has already observed, "a fair synthesis of prior decisions."[35] There is, finally, the imponderable alluded to above, that the Court was influenced by the possibility that Henry's prosecution was a consequence of his active participation in the civil rights movement.[36]

Nevertheless, there is as much and perhaps more reason to conclude that Mr. Justice Harlan's surmise regarding the Court's direction is well founded. If the Court's concern were with Henry as an individual, rather than with preparing the way for revision of the adequate state ground doctrine, avoidance of the bar to review posed by Henry's failure to comply with state procedure might as easily have been accomplished on the ground that the state supreme court's enforcement of its forfeiture rule was discriminatory and, therefore, inadequate under a long line of earlier cases.[37] Although a decision on that ground would have involved a minor inroad upon the adequate state ground doctrine,[38] it would have had the virtue of extremely limited precedential significance. The Court's failure to adopt that approach suggests that it had a more far-reaching objective.

There is additional evidence of the Court's direction in its curious insistence that the standard for determining adequacy stated in the opinion "will not inevitably lead to a plethora of attacks on the application of state procedural rules,"[39] a reassurance which would

---

[34] *Id.* at 452.

[35] Recent Developments, 65 COLUM. L. REV. 710, 713 (1965); see also Note, *supra* note 10, at 1388–91.

[36] Both the Petition for Certiorari and Petitioner's Brief on the Merits urged as a ground for reversal: "The State of Mississippi has used its criminal and judicial process as a punitive measure, to enforce racial segregation and to interfere with freedom of association. . . ." See Petition for Certiorari, p. 18; Brief for Petitioner, p. 36.

[37] See discussion in text *infra*, at note 143.

[38] See discussion in text *infra*, at notes 155–56.

[39] 379 U.S. at 448 n. 3. Rather more puzzling is the Court's statement in the same footnote that "where the state rule is a reasonable one and clearly announced to

hardly have been necessary if the Court contemplated merely the application of "settled principles." Moreover, the doubt cast upon the state's contemporaneous objection rule, the adequacy of which was hardly subject to question under earlier cases,[40] suggests at least that while the bottle—the verbal formulation for determining adequacy—is old, its contents may soon be replaced.

In a more political context, in sum, the Court's opinion might fairly be read as throwing up a "trial balloon." The implication that a change in doctrine is under consideration is manifest, yet the holding is sufficiently narrow that retreat is not foreclosed. A reconsideration of the adequate state ground doctrine is, therefore, plainly in order.

II. Substance and Procedure—and More Relevant Considerations

The Court's distinction between state substantive and procedural grounds has a surface plausibility that, on further examination, fails to withstand analysis. The distinction rests in part, it will be recalled, on the premise that determination of the federal question cannot affect disposition of the case if the state court decision on the question of state substantive law is allowed to stand. The premise is equally true, however, of a state court decision with respect to procedure. If *it* is allowed to stand, Supreme Court decision of the question of federal law cannot affect disposition of the case. In either event, whether the state ground is substantive or procedural, once the Supreme Court decided that it should be allowed to stand, the adequate state ground doctrine "is necessary to avoid advisory opinions."[41] The "advisory opinion" rationale, in other

defendant and counsel, application of the waiver doctrine will yield the same result as that of the adequate nonfederal ground doctrine in the vast majority of cases." At no point does the Court identify "the waiver doctrine" to which it refers; surely *Henry* does not in terms define such a doctrine. It seems a permissible inference, therefore, that "the waiver doctrine" is that laid down in *Fay v. Noia*, that, absent a knowing and intelligent waiver, failure to comply with state procedure respecting the presentation of federal claims does not bar review of such claims by a federal court.

[40] See discussion in text *infra*, at notes 171–77.

[41] 379 U.S. at 447. Significantly, Herb v. Pitcairn, 324 U.S. 117 (1945), in which the argument based upon avoidance of advisory opinions was apparently first articulated, involved a plainly procedural rule, the power of a state court to transfer a cause over which it lacked subject-matter jurisdiction. That this justification for

words, is concerned with the appropriate disposition of the case once it is determined that the state ground is adequate. It does not speak to the questions which state grounds are adequate or how that is to be determined.

The other basis for distinction suggested by the Court—that a procedural default held to bar assertion of a federal claim differs from a substantive ground because it prevents implementation of a federal right—is no more satisfactory. A state substantive ground may also bar implementation of a federal right.[42] The question before the Court is the same whether the state ground is substantive or procedural, i.e., whether it ought to preclude the Court's consideration of the federal claim.

The fact that but a single question is involved does not, obviously, mean that there must be a single answer to all the variant situations to come before the Court, nor does it mean that the Court must adopt the same premises or pursue the same policies in all situations. Differences in the intensity of the federal interest,[43] the extent to which the state ground interferes with that interest, and the importance to the state of the policy underlying the state ground of deci-

---

the adequate state ground doctrine applies equally to state substantive and procedural grounds was, moreover, explicitly recognized in Mr. Justice Brennan's opinion for the Court in Fay v. Noia, 372 U.S. at 429–30.

[42] See, e.g., Enterprise Irrigation Dist. v. Farmers' Mut. Canal Co., 243 U.S. 157 (1917); Gaar, Scott & Co. v. Shannon, 223 U.S. 468 (1912). The distinction between substance and procedure is as elusive here as in other contexts. For present purposes, however, state law prescribing consequences for prelitigation conduct, as in the cases just cited, may fairly be deemed substantive.

Cases raising the question whether a state has impaired the obligation of a contract or deprived a person of property without due process of law, while analytically distinguishable, also involve a risk that the state ground may interfere with the protection of a federal right. In such cases, where the Constitution protects a right created by state law, a determination by the state court that the right never existed at state law does not technically bar implementation of federal right, since the existence of the latter depends upon the former. Neverthless, power to avoid the federal right is inherent in the authority of the state court to decide the question of state law. See discussion in text infra, at notes 144–48.

[43] With rare exception, this factor has not been explicitly stressed in the Court's opinions. But cf. Brown v. Mississippi, 297 U.S. 278, 286–87 (1936). Nevertheless at least one commentator has observed that "the adequacy of a procedural bar to a federal claim seems to depend on the Court's assessment of the importance of the procedure when set against the federal claim." Note, supra note 10, at 1389. And, whatever the difficulties of such an assessment, appropriate accommodation of federal and state interests seems to require that it at least be attempted. See discussion in text infra, at notes 165–211.

sion call for differences in result. In assessing these differences, distinctions which might be made between substance and procedure seem of less importance than several others that might be suggested. Thus, the strength of the federal interest will vary according to whether the effect of the non-federal ground of decision is to produce a result the same as or different from that which would be produced by a decision sustaining the federal claim involved.[44] So also, different considerations are presented depending upon whether the state ground of decision concerns a refusal to adjudicate or leads to adjudication in a manner allegedly at variance with federal law.[45] Difference may perhaps also exist between those cases in which the party asserting the federal claim has invoked the jurisdiction of the state court and those in which he is in a defensive posture.[46]

The former alternative, in each instance, plainly presents a weaker basis for intervention by the Supreme Court. Yet, even in such cases, as subsequent discussion suggests, the exercise of jurisdiction may be warranted, although on grounds which deviate somewhat from traditional analysis. It is important at this point to note that the adequate state ground doctrine has two aspects. The first, which is emphasized by the traditional statement of the doctrine,[47] merely states the consequences of a determination that the state court judgment rests upon as adequate non-federal ground. The second and more important aspect of the doctrine is concerned with a definition of the circumstances under which the Court will re-examine the state court's determination of non-federal issues.

III. Review of Judgments That Protect Federal Rights

The justification for the Court's encroachment upon the function of state courts to declare authoritatively the content of state law[48] establishes the initial limitation of the Court's power: a non-federal ground of decision may be held inadequate to preclude review of a federal question only if a federal interest would be served thereby. Accordingly, a decision which upholds a state statute under the federal constitution while invalidating it under the state constitution is generally beyond the Court's jurisdiction. In such a case there is no danger of infringement of a federal right:

---

[44] See text *infra*, at notes 48–68.

[45] See text *infra*, at notes 68–121.   [47] See note 9 *supra*.

[46] See text *infra*, at note 211.   [48] See text *supra*, at note 10.

since the judgment gives no effect to the statute, the asserted federal right is accorded full protection and the federal interest is satisfied whether or not the state court was correct in its assessment of federal law. Similarly, the Court generally lacks jurisdiction when the state court has invalidated a state statute under both state and federal constitutions.[49] It is, of course, true that the Judiciary Act of 1914[50] recognizes a federal interest in freeing the states of restrictions imposed by state courts under the supposed obligation of federal law.[51] But a decision that the state court has incorrectly interpreted federal law will in no way advance that interest, since the statute will not be given effect in any event.

For these reasons, the Court's decision in *United States Mortgage Co. v. Matthews*[52] seems incorrect. In that case, the state court had construed a contract in the manner contended for by a party claiming rights under the Contract Clause and, on that basis, held a statute invalid as impairing the obligation of the contract. The Supreme Court reversed, disagreeing on the interpretation of the contract. Its power to consider this question of state law was affirmed summarily by reference to the "well established doctrine that where the contract clause is invoked this Court must determine for itself the nature and effect of the alleged agreement. . . ."[53] The Court seemingly failed to recognize that, in the cases that had established the doctrine, review of the state-law question by the Supreme Court was necessary, as Mr. Justice Roberts later put it, "in order that the constitutional mandate may not become a dead letter."[54] No such justification existed in *Matthews*. State law had been interpreted favorably to the federal right. *Matthews* can be justified, if at all, only on the ground that decision of the non-federal issue by the Supreme Court permitted it to avoid decision of a constitutional question.[55] Acceptance of that justification, which finds no support

---

[49] See ROBERTSON & KIRKHAM, *op. cit. supra* note 9, at § 98.

[50] See note 5 *supra*.

[51] See also Minnesota v. National Tea Co., 309 U.S. 551, 557 (1940).

[52] 293 U.S. 232 (1934).   [53] *Id.* at 236.

[54] Indiana ex rel. Anderson v. Brand, 303 U.S. 95, 100 (1938).

[55] The decision is to that extent distinguishable from those holding that a determination of the invalidity of a state statute under the state constitution is adequate to preclude review. See text *supra*, preceding note 49. In the latter cases, review of the state ground of decision would not permit the Court to avoid decision of the federal constitutional issue.

in other decisions of the Court,[56] would lead to a virtual reversal of *Murdock*. It would permit the Court, in effect, to exercise a general superintendence over matters of local law, a result having so profound an impact on the distribution of power between the states and the federal government that it is hardly to be justified by the desirability of avoiding constitutional questions.

In general, therefore, where the state court judgment protects the federal right asserted, a non-federal ground of decision is adequate to preclude the assertion of jurisdiction by the Supreme Court. Once it is concluded that the state ground ought not itself to be subject to re-examination by the Court, the "advisory opinion" rationale articulated by Mr. Justice Jackson in *Herb v. Pitcairn*[57] comes into play to preclude consideration of the federal question presented. Any discussion of that question would not alter the legal relationship of the parties, since the judgment rendered by the state court would stand whether or not it correctly ruled upon the federal question. All that would be accomplished by Supreme Court review would be an essay on the federal question, bearing the imprimatur of the Court but devoid of significance in the case at bar.

Yet even in such cases review of the federal question may occasionally be warranted. Although *Herb v. Pitcairn* contains overtones of constitutional or statutory limitations on the assertion of jurisdiction by the Court,[58] commentators have generally agreed that refusal to review a federal question where the judgment is based upon an adequate state ground rests upon a self-imposed rule of judicial administration.[59] Generally, nonetheless, the already heavy burdens on the Court[60] and the desirability of avoiding constitutional decisions will counsel against an assumption of jurisdiction. But cases may arise in which a statement by the Court on the federal issues presented would serve a useful purpose.[61] Perhaps the most

---

[56] See, *e.g.*, First Nat'l Bank v. Anderson, 269 U.S. 341, 346 (1926).

[57] 324 U.S. 117, 125–26 (1945).

[58] The reasons underlying the adequate state ground doctrine, Mr. Justice Jackson wrote, are "found in the partitioning of power between the state and federal judicial system and in the limitations of our own jurisdiction. Our only power over state judgments is to correct them to the extent that they incorrectly adjudge federal rights. And our power is to correct wrong judgments, not to review opinions. We are not permitted to render an advisory opinion. . . ." *Ibid.*

[59] Note, *supra* note 10, at 1377–79; Note, 49 YALE L.J. 1463 (1940).

[60] See Hart, *supra* note 8.   [61] See text *infra*, at notes 118–21.

frequently recurring of the situations in which an assertion of such power by the Court would be useful is that in which the state court has invalidated a statute under both state and federal constitutions. Although the state ground in that situation is, technically, both "independent" and "adequate," the frequency with which state courts, in interpreting state constitutions, rely on federal decisions construing a similar provision in the federal constitution suggests that the Court ought not to be blind to the leadership that it in fact exerts in this area.[62] Even when it does not seem likely that the judgment in the case at bar will be affected, thought must be given also to the potential impact in other cases and the desirability of assuring that "the responsibility for striking down or upholding state legislation be fairly placed."[63] In such cases, there is no overriding policy that requires the Court to stay its hand. The independence of state courts would not be sacrificed since the judgment would be undisturbed. Moreover, the record before the Court will normally be fully adequate to illumine the issues and the Court will frequently have the benefit of adversary proceedings,[64] thus removing the primary objections to "advisory opinions."[65]

Although the Court seems never to have taken jurisdiction for this purpose, several decisions suggest its power to do so.[66] In each, it was unclear whether the judgment below rested upon a state ground or upon a conclusion regarding the obligations imposed by federal law. Departing from its customary practice of declining to exercise jurisdiction until the ambiguity in the state court judgment is resolved,[67] the Court considered the federal issue on the merits, held that the state courts were free of federal compulsion, and vacated the judgment to permit a determination by the state court

---

[62] Note, 49 YALE L.J. 1463 (1940).

[63] Minnesota v. National Tea Co., 309 U.S. 551, 557 (1940).

[64] Petitioner's or appellant's interest in resolution of the issue by the Supreme Court is assured by the fact that it has invoked the Court's jurisdiction, presumably because its interest in the issue is continuing and not exhausted by a decision of the particular case. Respondent or appellee may of course also have such continuing interest in some situations.

[65] See LOCKHART, KAMISAR & CHOPER, CONSTITUTIONAL LAW 51–53 (1964).

[66] Perkins v. Benguet Consol. Mining Co., 342 U.S. 437 (1952); Missouri ex rel. Southern Ry. Co. v. Mayfield, 340 U.S. 1 (1950); cf. Patterson v. Alabama, 294 U.S. 600 (1935). See, also, discussion in text infra, at notes 118–21.

[67] Note, supra note 6.

whether non-federal grounds alone would sustain the judgment. A similar technique, but without the necessity of vacating the judgment, might be employed even where the grounds of decision are not ambiguous. Indeed, almost precisely this course was proposed in *Murdock*.[68]

IV. THE REFUSAL TO ADJUDICATE A FEDERAL CLAIM

Quite different questions are presented when the non-federal ground of decision consists of a refusal by the state court to grant a remedy for a claimed federal right or to exercise jurisdiction in a proceeding commenced to enforce such a right. If, by virtue of the Supremacy Clause or another provision of the Constitution, state courts must entertain an action based upon federal rights, the state court's refusal, being inconsistent with the Constitution, is plainly not adequate to support the judgment. The initial question, therefore, is whether the Constitution does impose such an obligation on the state courts. If (or to the extent that) the answer to that question is in the negative, there is a further question whether the state ground of decision may nonetheless be inadequate to preclude review by the Court.

Several lines of cases suggest that the state courts may not, consistently with the Constitution, decline to adjudicate a claim of federal right. Yet, both the precedents and the reasons in support of such a rule are sufficiently unclear that a fresh look at the question seems warranted.

A. THE SUPREMACY CLAUSE AND FEDERAL STATUTORY CLAIMS

Under prevailing doctrine, a state court may not decline to adjudicate a federal claim if it would enforce an analogous state-created right. It is still an open question, however, whether it must provide a forum for enforcement of the federal claim even when it does not entertain similar suits arising under local law. As an original matter, it might well be argued that the Constitution does not require the state court to hear the federal claim in either event. The Supremacy Clause does not, in terms, require it to do so. Historically, indeed, the concern was that the state courts would not be permitted to assume jurisdiction of actions to enforce federal rights[69] and it was not until 1876, in *Claflin v. Houseman*,[70] that the question

---

[68] 20 Wall. at 635–36.   [69] See Note, 73 HARV. L. REV. 1551 (1960).

[70] 93 U.S. 130 (1876).

of the power of state courts was finally put to rest.[71] Although the conversion of that power to a duty is now so firmly established that it is perhaps beyond reconsideration,[72] an examination of the cases establishing the duty, beyond suggesting what might have been, may illumine still unresolved questions.

In *Mondou v. New York, N.H. & H. R.R.*,[73] one of the questions presented was the duty of a state court "when its ordinary jurisdiction as prescribed by local laws is appropriate to the occasion and is invoked in conformity with those laws, to take cognizance of an action to enforce a right of civil recovery arising under the act of Congress and susceptible of adjudication according to the prevailing rules of procedure."[74] Although Congress had not, as the Court carefully observed, attempted to impose that obligation on state courts, the question was, nonetheless, answered affirmatively. The state court had declined to exercise jurisdiction because the policy manifested by the Act of Congress was not in accord with the policy of the state.[75] That reason, the Court said, was

> quite inadmissible, because it presupposes what in legal contemplation does not exist. When Congress, in the exertion of the power confided to it by the Constitution, adopted that act, it spoke for all the people and all the States, and thereby established a policy for all. That policy is as much the policy of Connecticut as if the act had emanated from its own legislature, and should be respected accordingly in the courts of the State.[76]

The Court went on to quote extensively from *Claflin v. Houseman* without, however, noting that that decision was concerned only

---

[71] The power of the state courts is, of course, subject to the power of Congress to confer exclusive jurisdiction on federal courts. See HART & WECHSLER, THE FEDERAL COURTS AND THE FEDERAL SYSTEM 373–74 (1953).

[72] In recent years, nevertheless, the Court has given renewed meaning to the maxim that constitutional questions are always open to re-examination. See Kurland, *Foreword: "Equal in Origin and Equal in Title to the Legislative and Executive Branches of the Government,"* 78 HARV. L. REV. 143, 164 (1964).

[73] 223 U.S. 1 (1912).   [74] *Id.* at 56–57.

[75] A second and somewhat related reason, that it would be "inconvenient and confusing" for the state courts to apply federal law to some cases and the differing standards of state law to similar cases not governed by the Act, was also advanced. The argument was rejected, partly because the Court doubted the factual premises on which it was based and partly because it apparently considered the justification impermissible in any event.

[76] 223 U.S. at 57.

with the *power* of state courts to adjudicate claims based on federal law, not with whether they had a duty to do so.

> The fact that a state court derives its existence and functions from the state laws is no reason why it should not afford relief; because it is subject also to the laws of the United States, and is just as much bound to recognize these as operative within the State as it is to recognize the state laws.[77]

Mondou is usually read as establishing only that a state must enforce a federally created right if it enforces analogous forum-created rights,[78] a proposition which was reaffirmed in *McKnett v. St. Louis & S.F. Ry.*[79] That reading is reinforced by the Court's subsequent decision in *Douglas v. New York, N.H. & H. R.R.*,[80] sustaining the refusal of a state court to exercise jurisdiction over a federal statutory claim under circumstances in which it would also have declined to adjudicate a state-created claim.

Yet, it seems plain that the reasons underlying the decision in *Mondou* will support a broader doctrine than the Court purported to lay down. If the duty of the state courts to accept jurisdiction flows from the obligation to respect federal policy, there is no apparent reason why the state should not be required to accept jurisdiction even though it would not entertain an analogous forum-created right. Federal policy is the same whatever lines the state has drawn in defining the jurisdiction of its courts over local claims. If the state may not assert a policy at variance with that expressed by the federal law, adjudication of the claim would seem to be required even in the absence of discrimination since, insofar as the local jurisdictional rule prevents adjudication, it is to that extent, under the reasoning of *Mondou*, inconsistent with the policy underlying the federal claim. Some support for this view may be found in *Testa v. Katt*,[81] the most recent of the Court's decisions touching the problem. There, a state court had declined to enforce a claim for treble damages provided by federal statute on the ground that it was contrary to state policy to enforce a foreign penal statute. Brushing aside the distinctions between "penal" and other claims

---

[77] *Id.* at 58.

[78] See, *e.g.*, Note, *supra* note 69, at 1553; Note, 47 Minn. L. Rev. 815, 827 (1963).

[79] 292 U.S. 230 (1934). See also Minneapolis & St. L. R.R. v. Bombolis, 241 U.S. 211, 221–23 (1916).

[80] 279 U.S. 377 (1929).   [81] 330 U.S. 386 (1947).

suggested by earlier decisions, the Supreme Court reversed, chiefly in reliance upon *Claflin* and *Mondou*. Although *Testa* in fact involved discrimination against a federal claim, since the state court did enforce "penal" claims under local law, the Court's reasoning was not dependent upon that fact: [82]

> [T]he policy of the federal Act is the prevailing policy in every state. . . . [A] state court cannot "refuse to enforce the right arising from the law of the United States because of conceptions of impolicy or want of wisdom on the part of Congress in having called into play its lawful powers."

These cases, then, may—though on their facts they need not—be taken to mean that the Constitution, presumably through the Supremacy Clause, directly imposes upon the states an obligation to enforce federal claims that Congress has not committed to the exclusive jurisdiction of the federal courts. Yet it is difficult to perceive the federal interest that justifies so substantial an intrusion upon the power of the states to determine the purposes to be served by agencies of state government. Article III of the Constitution confers upon Congress the power to establish a federal judicial system adequate to enforce claims of federal right. In both *Mondou* and *Testa* a federal court was open to the plaintiff, so that a decision sustaining the refusal to adjudicate would in no way have interfered with the vindication of federal rights. Conceding, therefore, that a state may not pursue a policy inconsistent with that established by federal law, it is by no means apparent that the state courts in *Mondou* and *Testa* had done so. Federal policy was substantive, that recovery should be permitted under specified circumstances. State policy, on the other hand, was concerned only with the use to be made of state courts, a matter not touched by the federal policy.

The Court's reliance on the Supremacy Clause appears to come to no more than it would be unseemly for the state to refuse recognition to rights conferred by federal law—particularly if similar rights under state law are adjudicated in state courts. In view of the rather substantial burden that the Court's current doctrine im-

---

[82] *Id.* at 393. The internal quotation is from *Bombolis, supra* note 79, where, however, it was coupled with a limitation to those cases in which the state enforced similar claims under local law.

poses upon the states,[83] that does not seem an adequate justification. It is, of course, true that if the states are free to decline jurisdiction over federal claims and if they exercise that option, the resulting burden on the federal courts may be extremely heavy. But the allocation of burdens between state and federal judiciaries seems peculiarly a matter for determination by Congress.[84] Recognition of congressional power to require the exercise of jurisdiction by state courts would permit ample protection of any federal interests. In the absence of a declaration by Congress that state courts must enforce rights that Congress has created, there appears to be no substantial reason why the Supreme Court should impose such an obligation.[85]

---

[83] The burden is primarily one of numbers. Although statistics on the federal claims adjudicated in the state courts are not available, the number is undoubtedly large. See Hart, *The Relations between State and Federal Law*, 54 COLUM. L. REV. 489, 507 n. 55 (1954). Moreover, if *Mondou* and *Testa* are extended to the limits of their rationale, there is a possibility of an additional burden, the necessity of administering remedies for which state courts are unprepared.

[84] Although congressional power to impose jurisdiction on state courts was denied as recently as 1944, see Brown v. Gerdes, 321 U.S. 178, 188–89 (1944) (concurring opinion), *Testa v. Katt* would seem to suggest the contrary. In the absence of any express limitation upon Congress' power, its authority "to make all laws which shall be necessary and proper for carrying into execution" its enumerated powers would appear to provide adequate authority. The existence of such authority might be implied also from the fact that Article III permits, but does not require, establishment of federal courts inferior to the Supreme Court, suggesting that Congress was to be free to make use of state judicial systems in the exercise of its powers under Article I.

[85] Since the rights involved are based upon Acts of Congress, there is no reason to fear that Congress would fail to give adequate protection to those rights. Compare discussion in text *infra*, at notes 86–92. In a few situations, nonetheless, it might be necessary, if the analysis suggested in the text were to be adopted, to infer a congressional intent to impose jurisdiction on the state courts. Under 28 U.S.C. § 1331, a federal district court may not exercise jurisdiction of a case arising under federal law unless the matter in controversy exceeds $10,000. Other statutes dispense with the necessity of this "jurisdictional amount" for most cases arising under federal law, see, *e.g.*, 28 U.S.C. §§ 1336–40, but a residuum of cases remain in which federal courts may not exercise original jurisdiction even though the case arises under a federal statute. See AMERICAN LAW INSTITUTE, STUDY OF THE DIVISION OF JURISDICTION BETWEEN STATE AND FEDERAL COURTS, Tent. Draft No. 3, pp. 94–97 (1965). In such cases, the intent of Congress to create a statutory right without providing a forum being unlikely, an inference that Congress intended state courts to exercise jurisdiction seems warranted.

B. ACTIONS AGAINST STATE OFFICIALS—IMPLICATIONS OF
THE CONSTITUTION

Some support for the view that state courts are under a general
obligation to entertain claims arising under federal law is provided
by several cases in which the Court has reviewed a judgment even
though it rested on a determination that under a nondiscriminatory
state rule the state courts lacked power to hear a federal claim
asserted by the plaintiff. In *General Oil Co. v. Crain*,[86] the state
court, under the compulsion of a statute which, as interpreted, deprived it of jurisdiction over suits against the state or any officer
acting under its authority, declined to hear a suit to enjoin collection of a tax allegedly inconsistent with the Commerce Clause.
The Supreme Court, with only Mr. Justice Harlan dissenting, held
that the state ground of decision was inadequate to preclude review,
apparently on the ground that the state could not constitutionally
refuse to hear the federal claim. The opinion is not, however, explicit about which provision of the Constitution deprived the state
of power to regulate the jurisdiction of its courts. If the obligation
is found in the Supremacy Clause, there would appear to be no
basis for distinction between constitutional and statutory claims;
state courts would be obligated to hear both. In that event, however,
Crain would be inconsistent with *Douglas v. New York, N.H. & H.
R.R.*[87]

Crain may be read, however, as resting upon the fact that the
plaintiff's claim arose under the Constitution. There is a faint suggestion in the opinion that the state's obligation to provide a remedy
derives not from the Supremacy Clause but as an implication from
the constitutional provision conferring the right. "It being then the
right of a party to be protected against a law which violates a
constitutional right . . . it is manifest that a decision which denies
such protection gives effect to the law. . . ."[88] Analytically, there

[86] 209 U.S. 211 (1908).

[87] See text *supra*, at note 80.

[88] 209 U.S. at 228. See also Poindexter v. Greenhow, 114 U.S. 270 (1884). *Cf.*
Lawrence v. State Tax Comm'n, 286 U.S. 276 (1932); Iowa–Des Moines Nat'l
Bank v. Bennett, 284 U.S. 239 (1931). But *cf.* Georgia R.R. & Banking Co. v.
Musgrove, 335 U.S. 900 (1949), in which on facts apparently indistinguishable
from *Crain*, the Court dismissed an appeal from a state court "for the reason
that the judgment of the court below is based upon a non-federal ground adequate to support it."

can be no objection to the implication of a remedy from the provision conferring the right; yet the question remains why the remedy must be available in a state court. A possible answer to this question is that if the states are not obligated to provide a remedy, the exercise by Congress of its power to limit the jurisdiction of federal courts could result in a denial of any remedy for violation of a constitutional right.[89] Such an analysis would provide a plausible basis for distinguishing between the obligation of state courts with respect to statutory and constitutional claims. It would, however, raise the question whether it is appropriate to fashion constitutional obligations of state courts on the remote possibility that Congress may act in a manner destructive of constitutional rights.[90] It is true that under existing legislation there may be some cases in which federal courts may not exercise jurisdiction over claims arising under the Constitution.[91] But the few instances in which Congress has failed to confer jurisdiction need not lead to a conclusion that state courts have a general duty to enforce federal constitutional claims. Exclusion of these cases from the federal courts might reasonably be read as a direction by Congress that state courts must assume jurisdiction over them and provide an appropriate remedy.[92]

---

[89] A related consideration appears to have had some influence on the Court. In an obvious reference to the argument for the state in Ex parte Young, 209 U.S. 123 (1908), which was decided the same day as *Crain*, the Court said: "If a suit against state officers is precluded in the national courts by the Eleventh Amendment to the Constitution, and may be forbidden by a State to its courts, as it is contended in the case at bar that it may be, without power of review by this court, it must be evident that an easy way is open to prevent the enforcement of many provisions of the Constitution. . . ." 209 U.S. at 226. The argument overlooks the fact that *Young* rejected the position that the Eleventh Amendment bars suit in a federal court against a state officer acting under an allegedly unconstitutional authority. Hence, the decision of a state to close the doors of its own courts to such suits would permit evasion of the Constitution only if Congress also excluded them from the jurisdiction of the federal courts.
On the power of Congress to limit the jurisdiction of the federal courts, see Hart, *The Power of Congress To Limit the Jurisdiction of Federal Courts: An Exercise in Dialectic*, 66 HARV. L. REV. 1362, esp. at 1386–1402 (1953).

[90] See discussion in text *infra*, at note 108. But *cf.* Martin v. Hunter's Lessee, 1 Wheat. 304, 339 (1816).

[91] Most, if not all, of the cases arising under the Constitution which are excluded from 28 U.S.C. § 1331 by reason of the "jurisdictional amount" specified therein come within 28 U.S.C. § 1343(3), which contains no requirement of a minimum amount in controversy. See AMERICAN LAW INSTITUTE, *op. cit. supra* note 85, at 95–96.

[92] See note 85 *supra*, and Hart, *supra* note 89, at 1399.

C. THE RIGHT TO BE HEARD AND THE OBLIGATION OF THE STATES
TO PROVIDE A POST-CONVICTION PROCEDURE

A third line of cases, involving the obligation of the states to provide a post-conviction remedy for state prisoners, deserves separate consideration. Last Term in *Case v. Nebraska*,[93] certiorari was granted to consider whether the Fourteenth Amendment requires that states afford state prisoners an adequate corrective process for the hearing and determination of claims of federal constitutional infirmity in the proceedings leading to their conviction. Although the question was avoided in that case, language in previous decisions strongly supports the conclusion that the Fourteenth Amendment does impose such a requirement.[94] The Court has not, however, gone beyond a statement of the obligation to an explanation of the basis upon which it rests. Nor, however frequently it has stated the obligation, has it ever required that the obligation be fulfilled. The consistent practice of the Court, on finding that a state provides no post-conviction remedy, has been to remit prisoners to the federal district court where federal habeas corpus is available.[95] And, although the writ of habeas corpus extends to a prisoner "in custody in violation of the Constitution,"[96] the issue in the federal court has always been viewed as the validity of the prisoner's underlying constitutional claim, not the failure of the state to provide post-conviction process.[97] If the latter were itself a violation of the Fourteenth Amendment, it alone would justify a discharge without the necessity of examining the underlying constitutional claim.[98] There is adequate justification, therefore, for the conclusion of one of our most respected state court judges that the Court's statements in this area ought not to be taken literally.[99]

Nevertheless, the notion that some post-conviction process must be afforded has so frequently been expressed by the Court that

---

[93] 381 U.S. 336 (1965).

[94] See cases collected *id*. at 343 n. 5 (Brennan, J., concurring).

[95] *Id*. at 343.

[96] 28 U.S.C. § 2241(c)(3).

[97] See, *e.g.*, Hawk v. Hann, 103 F. Supp. 138 (D. Neb. 1952), vacated as moot and remanded with directions to dismiss, 205 F.2d 839 (8th Cir. 1953).

[98] *Cf*. Dowd v. Cook, 340 U.S. 206 (1951).

[99] Schaefer, *Federalism and State Criminal Procedure*, 70 HARV. L. REV. 1, 16 (1956).

further consideration seems appropriate. The obligation might be justified on the ground that the states are under a general duty to provide a forum for claims of federal right.[100] The post-conviction cases do not, however, appear to rest on so broad a ground. A general duty to adjudicate federal claims would, presumably, flow from the Supremacy Clause. The obligation with respect to post-conviction process, however, appears to have been raised in the context of the Fourteenth Amendment and more specifically the Due Process Clause.[101] The precise question, therefore, is whether a prisoner incarcerated under a judgment allegedly violative of his federal constitutional rights is denied due process because of the state's failure to accord him a hearing on that claim. If the prisoner has not availed himself of a reasonable opportunity to assert those rights in the proceedings leading to his conviction, it seems clear that the state's refusal to afford post-conviction relief does not deny due process. A consistent line of decisions establishes that a state court's determination that a federal claimant has chosen an inappropriate remedy under state procedure—in this situation post-conviction relief rather than assertion at trial—is adequate to sustain a judgment of dismissal.[102]

A more troublesome issue is whether the state must provide post-conviction relief when the prisoner has not had a reasonable opportunity to assert his federal rights in the proceedings leading to his conviction. That issue, on analysis, is an aspect of a broader question: whether a state court must provide an appropriate remedy when, prior to the suit, it has acted against an individual—by judicial proceedings or otherwise—in a manner violative of his federal rights without affording an opportunity for their assertion. An affirmative answer to that question is suggested by the Court's decision in *Ward v. Love County*.[103] In that case the county had coerced the payment of certain taxes from which the taxpayers were constitutionally exempt. The state supreme court denied recovery on the ground that it had no authority under state law to require the county to repay the taxes when a portion of the taxes had already been paid

---

[100] See discussion in text *supra*, at notes 69–92.

[101] See Case v. Nebraska, note 93 *supra*, at 338; Taylor v. Alabama, 335 U.S. 252, 272 (1948) (concurring opinion).

[102] See Comment, 61 Colum. L. Rev. 255, 261 (1961).

[103] 253 U.S. 17 (1920).

over by the county to other governmental units. The Supreme Court reversed, invoking the Fourteenth Amendment:[104]

> To say that the county could collect these unlawful taxes by coercive means and not incur any obligation to pay them back is nothing short of saying that it could take or appropriate the property of these Indian allottees arbitrarily and without due process of law. Of course this would be in contravention of the Fourteenth Amendment, which binds the county as an agency of the state.

A state prisoner asserting that he is imprisoned in violation of his constitutional rights, under circumstances in which the proceedings leading to his conviction did not afford an opportunity to present that claim, is in an analogous position to that of the taxpayer in *Ward v. Love County*. In the one case the state has deprived a person of his liberty, in the other of his property, without affording him an opportunity to be heard in defense against its action.

There are at least two major difficulties with this argument. First, it proves too much. The "right to be heard" protected by the Fourteenth Amendment is not limited to federal defenses.[105] Thus, in *Ward v. Love County* the Court's conclusion that the state's refusal of a remedy violated due process did not rest upon the fact that the taxpayer's defense to the collection of the tax was based upon federal law. The Supreme Court assuredly has not, however, suggested that a state must afford post-conviction procedures permitting assertion of a violation of a prisoner's rights under state law.

Second, to derive a duty to provide post-conviction procedures from the right to be heard is merely question-begging. The premise that a prisoner has a "right to be heard" is merely another way of saying that the state is under an obligation to provide a post-conviction procedure. The "right" and the "duty," in other words, are correlative. The question presented by the post-conviction cases is whether that "right-duty" exists.

The notion that the prisoner has a right to be heard in a state

---

104 *Id.* at 24.

105 See, *e.g.*, Central of Georgia Ry. v. Wright, 207 U.S. 127 (1907), which held that a state may not, consistently with due process, assess a tax without affording the taxpayer an opportunity to assert that he is not subject to it, a proposition which was reaffirmed in Brinkerhoff–Faris Trust & Sav. Co. v. Hill, 281 U.S. 673 (1930). Neither case, however, is concerned with the question whether the state must provide a forum in which the taxpayer may assert and obtain a remedy for that violation of due process. See *id.* at 678–79.

court on his federal claim is derived from a quite different type of case. If, in a criminal trial, the defendant is denied the opportunity to present a defense, the denial of due process is clear.[106] Reversal of a conviction by the Supreme Court would be warranted because the Supremacy Clause requires that when a state undertakes to adjudicate a controversy it must do so in accordance with applicable federal law.[107] In the post-conviction cases, by contrast, the state has not undertaken to adjudicate the controversy.

There is no more compelling reason for imposing on the states an obligation to provide post-conviction process than there is for requiring them to adjudicate any other type of federal claim. The federal interest in the vindication of Fourteenth Amendment rights is adequately protected by the availability of federal habeas corpus. Congressional power to limit the availability of that remedy, a matter which itself raises unresolved constitutional questions,[108] is surely too slender a reed to support an argument that a state duty to provide post-conviction relief is necessarily to be implied from the constitutional provisions establishing rights against the state. Determination of the effect of a.limitation of the jurisdiction of federal courts upon the obligation of the states to provide a post-conviction remedy must await the event.

In these circumstances, the primary interest served by the provision of adequate corrective processes by the states is not the federal interest of assuring compliance with the Constitution but the state interest in retaining control of the administration of criminal justice.[109] Whether for that reason or, more laudably, simply to guard against the possible violation of fundamental rights, there

[106] *Cf.* Hovey v. Elliott, 167 U.S. 409, 417–18 (1897).

[107] Hart, *supra* note 83, at 507.

[108] See Oaks, *The "Original" Writ of Habeas Corpus in the Supreme Court*, 1962 SUPREME COURT REVIEW 153, 155–56; Hart, *supra* note 89, at 1397–98. Section 14 of the First Judiciary Act, 1 Stat. 81–82 (1789), expressly provided that the writ should not extend "to prisoners in gaol, unless they are in custody, under or by color of the authority of the United States or are committed for trial before some court of the same, or are necessary to be brought into court to testify," but the validity of that restriction seems never to have been determined.

[109] Under the principles laid down in Townsend v. Sain, 372 U.S. 293 (1963), a hearing need not be held on a habeas corpus petition if the state has provided adequate corrective process; hence, federal intervention in the administration of criminal justice by the state can be minimized if the state provides its own remedy. On the question when the state corrective process is adequate to obviate the necessity of a hearing in the federal court, see Note, 39 N.Y.U.L. REV. 78, 104–28 (1964).

is more than sufficient reason for the states to adopt adequate post-conviction remedies.[110] But it is difficult to find in the Due Process Clause any basis for compelling them to do so.[111]

In none of the situations that have reached the Court, therefore, was it necessary, in order to protect the federal interest in the vindication of federal rights, to construe the Constitution as imposing a self-executing obligation upon the state courts to hear claims arising under federal law. There may, of course, be other federal interests served by the state courts' assumption of jurisdiction over federal claims. In both *Henry*[112] and *Case*,[113] for example, Mr. Justice Brennan pointed to a reduction of tensions between state and federal judiciaries as a likely consequence of state court determination of issues that might be raised in a federal habeas corpus proceeding. To a lesser extent, that might be true whenever it became necessary to determine the constitutionality of state action. Initial decision of the issue by state courts represents an increase in state power, partly because some cases will never go beyond the state courts and partly because, even for those that do, the state courts will often be able significantly to shape the litigation. Beyond mere concern with ameliorating the possible sensitivity of state officials to federal intervention in the affairs of the state,[114] the exercise of jurisdiction by state courts allows them to play an important role in the task of integrating state and federal law, perhaps thereby hastening the

---

[110] See Meador, *Accommodating State Criminal Procedure and Federal Post-conviction Review*, 50 A.B.A.J. 928 (1964); Brennan, *Some Aspects of Federalism*, 39 N.Y.U.L. REV. 945, 957–59 (1964).

[111] In *Case*, petitioner's counsel urged the burden which federal habeas imposes upon the district courts and the friction which the exercise of that jurisdiction creates as grounds for imposing the obligation of providing a post-conviction remedy on the states. 381 U.S. at 344. The argument is, however, based on the assumption that the states are constitutionally required to provide corrective process and that the only question before the Court is whether it will enforce that obligation or continue to rely solely on federal habeas corpus. Brief for the Petitioner, pp. 30–38. If that premise falls, as suggested previously, the argument falls with it since it can hardly serve as independent basis for imposing the duty on the states.

[112] 379 U.S. at 452–53.   [113] 381 U.S. at 344–47.

[114] The attempt to formulate doctrine on the basis of a supposed reaction of state officials to federal intervention is hazardous at best. As Professor Amsterdam has recently suggested, it is at least plausible that federal intervention after a state court determination is more of an irritant to state judges than intervention at an earlier stage before state courts become deeply involved in the proceedings. See Amsterdam, *supra* note 13, at 835–36.

acceptance of federal law.[115] But the ability of the Court to contribute to a reduction of the friction resulting from the state's irritation over federal intervention in its affairs is limited to affording the state an opportunity to exercise jurisdiction over federal claims.[116] It can hardly achieve that goal by commanding the state to assume jurisdiction.[117]

D. INADEQUACY OTHER THAN CONSTITUTIONAL

Since the Supreme Court may not itself try the underlying federal claim, it normally will be required to choose between two positions when asked to review a judgment resting upon a state court's refusal to adjudicate. The refusal may be held unconstitutional, thereby imposing an obligation on the state court to try the case on remand, or the Court may hold the refusal permissible, thereby denying its own jurisdiction. Occasionally, however, a case may arise in which the Court is not limited to these alternatives. Such cases raise the question whether the state court's refusal to adjudicate may be inadequate to preclude review even though the refusal is not constitutionally infirm. Analysis of the constitutional obligation of state courts to afford a forum and a remedy for federal claims demonstrates that the traditional justification for a determination of inadequacy, the need to assure that rulings on state law do not interfere unduly with the vindication of federal rights, is not a factor in these cases. Other justifications for asserting jurisdiction may exist, however.

In *Liner v. Jafco, Inc.*,[118] a state trial court, rejecting a defense of federal preemption, enjoined peaceful picketing at a construction site. The state supreme court affirmed on the dual grounds that the preemption defense had been properly rejected and that the cause had become moot by reason of the completion of construction pend-

[115] *Id.* at 830–31.

[116] See, *e.g.*, Claflin v. Houseman, 93 U.S. 130 (1876); Ex parte Royall, 117 U.S. 241 (1886).

[117] Situations may be imagined in which the refusal of a state court to adjudicate a federal claim poses special problems, as where the state's refusal is announced for the first time in a case that would be time-barred if a new proceeding in a federal court were to be required. *Cf.* Herb v. Pitcairn, 324 U.S. 117 (1945). Solution of such problems is not likely to be beyond the Court's ingenuity. See Burnett v. New York Cent. R.R., 380 U.S. 424 (1965).

[118] 375 U.S. 301 (1964).

ing appeal. Without intimating that the latter, non-federal ground of decision was unconstitutional, the Supreme Court nonetheless held that it was inadequate to preclude review.[119] The issues were not moot, in the Court's view, because the defendant's right to recover on an injunction bond that had been required depended upon whether the injunction was wrongfully issued, a question that turned solely on federal law.

The justification for the Court's re-examination of what was plainly a matter of state law—the power of a state appellate court to consider an appeal it deemed moot—is far from clear. An analysis of the decision suggests that the Court's assumption of jurisdiction can be justified only by its desire to render an "advisory opinion" on the power of state courts to issue an injunction under the circumstances of the case. Acceptance of the state court's resolution of the mootness question would in no way have interfered with the vindication of the defendant's federal rights. As the case reached the Court, defendants had not yet attempted to recover on the bond. If at some later date they were to make such an attempt, the federal issue would still have been open for determination by the Court.[120]

The only purpose served by the Court's decision on the merits, therefore, was a clarification of federal law, partly for the potential benefit of the defendants at some later time, but more importantly for the education of state courts in connection with future and unrelated litigation. There is much in the Court's opinion, indeed, to indicate that the latter purpose was salient in its decision to treat the state ground as inadequate.[121] The only practical consequence

---

[119] See also Love v. Griffith, 266 U.S. 32 (1924), affirming a state court determination of mootness, but asserting the Court's power to treat such a determination as inadequate. But cf. Cramp v. Board of Public Instruction, 368 U.S. 278, 281 (1961).

[120] The Court's contrary assertion, that if the state court's determination of the federal "question may not be challenged here, the petitioners have no recourse against Jafco on the bond," 375 U.S. at 306, is plainly incorrect. If the federal issue were open in a subsequent state court proceeding on the bond, the Court's jurisdiction would be clear. Even if the state court were to treat the propriety of the injunction as foreclosed in a later proceeding, however, the power of the Court to consider the question at that time is well settled. See, e.g., New York Central R.R. v. New York and Pennsylvania Co., 271 U.S. 124 (1926).

[121] "It would encourage such interference with the federal agency's exclusive jurisdiction if a state court's holding of mootness based on the chance event of completion of construction barred this Court's review of the state court's adverse decision on the claim of federal preemption." 375 U.S. at 307.

of an explicit admission by the Court that its decision to review rested on that ground would have been the entry of a more appropriate order. Reversal and remand for further proceedings not inconsistent with the opinion, the order actually handed down by the Court, seems inappropriate in view of the fact that there appears to have been nothing in the Court's opinion that would require the state court to modify its original judgment. Accordingly, the state court's judgment might more appropriately have been left undisturbed.

V. ADJUDICATIONS INCONSISTENT WITH FEDERAL RIGHTS

In the situations considered thus far, discharge of the Court's responsibility for the protection of federal rights does not require a re-examination of non-federal grounds upon which the judgment may have rested: rights conferred by federal law are either protected by the judgment or, if the state has declined to adjudicate the controversy in which the federal claim is asserted, a federal forum for the assertion of those rights is available. But when a state court has undertaken to adjudicate a controversy and, though resting on a non-federal ground, has entered a judgment allegedly inconsistent with federal law, a re-examination of the non-federal ground by the Supreme Court is inescapable. "To hold otherwise," as Mr. Justice Holmes once wrote, "would open an easy method of avoiding the jurisdiction of [the] court."[122]

The Court's power to re-examine state grounds supporting a judgment allegedly inconsistent with federal law serves the additional purpose of permitting it to exercise final authority for the accommodation of interests required in the integration of state and federal law. State and federal law are complexly interrelated: federal law may protect legal relationships created by the state,[123] or confer immunity from state law,[124] or otherwise regulate the exer-

---

[122] Terre Haute & I. R.R. v. Indianapolis ex rel. Ketcham, 194 U.S. 579, 589 (1904).

[123] See, *e.g.*, Indiana ex rel. Anderson v. Brand, 303 U.S. 95 (1938) (Contract Clause protects obligation defined by state law); Fox River Paper Co. v. Railroad Comm'n, 274 U.S. 651 (1927) (Fourteenth Amendment protects property as defined by state law).

[124] See, *e.g.*, Ward v. Love County, 253 U.S. 17 (1920) (federal statute confers immunity from state taxation).

cise of state power.[125] State law may be urged in avoidance of a
federal claim,[126] and adherence to state procedure may have an
effect upon the substance of federal law.[127] The resting of a judgment upon a state ground, in the face of a claim that the effect of
the judgment is to deny rights conferred by federal law, necessarily
involves some accommodation of state and federal interests.[128]
Nevertheless, a re-examination of the state ground does not, as one
commentator has suggested, make of the Court merely "one more
court of appeals weighing factors of decision already judicially
considered."[129] The Court's power to declare the state ground inadequate exploits the institutional differences between it and the
state courts to assure that in the accommodation of state and federal
interests appropriate recognition will be given to the latter. In view
of the fundamental values embodied in the constitutional limitations
on state power, with which we are primarily concerned at this
point, and the deliberate decision in the constitutional convention to
accord supremacy to federal law, that power seems amply justified.

Criteria for determining adequacy must, therefore, serve two
purposes. First, they must assure that the Court will be able to exercise jurisdiction in at least a high proportion of those cases in
which a state ground is put forth with the intent to avoid a claim
of federal right. Second, they must strike an appropriate balance
between state and federal interests.

Recognition of the first purpose has led to the recurrent suggestion that a determination of adequacy involves an inquiry into the
question whether the non-federal ground was put forth with the
intent of evading the federal claim.[130] At the outset, it seems plain

---

[125] See generally, Hart, *supra* note 83, at 515–25.

[126] See, *e.g.*, Enterprise Irr. Dist. v. Farmers Mut. Canal Co., 243 U.S. 157 (1917)
(estoppel to assert denial of due process); Ward v. Love County, 253 U.S. 17
(1920) (voluntary payment claimed to avoid federal immunity from state taxation).

[127] See, *e.g.*, American Ry. Exp. Co. v. Levee, 263 U.S. 19 (1923) (burden of
proof).

[128] In *Henry*, for example, the decision of the state court to rest affirmance of
the conviction on the failure of Henry's counsel to interpose a timely objection
necessarily involved a determination that compliance with state procedure was
paramount to protection of a criminal defendant from the possibility of conviction upon unlawfully seized evidence.

[129] Note, *supra* note 10, at 1393.

[130] See, *e.g.*, ROBERTSON & KIRKHAM, *op. cit. supra* note 9, at § 96, and cases
cited therein.

that a determination of inadequacy is not dependent upon an affirmative conclusion to such an inquiry. Inadequacy has been found not only in its absence[131] but in cases in which the circumstances do not suggest intentional evasion.[132] A contrary doctrine would unduly limit the Court's power to protect claims of federal right by insulating from review state decisions resting on non-federal grounds which unjustifiably burden the assertion of such claims.[133] Moreover, the inevitable reluctance of the Court to find, except in the most extreme cases, that state judges had in effect violated their oaths of office[134] would result in an almost total insulation of state grounds from review.

There are equally persuasive objections to treating a finding of intent to deprive a litigant of his federal rights as one of the tests for adequacy.[135] Inquiry into the intent of a state court is sufficiently hazardous and the likely results of such doubtful utility that it ought not to be undertaken. The difficulties are amply demonstrated by *Henry*. Petitioner's counsel urged[136] that the change in the state decision was influenced by a statement in the Brief in Support of the Suggestion of Error of the affiliation of petitioner and his counsel with the NAACP.[137] In view of the apparent mistake of fact underlying the state court's first opinion, that inference is hardly compelling; yet, if the issue before the Court were the factual one whether the state court had the impermissible intent, the inference is surely not so unreasonable that it could have been rejected out of hand. If an inquiry into the "intent" of the state court is to be

---

131 See, *e.g.,* Lawrence v. State Tax Comm'n, 286 U.S. 276 (1932); American Ry. Exp. Co. v. Levee, 263 U.S. 19 (1923).

132 See, *e.g.,* Shuttlesworth v. Birmingham, 376 U.S. 339 (1964), discussed in text *infra,* at notes 199–204.

133 See discussion in text *infra,* at notes 166–78, 198–211.

134 U.S. CONST., art. VI.

135 Mr. Justice Clark, dissenting in Williams v. Georgia, 349 U.S. 375, 399 (1955), suggested the following formulation: "A purported state ground is not independent and adequate in two instances. *First,* where the circumstances give rise to an inference that the state court is guilty of an evasion—an interpretation of state law with the specific intent to deprive a litigant of a federal right. *Second,* where the state law, honestly applied though it may be, and even dictated by the precedents, throws such obstacles in the way of enforcement of federal rights that it must be struck down as unreasonably interfering with the vindication of such rights."

136 See Petition for Certiorari, p. 22; Brief for Petitioner, p. 36.

137 See note 21 *supra.*

undertaken, what weight is to be given the intimation that, in writing its first opinion, it may already have been aware of petitioner's participation in the civil rights movement?[138] Or, on the other hand, what weight is to be given to the fact that the second opinion substantially narrowed the state court's interpretation of a prior case defining the circumstances under which an appeal would be permitted notwithstanding failure to make timely objection?[139] In short, a determination of the intent with which the state ground of decision was put forward cannot be made on the basis of the materials normally available to the Court.[140]

The notion that the adequacy *vel non* of a state ground requires a determination in each case of the intent with which it has been put forth is, therefore, only a fiction, and not a particularly useful one.[141] A more appropriate inquiry would focus upon the establishment of workable criteria—applicable without reference to the unascertainable intent in particular cases—for distinguishing nonfederal grounds that ought to preclude Supreme Court review of federal questions from those that should not. The difficulty of establishing intent in a particular case does not, of course, require that in formulating criteria the Court ought to ignore the possibility of intentional evasion of federal rights by state court judges. Jurisdiction to review state court judgments has, from the very beginning, been justified in part upon the basis that it was necessary to protect against the potential hostility of state judges to federal rights.[142] More recent history does not inspire confidence that such concern is no longer necessary. The criteria, however, ought to be stated in terms susceptible of objective measurement.

A. CONSISTENCY WITH EARLIER DECISIONS

The Court traditionally has placed substantial weight on whether the non-federal ground put forth by the state court is consistent

---

[138] See note 19 *supra*.

[139] See text *supra*, at notes 19–22.

[140] The only exceptions are the extremely rare situations in which state law in terms discriminates against federal rights. See, *e.g.*, McKnett v. St. Louis & S.F. Ry., 292 U.S. 230 (1934); Mondou v. New York, N.H. & H. R.R., 223 U.S. 1 (1912).

[141] Few doctrines would be more destructive of harmonious relationships between federal and state judiciaries than one which requires the Supreme Court to inquire into the good faith of state judges.

[142] See, *e.g.*, Martin v. Hunter's Lessee, 1 Wheat. 304, 346–47 (1816).

with its earlier decisions.[143] A test of consistency serves several purposes, depending somewhat on the context in which it is employed. Initially, however, it serves generally as a fairly reliable discriminator. When a state ground of decision is supported by a history of consistent application, even in cases that do not involve a federal claim, it is not likely to have been used by the state court simply as a device to defeat the Court's jurisdiction. The converse, of course, is not necessarily true. A non-federal ground departing from previous state authority may have been put forth for wholly innocent purposes. Nevertheless, the risk that it was put forward for an illicit purpose is sufficiently substantial that the Court may be justified in treating it as inadequate.

The danger, of course, is that the Court will unwarrantedly interfere with the power of the state court to formulate state law. But that danger is not great in view of the minimal interference with state interests resulting from the determination of inadequacy. If the determination rests solely upon inconsistency with earlier state decisions, the state will be able to apply its new rule to future litigation. The effect of the determination, therefore, is limited to the case at hand and though that may be a matter of some moment to the state, its primary interest, control over the ongoing definition of state law, is respected.

In most situations, moreover, inconsistency with earlier decisions will be significant for reasons other than as an indicator that the state court has attempted to defeat a federal right by evasion of the Court's jurisdiction. For example, when federal law protects interests created by state law, the non-federal issue concerns the content of state law at a time prior to the litigation.[144] A state court's redefinition of the state right may effectively frustrate that protection, whether or not it was put forward in an attempt to evade the Court's jurisdiction. Other considerations support a determination of inadequacy when the state ground represents a departure from previously settled rules of procedure. In such cases, the effect of the new procedural ruling may be to deny any opportunity for the

---

[143] *Compare* Barr v. City of Columbia, 378 U.S. 146 (1964), *with* Wolfe v. North Carolina, 364 U.S. 177 (1960), *and* Indiana ex rel. Anderson v. Brand, 303 U.S. 95 (1938), *with* Fox River Paper Co. v. Railroad Comm'n, 274 U.S. 651 (1927). See generally, Note, *supra* note 10 at 1385; Comment, *supra* note 102, at 264–72.

[144] See HART & WECHSLER, *op. cit. supra* note 71, at 466.

assertion of federal rights.[145] In either event due regard for federal rights requires that the Court review the state judgment undeterred by the fact that it rests upon a non-federal ground.

Departures from previous authority do not, typically, involve an explicit overruling of earlier decisions. The state court or counsel for the prevailing party may be able to present a plausible argument for reconciling the non-federal ground of decision and earlier decisions allegedly inconsistent with it. In such cases, the Court must determine how much deference is to be given the state court. The answer, it seems, ought to depend upon the context in which the problem is presented. Opinions in cases involving federal protection of rights created by state law have, at least verbally, manifested substantial deference. Where the state ground concerns the existence of a contract obligation, for example, the Court has said that it accords "respectful consideration and great weight to the views of the State's highest court"[146] or, even more deferentially, that it leans "toward agreement with the courts of the state, and accept[s] their judgment as to such matters unless manifestly wrong."[147] The effect of such deference is to allow the state court considerable leeway: its determination with respect to the existence and meaning of the contract will stand if it can plausibly be reconciled with previous authority. Since, in this area, federal law attempts only to protect a justified reliance on rights conferred by the state, the allowance of that leeway is appropriate. Unless the earlier state law relied upon by the federal claimant has crystallized to the point that it must be overruled or can be distinguished only on tenuous

---

[145] The Court has held on at least one occasion that such a ruling constitutes a denial of due process. Brinkerhoff–Faris Trust & Sav. Co. v. Hill, 281 U.S. 673 (1930). See also Bouie v. City of Columbia, 378 U.S. 347, 354–55 (1964). More frequently, however, it has merely declared the procedural ruling inadequate to preclude its review. See, e.g., Barr v. City of Columbia, 378 U.S. 146 (1964); N.A.A.C.P. v. Alabama ex rel. Flowers, 377 U.S. 288 (1964); Wright v. Georgia, 373 U.S. 284 (1963); N.A.A.C.P. v. Alabama ex rel. Patterson, 357 U.S. 449 (1958); Staub v. City of Baxley, 355 U.S. 313 (1958).

More than a technical distinction is involved. If the application of a new procedural rule that forecloses a claim is treated as a denial of due process, rights under state law are protected equally with federal rights.

[146] Indiana ex rel. Anderson v. Brand, 303 U.S. 95, 100 (1938).

[147] Hale v. State Board, 302 U.S. 95, 101 (1937). Deference has also been expressed with respect to the question whether state law recognizes a property interest for which Fourteenth Amendment protection is sought. See, e.g., Broad River Power Co. v. South Carolina ex rel. Daniel, 281 U.S. 537, 540 (1930) (state court's determination must be upheld if it rests on "a fair or substantial basis").

grounds, the normal leeways in our legal system are such that reliance on it is not justified.[148]

A similar degree of deference will normally be inappropriate when the state ground of decision involves an arguable departure from previously established procedural rules. *N.A.A.C.P. v. Alabama ex rel. Patterson*[149] teaches that a novel state procedural rule that bars consideration of a federal claim ought not to be treated as adequate merely because it can be reconciled with previous state authority. In that case the state court refused to review a contempt conviction on the ground that the wrong appellate procedure had been employed. Language in earlier state opinions indicated that the procedure used was permissible, but the state urged that those cases were distinguishable. The state ground was nonetheless held inadequate because, even if in retrospect there appeared to be a consistent pattern of procedure to obtain appellate review, "petitioner could not fairly be deemed to have been apprised of its existence."[150]

N.A.A.C.P. v. Alabama ex rel. Patterson may be read narrowly to mean that a local procedural rule barring assertion of a federal claim will be held inadequate only if it appears that the federal claimant may have been affirmatively misled by prior decisions[151] or it may be read more broadly as requiring a determination of inadequacy whenever the state has failed to provide notice of the requirement. The former reading is suggested by an earlier decision, *Brinkerhoff–Faris Trust & Sav. Co. v. Hill*,[152] in which the Court said that where procedure was prescribed by an uninterpreted statute a federal claimant would have "to assume the risk that the ultimate interpretation by the [state's] highest court might differ from its own."[153] Nevertheless, if the Court determines that a federal claimant has reasonably interpreted earlier state law, the differ-

---

[148] In Adam v. Saenger, 303 U.S. 59, 64 (1938), involving the obligation of a state under the Full Faith and Credit Clause to enforce a judgment rendered by another state, the Court suggested that it re-examines "with deference" the non-federal ground of the effect which the latter state would accord the judgment. On that issue, however, the basis for a display of deference is far from clear. The Court is after all, as competent as the state court to ascertain the law of another state. See HART & WECHSLER, *op. cit. supra* note 71, at 469–70.

[149] 357 U.S. 449 (1958).

[150] *Id.* at 457.

[151] Thus, immediately following the statement quoted in the text, the Court referred to petitioner's "justified reliance on prior decisions. . . ." *Ibid.*

[152] 281 U.S. 673 (1930).   [153] *Id.* at 682 n. 9.

ing interpretation by the state court should not preclude review even though it also is reasonable. Due recognition of the supremacy of federal law would seem to require at least that a reasonable opportunity for its assertion be made available. When the state refuses to hear the federal claim because of a procedural rule of which it did not afford adequate notice, that opportunity has not been provided.[154]

These considerations are relevant, however, only when the state procedural rule is of a character to induce reliance on the part of the litigants. Not all procedural rules are of that character and more deference to the state court's attempt to reconcile its decision with previous authority may be appropriate where the procedural rule involved is not one on which the federal claimant may reasonably be deemed to have relied. The state supreme court's first opinion in *Henry*, it will be recalled, indicated that when fundamental rights were involved, state law recognized an exception to the rule that errors to which timely objection had not been made were foreclosed on appeal.[155] In its second opinion, however, the earlier decision which had established the rule was interpreted as resting upon the incompetence of trial counsel, a factor not present in *Henry*.[156] An examination of the earlier decision indicates that either reading is permissible.[157] Since Henry's counsel were not likely to have re-

---

[154] In *Brinkerhoff–Faris*, the Court was concerned with due process, not simply the adequacy of a state ground to preclude its own review of a federal question. Since a decision on due process grounds would protect state rights adversely affected by the state procedure as well as federal rights, see note 145 *supra*, a test more restrictive than that suggested in the text may well have been appropriate.

[155] See text *supra*, at note 20.   [156] See text *supra*; at notes 20–21.

[157] See Brooks v. State, 209 Miss. 150 (1950). In two previous cases cited in Mr. Justice Black's concurring opinion, Carter v. State, 198 Miss. 523 (1945), and Fisher v. State, 145 Miss. 116 (1926), the Mississippi Supreme Court reversed for error that had not been appropriately challenged at trial without any suggestion of the incompetence of trial counsel. These cases, however, are distinguishable from *Henry* in that the errors involved, the capacity of the defendant to stand trial and the admissibility of a coerced confession, were relevant to the integrity of the trial process, a claim which cannot be made concerning the alleged error in *Henry*. See discussion in text *infra*, at notes 205–07. Although the state court did not mention these decisions in its second *Henry* opinion, the ground upon which they can be distinguished is sufficiently close to the ground on which the *Brooks* decision was distinguished that it would be difficult to argue that the refusal to hear Henry's objection on appeal was inadequate simply on the basis of inconsistency with earlier decisions. At most, the earlier cases indicated, as Mr. Justice Black argued, that the state court had discretion to consider errors not appropriately raised at trial. See discussion in text *infra*, at notes 158–62.

lied on the exception and since the basis for the distinction is more than adequate to preclude suggestion of an inconsistency indicative of hostility to federal rights, it would seem that *Henry* was not an appropriate case for finding inadequacy simply on the basis of inconsistency with earlier decisions.

The earlier decision did, however, establish that the state supreme court had power to consider objections not timely raised at trial. Accordingly, refusal to consider Henry's constitutional claim may, as Mr. Justice Black contended, be viewed as involving the exercise of discretion. The adequacy of a discretionary determination to refuse consideration of a federal claim to prevent the exercise of jurisdiction by the Supreme Court has occasioned some confusion in the past. Earlier decisions may be read as holding that such a determination is adequate if it is consistent with the exercise of discretion in other cases.[158] In that event, the fact that the state court has discretion adds nothing to the analysis, since consistency with previous cases is a relevant test of adequacy even if the state court purported not to have discretion. Some support may be found, however, for the broader proposition that the very existence of discretion in the state court requires a determination of inadequacy.[159] Since state courts commonly exercise discretionary authority to waive procedural irregularities in the interest of justice, the existence of such authority, under the latter approach, would be of substantial significance. A conclusion that the state court's power to waive procedural irregularity permits the Court to assume jurisdiction, even though the state court has not exercised the power, might be supported on several grounds. Initially, the existence of the power suggests that no vital state interest is at stake. If some deviations from regular procedure can be tolerated, a few more can hardly be seriously disruptive. Moreover, it might be thought inappropriate for the state court to pick and choose among federal rights, deciding that only some were sufficiently important that a failure to raise them properly under state procedure ought to be excused. Finally, even if some such discrimination among federal rights is deemed appropriate, the power ought to rest in the Supreme

---

[158] See Wolfe v. North Carolina, 364 U.S. 177, 191 (1960).

[159] See Shuttlesworth v. City of Birmingham, 376 U.S. 339 (1964); Williams v. Georgia, 349 U.S. 375, 388–89 (1955). *Williams* may be read more narrowly as requiring a determination of inconsistency with earlier cases. See 349 U.S. at 383.

Court as the judicial body ultimately responsible for the accommodation of state and federal law.

Assessment of these arguments requires a closer examination of the discretion exercised by state courts. Discretion, the power to choose among alternatives, may be either what Professors Hart and Sacks have termed "a power of reasoned elaboration" or "a power of continuing discretion."[160] The latter connotes *"ad hocness"*— a power to decide one way on one occasion and differently on another without obligation for explanation. Not surprisingly, in view of the general postulates of our judicial system, neither *Henry* nor any of the other cases that have reached the Court is of this type.[161] Each involved discretion in the former sense. In that sense, however, discretion is nothing more than the judicial formulation of law. The latitude of choice, the recognition of an obligation for reasonable consistency and of the obligation to explain the decision, including the reason for according different treatment to the instant case and those previously decided, is the same whether the state court casts its decision in terms of discretion or in terms of a limitation on its power. Insofar as discretion involves "a power of reasoned elaboration," the conclusion of a state court that it lacks power to waive noncompliance with procedural rules, except under specified circumstances, is for present purposes the equivalent of a statement that it will exercise a discretionary power to waive noncompliance only under those circumstances.[162] Neither the intensity of the state's interest, the propriety of discrimination among federal rights, nor the Supreme Court's ultimate authority for accommodating state and federal law is affected by the formulation adopted by the state court to express what it has done.

---

160 HART & SACKS, THE LEGAL PROCESS: BASIC PROBLEMS IN THE MAKING AND APPLICATION OF LAW 161, 168–79 (tentative ed. 1958).

161 But *cf.* Brown v. Allen, 344 U.S. 443, 533, 556–59 (1953) (dissenting opinions). Mr. Justice Black's statement in *Henry*, that he would not allow petitioner's constitutional rights to "be cut off irrevocably by state-court discretionary rulings which might be different in particular undefined circumstances in other cases," 379 U.S. at 457, suggests that he perhaps viewed *Henry* as a case involving a "power of continuing discretion." That view is difficult to reconcile with the state court's reasoned distinction between *Henry* and its earlier cases.

162 Nor does it seem relevant that limitations on the state court's power are defined by legislation rather than self-imposed. Whether a state acts by its legislature, its executive, or its judiciary, is generally a matter of indifference under federal law. See, *e.g.*, Dreyer v. Illinois, 187 U.S. 71 (1902).

B. THE ACCOMMODATION OF STATE AND FEDERAL LAW

Although consistency with previous decision has been an important determinant of adequacy, there is no doubt that an inquiry into consistency does not describe the reach of the Court's power to re-examine state grounds put forth in support of a judgment that fails to recognize a claimed federal right. In part, the exercise of a broader power is necessary to guard against the possible hostility of state courts to federal rights. A federal right may be avoided by state grounds that lack a foundation in the record as well as by those that depart from earlier law. The Court has, in consequence, consistently asserted its power to review the factual basis for the state ground.[163]

When the state ground is unrelated to the asserted federal right,[164] a determination that it accords with previous state authority and that it is supported by the record should be sufficient to establish its adequacy. In such a case, the only justification for re-examination of the state ground is to guard against the possibility that it was put forward merely to defeat the federal right. A similar restriction on the Court's inquiry is appropriate when the state ground concerns the existence of a state right for which federal protection is claimed. Consistency with previous state authority and a foundation in the record are sufficient to safeguard against the potential hostility of state courts to federal rights and to protect the reliance with which federal guarantees are concerned.[165]

When, on the other hand, state law purports to regulate the circumstances under which federal rights may be established—either by recognition of defenses based upon pre-litigation conduct or by procedural doctrines—a determination of adequacy requires a more searching inquiry by the Court. In such cases, the Court's concerns are not limited to the potential hostility of state courts to federal rights or to the effect which a frustrated reliance on state

---

[163] See, *e.g.*, Ancient Egyptian Order v. Michaux, 279 U.S. 737 (1929); Creswill v. Knights of Pythias, 225 U.S. 246 (1912).

[164] See, *e.g.*, Leathe v. Thomas, 207 U.S. 93 (1907) (state court's allowance of set-off adequate to preclude review of claim that full faith and credit had not been given to judgment on which suit was based); Chapman v. Goodnow, 123 U.S. 540 (1887) (state court's judgment allegedly inconsistent with earlier decree of Supreme Court adequately supported by finding of liability distinct from that involved in original proceeding before Supreme Court).

[165] See text *supra*, at notes 143–48.

law may have on the vindication of federal rights. It must assure also that state law, though evenly applied, does not unduly burden federal rights.[166]

As an original proposition, it might be argued that defenses to a federal right or the avoidance of a federal defense raise questions of federal law. The Court has not followed that path. Numerous decisions sustain as an adequate non-federal ground a determination that under state law the pre-litigation conduct of the federal claimant resulted in a loss of his federal rights.[167] Yet, the Court has not hesitated to declare such grounds inadequate, not only for inconsistency with earlier state law or insufficient support in the record, but because they cut too deeply into rights conferred by federal law.[168] A similar power has been asserted by the Court in connection with state procedural doctrines. When a state rule, though denominated procedural, narrows the protection afforded by federal law—as, for example, by placing the burden of proof on the federal claimant[169]—justification for displacement of the state rule is precisely the same as in the cases holding a state substantive ground inadequate. In all such cases, it seems fair to conclude, the accommodation of state and federal law is dictated by the Supremacy Clause. The state ground is not independent of the federal right; the policy it expresses is in conflict with federal policy and, therefore, may not be given effect.

The Supremacy Clause provides a less certain answer with respect to the adequacy of state grounds that do not purport to limit the rights conferred by federal law, but merely to establish the manner in which they are to be presented to and determined by the state court. A variety of factors support federal respect for procedural rules of this type. Generally, they do not express a policy at variance with the substance of the claimed federal right[170] and, if they are evenly applied, there is no need for concern about hos-

---

166 See note 135 *supra*.

167 See, *e.g.*, Utley v. St. Petersburg, 292 U.S. 106, 111–12 (1934) (laches); Enterprise Irr. Dist. v. Farmers Mut. Canal Co., 243 U.S. 157 (1917) (estoppel).

168 See, *e.g.*, MacGregor v. Westinghouse Elec. & Mfg. Co., 329 U.S. 402 (1947); Abie State Bank v. Bryan, 282 U.S. 765 (1931); Union Pac. R.R. v. Public Serv. Comm'n, 248 U.S. 67 (1918).

169 See, *e.g.*, American Ry. Exp. Co. v. Levee, 263 U.S. 19 (1923).

170 When federal policy extends to the procedure by which the federal claim is to be determined, a state that undertakes to adjudicate that claim must, of course, respect that policy. Dice v. Akron, C. & Y. R.R., 342 U.S. 359 (1952).

tility to federal rights. Further, distribution of authority between the federal government and the states might be thought to require that, so long as these conditions and constitutional standards of fairness are satisfied, states ought to be free to define the procedures by which their courts are to be operated. There is, however, another dimension to the problem. Emphasis upon the distribution of power in a federal system ought not to obscure the fact that deference to state procedures will sometimes result in frustration of important federal policies. The tendency of our legal system for more than a century has been toward securing the disposition of lawsuits on the merits. A determination of the adequacy of state procedural grounds requires some consideration of the extent to which the Court ought to permit a state's imperviousness to this tendency, either generally or in particular instances, to affect the enforcement of federal policy.

1. *The traditional approach.* In general, the Court has held that state law determines "the time when and the mode by which federal claims must be asserted and preserved."[171] And a state court's refusal to consider a federal claim because of the claimant's failure to comply with such rules has frequently been treated as an adequate state ground.[172] Nevertheless, when state courts have applied local procedural rules with pointless severity to foreclose consideration of federal claims, the Court has on occasion held the state ground inadequate for that reason.[173] The principle stated by the majority in *Henry*, "that a litigant's procedural defaults in state proceedings do not prevent vindication of his federal rights unless the State's insistence on compliance with its procedural rules serves a legitimate state interest,"[174] is therefore, amply supported by previous case law. Viewed as an accommodation of state and federal interests,

---

[171] HART & WECHSLER, *op. cit. supra* note 71, at 500.

[172] See, *e.g.*, Wolfe v. North Carolina, 364 U.S. 177 (1960); Pennsylvania R.R. v. Illinois Brick Co., 297 U.S. 447 (1936); Central Union Co. v. Edwardsville, 269 U.S. 190 (1925).

[173] Douglas v. Alabama, 380 U.S. 415 (1965); Davis v. Wechsler, 263 U.S. 22 (1923); Rogers v. Alabama, 192 U.S. 226 (1904). See also, N.A.A.C.P. v. Alabama *ex rel.* Flowers, 377 U.S. 288 (1964); Wright v. Georgia, 373 U.S. 284 (1963); Staub v. City of Baxley, 355 U.S. 313 (1958). Although the determination of inadequacy in each of the last three cases rested in part on other grounds, such as inconsistency with previous state authority, the Court appears to have been influenced in each by a belief that to require adherence to the state procedure "would be to force resort to an arid ritual of meaningless form." 355 U.S. at 320.

[174] 379 U.S. at 447.

moreover, the principle is unexceptionable. If no state interest is served by requiring adherence to the state procedure, the sacrifice of federal rights plainly is not justified.

It is only the aberrant case, however, that involves a procedural rule that serves no legitimate state interest. The important question is whether, assuming that the rule is supported by permissible state policies, the Court ought to permit a loss of federal rights to result from a procedural default. Decisions before *Henry* consistently answered that question in the affirmative. Moreover, if the procedural rule invoked by the state court is one generally supported by state policy, the Court's tendency has been to avoid close scrutiny of whether the policy is served by invoking the rule in the particular case.[175] The resulting doctrine comes to this: a state procedural rule that bars assertion of a federal right will be adequate to deprive the Court of jurisdiction if the rule is evenly applied,[176] serves a legitimate state interest, and (assuming the rule is of a character to induce reliance) has been clearly announced in earlier decisions.[177]

Such a doctrine permits the state courts to exercise primary responsibility for accommodating relevant state and federal law. In effect, the power of the state to require adherence to its established procedure is treated as paramount in importance to the protection of federal rights. Even if it is conceded that that may sometimes be appropriate,[178] the general importance of federal rights and the supremacy of federal law suggest that it is unlikely that such deference to state procedure is always appropriate. Nor is there any apparent reason for conferring upon state courts the ultimate responsibility for striking a balance between federal policies and the state's interest in the integrity of its procedures. Insofar as state policies impinge upon federal policies, ultimate responsibility for their accommodation is normally exercised by the Supreme Court.

2. *The impact of Fay v. Noia.* Continued adherence to the Court's traditional approach to determining the adequacy of state procedural grounds is, additionally, more than a little anomalous in view of the decision in *Fay v. Noia.*[179] In *Fay* the Court rejected the

---

175 See, *e.g.,* Wolfe v. North Carolina, 364 U.S. 177 (1960); Parker v. Illinois, 333 U.S. 571 (1948).

176 See discussion in text *supra,* at notes 143–45.

177 See discussion in text *supra,* at notes 149–54.

178 See text *infra,* at notes 205–11.   179 372 U.S. 391 (1963).

position that a state procedural ground adequate to deprive it of jurisdiction on direct review was also a bar to the exercise of habeas corpus jurisdiction by the district courts. It held that a state prisoner claiming a constitutional infirmity in the proceedings leading to his conviction could be denied relief only if he had deliberately bypassed orderly state procedure for the presentation of that claim.[180] In the limited area which it affects—state criminal proceedings—*Fay* thus strikes a balance between state and federal interests which is quite inconsistent with that struck by the Court's traditional approach to determining the adequacy of state grounds to preclude its own jurisdiction. In effect, *Fay* represents a determination that protection of federal rights—at least in criminal cases—is paramount to the interests served by the state's insistence on a litigant's adherence to established procedure, a determination diametrically opposed to that which underlies the traditional adequate state ground doctrine. The extent of the anomaly is demonstrated by the fact, noted by the Court in *Henry*, that even if it had held the state court's refusal to consider Henry's constitutional claim adequate to preclude its own jurisdiction, the claim would have been open in a federal habeas corpus proceeding unless the district court were to determine that Henry had deliberately bypassed the state procedure.[181]

To suggest the necessity of a redefinition of the adequacy of state procedural grounds to foreclosure review of claimed federal rights because of the decision in *Fay* is not without irony. Several years before *Fay* was decided, Professor Hart had suggested that state grounds adequate to prevent the Court from taking jurisdiction or direct review ought also to be a bar to the assertion of habeas corpus jurisdiction.[182] In rejecting that position both the majority in *Fay*, and Professor Reitz in his influential article preceding that decision,[183] were at pains to distinguish habeas corpus from direct review for the purpose of demonstrating that doctrines limiting the Court's jurisdiction in the latter situation were not controlling in the former. And yet, the arguments advanced for rejecting the limitation on habeas corpus jurisdiction proposed by Professor Hart appear, on examination, to be equally applicable to direct review.

---

[180] *Id.* at 438–39.   [181] 379 U.S. at 452.   [182] Hart, *supra* note 8, at 118–19.

[183] Reitz, *Federal Habeas Corpus: Impact of an Abortive State Proceeding*, 74 HARV. L. REV. 1315 (1961).

Both the Court and Professor Reitz, for example, condemned the exaltation of procedure over substance that would result from denying relief to a prisoner claiming violation of his constitutional rights merely because of a failure to comply with state procedure.[184] But that is as much a consequence of the Court's traditional approach to determining the adequacy of state procedural grounds to foreclose review as it would have been a consequence of importing the adequate state ground doctrine into habeas corpus. In both situations— as the Court and Professor Reitz argued in connection with habeas corpus—a litigant in a state proceeding is unlikely to forgo compliance with state procedure, thereby losing the opportunity for a determination of the federal claim by the state courts, merely because a federal court may at some later date provide a remedy for the federal claim. To do so would not only ignore the risk that the federal claim might be overlooked in the flood of applications for federal relief but would ignore the advantage of having that claim passed on by state courts as well as federal. In both situations, moreover, a doctrine permitting forfeiture of constitutional rights because of a failure to comply with state procedures will weigh heavily on those whose only fault is inadvertence or neglect. If the state's interest in requiring adherence to its procedures is insufficient to bar habeas corpus, it is difficult to see why it is sufficient to bar direct review.

The Court's opinion in *Fay* suggests, however, that there are technical reasons, inapplicable to habeas corpus, that prevent it from asserting jurisdiction over state court judgments that rest on state procedural grounds.[185] Unfortunately, the precise nature of the technical distinctions is not articulated. It is true, of course, that on direct review, unlike in habeas corpus, the Court is concerned with the "correctness" of the state court's judgment. The judgment is not "correct," however, unless the procedural ground is adequate, and adequacy, as we have seen, is not established merely by a demonstration that the state court refused consideration of a federal claim under a state rule of procedure.[186] The question, therefore, is whether there are reasons for finding state procedural grounds ade-

---

184 *Id*. at 1350–52; 372 U.S. at 431–34.

185 372 U.S. 429–30, 433; see also Reitz, *supra* note 170, at 1344–45.

186 See cases cited at note 162 *supra*, and text *supra*, at notes 149–53.

quate to insulate the state court judgment from reversal on direct review even though habeas corpus is available.[187]

In arguing that the adequate state ground doctrine should not be carried over to habeas corpus, Professor Reitz urged that a determination of inadequacy involved a more substantial interference with state judicial procedures than a failure to bar habeas corpus because of noncompliance with state procedures. In the latter situation, the state is free in future litigation to continue to insist upon adherence to its procedural rule, while if the state ground is declared inadequate, he argued, the state court cannot properly rest a decision on that rule in subsequent similar circumstances.[188] It is not clear, however, that a determination of inadequacy has that effect. There appears to be no decision that so holds. On principle, the issue that the Court decides when it determines the adequacy of a state procedural rule is not whether the state may adhere to the rule in future cases but whether, even in view of the state court's adherence to the rule, the Court should not consider the federal claim. In any event, the practical effect of ignoring the state procedural determination would be the same in both situations: to put extreme pressure on the state courts to ignore their procedural rules in deference to the federal claim.

Professor Reitz also urged that direct review differed from a habeas corpus proceeding because the latter is independent of state judicial processes, while in the former situation the Court remands

---

[187] A possible justification for such a distinction, suggested by the Court's reference in *Fay* to "the web of rules and statutes that circumscribes our appellate jurisdiction," 372 U.S. at 433, is that the statute defining the Court's jurisdiction limits it to consideration of federal questions presented in the state courts in accordance with state law. The current statute, 28 U.S. § 1257, as its predecessors, see ROBERTSON & KIRKHAM, *op. cit. supra* note 9, at App. A, requires that the federal question have been "drawn in question" or "specially set up and claimed" in the state court, in terms suggesting only that the issue must have been raised in the state courts. See Note, 33 COLUM. L. REV. 316, 318 (1933). Nevertheless, there is authority that the quoted language "means that the claim must be asserted at the proper time and in the proper manner by pleading, motion or other appropriate action under the state system of pleading and practice. . . ." Atlantic Coast Line R.R. v. Mims, 242 U.S. 532, 535 (1917). To construe the statute in that manner, however, would require a conclusion that earlier cases in which a state procedural ground was held inadequate rested upon a determination that the procedure violated due process, a position that the Court plainly has rejected. See Davis v. Wechsler, 263 U.S. 22 (1923).

[188] Reitz, *supra* note 170, at 1347–48.

to the state court for entry of an appropriate judgment, thus effectively requiring the state court to consider a federal claim barred by its own procedure.[189] The primary concern, apparently, is the potential refusal of state courts to comply with the Court's mandate,[190] a problem that need not be considered in a habeas corpus proceeding because the district court's writ is addressed to the state's custodial officer.[191] At least two relatively recent cases suggest that this concern is not fanciful.[192] Yet, the problem is no different from that which the Court now faces when, under its traditional tests, it holds a state ground inadequate. Normally state courts will obey the Court's mandate. In the rare situations in which they decline to do so, the Court's power to enter judgment or to take other appropriate corrective measures are adequate to protect the federal right.[193]

The distinctions between habeas corpus proceedings and direct review are largely illusory. Even if I have overstated the similarities in the two situations, however, it seems plain that the Court's decision in *Fay v. Noia* severely undercuts its traditional deference to state procedural grounds that foreclose consideration of federal claims. The subordination of federal rights to state procedure on direct review cannot be reconciled with the paramount position given them in habeas corpus proceedings. The impact of *Fay*, moreover, is not limited to criminal cases. If the state's interest in a system of forfeitures is not adequate to outweigh federal rights in criminal litigation, it is not easy to see why it should outweigh such rights in a civil context. Surely it cannot seriously be contended that every violation of constitutional right in a criminal case is more important than any violation in a civil case.[194]

---

189 *Id.* at 1342, 1347. Insofar as the argument rests upon concern for the sensibilities of state judges, it must at least be weighed against the increased irritation over federal habeas corpus jurisdiction resulting from *Fay*. See *e.g.*, Desmond, *Federal Habeas Corpus Review of State Court Convictions—Proposals for Reform*, 9 UTAH L. REV. 18 (1964).

190 Reitz, *supra* note 170, at 1347, 1354.

191 *Id.* at 1347 n. 115.

192 See Williams v. State, 211 Ga. 763 (1955); Johnson v. Radio Station WOW, 146 Neb. 429 (1945).

193 See HART & WECHSLER, *op. cit. supra* note 71, at 420–21.

194 *Compare*, for example, the asserted violation of constitutional right in *Henry* —the introduction of unlawfully seized but clearly relevant evidence—*with* the infringement of the First Amendment rights found in N.A.A.C.P. v. Alabama ex rel. Patterson, 357 U.S. 449 (1958). A comparison of the penalties in the two cases—

3. *A proposed intermediate position.* The implications of *Fay*, accordingly, provide ample warrant for Mr. Justice Harlan's concern that the Court is moving toward "a severe dilution, if not complete abolition, of the concept of 'adequacy' as pertaining to state procedural grounds."[195] I have previously attempted to demonstrate that some dilution of the concept would be desirable.[196] If the Court continues to adhere to its decision in *Fay*, even complete abolition might seem appropriate—save only for the exception now recognized in habeas corpus proceedings, that a deliberate bypassing of state procedure might continue to be adequate to insulate the state court's judgment from reversal. That extreme a position, however, is hardly more satisfactory as an accommodation of the relevant interests than the Court's traditional approach to state procedural grounds that purport to prevent consideration of federal claims. A doctrine that procedural default will never foreclose substantive claims—such as that announced in *Fay*—ignores the values served by orderly procedure. Rules similar to those employed by state courts to foreclose federal claims are regularly enforced in federal courts. Abolition of the adequate state ground doctrine as applied to state rules of procedure can hardly fail to call the validity of similar federal rules into question. Yet, procedural values of administrative efficiency and fairness to adversaries are surely entitled to some weight. Not all federal rights, moreover, are of equal importance. In at least some situations, to state the strongest case, federal policies would not be significantly thwarted by recognizing a state forfeiture rule as adequate to bar the exercise of the Court's jurisdiction.[197] In others, the federal substantive policy seems entitled to less weight than the interests served by the state's procedural rule.

The need, therefore, is for an approach to the determination of adequacy that strikes an appropriate balance between substantive rights and orderly procedure. That problem is not, obviously, a product of federalism. As suggested above, it exists also when federal rights are enforced in federal courts.[198] Considerations of fed-

---

sixty days' imprisonment and a $500 fine in *Henry* and permanent loss of the right to continue operations within the state in *Patterson*—is also relevant in determining whether constitutional violations in criminal cases are always of more importance than in civil cases.

[195] 379 U.S. at 457.   [196] See text *supra*, at notes 177–79.

[197] See text *infra*, at notes 205–06.

[198] See James, Book Review, 78 HARV. L. REV. 1296 (1965).

eralism do, nevertheless, make the problem more complex. The accommodation of federal rights and state procedure must proceed with due recognition that the Court does not have the authority, as it does for the federal judicial system, to lay down a code of procedure for the state courts. The fact that every state rule need not be respected does not require that all must be ignored.

The difficulty is in formulating criteria that will strike an appropriate balance. That cannot, obviously, be accomplished in the abstract. Such criteria must be developed by consideration of concrete situations, just as the Court's present doctrines concerning adequacy have evolved by decision of particular cases. Any attempt to lay down over-all solutions to the multiple problems that would be likely to arise under such an approach would, therefore, be premature. It seems appropriate, nevertheless, to suggest, by consideration of several recent cases, including *Henry*, at least some of the relevant criteria.

In *Shuttlesworth v. City of Birmingham*,[199] petitioner's conviction for resisting arrest was affirmed by a state intermediate appellate court on the ground that the evidence disclosed he was guilty of assault, a distinct offense.[200] His attempt to invoke the jurisdiction of the state supreme court, on a claim that affirmance on that basis constituted a denial of due process,[201] was unsuccessful because his petition for review had not been filed on paper of the type and size required by the court's rules.[202] Although the state's rule did serve a legitimate interest, as petitioner's counsel conceded,[203] it seems hardly debatable that so trivial a default ought not to result in the loss of a constitutional right of such vital significance to the integrity of the proceedings. Even if forfeiture of constitutional rights in con-

---

[199] 376 U.S. 339 (1964).

[200] 149 So.2d 921 (Ala. 1962).

[201] See Cole v. Arkansas, 333 U.S. 196 (1948).

[202] 149 So.2d at 923. The Supreme Court reversed without opinion, citing Cole v. Arkansas, note 188 *supra*, and Williams v. Georgia, 349 U.S. 375 (1955). The latter citation was presumably intended to convey the reason for finding the state ground inadequate, that the state court had discretion to waive the procedural default. The Alabama Supreme Court had, however, consistently refused to hear petitions filed on the wrong paper, see 149 So.2d at 923 and cases cited therein, and petitioner was unable to cite a single case representing a clear departure from that practice. See Petitioner's Brief at pp. 26–29, Shuttlesworth v. City of Birmingham, 376 U.S. 339 (1964).

[203] *Id.* at p. 30.

sequence of a procedural default can sometimes be justified, there is no reason why "every last technicality of state law must be sacrosanct."[204] *Shuttlesworth* suggests two of the factors relevant to a determination of adequacy. The federal right asserted concerned the fundamental fairness of the proceedings. The state's procedural rule, on the other hand, involved only a matter of administration collateral to the primary purpose of the litigation. When both factors are combined in a single case, appropriate accommodation of state and federal law requires a determination that the state ground is inadequate to prevent protection of the federal right by the Supreme Court.

Shuttlesworth may profitably be contrasted with the situation that confronted the Court in *Henry*. The precise question presented in *Henry* was the admissibility of testimony that was concededly relevant but which was arguably the product of an unlawful search and, therefore, inadmissible under the Court's decision in *Mapp v. Ohio*.[205] Only last Term, in declining to apply *Mapp* retroactively, the Court recognized that the justification for the exclusionary rule is the deterrence of unlawful conduct by the police.[206] Deterrence is not likely to be lessened, however, by the state's forfeiture rule or the Court's acceptance of it as an adequate state ground. Whatever the impact of the exclusionary rule on the behavior of the police, the remote possibility that counsel may fail to make timely objection at the trial is not likely to provide incentive to the police to engage in an unlawful search.

The procedural default in *Henry* was, moreover, of rather more significance than that in *Shuttlesworth*. A requirement of contemporaneous objection to the introduction of evidence is plainly relevant to the just disposition of litigation, since timely objection may affect presentation of the opposing party's case. The importance of that effect under our adversary system indicates the weight that a contemporaneous objection rule ought to be accorded. There may be situations, however, in which even the failure to make a timely objection ought not to result in forfeiture of a federal right, as, for example, where the federal issue involves the fundamental fairness of the proceedings.[207]

---

[204] Hart, *supra* note 8, at 118.

[205] 367 U.S. 643 (1961).

[206] Linkletter v. Walker, 381 U.S. 618 (1965).

[207] *Cf.* Brown v. Mississippi, 297 U.S. 278 (1936).

Additional factors relevant to a determination of adequacy are suggested by *Brown v. Western Ry.*,[208] an FELA action dismissed by the state court on the ground that the complaint did not allege negligence with adequate particularity. The Supreme Court, holding that it must construe for itself the adequacy of an allegation claiming a federal right, reversed the state court. There is a possibility that *Brown* should be read as a substantive determination concerning quantum of evidence needed to support a claim under FELA.[209] The Court did not purport to rest on that ground, however. It held, instead, that "strict local rules of pleading cannot be used to impose unnecessary burdens upon rights of recovery authorized by federal laws."[210] On that basis, the decision seems questionable. The degree of particularity required in a complaint is necessarily interrelated with other procedures in the forum. Loose pleading in the federal courts is justifiable, in large measure, because of the availability of pre-trial and discovery under the Federal Rules. States that have not adopted those procedural reforms may reasonably require more particularistic pleading. It seems relevant also, as Mr. Justice Frankfurter suggested in dissent, that plaintiff was not forced into a state court but freely chose to enforce his federal claim there.[211] By ignoring that fact and the interrelationship between pleading and other procedural rules the Court's decision in effect permits a plaintiff to frustrate the common objectives of both state and federal courts.

An attempt to formulate additional factors relevant to a determination of adequacy would unduly lengthen an already overly long article. The main burden of this section has been to demonstrate that appropriate accommodation of state and federal law is not accomplished by either the Court's traditional approach or, at the other extreme, an extension to direct review of the doctrine announced in *Fay v. Noia*. Careful attention to the particular interests at stake should, however, yield more satisfactory results.

---

[208] 338 U.S. 294 (1949).

[209] See Hill, *Substance and Procedure in State FELA Actions—The Converse of the Erie Problem,* 17 Ohio St. L.J. 384, 407 (1956).

[210] 338 U.S. at 298.

[211] 338 U.S. at 300. See also Hart, *supra* note 83, at 508.

VI. Conclusion

It is nearly forty years since Professors Frankfurter and Landis cautioned against consideration of "jurisdictional questions . . . in isolation from the purposes of the legal system to which they relate."[212] An analysis of the adequate state ground doctrine based upon a pragmatic assessment of the varied interests which it affects indicates that the doctrine is in need of modification. On the one hand, by imposing upon the state courts an obligation to adjudicate federal claims, the Court has unnecessarily interfered with the power of the states to regulate their judicial systems. No federal interest adequately justifies that interference. In other contexts, where federal interests are threatened, the Court has taken too restrictive a view of its powers. The primary difficulty is the Court's traditional willingness to permit a forfeiture of federal rights for noncompliance with established state procedure. A general subordination of federal rights to state procedure, the consequence of the Court's traditional approach, is difficult to justify on any assessment of the competing interests.

Henry suggests that the Court may be prepared to modify its traditional position. The danger is that it will swing to the other extreme, abolishing the concept of adequacy so far as state procedural grounds are concerned. The main criticism of that position is not that it fails to accord sufficient weight to the states' interests, though it may justly be criticized on that ground, but that it ignores the interests of both the litigants and the judicial system in orderly procedure.

Determination of the adequacy of state procedural grounds, as most other problems in the law, requires a more particularistic assessment of the affected interests. An attempt by the Court to undertake such an assessment will undoubtedly lead to a period of uncertainty while principles are evolved, but uncertainty during a time of fruitful inquiry seems preferable to certainty that produces undesirable results.

---

[212] Frankfurter & Landis, *op. cit. supra* note 5, at 2.

ARTHUR SELWYN MILLER

TOWARD A CONCEPT OF

CONSTITUTIONAL DUTY

I. INTRODUCTION

Many years ago, before the public law explosion had begun,
Léon Duguit asserted: "Any system of public law can be vital only
so far as it is based on a given sanction to the following rules: First,
the holders of power cannot do certain things; second, there are
certain things they must do."[1] Most of American constitutional
history has emphasized that "cannot do." The law as created by the
Supreme Court has been nay-saying in fact and in effect, stating in
specific instances a series of "thou shalt nots." Not entirely, to be
sure, as the cases illustrating *raison d'état* in American constitutional
law tend to indicate,[2] but enough to make the generalization valid.

Arthur Selwyn Miller is Professor of Law, George Washington University.

[1] DUGUIT, LAW IN THE MODERN STATE 26 (Laski trans. 1919). See Howell, *The
Search for Jurispolitical Philosophy*, 44 VA. L. REV. 409 (1958).

[2] This is not to suggest that *raison d'état* is an avowed principle, but that such
cases (to take but two instances) as the Prize Cases, 2 Black 635 (1863), and Korematsu v. United States, 323 U.S. 214 (1944), may be said to enunciate a principle
that "constitutional reason of state" does exist in American constitutional law. *Compare* FRIEDRICH, CONSTITUTIONAL REASON OF STATE (1957), *with* CORWIN, THE PRESI-
DENT: OFFICE AND POWERS 1787–1957 (4th rev. ed. 1957). A rather different viewpoint may be found in Wormuth, *The Vietnam War: The President versus the
Constitution* (OCCASIONAL PAPER, CENTER FOR THE STUDY OF DEMOCRATIC INSTITU-
TIONS, 1968). See United States v. O'Brien, 391 U.S. 367 (1968). There, as Mr. Justice Douglas cogently pointed out in dissent, the majority of the Court accepted
the notion that the "power of Congress to classify and conscript manpower for
military service is beyond question," even though the Court had never so held. That
validation of congressional power by Chief Justice Warren is reminiscent of what

The classic text by Cooley was aptly named: *Constitutional Limitations*. In recent years, however, since the coming of the Positive State, a subtle but definite change is apparent. While still speaking negatively, in terms of limitations, the Supreme Court has begun to construct a set of affirmative constitutional doctrines. It has, in other words, become more interested in the "must do" part of Duguit's formulation. The purpose of this paper is to invite attention to this emergent development, to attempt to outline its contours, and to indicate some of the problems involved. The development goes beyond that of opening up § 5 of the Fourteenth Amendment and § 2 of the Fifteenth Amendment to congressional actions. That, as such decisions as *Katzenbach v. Morgan*[3] and other recent cases tend to show, is now an accomplished fact. The resurrection by the Court in June, 1968, of an 1866 statute, so as to uphold Congress' power to enact "open housing" laws, is merely another milestone in a journey already begun.[4]

The basic proposition suggested here is that a judicial concept of constitutional duty, of obligation to take action, is being evolved out of a series of decisions rendered in the past three decades—a time of turmoil and stress, actual and potential, paralleled in American history only by the era of the Civil War. Included are cases on racial relations, legislative reapportionment, administration of the criminal law, and (less directly) administrative law. All are familiar. What will be stressed is their implication, rather than the specific doctrines enunciated. Taken together, they add up at least to a strong suggestion, if not a command, by the judiciary to the political branches of government on how they must behave in certain instances. That those admonitions have not been empty words may be seen in a number of political programs promulgated after the Court had energized what Lord Bryce (in a different context)

----

the Court did in 1886 when it accepted without argument that a corporation was a person within the meaning of the Fourteenth Amendment. Santa Clara County v. Southern Pacific R.R., 118 U.S. 394 (1886). Both instances might well be called lawmaking by inadvertence. Perhaps, however, it was not done inadvertently, but by design, in which event it is as casual a piece of lawmaking as one is likely to find. Is it too much to ask of our judicial lawmakers that they act with more deliberation?

[3] 384 U.S. 641 (1966). See also South Carolina v. Katzenbach, 383 U.S. 301 (1966); United States v. Guest, 383 U.S. 745 (1966); *cf.* United States v. Price, 383 U.S. 787 (1966). For discussion, see Cox, *Foreword: Constitutional Adjudication and the Promotion of Human Rights*, 80 HARV. L. REV. 91 (1966).

[4] Jones v. Alfred H. Mayer Co., 392 U.S. 409 (1968).

called "the conscience of the people." If the thesis is valid, it marks an exponential jump in the jurisprudence of the Supreme Court, though the development is far from complete.

The change has come unheralded. The Court has not announced a shift in emphasis (and the Justices would be quite reluctant to do so). In the great bulk of its work, the Court still operates in its traditional way. But a growing number of decisions now exemplify how the Justices, as Alexander Pekelis advocated, have immersed themselves in "the travail of society" and are helping to build a "jurisprudence of welfare" to complement the political programs of the Positive State.[5] It is an illustration of the validity of what Henry George once called "an axiom of statesmanship . . . that great changes can be brought about under old forms."[6] Change, of course, is built into the very process of constitutional interpretation.[7] Usually, however, it is of an evolutionary, not revolutionary, nature. The point is that the concept of constitutional duty is of considerably greater magnitude than the routine progression of doctrine. It is the judicial counterpart of the fundamental change in the nature of political government, often called the "constitutional revolution of the 1930's," that ushered in the Positive State. The development presents novel problems to the high bench, a supreme tribunal in a government with affirmative responsibilities for the well-being of the people. As such, it requires a reexamination of the very concept of judicial review—not so much to say what the Supreme Court should not do, as did Judge Learned Hand,[8] but rather to try to find out what it can do, and to develop institutional techniques to assist it.

In analyzing the idea of constitutional duty, attention must be paid to the effects of judicial decisions as well as to the abstract statements of principle set out in the opinions. The need is for a jurisprudence of consequences in which an effort is made to assess the societal impact of judicial decrees, particularly the extent to which the political branches of government follow the Court's par-

---

[5] See Pekelis, *The Case for a Jurisprudence of Welfare*, in KONVITZ, ed., LAW AND SOCIAL ACTION 1 (1950).

[6] PROGRESS AND POVERTY c. 8 (1879).

[7] See Miller, *Notes on the Concept of the "Living" Constitution*, 31 GEO. WASH. L. REV. 881 (1963); Miller, *Technology, Social Change, and the Constitution*, 33 GEO. WASH. L. REV. 17 (1964).

[8] HAND, THE BILL OF RIGHTS (1958).

ticular norm with promulgation of a general norm. A "jurisprudence of consequences" or "impact analysis" requires also that the
Court have an institutional means of forecasting the probable effects
of consequences of given decisions.

From the standpoint of the commentator, the inquiry involves,
in the first place, the more basic question of the operative effect of
a Supreme Court decision. Who in fact is bound? To what extent?
It may seem odd to raise such questions so long after *Marbury v.
Madison*.[9] But they are fundamental in at least the same way as a
somewhat analogous question of current vintage is, the problem of
"prospective overruling,"[10] which is also an aspect of a reexamination of the basic doctrine of *Marbury*. There has been much loose
talk in recent years about "judicial legislation" and about the Supreme Court acting as a "superlegislature." Proponents of such notions can only be writing on the assumption that the Court in its
decisions states a general norm or, as it is sometimes put, "the law
of the land." But that can hardly be accurate, however much one
may applaud or deplore certain decisions. The answer to the question of the scope of Court decisions must be, at least on the historical record, that only the parties before the Court are bound
unless it is a class action. At the most, a "Supreme Court pronouncement in a constitutional case . . . delegates authority to others—
legislature, executives, administrators, and judges in lower courts
(federal and state)—to carry out the terms of the edict in other
situations. Other than judges in lower federal courts, whether they
do so is required neither by the Constitution nor the Court decision;
nor is it a requirement of statutes, discretion in the delegate being
the rule."[11]

---

[9] 1 Cranch 137 (1803).

[10] See, *e.g.*, Linkletter v. Walker, 381 U.S. 618 (1965). That decision has been
criticized for purportedly jeopardizing the Court's symbolic position with the
American people. See Mishkin, *Foreword: The High Court, the Great Writ, and
Due Process of Time and Law*, 79 HARV. L. REV. 56, 62–70 (1965). For a statement
disputing Professor Mishkin's assertions, see Miller & Scheflin, *The Power of the
Supreme Court in the Age of the Positive State*, 1967 DUKE L.J. 273, 522.

[11] Miller & Scheflin, note 10 *supra*, at 290. But see Cooper v. Aaron, 358 U.S. 1
(1958) (asserting, in a unique opinion signed by the entire Court, that the governor
and legislature of Arkansas were bound by the Court's decision in *Brown v. Board
of Education*, 347 U.S. 483 (1954), even though none of the several cases consoli-
dated in the *Brown* decision emanated from Arkansas). That opinion, even as aided
by Mr. Justice Frankfurter's separate concurrence, 358 U.S. at 20, hardly disposed
of the issue. What the Court did in *Cooper* was to pose the question; its answer has
yet to be developed.

That is the technical legal answer. But it is without reference to what the delegates do in fact or to what lawyers do in advising clients. When human conduct is actually influenced by lawyers' interpretation of court decisions, in private practice or in government, then it may be said that the decision has a wider impact than on the litigants before the bench in the original decision. "Impact analysis" —the extent to which compliance takes place—is, however, still *terra incognita*. There have been few factual studies of the manner in which judicial decrees have been obeyed. Those that have been made, principally in the field of church-state relations, tend to reveal a spotty or uneven record. Some non-parties comply but others do not.[12] Some notorious refusals to adhere to decisions, as in racial desegregation (*de jure* or *de facto*), require no documentation. If the law is looked upon as did Holmes—through the eyes of the "bad man"—one answer may be forthcoming. But if one takes, following H. L. A. Hart's conception, the "good man" theory of law, quite another may be evident.[13] The role of law in society is rather more than a prophecy of what a court will do with a given set of facts. But how much more we really do not know, save by intuition or rough observation. The dearth of empirical data is the barrier. In sum, my conclusion is that the technical legal answer is the only reliable one—and even there it may at times be inconclusive.[14]

The technical legal answer also does not come to grips with the question whether the Court is trying to alter the operative impact of its decisions. The evidence is sparse and it possibly may be premature to read much into a handful of decisions, important though they may be as specific instances of judicial craftsmanship. But the Justices do seem to be moving toward a situation where they will

---

[12] For recent discussion, see MUIR, PRAYER AND THE PUBLIC SCHOOLS: LAW AND ATTITUDE CHANGE (1968); Beaney & Beiser, *Prayer and Politics: The Impact of Engel and Schempp on the Political Process*, 13 J. PUB. L. 475 (1964).

[13] See HART, THE CONCEPT OF LAW (1961). Holmes's idea is set out in Holmes *The Path of the Law*, in COLLECTED LEGAL PAPERS 167 (1920).

[14] This is particularly to be noted in cases remanded to administrative agencies for action, "not inconsistent with this opinion, as may be appropriate." JAFFE, JU-DICIAL CONTROL OF ADMINISTRATIVE ACTION 589 (1965) (talking about the "utility or futility" of such judicial action). A recent example is Cascade Natural Gas Corp. v. El Paso Natural Gas Co., 386 U.S. 129 (1967), in which Douglas, J., asserted that the antitrust division of the Department of Justice had "knuckled under" to one of the litigants. And see *Evasion of Supreme Court Mandates in Cases Remanded to State Courts Since 1941*, 67 HARV. L. REV. 1251 (1954); *State Court Evasion of United States Supreme Court Mandates*, 56 YALE L.J. 574 (1947).

be promulgating a general norm. Put another way, the suggestion is that the Court has begun to issue what might be called a type of "advisory opinion" covering a wider scope than the precise issue before it. Of course, it is hornbook constitutional law that the Supreme Court does not render advisory opinions at the request of other governmental officials or of private litigants. But once it has found a justiciable controversy, itself an expanding concept, then more generalized pronouncements are at times made. The style of judicial creativity has become more broad-gauged than in the past, at least sufficiently to reveal an emergent trend. To be sure, any decision on the merits tends to be creative, as Justice Walter V. Schaefer has said,[15] simply because a choice must be made between conflicting doctrinal principles. But that is a limited type of creativity, basically different from the "new look" in judicial opinion-writing. Clearly the Court has widened the type of controversy dealt with (by making more issues "justiciable") and broadened the scope of its decisions.

II. Lines of Doctrinal Development

It is hoped that these remarks will both introduce the thesis of this paper and provide a testing board against which individual decisions and language in opinions may be evaluated. Several doctrinal areas will be suggested. The development will perforce be impressionistic rather than exhaustive.

A preliminary observation is desirable: The coming of the Positive State as a form of affirmative government with self-imposed duties has been "constitutionalized" to the extent that the programs of that state have received the imprimatur of the Supreme Court.[16] The Court, thus, may be said to have cooperated in the promulgation of a set of obligations enunciated by the political branches of government. That exemplifies, it is meet to note, the other side of "separation of powers"—cooperation rather than conflict. The disputes between branches of government receive attention, but they should not be allowed to hide the more pervasive and more important cooperative activitie;. Cooperation among the various organs

---

[15] Schaefer, *Precedent and Policy*, 34 U. Chi. L. Rev. 3, 4 (1966).

[16] This is discussed in Miller, The Supreme Court and American Capitalism c. 3 (1968); Kurland, *Guidelines and the Constitution: Some Random Observations on Presidential Power to Control Prices and Wages*, in Schultz & Aliber, eds., Informal Controls and the Market Place 209 (1966).

of government is a necessity and their warfare "fatal," as Woodrow Wilson averred. The genesis of the concept of constitutional duty, accordingly, may be traced to decisions finding no objection in the fundamental law for politically articulated duties. Those cases changed the nature of liberty, of government itself, under the Constitution. "From being a limitation on legislative power," Professor Edward S. Corwin said, "the due process clause became an actual instigation to legislative action of a leveling character."[17]

Usually the *Jones & Laughlin* case,[18] which upheld the Wagner Act, is said to be the turning point. Not to minimize its importance, a more likely candidate is a decision rendered shortly before. In his majority opinion in *West Coast Hotel Co. v. Parrish*,[19] Chief Justice Hughes crossed over the Great Divide between the Negative and Positive States with this statement:[20]

> The principle which must control our decision is not in doubt. The constitutional provision invoked is the due process clause of the Fourteenth Amendment governing the States, as the due process clause invoked in the *Adkins* case governed Congress. In each case the violation alleged by those attacking minimum wage legislation for women is deprivation of freedom of contract. What is this freedom? The Constitution does not speak of freedom of contract. It speaks of liberty and prohibits the deprivation of liberty without due process of law. In prohibiting that deprivation, the Constitution does not recognize an absolute and uncontrollable liberty. Liberty in each of its phases has its history and connotation. But the liberty safeguarded is liberty in a social organization which *requires* the protection of law against the evils which menace the health, safety, morals and welfare of the people. *Liberty under the Constitution is thus necessarily subject to the restraints of due process,* and regulation which is reasonable in relation to its subject and is adopted in the interests of the community is due process.

The first step toward creating constitutional duties had been taken. Liberty, to repeat Hughes's words, is "necessarily subject to the restraints of due process." Theretofore, liberty had been protected by due process from governmental action. It was viewed in an individualistic manner, not as an aspect of "a social organization which requires the protection of law against evils." At the mini-

---

[17] CORWIN, LIBERTY AGAINST GOVERNMENT 161 (1949).

[18] NLRB v. Jones & Laughlin Corp., 301 U.S. 1 (1937).

[19] 300 U.S. 379 (1937).   [20] *Id.* at 391. (Emphasis added.)

mum, the new conception meant that the Constitution permitted social welfare legislation. But even more, it seems a not-too-subtle hint that the Constitution might require it. In 1937 the Court, thus, acknowledged what John D. Rockefeller had said at the turn of the century: "Individualism has gone, never to return."[21] Liberty had become a matter of which group to join (and freedom of contract had become a matter of which "contract" to adhere to). Note particularly that the Chief Justice said that due process was a restraint on liberty, not an aspect of it. In this, he could only have been talking about the "liberties" of those collectivities called corporations.[22] The 1968 decision on open housing that placed limits on an individual's power of sale of real property,[23] however, may be said to fall within the broad conception. The liberties of natural as well as artificial persons can be limited through enforcement of § 1 of the Fourteenth Amendment.

The hint by Hughes lay dormant for a number of years. Hitler's war, plus the progressive enactment of social welfare programs uniformly upheld by a Supreme Court as quick to recognize the rigors of an urbanized and industrialized nation as were the Congress and the President, made it unnecessary to employ judicial power to effect the Hughes suggestion. Duguit's formulation was being met. The "must do" part of public law grew apace—save in the area of civil rights and civil liberties. There the Court finally found a new role in the twentieth-century phenomenon of concern for human rights and liberties. A means was provided for expansion of the Delphic language of Hughes. Having relinquished its position as "the first authoritative faculty of political economy,"[24] the Court in the postwar years has become an authoritative faculty of social ethics. Throwing over the idea that the Constitution enacted Mr. Herbert Spencer's *Social Statics*, it found that the Constitution in effect enacted Thomas Hill Green's concept of positive freedom

---

[21] Quoted in 1 Nevins, John D. Rockefeller 622 (1940).

[22] Corporations are, by lawyers' legerdemain, "persons" within the meaning of the Constitution, a conception now so accepted in law that it seems beyond challenge. See, however, Black, J., dissenting, in Connecticut General Life Insurance Co. v. Johnson, 303 U.S. 77, 85 (1938), and Douglas and Black, JJ., dissenting, in Wheeling Steel Corp. v. Glander, 337 U.S. 562, 576 (1949).

[23] Note 4 *supra*.

[24] Commons, Legal Foundations of Capitalism 7 (1924).

and of collective well-being.[25] The idea of positive freedom as enunciated by the English philosopher, "reflected the rediscovery of the community as a corporate body of which both institutions and individuals are a part, so that the idea of collective well-being or the common good underlies any claim to a private right."[26] Since "necessitous men cannot be free men," this idea is an assertion of the philosophical basis for positive government and for social insurance programs that provide the economic foundation for more people to be free—if they so desire. The duty of government, in this conception, is not so much to maximize individual liberty per se but rather "to insure the conditions for at least a minimum of well-being—a standard of living, of education, and of security below which good policy requires that no considerable part of the population shall be allowed to fall."[27] This is not to say that the Justices openly avowed the almost forgotten Green, but it is to say that freedom had become a social right as well as something of value for the individual. Green sought to reunite the individual with the social order of which he was a member and without which his existence has no meaning. Rather than an absolute and doctrinaire individualism, based on a theory of natural rights, he considered individual freedom to be a social phenomenon, one protected by the legal and other institutions that can only be provided by the community. "When we speak of freedom as something to be so highly prized," said Green, "we mean a positive capacity of doing or enjoying something worth doing or enjoying, and that, too, something that we do or enjoy in common with others. We mean by it a power which each man exercises through the help or security given him by his fellow men, and which he in turn helps to secure for them."[28]

---

25 I suggested this in a previous paper. Miller, *An Affirmative Thrust to Due Process of Law?* 30 GEO. WASH. L. REV. 399 (1962). The idea has been challenged. See Murphy, *Deeds under a Doctrine: Civil Liberties in the 1963 Term,* 59 AM. POL. SCI. REV. 64 (1965).

26 SABINE, A HISTORY OF POLITICAL THEORY 674 (1937).

27 *Id.* at 676. See Holloway, *Mill and Green on the Modern Welfare State,* 13 W. POL. Q. 389 (1960); Jones, *The Rule of Law and the Welfare State,* 58 COLUM. L. REV. 143 (1958).

28 3 GREEN, WORKS: MISCELLANIES AND MEMOIRS 371 (3d ed. 1891). See RICHTER, THE POLITICS OF CONSCIENCE: T. H. GREEN AND HIS AGE (1964); BAY, THE STRUCTURE OF FREEDOM c. 3 (1958); BOSANQUET, THE PHILOSOPHICAL THEORY OF THE STATE (1899); CHIN, THE POLITICAL THEORY OF THOMAS HILL GREEN (1920).

How has the Supreme Court fulfilled that conception? Not expressly but only indirectly, as the following categories of decisions indicate.

A. RACE RELATIONS

The key case is *Shelley v. Kraemer*,[29] which dealt a mighty blow to the state-action concept. If restrictive covenants are unenforceable in equity or at law,[30] then the judicial attitude that manifested itself in 1954 in *Brown v. Board of Education* was easily visible, particularly when *Shelley* was buttressed in the interim by such decisions as *Terry v. Adams*[31] and *Sweatt v. Painter*.[32] The wave that had its beginnings in 1938 in the Missouri law school case[33] and that quickened with *Smith v. Allwright*[34] and in such presidential actions as Executive Order 8802,[35] peaked in *Brown* and has swept on since, tumbling all officially imposed racial barriers in its path. In so doing, the Court has so diluted the concept of officiality that it has become all but moribund.[36] The importance of the school desegregation decision, for present purposes, is in *Brown* II,[37] the case that translated the principle of desegregation as an individual right into a judicially enunciated command to do so "with all deliberate speed." The particular norm of the initial decision a year before had become a general command. It was left to the buck privates of the judiciary, the judges in the trial courts (mainly federal district judges), to translate the grand pronouncement into operational reality.[38] That different judges read it differently is not astonishing. As with general orders in all milieus, those who are called upon to put them into effect have tactical discretion. Professor

---

[29] 334 U.S. 1 (1948).

[30] Barrows v. Jackson, 346 U.S. 249 (1953).

[31] 345 U.S. 461 (1953).   [32] 339 U.S. 629 (1950).

[33] The Missouri law school case was the first breakthrough of importance in the judicial enforcement of Negro rights under the Equal Protection Clause. Missouri *ex rel.* Gaines v. Canada, 305 U.S. 337 (1938).

[34] Smith v. Allwright, 321 U.S. 649 (1944), is a leading "white primary" case.

[35] Executive Order 8802 required a nondiscrimination-in-employment clause to be inserted in all federal contracts. It was the first important breakthrough in executive protection of Negro rights. See RUCHAMES, RACE, JOBS, AND POLITICS (1953).

[36] See, *e.g.*, Evans v. Newton, 382 U.S. 296 (1966).

[37] Brown v. Board of Education, 349 U.S. 294 (1955).

[38] See PELTASON, FIFTY-EIGHT LONELY MEN (1961).

Walter F. Murphy has termed this to be a "lower court check on Supreme Court power," and that it is.[39]

Laws, no matter who first announces them, do not enforce themselves. It takes the active intervention of some human force—a plaintiff for judicially created norms, an administrator for many legislative commands—for laws to be put into effect. In this connection, the power to do nothing is itself a significant power. As Mr. Justice White said in *Avery v. Midland County*[40] in which the *Reynolds v. Sims*[41] rule was applied to a local government unit: "And we might point out that a decision not to exercise a function within the court's power—a decision, for example, not to build an airport or a library, or not to participate in the federal food stamp program—is just as much a decision affecting all citizens of the county as an affirmative decision."

By 1967, however, the standard erected in *Brown* had been accepted and acted upon by Congress and the President and the majority of state governments. The culmination came in 1964 with the enactment of the Civil Rights Act. There are some statutes—the Sherman Act is one, the Employment Act of 1946 another—that are so fundamental that they should be thought of as "quasi-amendments."[42] So it is with the Civil Rights Act of 1964. Title VI of that act, authorizing withholding of federal funds from noncomplying school districts, is particularly noteworthy. The power of the purse had been added to the power of judicial exhortation. Title VI became even more important when the Department of Health, Education, and Welfare read its mandate broadly and purposively so as to include the power to issue "guidelines" for school administrators to follow. Political acceptance seems to be an important factor

---

[39] Murphy, *Lower Court Checks on Supreme Court Power*, 53 AM. POL. SCI. REV. 1017 (1959).

[40] 390 U.S. 474, 484 (1968).   [41] 377 U.S. 533 (1964).

[42] In other words, the custody of constitutional law is not solely in the hands of the judiciary, despite Chief Justice Marshall's fervent assertion in *Marbury v. Madison* that it was "emphatically" the province of courts to say what the law is. That contention was answered by Justice Stone, dissenting in United States v. Butler: "Courts are not the only agency of government that must be assumed to have capacity to govern." 297 U.S. 1, 87 (1936). *Nota bene:* This is not an argument for judicial self-restraint, à la Frankfurter, J., but merely to say that others than the Supreme Court can make constitutional decisions. As Professor Robert McCloskey has said, "the meaning of the Constitution is profoundly influenced by the actual course of legislative and executive action, . . . [and] constitutional interpretation is *not* a judicial monopoly." McCLOSKEY, ESSAYS IN CONSTITUTIONAL LAW 183 (1957).

in making the judiciary less circumspect, or at least more willing to tackle abrasive problems of the human condition and to state their decrees in sweeping affirmative language.

Witness in this connection the decision of the Court of Appeals for the Fifth Circuit in *United States v. Jefferson County*,[43] in December, 1966, affirmed *en banc* in March, 1967, and accepted by the Supreme Court in December, 1967.[44] After disposing of an alleged difference between "desegregation" as a personal right as compared to "integration" as a group right (which Judge Cox relied on in dissent), the lower court asserted that the Constitution, "as construed in *Brown, required* public school systems to integrate students, faculties, facilities, and activities."[45] "The two *Brown* decisions," said Judge Wisdom, "established equalization of educational opportunities as a high priority goal for all of the states and *compelled* seventeen states which by law had segregated public schools, to take *affirmative* action to reorganize their schools into a unitary, non-racial system."[46] In reaching that result, the court of appeals relied heavily both on an expansive reading of the *Brown* (and subsequent) decisions and on the manner in which the political organs of government had accepted the principle: "We read Title VI [of the Civil Rights Act of 1964] as a congressional mandate for change—change in the pace and method of enforcing desegregation."[47] By that tactic, the lower court built the strongest possible case for its decision—and made it a foregone conclusion that the Supreme Court would not reverse. To do so would have meant, not merely a repudiation of the court of appeals, but also of Congress and the President. A group of Justices already predisposed toward improving the status of the Negro used both the "certiorari denied" technique and a per curiam affirmance to make a "mutational leap."[48] (Worth at least passing mention is the way in which Mr. Justice Harlan could swallow this without public disagreement,

---

[43] 372 F.2d 836 (5th Cir. 1966), *affirmed en banc*, 380 F.2d 385 (5th Cir. 1967), *cert. den.*, 389 U.S. 840 (1967).

[44] Lee v. Macon County Board of Education, 267 F.Supp. 458 (M.D. Ala. 1967), *affirmed sub nom.* Wallace v. United States, 389 U.S. 215 (1967).

[45] 372 F.2d at 846. (Emphasis added.)

[46] *Id.* at 847. (Emphasis added.)   [47] *Id.* at 852.

[48] The term comes from McCloskey, *Reflections on the Warren Court*, 51 Va. L. Rev. 1229, 1240 (1965). See Miller, *The Changing Role of the United States Supreme Court*, 25 Modern L. Rev. 641 (1962).

although the reapportionment situation caused him to utter anguished dissents.)

The jump in *Jefferson County* is matched by Judge J. Skelly Wright's decision outlawing *de facto* segregation in the District of Columbia. Sitting as a district judge because the peculiarities of District of Columbia law had made all the district judges defendants, Judge Wright in *Hobson v. Hansen*[49] drew heavily on the Fifth Circuit's handling of desegregation, as well as a distillation of cases since *Shelley*, to indicate that the equal protection clause was "the cutting edge of our expanding constitutional liberty."[50] In making this statement, he cited *Reitman v. Mulkey*,[51] which affirmed the California Supreme Court's invalidation of Proposition 14, as well as *Reynolds v. Sims*,[52] *Griffin v. Illinois*,[53] and Justice Goldberg's New York University address on equality.[54] The liberty protected by the Due Process Clause was thereby merged into a concept of equality—a variation on what Chief Justice Hughes had suggested in *Parrish* thirty years before. The hint by Hughes had been accepted by leading figures in the federal judiciary.

Reitman, which got a bare majority of the Supreme Court, is surely interpretable as a decision that liberty is indeed "liberty in a social organization which requires the protection of law." (Mr. Justice Harlan, it is relevant to note, wrote the dissenting opinion. How he can square the philosophy of that dissent with his silence in the Alabama cases is something not yet explained. The same may be said of Justices Black and Stewart, who agreed with the dissent in *Reitman*, but who did not balk at the Alabama decision.) Desegregation had become integration, both *de jure* and *de facto*. The right of an individual had been translated into the right of a group (the Alabama case was a class action); negative nay-saying had be-

---

[49] 269 F. Supp. 401 (D.D.C. 1967). Judge Wright sat by designation pursuant to 28 U.S.C. § 291(c).

The Court of Appeals for the District of Columbia will be given an opportunity to rule in *Hobson v. Hansen*—and thus to contribute, in one way or another, to the concept of duty—following Judge Wright's decision to permit Hansen, the former Superintendent of Schools who was defendant in the original action, to appeal even though the Board of Education had voted not to appeal and had entered into a course of compliance with the original decree. Hobson v. Hansen, Civil Action No. 82–66, District Court of the District of Columbia, Feb. 19, 1968.

[50] 269 F. Supp. at 493.   [52] Note 41 *supra*.

[51] 387 U.S. 369 (1967).   [53] 351 U.S. 12 (1956).

[54] Goldberg, *Equality and Government Action*, 39 N.Y.U. L. Rev. 205 (1964).

come an affirmative command. The concept of constitutional duty
was full blown.

The denouement of the affirmative duty concept in race relations
came in May, 1968. In *Green v. County School Board*,[55] *Raney v.
Board of Education*,[56] and *Monroe v. Board of Commissioners*,[57]
the Court without dissent extended and clarified *Brown* II. In so
doing, Mr. Justice Brennan used language of express duty:[58]

> *Brown-II* was a call for the dismantling of well entrenched dual
> systems tempered by an awareness that complex and multi-
> faceted problems would arise which would require time and
> flexibility for a successful resolution. School boards such as
> respondent [in *Green*] then operating state-compelled dual
> systems were nevertheless clearly charged with the affirmative
> duty to convert to a unitary system in which racial discrimi-
> nation would be eliminated root and branch.

To that end, said Mr. Justice Brennan, school boards were com-
manded to bend their efforts. That, in short, was the articulation
by a unanimous Court that it does state general norms and that all
in similar circumstances to given cases are required to obey. The
school board in *Green* gave at least partial recognition that it was
bound, when it argued that its "obligation" under *Brown* II was
fulfilled by a so-called freedom-of-choice plan. This does not definitively assure the power of the Court to state general norms, but it
is a clear indication of the direction the Justices are taking. Whether
they will prevail in this movement is, however, even now problem-
atical. The net effect may well be, in the words of Brooks Adams,
"a delusion."

The technique is not universally used. Of interest in this connection is the statement of Mr. Justice Marshall speaking for the Court
in *Pickering v. Board of Education*,[59] concerning a teacher's First
Amendment right publicly to criticize his Board of Education:[60]

> Because of the enormous variety of fact situations in which
> critical statements by teachers and other public employees
> may be thought by their superiors, against whom the state-
> ments are directed, to furnish grounds for removal, we do

---

55 391 U.S. 430 (1968).   58 391 U.S. at 437–38.

56 391 U.S. 443 (1968).   59 391 U.S. 563 (1968).

57 391 U.S. 450 (1968).   60 *Id.* at 569.

not deem it either appropriate or feasible to attempt to lay down a general standard against which all such statements may be judged.

He then set forth some of the ways which analyses of such situations should be conducted. It is evident that the Court—as always—will vary its technique to suit the case at bar.

Another issue not yet presented may well come out of the parlous situation in Alabama. To what extent, if at all, do other federal organs, particularly the President, have a duty to take action to assure that the law as enunciated by the Supreme Court is "faithfully executed"? The road from President Jackson's perhaps apocryphal sneer at Chief Justice John Marshall's lack of power to enforce a decision leads to Governor Wallace's revival in 1967 of the same flouting words. But it leads past Little Rock, Arkansas, and Oxford, Mississippi, and Birmingham, Alabama, where Presidents used the military to enforce judicial decisions. The Supreme Court, the Fifth Circuit, and Judge Wright have all struck at "practical nullification." Whether the Executive can safely ignore the Court's commands will depend on as yet unknown factors, including the willingness of a sufficient number of Negro citizens to present themselves for integration in compliance with the Court's order and whether the governor's defiant language is to be matched by action. That a presidential duty to obey the decree exists (whether or not he is amenable to judicial process) seems clear. The duty runs, it seems, to taking action to insure that executive agencies comply affirmatively with the principle of desegregation, particularly in spending (contracts and grants).[61] And if the use of federal troops during recent years to enforce court orders may be taken to be an example of the "practical" Constitution in action, then precedent exists. Whatever discretion a President may have, and it no doubt is very great, it should not go so far as to permit him to flout a judicial decision, to do nothing. The response from the Executive to decisions not liked should be to try to get them overruled—either by the Court itself or by Congress (as in the case of statutory interpretation) or by constitutional amendment. The duty is clear, albeit not in a Hohfeldian sense. No one can force the President to act.

---

61 See Simkins v. Moses H. Cone Memorial Hospital, 323 F.2d 959 (4th Cir. 1963), cert. den., 376 U.S. 938 (1964); Miller, Presidential Power to Impound Appropriated Funds: An Exercise in Constitutional Decision-Making, 43 No. Car. L. Rev. 502, 533–34 (1965).

What this means is that the arena in which the conflict takes place shifts from the judicial to the political. If the plaintiffs in the Alabama case and in *Hobson v. Hansen* want further relief, they will have to trigger responses from the politicians and the bureaucrats. The Court can do little more. But what it has done is considerable. The little more that it can do is to extend and amplify the decision of the Court of Appeals for the Fourth Circuit in the *Cone Hospital* case which invalidated disbursements under the Hill-Burton Act to an assertedly "private" hospital.[62]

A by-product of the development, quite important in itself, is the possible resurrection of the long-dormant § 5 of the Fourteenth Amendment. As Professor Archibald Cox has persuasively argued, it now provides a constitutional peg on which to hang a variety of congressional actions affirmatively protecting liberty and equality.[63] And a serendipitous effect from the Negro (and other) cases may be such new developments as the enforcement of the First Amendment against the mass media, which, if done, would mean that constitutional duties would be imposed on private entities.[64] What this portends is the demise of the state-action concept, in effect if not in form. Already reeling from the evolution that peaked in *Shelley* and the various sit-in cases, a principle that had been judicially read into the Constitution in 1883 seems now to be at the end of its life. As Professor Jerre Williams has said, it is in its "twilight."[65] It is no longer a barrier of consequence to what a Supreme Court majority might want to do. *Evans v. Newton*[66] and Mr. Justice White's majority opinion in *Reitman* are ample evidence of that. Orthodoxy would have called for Mr. Justice White to write an opinion (and decision) more in accord with Mr. Justice Harlan's plaintive dissent, for the California Supreme Court's opin-

---

[62] Note 61 *supra*.

[63] Cox, *supra* note 3. Professor Cox's position is thus intermediate between the Constitution as negative limitation and the notion of constitutional duty. He does not suggest the latter, although some language in his article might be so interpreted.

[64] See Barron, *Access to the Press—a New First Amendment Right*, 80 Harv. L. Rev. 1641 (1967). In this seminal article, Professor Barron suggests that the First Amendment should be read to impose "affirmative responsibilities," the mass media being "quasi-public instrumentalities." *Id.* at 1675.

[65] Williams, *The Twilight of State Action*, 41 Texas L. Rev. 347 (1963).

[66] 382 U.S. 296 (1966). *Cf.* Marsh v. Alabama, 326 U.S. 501 (1946); Bell v. Maryland, 378 U.S. 226 (1964).

ion did not "opine" in the traditional sense. But it was not to be. In an opinion that is logically arbitrary but sociologically non-arbitrary,[67] Mr. Justice White and four of his colleagues simply swept the state-action argument aside. The report of its death may be premature, but surely it is gasping out its life in the affirmative judicial jurisprudence of race relations. The line between public and private in American society, never as sharp as some have thought, is being progressively blurred, even erased.

Of more than passing interest is a statement by Mr. Justice White in *Reitman*. Speaking of the state-action cases and conceding that none squarely controlled the situation at bar, he went on to say: "They do exemplify *the necessity for a court to assess the potential impact* of official action in determining whether the State has significantly involved itself with invidious discriminations."[68] He thereby echoed Justice McKenna, who more than a half-century before had said:[69]

> ... constitutions ... are not ephemeral documents, designed to meet passing occasions. They are, to use the words of Chief Justice Marshall, "designed to approach immortality as nearly as human institutions can approach it." The future is their care and provision for events of good and bad tendencies of which no prophecy can be made. In the application of a constitution, our contemplation cannot be only of what has been but of *what may be*.

But how is a judge to assess "impact" or "what may be"? What techniques of argumentation will, within the confines of the adversary system, bring to the bench the data necessary to evaluate what might take place after a given policy, executive or legislative or judicial, is enunciated? And where do judges acquire the competence to make such evaluations? These and other questions are squarely presented by the movement into affirmative jurisprudence by the Court. They will be dealt with shortly.

---

[67] See Miller, *Mulkey v. Reitman: A Brave but Futile Gesture?* 14 U.C.L.A. L. REV. 51 (1966). See also CRAWSHAY-WILLIAMS, METHODS AND CRITERIA OF REASONING: AN INQUIRY INTO THE STRUCTURE OF CONTROVERSY 195 n. 1 (1957), speaking of the "apparent paradox" that decisions can be "logically arbitrary, but sociologically unarbitrary." For discussion of the *Reitman* case, see Karst & Horowitz, *Reitman v. Mulkey: A Telophase of Substantive Equal Protection,* 1967 SUPREME COURT REVIEW 39.

[68] 387 U.S. at 380. (Emphasis added.)

[69] Weems v. United States, 217 U.S. 349, 373 (1910). (Emphasis added.)

B. LEGISLATIVE REAPPORTIONMENT

"It is regrettable," said Judge Wright in *Hobson v. Hansen*, "that in deciding this case this court must act in an area so alien to its expertise. It would be far better indeed for these great social and political problems to be resolved in the political arena. . . . But there are social and political problems which seem at times to defy such resolution. In such situations, under our system, the judiciary must bear a hand and accept its responsibility to assist in the solution where constitutional rights hang in the balance."[70] The point is not that the courts will or should have to shoulder the entire burden, but that they do what they can in such extraordinary situations. The resolution of some social problems takes the cooperative action of all the branches of government. When the political branches are stymied, then the judiciary is the government's only lawful way out. This may clearly be seen in the racial situation, but an even clearer example may be found in the problem of the "rotten borough" resulting from the urbanization of American society. Possibly Congress could have acted pursuant to the Guarantee Clause of Article IV. But it was most unlikely to do so. And despite Justice Frankfurter's fervent assertion that the remedy for malapportionments lay in the state legislatures, even a federal judge who was once a professor should have been able to recognize

---

[70] 269 F. Supp. at 517. *Cf.* Harlan, J., in *Reynolds v. Sims:* ". . . these decisions give support to a current mistaken view . . . that every major social ill in this country can find its cure in some constitutional 'principle,' and that this Court should 'take the lead' in promoting reform when other branches of government fail to act. The Constitution is not a panacea for every blot upon the public welfare, nor should this Court, ordained as a judicial body, be thought of as a general haven for reform movements. . . . This Court . . . does not serve its high purpose when it exceeds its authority, even to satisfy justified impatience with the slow workings of the political process." 377 U.S. at 624–25. The trouble with Mr. Justice Harlan's position is multiple: (*a*) Who believes that "*every* major social ill" can be constitutionally resolved? And what are a Constitution and its authoritative interpreter for, if not to deal with social problems juristically? Alexis de Tocqueville noted that tendency in American government well over a century ago. If the view is mistaken, as Mr. Justice Harlan says, it can hardly be called "current." (*b*) What is the difference between the Court trying to rectify ethnic ills, as in the segregation situation, and trying to remedy apportionment imbalances? If anything, the latter is the more easily resolved. It has so been proved. (*c*) The Justice assumes the answer in the last sentence quoted above; he begs the question: the problem is the extent and nature of judicial authority; it simply will not do to assert judicial impropriety when that is the very question at issue. It would be useful if attention were to be paid to the nature and limits of judicial lawmaking, not by way of a priori assertion, but through a careful analysis of the role of the Supreme Court in the modern era.

that politicians are not going to vote themselves out of office. The breakthrough in *Baker v. Carr*[71] was necessary if the spirit of the Constitution was to be fulfilled. The case (and its progeny) has been criticized as being "judicial fiat"—but such criticisms could have been (and were) leveled against *Marbury v. Madison* and many decisions since 1803. The critics of *Baker* have yet to point to a period when the Court operated in any other way. They cannot, for it is the nature of the constitutional adjudicative process to exhibit that pseudo-logic that so delights and comforts lawyers (because it is familiar) while simultaneously permitting the Justices to reach their conclusions and to make law for other reasons (not necessarily known even to them).

When *Baker* was followed by *Wesberry v. Sanders*[72] and *Reynolds v. Sims*, not only was the "one person–one vote" formula enshrined in constitutional doctrine; there was also the clear illustration of an affirmative constitutional duty on state legislatures to act, and act quickly, often under the threat of judicial reapportionment if they failed to do the job.[73] Oddly enough, save for some disgruntled politicians who would have been voted out of office and some professors who thought the Supreme Court had not exemplified "sovereign Reason" in its decisions and had also transgressed the proper boundaries of judicial action, the decisions have been accepted. By and large, they have been acted upon with celerity, despite the breathless misgivings of Justice Frankfurter and the impassioned warnings, rather reminiscent of Justice McReynolds in the early 1930's,[74] of Mr. Justice Harlan. The courts have shown that they can fashion a remedy in apportionment situations. The task was not easy. There has been considerable experimental prob-

---

[71] 369 U.S. 186 (1962).　　　　[72] 376 U.S. 1 (1964).

[73] Recent analyses of the apportionment situation may be found in DIXON, DEMOCRATIC REPRESENTATION: REAPPORTIONMENT IN LAW AND POLITICS (1968); McKAY, REAPPORTIONMENT (1965).

[74] See, *e.g.*, Norman v. Baltimore & Ohio R.R., 294 U.S. 240, 361, 381 (1935). "Loss of reputation for honorable dealing will bring us unending humiliation; the impending legal and moral chaos is appalling." *Cf.* Harlan, J., in Wesberry v. Sanders, 376 U.S. at 48: "What is done today saps the political process. The promise of judicial intervention in matters of this sort cannot but encourage popular inertia in efforts for political reform through the political process, with the inevitable result that the process is itself weakened." Mr. Justice Harlan forgets that the Supreme Court is, and always has been, a part of the political process. See SHAPIRO, LAW AND POLITICS IN THE SUPREME COURT (1964); KRISLOV, THE SUPREME COURT IN THE POLITICAL PROCESS (1965).

ing to try to fit the particularities of local situations within the general principle. And, in all probability, the courts will have a continuing job in that every census will pose anew the question of voting equality. But the lesson is unmistakable. Here is a classic enunciation of an affirmative duty imposed by the judiciary on the political branches of government. The consequence is a widespread restructuring of the state legislatures and of the House of Representatives. The logical end of the process begun with *Baker v. Carr* came in April, 1968, when *Avery v. Midland County* extended one person–one vote to local governments.[75]

Unanswered questions about reapportionment remain, in addition to the knotty problems of translating the Delphic one person–one vote formula into operational reality. For example, will the difference in representation, from rural to urban, mean a difference in the kind of legislation enacted by reapportioned legislatures? The answer is by no means clear, although it might be hypothesized that it is far too simplistic to suggest a rural-urban dichotomy in legislative action. From what is known about the "group basis of politics," it may well be that in the long run there will be little or no change in product.[76] That, however, will never be known. Second, how can the greater judicial success in reapportionment be explained, as compared with that in racial desegregation? Not, surely, on the basis of arguments about the abstract power of the Court. We know little about the sociology of judicial decision-making.[77] What is known is that the Court's power varies with the issues it decides. Few studies have been made of the impact of Court decisions and of when and why people obey judicial commands. It is common knowledge that at times not even the litigant before the Court adheres to the decision, as *Cascade Natural Gas Co. v. El Paso Natural Gas Co.*[78] evidences. A comparison of desegrega-

---

[75] Note 40 *supra*. See also Sailors v. Board of Education, 387 U.S. 105 (1967); Dusch v. Davis, 387 U.S. 112 (1967).

[76] See, *e.g.*, TRUMAN, THE GOVERNMENTAL PROCESS (1951); McCONNELL, PRIVATE POWER AND AMERICAN DEMOCRACY (1966).

[77] See Miller, *On the Need for "Impact Analysis" of Supreme Court Decisions*, 53 GEO. L.J. 365 (1965).

[78] 385 U.S. 129 (1967). *Compare* Greene v. McElroy, 360 U.S. 474 (1959), *with* Greene v. United States, 376 U.S. 149 (1964). In the first *Greene* case, the Court found that petitioner had been improperly discharged from his position with a navy contractor. The government, nevertheless, took the position that he was not entitled to back pay, but would have to go through the process of obtaining a security clearance first. It took the second Court decision to get the matter rectified.

tion with reapportionment reveals that both the affirmative commands (the general norms) and the traditional "thou shalt nots" of the Supreme Court are followed at times and ignored at times.

C. ADMINISTRATION OF THE CRIMINAL LAW

The development of a concept of constitutional duty may also be seen in recent criminal law cases, notably *Johnson v. New Jersey*[79] and *Miranda v. Arizona*.[80] Also relevant are the "prospective overruling" cases, such as *Linkletter* and *Tehan*.[81] These decisions purport to settle a general, as distinguished from a particular, norm. They are a form of advisory opinion, of a legislative character, binding insofar as they determine the fate of all those caught by the rulings without the benefit of a specific determination of the merits of each individual case. In *Johnson* and *Miranda* the Court took the opportunity to promulgate rules of general applicability with respect to the treatment of those caught in the enforcement of the criminal law. The Justices exhibited an impatience with the slow case-by-case development of the law—and quite possibly also with techniques of sophisticated evasion of the spirit of *Miranda* by law-enforcement officials.

Criminal-law administration, as an example of constitutional duty, differs from race relations and reapportionment in that the judicial pronouncement was not directed to any political or administrative official. Rather, the Court made an announcement, somewhat similar to a code, of what should be done with respect to the right to counsel of persons accused of crimes. It imposes affirmative obligations because it is clear and unmistakable indication of what the Court would do if the guidelines are not followed. The binding effect of such statements is not at all certain. Technically, the *Johnson-Miranda* "code" of conduct for police officials falls into the category of *obiter dicta*. But surely it is more than that. It provides a basis for lawyers to predict what the Court will do in future cases, and thus is law under the Holmes-Cardozo concept.[82] Those standards are certainly more binding than the now moribund wage-price guidelines issued by the Council of Economic Advisers, and are to be compared with the guidelines promulgated by the Department

---

[79] 384 U.S. 719 (1966).

[80] 384 U.S. 436 (1966).   [81] See note 10 *supra*.

[82] The Holmes-Cardozo concept, in short, is the "prediction" theory of law, law being a prediction of what a court will do with a given set of facts. That law is something more than such a prediction seems to be a self-evident proposition.

of Health, Education, and Welfare under Title VI of the Civil Rights Act of 1964.

It is of interest also to note that the function of a litigant in a constitutional case is solely that of getting the case to the Court and triggering the judicial process. The Court cannot operate without that external stimulus. Once, however, the Court is energized, the litigant largely becomes irrelevant, even though the decision will affect him directly. On the other hand, legislatures and administrators are self-starters. Their failures, at times, to do so is the factor that leads to judicial attempts to stimulate them through the concept of constitutional duty. The Court, as Mr. Justice Harlan has said, chooses its cases "in the interests of the law, its appropriate exposition and enforcement, not in the mere interest of the litigants."[83] Justice Frankfurter put it a little differently: "We do not sit like a kadi under a tree," he said, "dispensing justice according to considerations of individual expediency."[84] That is to say, the Justices are interested in the generality of the law. Litigants are important only when they can fit within an "appropriate exposition of general principles."[85]

D. ADMINISTRATIVE LAW

One further area deserves mention: judicial review of the public administration. In this, the largest single category of cases that the Court decides, a marked change in judicial philosophy from the 1930's and early 1940's is apparent. When the Positive State first came into being, much was made of "government by expert."[86] The courts by and large abdicated to the administrators, viewing the technical problems as too complex for determination by judges.[87] Deference to administrative judgment was the hall-

[83] Harlan, *Manning the Dikes,* 13 RECORD 541, 551 (1958), quoting Chief Justice Hughes.

[84] Terminiello v. Chicago, 337 U.S. 1, 11 (1949). Of course, Justice Frankfurter was talking mainly about the methodology of judicial decision-making, and not so much the idea of who can get a decision. But his well-known aversion to "judicial activism" seems evident in *Terminiello.*

[85] This may be the burden of the complaint in the well-known article, Wechsler, *Toward Neutral Principles of Constitutional Law,* 73 HARV. L. REV. 1 (1959), even though the article has been called "verbally muddled" by Professor Anthony Blackshield of the University of Sydney, quoted in Miller & Scheflin, note 10 *supra,* at 308.

[86] See, *e.g.,* LANDIS, THE ADMINISTRATIVE PROCESS (1938).

[87] *E.g.,* Railroad Comm'n v. Rowan & Nichols Oil Co., 311 U.S. 570 (1941).

mark of the period. That attitude still exists, but it seems to be changing. Here too may be seen signs of judicial enunciation of affirmative obligations, but with a difference. Here the task of the Court is to interpret statutes, not the Constitution, and this affords a different milieu in which to operate.

The context is different because the Court, when it interprets statutes, is always subject to reversal by Congress. As Justice Jackson said in 1953: "If Congress does not like our legislation, it can repeal it—as it has done a number of times in the past."[88] There is in fact considerable evidence that Congress is taking on a new role in the changing alignments of the misnamed separation of powers, that of being a "super court of appeals." Not only judicial legislation, but also administrative rule-making, is subject at times to review by Congress, sometimes by prior statutory command, as in the "come-into-agreement" provisions of some bills,[89] and sometimes when Congress is displeased at a given administrative decision and "reverses" it. An example of the latter is the action taken when the Federal Communications Commission sought to enact into administrative rule the code of ethics of the National Association of Radio and Television Broadcasters. The networks went to Congress, not to a Court of Appeals as provided by statute, with the result that the FCC saw new light and quickly (and apparently permanently) rescinded its proposed rules.

The context of "administrative law"[90] is also different because the Court (thus far at least) has not promulgated norms of general

---

[88] United States v. Public Utilities Comm'n, 345 U.S. 295, 320–21 (1953).

[89] See HARRIS, CONGRESSIONAL CONTROL OF ADMINISTRATION (1964).

[90] Whether "administrative law" exists at all, save in the minds of casebook editors, textbook writers, and those who write headnotes for the key numbers of the West Publishing Company, is itself a good question not yet answered. Some lawyers insist that administrative law does not exist apart from the substantive content of the rules and practice of each agency. It is not a single subject, but a congeries of separate subjects. See, e.g., Westwood, The Davis Treatise: Meaning for the Practitioner, 43 MINN. L. REV. 607 (1959). See also Miller, Book Review of Jaffe, Judicial Control of Administrative Action, 34 GEO. WASH. L. REV. 970 (1966). One reason for the lack of a generalized body of doctrine that can meaningfully be called "administrative law" is the failure, so far at least, of legal scholars to see administration, wherever conducted, as the marriage of politics and law. Compare Bernstein, The Regulatory Process: A Framework for Analysis, 26 LAW & CONTEMP. PROB. 329 (1961), with Massel, The Regulatory Process, 26 id. 181 (1961), and Miller, "Malaise in the Administrative Scheme": Some Observations on Judge Friendly's Call for Better Definition of Standards, 9 HOWARD L.J. 68 (1963).

applicability (as in race relations and the criminal law). Rather, it has tended to act in individual disputes in the time-honored case-by-case manner, settling the situation before it without regard to Mr. Justice Harlan's "appropriate exposition" of the law. It has considered appropriateness in this area to mean the application of the decisional process to the litigants only. In any event, it is relevant to mention that the Court has been criticized because it has not developed a systematic and comprehensive corpus of administrative law—a notion that may be based on the assumption that the task of the Court is to "enact" what might be called codes of law in specific areas.[91]

What is taking place is a change in judicial attitude, in the direction of holding public administration to higher standards of performance. And that is a constitutional development, even though usually it does not concern the interpretation of the fundamental document. It does change the balance of power among the branches of government, and, accordingly, may be thought to be within the framework of "separation of powers."

The movement may be traced at least as far back as Justice Jackson's concurring opinion in the *Hope Natural Gas* case.[92] There, in the context of a question of public utility rate-making, he asserted that "the question is . . . whether price control shall have targets at which it deliberately aims or shall be handled like a gun in the hands of one who does not know that it is loaded."[93] He conceded that the task was that of the Federal Power Commission, not the courts, but he would have the FPC "make sound economic considerations, instead of legal and accounting theories, the foundation of federal policy."[94] Such views led one commentator to maintain that, in Justice Jackson's view, judicial intervention in governmental affairs is necessary both to check excesses of

---

[91] See DAVIS, ADMINISTRATIVE LAW TREATISE iii (1958). I am not suggesting that Professor Davis is outwardly calling for the "enactment of codes of law." On the contrary, he pleads for a better case-by-case development. But how can this be done, given the plethora of administrative decisions and the crowded docket of the Supreme Court? Even though the Court may devote about 40 percent of its time to judicial review of administration, it can scarcely construct a systematic body of law except over decades of time. Events will not wait for such action. Furthermore, if one is to accept the view of the practitioner, see Westwood, note 90 *supra*, then the Davis definition of administrative law as being "especially . . . judicial review" seems rather awry.

[92] FPC v. Hope Natural Gas Co., 320 U.S. 591 (1944).

[93] *Id.* at 653.   [94] *Id.* at 660.

power against individuals and also "to see that the tasks delegated to the administrative agency are more fully activated and enforced, that the general interest, broadly conceived, is better served."[95] Ten years later the Court decided in *Phillips Petroleum Co. v. Wisconsin*[96] that the FPC must exercise jurisdiction over producers of natural gas, even though the Commission did not want to do so. That the FPC for years failed to adhere to the judicial command[97] does not alter the point being made: that the federal judiciary is assuming a new posture vis-à-vis the public administration. As the Court of Appeals for the District of Columbia said in 1960:[98]

> We believe that the Supreme Court [in the *Catco* case] meant to impress upon the Commission an interpretation of the "public interest" which, in the context of a rising natural gas market, demands a real administrative effort to hold back prices. We find nothing in the record before us which would justify the conclusion that the Commission had adequately performed this duty.

In brief, the Court imposed an affirmative duty on the FPC to improve its performance. The technique, however, was that of reading content into statutes, rather than the Constitution. The *Permian Basin* case in 1968 is a further extension of the idea.[99]

Two recent decisions in the Courts of Appeals deserve mention: the *Church of Christ* case in the District of Columbia Circuit[100] and the *Scenic Hudson Preservation Conference* case in the Second Circuit.[101] In those, the two courts considerably expanded the concept of standing to challenge administrative action, in the first by

---

[95] Solo, *The New Look in the Constitutional Structure of Public Regulation*, 4 ANTITRUST BULL. 503, 509 (1959).

[96] 347 U.S. 672 (1954).

[97] As noted in the so-called Landis Report. See Subcommittee on Administrative Practice and Procedure of the Senate Committee on the Judiciary, 86th Cong., 2d Sess., Report on Regulatory Agencies to the President-Elect (Comm. Print 1960).

[98] Public Service Comm. v. FPC, 287 F.2d 146, 150 (D.C. Cir. 1960). The "Catco" case is Atlantic Refining Co. v. Public Service Comm'n of New York, 360 U.S. 378 (1959).

[99] Permian Basin Areas Cases, 390 U.S. 747 (1968). In the *Permian Basin* case, however, the Court upheld an assertion of power by the FPC, over the protests of the industry, to set area prices, the FPC having had something of a change in attitude toward regulation.

[100] Office of Communication of the United Church of Christ v. FCC, 359 F.2d 994 (D.C. Cir. 1966).

[101] Scenic Hudson Preservation Conference v. FPC, 354 F.2d 608 (2d Cir. 1965).

giving "consumers" (a group of Negroes) status to contest re-
newal of a television license and in the second by permitting a
conservation group to challenge the grant of a license to construct
a power plant on the Hudson River. The latter is perhaps of more
interest for present purposes. In *Scenic Hudson*, Judge Hays, after
finding that the group had standing, went on to state that the FPC
had to take "aesthetic" considerations into account in licensing the
plant. This, then, was another instance of a court interpreting "the
public interest" in a manner different from the agency. In so
doing, the court tried to put some content into what has always
been a nebulous and ill-defined concept.[102] The "public interest"
may be to the bureaucracy, as one observer has said, what "due
process" is to the judiciary, but there have been few efforts to
determine its substantive content. The concept has been used as a
means of transferring governing power to the bureaucracy, and not
much more.[103] But the time has come, and the judiciary seems to be
recognizing it, for it to be canalized within some broad boundaries.
As matters stand now, power to regulate in the public interest means
uncontrolled discretion in the administrator, with a consequent politicization of the administrative process.[104] When *Church of Christ*
and *Scenic Hudson* are seen as part of a progression of cases that
exhibit a new judicial attitude, they become more important than
they would be if viewed in isolation.

The success of the movement toward greater supervision of the
public administration by the judiciary (and by Congress, for that
matter) is by no means a foregone conclusion. Pronouncements
may be issued by the judges to the bureaucracy, but it will take an
affirmative attitude of compliance for them to be translated into
reality. Here, an impressionistic view shows a spotty record. The
refusal of the FPC to follow the spirit and letter of the *Phillips*
decision is notorious. And other cases exist which show clearly that
the bureaucrat resists and tries to avoid or evade the judicial decree.
Greene v. McElroy is a good example.[105] Furthermore, there can

---

[102] See Miller, *Foreword: The Public Interest Undefined*, 10 J. Pub. L. 184 (1961)

[103] *Cf.* 1 Davis, Administrative Law Treatise c. 2 (1958).

[104] See Horsky, The Washington Lawyer 68 (1952), for a lucid discussion of
what he terms to be "emphatically a government of men, not of laws."

[105] Note 78 *supra*. I know of one instance where a government agency circulated
a memorandum following a decision adverse to it, stating (confidentially) that the
agency would not follow the majority opinion, but would adhere to the dissent. It
would be instructive to follow up on cases remanded to the agencies for action "not
inconsistent with this decision," to find out what actually happened within them.

be no doubt that a decision about Agency A is not considered by Agency B to be binding. On the other hand, the passport cases seem to have worked a change in the issuance of passports.[106] Here as elsewhere, however, there have been few empirical studies made of compliance, so conclusions at best must be intuitive. The alteration in judicial attitude seems clear. But what difference will it make?

III. AN EVALUATION

This brief rundown of some recent well-known decisions neither exhausts all possible areas nor does it plumb each category considered. Furthermore, it is not suggested that the concept of "duty" is the norm of decision-making, even in constitutional cases. Quite the contrary. Even though it may be called a tendency or an exception, however, it seems to be growing. The examples mentioned are instances of judicial statesmanship of a high order, indicating that the Supreme Court is not a passive organ of government. It is rather an institution and an instrument of government with "a legitimate political function to perform."[107] Or, as Lord Bryce said: "The Supreme Court is the living voice of the Constitution . . . the conscience of the people, who have resolved to restrain themselves from hasty or unjust action by placing their representatives under the restriction of a permanent law."[108] The concept of constitutional duty, however, goes beyond Lord Bryce's idea of the Court as national conscience. He spoke about the Court being a restraint on the "impatient vehemence of a majority." He was talking about "constitutional limitations," in Cooley's classic formulation. What the Court is doing now is to trigger the conscience of the people by erecting a standard of behavior to which the nation can aspire in its struggle to achieve the values of human dignity and freedom. In Professor Lawrence Friedman's terminology, these rules promulgated by the Court under the rubric of constitutional duty are "quantitative" rather than "qualitative," but in a sense they go beyond Friedman's idea.[109]

---

106 *E.g.*, Kent v. Dulles, 357 U.S. 116 (1958); Aptheker v. Secretary of State, 378 U.S. 500 (1964).

107 Alfange, *The Relevance of Legislative Facts in Constitutional Law*, 114 U. PA. L. REV. 637, 639 (1966).

108 BRYCE, THE AMERICAN COMMONWEALTH 273 (1914 ed.). See Howell, *James Bryce's "The American Commonwealth,"* 9 J. PUB. L. 191 (1960).

109 Friedman, *Legal Rules and the Process of Social Change*, 19 STAN. L. REV. 786 (1967).

The concept of duty under the Constitution is not exhausted by the extent and nature of what the Supreme Court can do. Individuals, as well as government officials, have duties as well as rights under the fundamental law, as the selective service laws evidence. And as the Supreme Court told the Americans who had the lack of foresight to be born into families of Japanese ancestry, citizenship has its responsibilities as well as rights.[110] Therefore, said Mr. Justice Black for the Court, they should not complain about being penned up in concentration camps during World War II. Moreover, in some relatively rare instances corporations have had duties imposed both by judicial decree, as in *Marsh v. Alabama*[111] and *Amalgamated Food Employees Union v. Logan Valley Plaza, Inc.*,[112] and legislative action, as in the Civil Rights Act of 1964,[113] and also by executive action, as in the nondiscrimination in employment clause in federal contracts. These duties are "constitutional" in that they are in accord with constitutional norms. It is inconceivable that they would be changed politically.

It is even possible to argue that Congress could not constitutionally repeal the Civil Rights Act of 1964. Suggested here is that once government has undertaken a certain program designed to further the norms of the Constitution as enunciated by the Supreme Court—which is what Congress did in the Civil Rights Act of 1964—then Congress cannot validly repeal such legislation. *Shelley v. Kraemer* plus *Reitman v. Mulkey* and the *Prince Edward County*[114] school case seem to lead to such a conclusion. But is the lesser position, if that be granted, equally valid: Did Congress have a duty under the interstate commerce clause (and perhaps pursuant to § 5 of the Fourteenth Amendment) to enact the statute? Putting the question in such a way asks for a quick negative. But it is also obvious that Congress has to adhere to constitutional precepts when it does choose to regulate commerce. As Walter Gellhorn recently put it: "[G]overnment can decide to do nothing whatsoever to relieve misery [and presumably, other adverse social circumstances]. But

---

110 Korematsu v. United States, 323 U.S. 314 (1944).

111 326 U.S. 501 (1946). See Berle, *Constitutional Limitations on Corporate Activity—Protection of Personal Rights from Invasion through Economic Power*, 100 U. PA. L. REV. 933 (1952).

112 391 U.S. 308 (1968).   113 78 Stat. 241 (1964).

114 Griffin v. County Board of Prince Edward County, 337 U.S. 218 (1964).

having chosen to do something, it cannot do anything at all, regardless of constitutional limitations."[115]

Can it be argued, however, that Congress and the state legislatures have an obligation, undertaken when the individual member of the nation's legislature is sworn to defend and uphold the Constitution? If the Constitution means what the Supreme Court says it means, does not this in effect create the same sort of duty that the President has to "faithfully execute the laws"? In this instance, the "laws" are the norms stated by the Supreme Court. Once the Court has said, as it did in *Cooper v. Aaron*[116] and in *Bailey v. Patterson*,[117] that all officially imposed racial discriminations are invalid, can it be said that the words of limitation then become a command—in this instance, to take action to further the principles enunciated in *Brown v. Board of Education, Bolling v. Sharpe*,[118] and their progeny? Furthermore, the Court had previously said that state segregation laws were an unconstitutional burden on interstate commerce.[119] The power of Congress to alter constitutional decisions may receive a definitive test when the Crime Control Bill of 1968, certain parts of which seek to change the result in the *Miranda* and other cases, is litigated. If the Constitution commands certain action in the administration of the criminal law, how can Congress by merely passing a statute change the fundamental law? The answer is by no means self-evident.

The net result, not yet fully enunciated in constitutional doctrine, is that Congress and the states must act in certain circumstances. Racial discrimination is only one of the circumstances. Something similar to the express statements in the constitutions of India and of Pakistan may well be in the making.[120] By a process of slow accretion rather than a single thunderbolt of amendment or of sweeping judicial pronouncement, affirmative obligations of government are being recognized. It may not, even today, be wholly

---

[115] Gellhorn, *Poverty and Legality: The Law's Slow Awakening,* 112 PROC. OF AM. PHIL. SOC'Y 107, 109 (1968).

[116] 358 U.S. 1 (1958).

[117] 369 U.S. 31 (1962). In the *Bailey* case, the Court said that officially imposed racial discrimination was no longer a litigable issue.

[118] 347 U.S. 497 (1954).

[119] Morgan v. Virginia, 328 U.S. 373 (1946).

[120] See Constitution of India, Part IV, Articles 42, 43, 45, 47; Constitution of Pakistan, Part II, chap. 2.

accurate to assert that "government can decide to do nothing what-soever." Modern government is responsible government—and that responsibility runs far beyond the housekeeping functions of yes-teryear. Government can either act or fail to act. In some instances, as we have seen, the Supreme Court may attempt to create a duty to act. If government acts, then it must, as Gellhorn says, obey the command of the Constitution. Furthermore, once government has acted, the suggestion is that it cannot constitutionally change its mind—unless and until the Supreme Court changes the interpreta-tion of the Constitution or an amendment is promulgated. The last step is that of duties imposed by the Court—and that, it is submitted, is the direction in which the doctrine is moving.

Furthermore, the President has, by constitutional practice at least, the awesome responsibility of taking action to insure the very sur-vival of the nation: "constitutional reason of state" is a viable prin-ciple of American constitutional law, although it seldom gets liti-gated.[121] That, too, is a "constitutional duty," even though it is not judicially cognizable.

In a comprehensive delineation of the concept of duty, these (and other) matters would have to be fully considered. In this paper, the focus is mainly on only one facet of constitutional duty, ex-emplified by judicial decision-making. That development brings with it serious problems and poses basic questions about the role of courts and their relationships to the political mechanisms. In brief, it presents the need for a re-examination of the premises of *Mar-bury v. Madison.* Learned scholars in recent years have struggled with that need, but have not as yet produced a systematic, viable conceptualization. Problems of American constitutionalism are never finally answered. The law is always in a state of becoming, open-ended and fluid. Government institutions do not remain static; social change begets legal change. The law must be stable, yet it cannot stand still. Where do the courts—where does the Supreme Court—fit into this process? The Court must answer that question anew in each succeeding generation. It is answering it now, in part, by constructing a concept of constitutional duty. But here, as else-where, "the fleas come with the dog."

---

[121] Professor Carl J. Friedrich has defined constitutional reason of state as "the doctrine that whatever is required to insure the survival of the state must be done by the individuals responsible for it, no matter how repugnant such an act may be to them in their private capacity as decent and moral men." FRIEDRICH, note 2 *supra,* at 4–5. See ROSSITER, CONSTITUTIONAL DICTATORSHIP pt. IV (1948).

IV. PROBLEMS AND QUESTIONS

The law, Justice Frankfurter once said, "presupposes socio-logical wisdom as well as logical unfolding."[122] In the developing law of constitutional duty the Supreme Court must of necessity be as concerned with "sociological wisdom" as it is with the "logical unfolding." This means that it must be forward-looking, purposive in its outlook, teleological in posture, as well as backward-looking (to a corpus of established doctrine or precedent). Such a conception of the adjudicatory function is wholly different from the received wisdom about courts and their role. Orthodoxy would confine the judge to the Blackstone "declaratory" theory, under which the judge is "sworn to determine, not according to his own private judgment, but according to the known laws and customs of the land; not delegated to pronounce a new law, but to maintain and expound an old one."[123] The theory has long been dead, although it may still rule from its grave.[124] Attention must accordingly be paid, as Wolfgang Friedmann has said, not to "the stale controversy over whether judges make law [but] to the much more complex and controversial question of the limits of judicial law-making."[125] This is but one of the problems raised by the new teleological jurisprudence of the Court. In order to put it into perspective, it will be discussed with others that are now evident.

A. PROPRIETY OR LEGITIMACY

Perhaps the most basic of the problems raised by the new style of decision-making is whether it is proper or not. Strong and vociferous critics of the Court speak seriously of "usurpation" of power. Others spring to its defense. Both are correct and both are wrong. There is no settled concept of the judicial process, even after almost 180 years of Supreme Court history. The critics are correct because the Justices do seem to have made a mutational leap, and thus have poached on what hitherto have been the preserves of other governmental organs. But the defenders are also

---

[122] Frankfurter, *The Judicial Process and the Supreme Court*, in FRANKFURTER, OF LAW AND MEN 35 (Elman ed. 1956).

[123] 1 BLACKSTONE, COMMENTARIES 69.

[124] See Miller & Scheflin, note 10 *supra*.

[125] Friedmann, *Limits of Judicial Lawmaking and Prospective Overruling*, 29 MODERN L. REV. 593, 595 (1966).

correct. As Professor Friedman has said: "The courts do not inno-
vate certain kinds of new programs because they lack power—in
the sense of legitimate authority—to do so. . . . There is nothing
inherent in a 'court' to prevent it from devising new programs
and, specifically, from promulgating rules in precise, quantitative
terms."[126] Legitimacy, as a concept in political theory, pertains to
the right or title to rule. In the past, it has been founded on a number of beliefs (which in turn are based on a range of religious and
metaphysical notions). These include a magical belief in descent
from the gods, blood descent which equates rules with the right of
property, the divine right, custom and tradition, and by those who
are being ruled expressing a preference for the ruler (or the rule)
by voting for him (or it).[127]

Normally, the ruler in the American system achieves legitimacy
because he has been elected to office or is responsible to someone
who has been elected. Much of the talk about judicial usurpation
derives from the nonrepresentative character of the Supreme Court.
The Court is, as Justice Frankfurter once said, essentially "oli-
garchic."[128] But that seems too simplistic, even though it has the
weighty authority of Judge Learned Hand behind it. Hand, in
1958, maintained that the task of the Court was that of determining the "competence" under the Constitution of other government
institutions to deal with a problem. Once competence was found,
then the Court was not authorized to reweigh what already had
been weighed by a competent authority.[129] Presumably, this would
mean that each of the four categories mentioned above would be,
in Hand's view, beyond the authority of the Supreme Court. Its
legitimacy did not go that far. That conception is hardly accurate,
either on the historical record or as a matter of theory. The Supreme Court can issue decrees establishing constitutional duties.
Whether it does so or not depends less on its legitimacy or authority
than on an implicit evaluation of how given decisions will be received. Holmes and Frankfurter and Hand (and their followers in

---

126 Friedman, note 109 *supra*, at 822.

127 See FRIEDRICH, MAN AND HIS GOVERNMENT: AN EMPIRICAL THEORY OF POLITICS
233 (1963).

128 A. F. of L. v. American Sash & Door Co., 335 U.S. 538, 555 (1949). See
CAHILL, JUDICIAL LEGISLATION 9 (1952); Miller, *Some Pervasive Myths about the
United States Supreme Court*, 10 ST. LOUIS U. L. J. 153, 159–62 (1965).

129 HAND, note 8 *supra*.

the profession) would limit judicial creativity to incremental change. The courts would be permitted to legislate only interstitially. They would be confined from molar to molecular motion.

That, at its best, is a statement of a value judgment or preference. For the Supreme Court to issue norms of general applicability is dependent, not upon a commonly accepted theory of the proper scope of judicial activity, but upon an evaluation, intuitive to be sure, for the Court has no means for the accurate prediction of impact upon the public of its decisions, of how a decision may be received by the American people. Legitimacy ultimately relates as much to current public acceptance as it does to the representative character of the decision-maker. There being no settled conception of what adjudication should consist of, the problem devolves, to put it in its lowest terms, to what the Court can "get away with." Or, as it was recently put: "The turning-point [in Supreme Court activity] came . . . when the court, walking on eggs in the School Segregation Cases, found that its public image was such that it *could* get away with revolutionary changes . . . in the areas of criminal-law enforcement and reapportionment. . . . Moreover, the court's public image is sustained and fostered each time it has one of the successes. . . . Success begets success; more power begets more power."[130] Gunnar Myrdal has given a label to this phenomenon, "the principle of cumulative social causation," by which he means that social affairs are never in equilibrium but always in flux or in "process" in an upward or downward cycle.[131] Perhaps an apt analogy is the manner in which the warmaking power has flowed to the President, despite the express constitutional provision to the contrary.

The point is not to state the bases of legitimacy for judicial promulgation of norms of constitutional duty but rather to underscore the fact that it presents a continuing problem for constitutional scholars. The complex and controversial question of the limits of judicial lawmaking has not yet been settled. It might be said, however, that the Court in one sense is representative even though it is not elected, because it is the only institution other than the presidency that has the entire nation as its constituency.

Furthermore, there is a basic difference between the actions of

[130] Quoted in Miller & Scheflin, note 10 *supra*, at 318-19.

[131] See MYRDAL, THE INTERNATIONAL ECONOMY 15-16 (1956); MYRDAL, AN AMERICAN DILEMMA 75, 1065-70 (1944).

the modern Court in "duty" cases and those of the "nine old men" in the pre-1937 Court. Efforts to compare the two periods will not wash, for today the Justices are trying to further social change, not halt it. There may be some merit in Adolf Berle's breathless, albeit belated, discovery that the Court in recent years has functioned as a "revolutionary committee."[132] Legitimacy, always a problem with the Court, is not absent in the "constitutional duty" situations, but it surely is no greater, and indeed may be rather less, than when the Justices were saying no to legislative programs.

B. THE AUTONOMY OF LAW AND LAWYERS

Courts, to use Aristotle's classification, have traditionally engaged in dispensing *corrective* justice. The concept of constitutional duty calls for them to assist in the dispensation of *distributive* justice. Legitimacy may possibly be a lesser problem, even though it is basic, because the institutional characteristics of courts make distributive justice difficult indeed. Law and lawyers become merged in the political process. There is a certain danger in this, a danger that may be labeled the "loss of autonomy of law and lawyers" or, perhaps better, the "politicization of law and the legal process." Norman S. Marsh, now a parliamentary law commissioner, writing in 1959, put the problem in these terms:[133]

> On the one hand if the ideal of a Free Society is accepted as the basis of the conception of the Rule of Law, it is impossible to ignore that aspect of man's dignity and worth which finds expression in a demand for a minimum standard of material well-being and educational opportunity. On the other hand, it is precisely the so-called positive rights which the traditional legal machinery is ill adapted to enforce, except sometimes indirectly by insisting that whatever benefits the State may bestow, it distributes them equally between its citizens. Moreover, there is a danger that an interpretation of the Rule of Law which lays too great an emphasis on what the State should do for the individual may end by forgetting the individual in its enthusiasm for its plans of collective welfare, the development of which would mark the decline of a Free Society into something similar to the typical totalitarian State. It must also be recognized that there is a danger, if the Rule of Law is to include, or at all events to assume, a basis of economic and social justice, that the law and lawyers may

---

[132] Berle, The Three Faces of Power (1967).

[133] Marsh, *The Background of the Congress of New Delhi*, 2 J. Int'l Comm. of Jurists 43, 53–54 (1959).

find it difficult to assert that measure of detachment from the immediate policies of a party or group in power which is an important aspect of the legal function in society.

It would be wrong to claim that there is a neat and conclusive answer to these problems. The most that can be expected is that different dangers are always kept in mind.

Marsh was alluding to a conception of the "Rule of Law" enunciated by the International Congress of Jurists in 1959. At that time, in the so-called Declaration of Delhi, it was said that "the Rule of Law is a dynamic concept . . . which should be employed not only to safeguard and advance the civil and political rights of the individual in a free society, but also to establish social, economic, educational and cultural conditions under which his legitimate aspirations and dignity may be realized."[134] In some respects, it may be said that the Supreme Court is furthering that concept of the Rule of Law in its promulgation of constitutional duties.

But if so, this means that law has become openly instrumental, goal-seeking as well as interdictory, an active instrument for the furtherance of postulated or assumed goals. Once the goals are set—and this in itself is a large task, but one in which the Court lends a hand—the requirement is for the development of alternative ways of achieving them. In such a job, the traditional way of thinking of lawyers (backward, to see what has been done) must perforce be supplemented by "forward thinking."[135] A satisfactory theoretical formulation of the twin demands on law, however, has not yet been made. No one has adequately combined law as normation (the historical view) with law that is positive and goal-seeking. Put another way, the advent of public law as the dominant part of the legal system has not yet been assimilated into legal philosophy.

That is one aspect of the politicization of law. Another is the merger of law and politics. As the Supreme Court is openly recognized as a political organ,[136] it presents serious problems of what Marsh calls "that measure of detachment" from the immediate demands of the state. This is not to say that the Court did not at times, in the past, become in effect an arm of the political branches of

[134] INTERNATIONAL COMM'N OF JURISTS, THE RULE OF LAW IN A FREE SOCIETY 3 (Marsh ed. 1960). See Thorson, *A New Concept of the Rule of Law*, 38 CAN. B. REV. 238 (1960).

[135] See Miller, *Science versus Law: Some Legal Problems Raised by "Big Science,"* 17 BUFFALO L. REV. 591 (1968).

[136] *Compare* SHAPIRO, note 74 *supra*, *with* BICKEL, THE LEAST DANGEROUS BRANCH (1962).

government. As Alpheus Thomas Mason has shown, during World War II the Court came perilously close to becoming a part of the "executive juggernaut."[137] That was during a period of emergency. Whether the Justices should be excused for having taken the easy (and popular) way out when presented with situations which in other circumstances would have been decided differently is itself a complex question. But the concept of constitutional duty places even greater demands on the legal system. It not only immerses the judiciary deeply into the "travail of society," it asks of the legal profession that it abandon its posture of "professional" detachment and help in the attainment of postulated goals. Those goals are not necessarily those of the "party or group in power" but are the ideals subsumed under the concept of human dignity. Merely stating such a proposition reveals the staggering enormity of the problem. Politicized law under a constitutional order can only mean that the law is to be used to further the ideals of the Constitution. The Court can help to articulate those ideals, but they will be hollow unless they are followed by affirmative action on the part of other governmental organs. In this activity, the legal profession cannot remain quiescent—and it cannot be neutral.[138] The task of social engineering to achieve the ideals is no doubt of far greater magnitude than any other intellectual task. Alongside it, the problems of natural scientists are relatively simple and manageable.[139] Let no one be sanguine about such matters. But it is necessary to try. And lawyers are among those fated to do so, simply because law is the instrument through which social changes can be engineered. "The challenge facing America," Michael Shanks has said, "is not a technical one, it is a challenge of social, political and psychological adjustment, to adapt the ideals of the eighteenth century to the facts of the twentieth."[140] That process of adaptation must have the lawyer as social engineer in the forefront.

---

137 MASON, HARLAN FISKE STONE: PILLAR OF THE LAW 666 (1958).

138 See F. COHEN, ETHICAL SYSTEMS AND LEGAL IDEALS (1933); Miller, *Science and Legal Education*, 19 CASE WEST. RES. L. REV. 29 (1967).

139 "Good scientists study the most important problems they think they can solve. It is, after all, their professional business to solve problems, not merely to grapple with them." MEDAWAR, THE ART OF THE SOLUBLE 7 (1967). In comparison with the problems of social engineering, even the most difficult problems tackled by natural scientists seem relatively easy. See Weinberg, *Can Technology Replace Social Engineering?* UNIVERSITY OF CHICAGO MAGAZINE 6 (October 1966).

140 SHANKS, THE INNOVATORS 10 (1967).

C. INSTITUTIONAL ADEQUACY

The loss of autonomy of law and lawyers presents, as has been said, what may be the greatest problem of affirmative constitutional jurisprudence. The idea of an autonomous law supposes a set of precepts that are applicable, at least in theory, without regard to values and value preferences. The new jurisprudence avowedly makes values an integral part of the concept of law. It makes it necessary for the legal profession, not least the courts, to know what is wanted—which in turn presupposes that the American people know what they want. Historical Supreme Court adjudication was based on the premise that the ultimate ends or values of society were fairly clear and widely accepted and understood, even if not expressly stated. As Yves Simon has said, in a democratic state "deliberation is about means and presupposes that the problem of ends has been settled."[141] The "problem of ends" is precisely that posed by the concept of constitutional duty and it presents in addition the further question of adequacy of existing institutions to deal with that problem. The "duty" cases involve the substance and not the form of governmental action. They reflect, not acceptance of final ends, but clashes of warring views on what those ends should be.[142] "*De facto* segregation" provides apt illustration. It is in that context that the question of the limits of judicial lawmaking must be seen. The answer depends not only on the social milieu in which the Court acts but also the extent to which the Court has achieved legitimacy in the sense of social acceptance.

The question of institutional adequacy may be analyzed in two contexts: first, the extent to which the adversary system is sufficient to the need, and, second, the manner in which lawyers are educated (*i.e.*, the system of legal education in the nation's law schools). Both can be only briefly discussed. The concept of constitutional duty involves the legal profession in a much larger intellectual move-

---

[141] SIMON, PHILOSOPHY OF DEMOCRATIC GOVERNMENT 123 (1951).

[142] One such clash of opinion is set out in the REPORT OF THE NATIONAL ADVISORY COMMISSION ON CIVIL DISORDERS (1968). *Cf.* BENNETT, CONFRONTATION: BLACK AND WHITE 5-6 (1965): "The basic fact of the Negro situation is shattered community. Negro and white Americans do not belong to the same social body. They do not share that body of consensus or common feeling that usually binds together people sharing a common land. . . . Black man is incomprehensible to white man in America, and vice versa: this is the root cause of the rebellion—broken community and the failure of Americans to create a single social organization." See also PARSONS & CLARK, eds., THE NEGRO AMERICAN (1966).

ment, away from mechanism and breaking away from an obsession with the past, generated in large part by the impact of science and technology on the social order. "Forward" or "future" thinking thus becomes an integral part of many disciplines, not excluding law.[143] But lawyers, since they have always looked to the past for guidance, are particularly inept in "forecasting" or "guiding" the future. Their institutions are not sufficient to the need.

The adversary system, for example, is a product of a feudalistic, preindustrial, and prescientific age. Its techniques and personnel are those that can cope with the familiar or the already known. The point can be illustrated in several ways. First, the widespread acceptance that "policy" considerations play as large a part as "doctrinal" matters in the resolution of controversies brought to courts reveals a need for a breakaway—unannounced, to be sure—from the traditional methodology of the adversary system. For what are "policy" considerations? Often employed but never defined, the term is one of the most loosely used in legal terminology. Where in the immense literature of law is there a coherent account of what the generic concept of "policy" means for law and lawyers? The literature, official (as in court reports) and unofficial (as in law review commentary), is replete with mention of policy (sometimes called public policy). But there is a dearth of analysis of the concept, as distinguished from its particular applications. The term "policy" at the very least is one of multiple reference. It concerns not only the *outcomes* of the judicial process (the "policy-making" powers of court) but also one of the *inputs*. It is the input to the judicial decision-making process that lacks systematic and comprehensive analysis. A plethora of writings exist on policy as outcome, although much of that literature is purely doctrinal. In terms of high-level abstraction, policy considerations require judges to weigh the social advantage of alternative holdings. Writing in 1897, Justice Holmes put the matter well—in terms bridging both the adversary system and legal education:[144]

> I think that the judges themselves have failed to recognize their duty of weighing considerations of social advantage. The duty is inevitable and the result of the often proclaimed judicial aversion to deal with such considerations is simply

---

[143] *Cf.* Mayo & Jones, *Legal-Policy Decision Process: Alternative Thinking and the Predictive Function,* 33 Geo. Wash. L. Rev. 318 (1964).

[144] Holmes, note 13 *supra,* at 184.

to leave the very ground and foundation of judgments inarticulate, and often unconscious. I cannot but believe that if the training of lawyers led them habitually to consider more definitely and explicitly the social advantage on which the rule they lay down may be justified, they sometimes would hesitate where now they are confident, and see that really they were taking sides upon debatable and often burning questions.

As now constituted, the adversary system in constitutional adjudication is not adequate for the satisfactory resolution of policy questions. It does not provide the relevant data and criteria and it does not insist upon a high quality of talent in judges. Furthermore, there is no present way that judges can effectively assess the "impact" or "social advantage" of their decisions, save by intuition or by common sense (that most uncommon of all the senses). Much the same may be said for legal education. Neophytes to the profession of law are not given an adequate assessment of policy data and criteria, whatever may be said of the doctrine they absorb. Nor do they get expertise in weighing considerations of social advantage or of assessing the impact of legal norms. "How to inform the judicial mind," said Justice Frankfurter, ". . . is one of the most complicated problems."[145] In the informing process, the idea that the Supreme Court depends on orthodox notions of the adversary system to furnish it with the data considered relevant and necessary to a decision is an obvious fiction. Information can and does flow to the Court outside of the "normal" paths of record, briefs, oral argument, and the concept of judicial notice. The Justices "supplement those materials," as Mr. Justice Brennan has said, "with independent research."[146] Or as Judge Charles Wyzanski has put it:[147]

This tendency of a court to inform itself has increased in recent years following the lead of the Supreme Court of the

---

[145] Frankfurter, J., quoted from oral argument (in *Brown v. Board of Education*), in MURPHY & PRITCHETT, COURTS, JUDGES, AND POLITICS 318 (1961). For a discussion of how Justice Frankfurter used extra-record materials, see Wormuth, *The Impact of Economic Legislation upon the Supreme Court*, 6 J. PUB. L. 296 (1957). See also Karst, *Legislative Facts in Constitutional Litigation*, 1960 SUPREME COURT REVIEW 75.

[146] Brennan, J., quoted in WESTIN, ed., AN AUTOBIOGRAPHY OF THE SUPREME COURT 303 (1963).

[147] Wyzanski, *A Trial Judge's Freedom and Responsibility*, 65 HARV. L. REV. 1281, 1295 (1952).

United States. Not merely in constitutional controversies and in statutory interpretation but also in formulation of judge-made rules of law, the justices have resorted, in footnotes and elsewhere, to references drawn from legislative hearings, studies by executive departments, and scholarly monographs. Such resort is sometimes defended as an extension of Mr. Brandeis' technique as counsel for the state in Muller v. Oregon. In Muller's case, however, Mr. Brandeis' object was to demonstrate that there was a body of informed public opinion which supported the reasonableness of the *legislative* rules of law. But in the cases of which I am speaking these extra-judicial studies are drawn upon to determine what would be a reasonable *judicial* rule of law. Thus the focus of the inquiry becomes not what judgment is permissible, but what judgment is sound. And here it seems to me that the judge, before deriving any conclusions from any extra-judicial document or information, should lay it before the parties for their criticism.

"Laying it before the parties," however, is precisely what is *not* done when judges conduct independent research or when they use expansive notions of judicial notice.[148] The implication is clear. The Justices themselves are recognizing the inadequacies of the adversary system in an era of affirmative jurisprudence. But their actions to rectify the situation leave a great deal to be desired.

The informing process in adjudication is only one of the faults of the adversary system. It obtains in all types of judicial decision-making but is particularly evident when the Court acts affirmatively. Another shortcoming is the lack of any systematic delineation of the "policy" considerations—the "social advantages"—that judges should take into account. Here the judiciary is thrown back upon its own subjective resources. The situation is evident, for example, in due process decisions, those in which the *Palko*[149] rule prevails. Does the conduct complained of violate fundamental canons of decency and justice of the English-speaking peoples? The essence of this formulation is that it allows Justices to read their notions of good social policy—sometimes called "natural law"—into the Constitution.[150] Constitutional law and policy, to a marked extent, is

---

[148] And of course "laying it before the parties" is an impossibility when the Court writes an opinion such as it did in *Miranda*, there being no parties before whom the data or questions could be laid.

[149] Palko v. Connecticut, 302 U.S. 319 (1937).

[150] This is the essence of the famous Black-Frankfurter argument in such cases as Adamson v. California, 332 U.S. 46 (1947), a debate continued in 1968 in BLACK, A CONSTITUTIONAL FAITH (1968).

dependent on the accident of appointment to the bench, something that has long been known but which has had too little attention from legal scholars.[151] Of interest also is the fact that argument of "policy" by adversaries is not guided by any known set of procedural rules or criteria of relevance. Lawyers must bring such matters to the Court, if they are to do their job properly, but must operate largely in the dark when so doing.

Furthermore, the adversary system is predicated on the dubious assumptions that, first, judges have the personal expertise sufficient to making important law-creating pronouncements (in present context, that of constitutional duty) and, second, that they have the means available to predict with some certainty the impact of alternative decisions on the social order. The very statement of such assumptions is their own refutation. The "statesmanship" which Woodrow Wilson said Americans look for in their judges tends to be catch-as-catch-can forays in the dark. Not always, to be sure. For the judges themselves have recognized in one way or another their lack of competence to deal with many matters and have left them to settlement or resolution by the political organs of government. It is no longer possible, as it once was, for American monetary policy to be set in a private lawsuit involving the astronomical sum of $15.60.[152] The Justices evade involvement in many important present-day matters, so much so that the old Tocquevillean aphorism about most political questions tending to become judicial is no longer valid. At best, it is a half-truth. Despite the burst of activity of the Warren Court, a group of Justices the most "activist" since the time of Chief Justice Marshall, judicial review is a seldom used technique given the full sweep of public policy matters.

"The adversary principle," Philip Selznick has said, ". . . lends legitimacy to partisan advocacy within the legal process, allowing and even encouraging the zealous pursuit of special interest by

---

[151] The political science fraternity has been much quicker to look to the questions of the personality and background of the Justices. See SCHUBERT, CONSTITUTIONAL POLITICS (1960); MASON, note 137 supra; MURPHY, ELEMENTS OF JUDICIAL STRATEGY (1964). See, however, BICKEL, THE UNPUBLISHED OPINIONS OF MR. JUSTICE BRANDEIS (Phoenix ed. 1967).

[152] Norman v. Baltimore & Ohio R.R., 290 U.S. 398 (1934). See JACKSON, THE STRUGGLE FOR JUDICIAL SUPREMACY 94–104 (1941), discussing how astonished Europeans were that national monetary policy could be set in a lawsuit involving $15.60. "Why," he was asked, "should lawyer-judges be supreme over the national parliament, the President, the Treasury, and the whole government in a matter so vital to economic life?" Id. at 104.

means of self-serving interpretations of law and evidence."[153] That legitimacy, however, can be based only on the assumptions not only that such self-serving interpretations provide the data necessary for decision but also that the system by satisfying particular litigants can redound to the general good. The latter involves a conflict theory and is predicated on the untested belief that when two parties are at odds on constitutional questions and cannot settle their differences without reference to the machinery of the state, by some magic the Court's resolution will inure to the benefit of the nation. That is the legal counterpart of the classical economist's "invisible hand."

A failure properly to analyze and test the adversary system means that Justices of the Supreme Court, as well as judges generally, are not being given the type of assistance they need in order to make better, that is, wiser, decisions. The judge must rise above the narrow presentations of counsel if he is to make proper "policy" decisions, if he is to be able to forecast the probable impact of alternative decisions, and if the general good is to be served. Professor Lon L. Fuller has said that the moral force of a judgment is maximized if a judge decides solely on the basis of arguments presented to him. "Because if he goes beyond these he will lack the guidance given by the parties and may not understand the interests that are affected by a decision rendered outside that framework."[154] That is what judges often must do, however, particularly in the area of pronouncements of general norms. Here the bar has not been as helpful as it could be, as witness the antitrust field.[155]

Other institutional shortcomings are visible within the profession. To the extent that the judiciary has moved into a new type of decision-making, the organized bar has not proceeded along parallel lines. Bar associations, local and national, with rare exceptions confine themselves to the esoterica of the craft and to the protection of the guild. Even the prestigious American Law Institute still is largely engaged in "restating" the law—an intellectual endeavor that comes at the very point in history when law is fluid and cannot be restated with any marked success. Would it not be far better if

---

[153] Selznick, *Sociology of Law*, INT. ENCYC. SOC. SCI. (1968). See also BROOM & SELZNICK, SOCIOLOGY: A TEXT WITH ADAPTED READINGS 386–88 (4th ed. 1968).

[154] FULLER, THE PROBLEMS OF JURISPRUDENCE 707 (1949).

[155] See, *e.g.*, Massel, *Economic Analysis in Judicial Antitrust Decisions*, 20 A.B.A. SECTION OF ANTITRUST LAW 46 (1962).

230 ARTHUR SELWYN MILLER

those keen legal minds addressed themselves to the real problems of real people, not to the delineation of black-letter "rules"? Of what use, for example, is the *Restatement of Foreign Relations Law?* In torts, to take another example, would it not be better to spend time on such matters as automobile accidents and even sonic booms and other human problems than to publish a restatement? Now and then an exception appears, one that suggests that the organized bar could do much more if the will were present. For example, Professor Alan Westin's fine study on privacy was written for the Association of the Bar of the City of New York.[156] Ralph Nader's impact in the field of safety is revealing testimony of what one lawyer, working alone, is able to do.

If the objection is made, as surely it will be, that it is puerile to think that lawyers can or will want to rise above the narrow interests of their clients so as to pursue the general good, the answer can only be that it is not naïve to suggest that the lawyers may well be on the way to becoming more and more irrelevant in a scientific-technological age.[157] They are tending to become mere technicians, practicing "a rather esoteric craft of limited social value."[158] The fault may be traceable to the way that legal education has developed in the United States. It is looked upon vocationally, as training for private practice—and for a practice, be it noted, likely to have little resemblance to what today's lawyers do in fact. Institutionally, furthermore, American law schools are not preparing their students for the affirmative jurisprudence of the day. In a time when scientists and technologists are forecasting and even molding the future, legal educators think mainly in terms of what has been. At most, they are contemporaneous. That is not enough. Required is a sustained effort to assist in the attainment of the values of a democratic polity. A part of that effort must surely be directed toward an evaluation of the role and nature of government in the age of the Positive State—including that very "special type of court"—the Supreme Court of the United States. Scientists and technologists, with the *hubris* that seems to infect that fraternity, claim an ability to "invent the future." That they may be able to do, but are we preparing lawyers for it?

---

[156] WESTIN, PRIVACY AND FREEDOM (1967).

[157] See Miller, *Public Law and the Obsolescence of the Lawyer*, 19 U. FLA. L. REV. 514 (1967).

[158] ROSTOW, REPORT OF THE DEAN OF THE YALE LAW SCHOOL 16 (1966).

D. OTHER PROBLEMS

There are additional problems involved in the concept of constitutional duty, problems that may be somewhat more technical than those already set out. They can be briefly delineated. Included among these are (*a*) the criteria for determining affirmative governmental duties, (*b*) who is to be permitted to bring actions (the question of standing), and (*c*) enforcement of the Court's decrees.

What may be said about all of them? Four things, at least. First, and most obvious, each is not unique to the enunciation of constitutional duties by the Supreme Court. The criteria of constitutional adjudication—what the proper ingredients and methodology of an opinion are and should be—has been argued by Americans, lay and professional, throughout the stormy history of the Court. What part should history (as precedent, as intention of the framers, or whatever) play in the decisional process? The question cannot be answered definitively. What may be said is that the Justices are free to use such criteria as they think are relevant, there being no settled conception of the nature of the judicial process. So it is with that nebulous concept of standing. One of the identifying characteristics of the concept of constitutional duty is a tendency to expand the class of those who may trigger a judicial response. *Baker v. Carr* is the ready illustration. Problems of standing are present, however, in most, possibly all, cases. Accordingly, there is nothing new or onerous imposed on the Justices in this respect when they are dealing with purported duties or obligations of government. No judicial decision is self-executing. It requires positive action (usually forthcoming) of some other governmental official to translate a court decision into operational reality. This is particularly true of the Supreme Court, which must rely on delegated commands or admonitions to others if compliance is to be attained.[159] In "duty" cases, as elsewhere, the delegates have discretion. Only those directly before the bar of the Court in a specific case can be said to be under a legal obligation to comply (unless, of course, the case falls within the nebulous realm of class actions).[160] In sum, the problems of criteria, of standing, as of this moment at least,

---

[159] See Miller & Scheflin, note 10 *supra*, at 288–94.

[160] On class actions, see *Multiparty Litigation in the Federal Courts*, 71 HARV. L. REV. 874, 928–43 (1958). See also the newly amended FED. R. CIV. PROC., Rule 23, and notes of the Advisory Committee thereon.

and of enforcement, do not present the Justices with questions that differ essentially from what their predecessors decided.

Second, even if the problems are not dissimilar from those in other areas and other times, they are harder to resolve. They call for a high quality of capacity on the part of both bench and bar, a quality that is not in particularly ample supply. They call as well for an appreciation of social conditions and an evaluation of the impact that a given decision will be likely to make on the behavior of Americans. The institutional inadequacy of the law, already discussed, makes the problem doubly difficult—to the point where one may well suggest a coming desuetude of the Supreme Court.[161] By no means is it clear that the American people will continue to accept that institution as a norm-setter or rule-maker in the nation. The massive retreat that the Court made in the late 1930's and early 1940's in economic policy questions is revealing testimony to buttress the proposition that the locus of governmental power is to be found ever increasingly within the amorphous confines of the executive-administrative branch and that the Court, as a consequence, may now be engaged in a burst of activity comparable to that of stars that flare up and burn fiercely just before they die. The very difficulty of "duty" problems makes it necessary to pose the question of the continuing viability of the Supreme Court. If, as Justice Frankfurter said, it is necessary for law to display "sociological wisdom," can we continue to rely on the nine men who sit on that tribunal to be sociologically wise?[162] The answer is far from self-evident.

Third, it seems equally clear that no guarantees are built into the system to insure that the Court will continue to follow a given line of doctrine. Quite the contrary. The laissez faire Court of the pre-1937 period gave way to the permissive and libertarian Court of the modern era. That violent swing in doctrine may be attributed to "Mr. Zeitgeist," as Charles Wyzanski observed after winning the labor cases of 1937,[163] more than to a change of personnel or to the Justices' sudden discovery of revealed truth. Whatever the causes, and surely they are multiple and not simple, that sort of

---

[161] See MILLER, note 16 *supra*, at c. 6.

[162] How wise, to take just one example, was *Korematsu,* note 110 *supra?*

[163] Letter of Apr. 14, 1937, Learned Hand Papers, Harvard Law School Library, quoted in Freund, *Charles Evans Hughes as Chief Justice,* 81 HARV. L. REV. 4, 35 n. 112 (1967).

fluctuation could be repeated. A new set of doctrines and a new judicial posture could be created. Change may be foreseen but its nature and direction are unforeseeable. Possibly the category of those having standing to challenge official action may be expanded. On the other hand, that group of litigants with "justiciable controversies" could be abruptly curtailed. *Flast v. Cohen* would seem to indicate the former.[164] What will happen, however, cannot be forecast, simply because the social context in which the Court (and other organs of government) operates cannot be foreseen with any degree of certainty. As Dean Don K. Price has recently asserted: "The main lines of our [public] policy, over the long run, are likely to be determined by scientific developments that we cannot foresee, rather than by political doctrines that we can now state."[165] If for "political" we read "political and legal," for the Supreme Court in constitutional matters deals essentially with juristic theories of politics, it may readily be perceived that what the Court may do in the future is an entirely unknown quantity. Those who applaud the "activism" of the Warren Court may be in for a rude shock some time in the future. The Court, until recent years, has never been noted either for its courage or for the protection of personal rights and liberties. This is neither to denigrate a group of dedicated men nor to predict an abrupt change, but merely to point out the possible.[166]

Finally, it will be necessary to identify problem areas ripe for and susceptible of judicial enunciation of affirmative goals or duties. This will be difficult, for if one surveys the field of possible activity it seems that the Court may be running out of fundamental constitutional issues. It may be increasingly concerned with the minutiae of already announced policies, with filling in their interstices, rather than with breaking new ground. At the seeming height of its powers, and at a time when it has been more "activist" than ever before in its history, it may in fact be diminishing in power. Already an inferior tribunal in economic policy questions, it may have reached its pinnacle as an arbiter of social ethics. Not that it

---

[164] 392 U.S. 83 (1968).

[165] PRICE, THE SCIENTIFIC ESTATE 186 (1965).

[166] A change in personnel of the Court could bring this about. Also, some of the Justices may change their minds about some matters. For example, Mr. Justice Black went to great lengths in his 1968 Carpentier Lectures at Columbia University to assert (and prove to his satisfaction) that he has not changed in recent years, as some have thought. BLACK, note 150 *supra*.

will dwindle overnight. Doubtless the Court will continue to sit and to issue its ostensibly portentous pronouncements on public policy. But in its constitutional role it may have shot its bolt. It may ever increasingly be a "supreme court of statutory interpretation." In the same manner that Congress in recent years has lost status and is searching for a new role in the technological age,[167] the Supreme Court could well be on the way to "running out of constitutional gas." The Justices may find it difficult to identify (and accept) new problem areas for determination. This is, after all, the age of executive hegemony in government, here and elsewhere. The concept of constitutional duty, in short, may be the last, brilliant contribution of America's unique development in the art of government.

V. Conclusion

Suggested in this paper is the idea that the Supreme Court is moving in the direction of changing the Constitution from one of limitations alone to one of limitations and duties. There is, of course, a semantic problem in seeing "duties" rather than "limitations" in the decisional areas mentioned. Even so, the change, subtle though it may be, does seem to be occurring. Students of the Court doubtless will differ strenuously over its propriety. As long as the new posture continues, continuing controversy about the Court may be forecast, for it involves, in essence, the Justices taking sides on burning questions of public policy, in areas where tempers and emotions run strong and deep. Not that the Court has not often been in controversy. Only time will tell if the new posture can or will continue. That it should continue is, to me, a necessary proposition. The continuing dialogue that is the American democracy can function better with guidance from the supreme tribunal.

What the Supreme Court is doing, as I see it, is to attempt to put content into the Constitution rather similar to that expressed in the Universal Declaration of Human Rights, adopted by the General Assembly of the United Nations in December, 1948. In that Declaration, certain economic and social rights are stated. For example, the rights to work, to equal pay for equal work, to rest and leisure, to an adequate standard of living, to education, to par-

---

[167] See, *e.g.*, the several essays in TRUMAN, ed., THE CONGRESS AND AMERICA'S FUTURE (1965).

ticipate in the cultural life of the community. Utopian though it may be, unratified by the United States as it is, unfulfilled for most of the peoples of the world, the Declaration[168] nonetheless helps point the way in which law and, I hope, society are moving. The Supreme Court is helping to create a law of the affirmative responsibilities of government. By doing so, it remains relevant to the needs and demands of the modern era.

---

[168] See POLITICAL THEORY AND THE RIGHTS OF MAN (Raphael ed. 1967). The Universal Declaration of Human Rights is reprinted at pp. 143–48. The several essays printed in the book discuss various aspects of the concept of "human rights," both with respect to the Declaration and otherwise. In *The People Left Behind: A Report of the President's National Advisory Commission on Rural Poverty* (September 1967), it is said that if private enterprise does not provide enough employment opportunity, "it is the obligation of government to provide it." And further: "The Commission believes it is the obligation of society and of government, to assure . . . people enough income to provide a decent living." P. xi. Although it is clear from that report that the Commission was talking of political programs, the apposite question posed here is the extent to which (if at all) the judiciary can aid in the articulation and the furtherance of such an obligation. See, however, Neumann, *The Concept of Political Freedom*, 53 COLUM. L. REV. 901 (1953).

PAUL BREST

PALMER v. THOMPSON: AN APPROACH TO THE PROBLEM OF UNCONSTITUTIONAL LEGISLATIVE MOTIVE

[W]e cannot shut our eyes to matters of public notoriety and general cognizance. When we take our seats on the bench we are not struck with blindness and forbidden to know as judges what we see as men. . . .[1]

[T]he Court ought to shut its mind to much of what all others think they see. That is precisely what courts are for. They try things out on evidence, by the process of proof and refutation, and shut their minds to the kinds of surmise by which the general public may reach politically sufficient conclusions.[2]

I. PALMER v. THOMPSON[3]

Almost everyone in Jackson, Mississippi, knew that the city closed its public swimming pools solely to avoid integration. In 1962, seven years after the Supreme Court held maintenance of segregated public facilities to be unconstitutional,[4] the city of Jack-

---

Paul Brest is Assistant Professor of Law, Stanford University.

[1] Ho Ah Kow v. Nunan, 12 Fed. Cas. 252, 255 (No. 6546) (C.C.D. Cal. 1879) (Field, J.).

[2] BICKEL, THE LEAST DANGEROUS BRANCH 220 (1962).   [3] 403 U.S. 217 (1971).

[4] Mayor and City Council of Baltimore v. Dawson, 350 U.S. 877 (1955); Holmes v. City of Atlanta, 350 U.S. 879 (1955).

son was still operating its parks, libraries, zoos, golf courses, playgrounds, and pools on a segregated basis.[5] A Mississippi statute required all political subdivisions "to prohibit . . . the causing of a mixing or integration of the white and Negro races in . . . public places of amusement, recreation or assembly."[6] In a decision enjoining the city of Jackson from maintaining separate waiting rooms in train and bus stations, the Court of Appeals for the Fifth Circuit took judicial notice of the state's "steel-hard, inflexible, undeviating official policy of segregation . . . , stated in its laws . . . , rooted in custom," and observed by the city.[7]

In 1962, black residents of Jackson brought an omnibus suit to desegregate the city's public facilities including its five swimming pools. In May 1962, nine days after the district court entered a declaratory judgment in plaintiffs' favor,[8] Jackson's mayor Allen Thompson announced: "We will do all right this year at the swimming pools . . . but if these agitators keep up their pressure, we would have five colored swimming pools because we are not going to have any intermingling."[9] The mayor added that the city had legislative authority to sell the pools or close them down.

One year later, the city's recreational facilities remained segregated.[10] Mayor Thompson announced that "neither agitators nor President Kennedy will change the determination of Jackson to retain segregation."[11] When a committee of black citizens re-

[5] 403 U.S. at 247 (White, J., dissenting). Mr. Justice White's opinion sets out all the salient facts in the record. For convenience I have referred to his opinion rather than the record.

[6] MISS. CODE ANN. § 4065.3 (1957), repealed, 1970 Laws, ch. 374, § 2 (1970 Cum. Supp.).

[7] United States v. City of Jackson, 318 F.2d 1, 5–6 (5th Cir. 1963).

[8] Clark v. Thompson, 206 F. Supp. 539 (S.D. Miss. 1962), aff'd per curiam, 313 F.2d 637 (5th Cir. 1963).

[9] 403 U.S. at 250.

[10] The district court had refused to grant an injunction against the city, stating that "the individual defendants in this case are all outstanding, high class gentlemen and in my opinion will not violate the terms of the declaratory judgment." 206 F. Supp. at 543. Only plaintiffs appealed from the judgment, alleging that declaratory relief was inadequate. As Mr. Justice White noted, none of the facilities was desegregated "until after the appellate proceedings in Clark v. Thompson were fully concluded. This was true despite the fact that . . . the only possible result of such review would have been a broadening of the relief granted by the District Judge." 403 U.S. at 249–50.

[11] Id. at 250.

quested that the facilities be desegregated, Mayor Thompson responded that "in spite of the current agitation" he and the commissioners were planning to build additional Negro parks, a Negro clubhouse, a Negro library, and other recreational facilities for Negroes.[12] Pressures from the black community persisted, and in the spring of 1963 Mayor Thompson announced that the pools would not be opened on schedule "due to some minor water difficulty."[13] Jackson did not reopen the swimming pools. The city canceled its lease on one pool owned by the YMCA and sold another to Jackson State College. The three pools owned by the city remain closed to this day.[14]

In 1965, the petitioners in *Palmer v. Thompson,* alleging that Jackson had closed its swimming pools solely to avoid integrating them, sued to compel the city to reopen the pools and operate them on a desegregated basis. Respondents conceded that the decision to close the pools was precipitated by the 1962 desegregation ruling. They claimed, however, that it was not the prospect of desegregation as such, but attendant physical and economic hazards, that underlay the decision. Mayor Thompson submitted an affidavit that stated: "Realizing that the personal safety of all of the citizens of the City and the maintenance of law and order would prohibit the operation of swimming pools on an integrated basis, and realizing that the said pools could not be operated economically on an integrated basis, the City made the decision."[15]

For some years, the city had operated its pools at a deficit, boasting that its fees were "the lowest to be found anywhere in the country . . . in order to serve as many people as possible."[16] The respondents offered no evidence supporting their predictions that the deficit would increase if the pools were desegregated. Nor did respondents provide any basis for the prediction that desegregation of the pools would lead to racial violence.[17]

---

[12] *Id.* at 250–51.   [13] *Id.* at 251.   [14] *Id.* at 252–53.

[15] *Id.* at 253. The director of the Department of Parks and Recreation similarly averred: "[I]t became apparent that the swimming pools owned and operated by the City of Jackson could not be operated peacefully, safely, or economically on an integrated basis." *Ibid.* The case was tried entirely on affidavits and documentary evidence.

[16] *Id.* at 251.

[17] In oral argument before the Supreme Court, counsel for respondents stated that "to his knowledge there has been no interracial violence in Jackson since the 1961 freedom rider incidents." *Id.* at 259, n.15.

The district court ruled in favor of the respondents, adopting their explanation for the decision to close the pools.[18] A closely divided Court of Appeals affirmed.[19] In June 1971, the Supreme Court affirmed, by a five-to-four decision.[20]

Mr. Justice Black's opinion for the Court gave short shrift to petitioners' argument that the closing of the pools was unconstitutionally motivated. He asserted that the Court has never "held that a legislative act may violate equal protection solely because of the motivations of the men who voted for it,"[21] distinguishing *Griffin v. Prince Edward County School Board*[22] and *Gomillion v. Lightfoot*[23] on the ground that "the focus in those cases was on the actual effect of the enactments" rather than on motivation.[24] As authority for the impropriety of judicial review of legislative motivation, he cited *Fletcher v. Peck*,[25] and he reiterated the concerns expressed in *United States v. O'Brien:*[26] it is difficult to ascertain motivation—especially the "sole" or "dominant" motivation of a group of legislators; and it is futile to strike down a law that would be "valid as soon as the legislature . . . repassed it for different reasons."[27] Mr. Justice Black found credible respondents' explanation for their decision to close the pool. And he concluded the discussion by asserting that no one was denied the equal protection of the laws "when the city has closed the public pools to black and white alike."[28] Chief Justice Burger and Mr. Justice Blackmun each wrote a short concurring opinion, expressing their common concern that, if petitioners prevailed, Jackson would "be 'locked in' with its pools for an indefinite time in the future, despite financial loss of whatever amount, just because at one time the pools of Jackson had been segregated."[29]

---

[18] Palmer v. Thompson, Civ. No. 3790 (J) (S.D. Miss., 14 August 1965).

[19] 391 F.2d 324 (5th Cir. 1967), *aff'd en banc*, 419 F.2d 1222 (5th Cir. 1969).

[20] 403 U.S. at 217.   [23] 364 U.S. 339 (1960).

[21] *Id*. at 224.   [24] 403 U.S. at 225.

[22] 377 U.S. 218 (1964).   [25] 6 Cranch 87 (1810).

[26] 391 U.S. 367 (1968). See Alfange, *Free Speech and Symbolic Conduct: The Draft-Card Burning Case*, 1968 SUPREME COURT REVIEW 1.

[27] 403 U.S. at 224–25.   [28] *Id*. at 226.

[29] *Id*. at 230 (Blackmun, J.). At oral argument, Mr. Justice Blackmun asked counsel for petitioners: "Now suppose you prevail, and suppose [respondents] . . . lose economically year after year by increasing amounts. My question is, are they

Mr. Justice White wrote the principal dissenting opinion, in which he proposed alternative grounds for reversal:[30] The record indicated that the city had closed its pools solely because of official opposition to integration. This action would violate the Fourteenth Amendment even if the decision operated equally on blacks and whites. But the city's decision operated unequally, for it stigmatized black citizens by expressing the "official view that Negroes are so inferior that they are unfit to share with whites this particular type of public facility."[31] Moreover, even accepting respondents' stated reasons for closing the pools, any state action designed to avoid integration bears a heavy burden of justification that is not satisfied by "vague speculation" about possible adverse consequences.[32]

II. INTRODUCTION TO THE PROBLEM OF LEGISLATIVE MOTIVE

Palmer v. Thompson is but the latest addition to one of the most muddled areas of our constitutional jurisprudence. The Court's opinion is typical of the current state of the art.

First, Mr. Justice Black's assertion that *Griffin v. County School Board* and *Gomillion v. Lightfoot* turned solely on effect rather than on motivation is untenable. In *Griffin*, the Court invalidated the closing of a county school system and the payment of tuition grants to students attending private schools. The Court held (per Mr. Justice Black):[33]

> [T]he record in the present case could not be clearer that Prince Edward's public schools were closed and private

---

locked in forever?" Counsel responded: "If the question is, are they locked in forever because of racial problems which cause a rise in economic difficulties in operating the pool, my answer is that they would be locked in." *Id.* at 230 n. *Cf.* text *infra*, at notes 151–57.

[30] 403 U.S. at 240. Justices Brennan and Marshall joined Mr. Justice White. Mr. Justice Marshall also wrote a short separate dissenting opinion. Mr. Justice Douglas dissented separately, relying chiefly on the Ninth Amendment.

[31] *Id.* at 266. Mr. Justice White also suggested that an official policy of closing public facilities after they were ordered desegregated would deter Negroes from asserting their constitutional rights. *Id.* at 269. See text *infra*, at notes 178–79.

[32] 403 U.S. at 260.

[33] 377 U.S. at 231. See also Hall v. St. Helena Parish Sch. Bd., 197 F. Supp. 649 (E.D. La. 1961), aff'd, 368 U.S. 515 (1962); Bush v. Orleans Parish Sch. Bd., 187 F. Supp. 42 (E.D. La. 1960), aff'd, 365 U.S. 569 (1961); Ely, *Legislative and Adminis-*

schools operated in their place with state and county assistance, for one reason, and one reason only: to ensure through measures taken by the county and the State, that white and colored children in Prince Edward County would not, under any circumstances, go to the same school. Whatever non-racial grounds might support a State's allowing a county to abandon public schools, the object must be a constitutional one, and grounds of race and opposition to desegregation do not qualify as constitutional.

In *Gomillion*, the Alabama legislature had altered the shape of the city of Tuskegee from a square to an "uncouth twenty-eight-sided figure,"[34] with the effect of removing all but a handful of black voters (but not a single white voter) from the city limits. The Court sustained an action to set aside the change, finding these facts "tantamount for all practical purposes to a mathematical demonstration, that the legislation is solely concerned with segregating white and colored voters by fencing Negro citizens out of town."[35]

Although Mr. Justice Black made no mention of it, the Court has inquired into legislative motivation in areas other than equal protection. The Court's current standard of review under the Establishment Clause, for example, calls for an inquiry into "the purpose and the primary effect of the enactment. . . . If either is the advancement or inhibition of religion then the enactment exceeds the scope of legislative power as circumscribed by the Constitution."[36] As recently as 1968, the Court invalidated a state law forbidding the teaching of Darwinian theory in the public schools, solely on the ground that the law's purpose was "to blot out a particular theory because of its supposed conflict with the Biblical account."[37]

Second, Mr. Justice Black's reliance on *Fletcher v. Peck* was misplaced. The Georgia legislature there rescinded an enormous land

---

trative Motivation in Constitutional Law, 79 YALE L.J. 1205, 1295–96 (1970) (hereafter cited as Ely).

[34] 364 U.S. at 340.

[35] *Id.* at 341. See also Ely, at 1255–61.

[36] Abington School District v. Schempp, 374 U.S. 203, 222 (1963). See also Lemon v. Kurtzman, 403 U.S. 602 (1971); Tilton v. Richardson, 403 U.S. 672 (1971).

[37] Epperson v. Arkansas, 393 U.S. 97 (1968). The Court has also inquired into motivation to determine whether a statute has punitive intent under the Bill of Attainder Clause, see United States v. Lovett, 328 U.S. 303 (1946), and the Due Process Clause, see Kennedy v. Mendoza-Martinez, 372 U.S. 144, 169–84 (1963).

242   PAUL BREST

grant made by an earlier session of the legislature, members of which had been bribed to vote for the grant. Fletcher was the bona fide purchaser of a parcel of this land from Peck. Alleging that the bribery nullified the grant, Fletcher sued Peck for breach of a covenant that all of the state's title in the premises had been conveyed to Peck. Chief Justice Marshall, after mentioning the problems that a judicial inquiry into political corruption would present if the issue were properly raised, held that it could not be raised "collaterally and incidentally" in a private action for breach of covenant. (The Court went on to hold that the state could not, in any case, impair the interests of bona fide purchasers by rescinding the grant.)

Although the Chief Justice did not clearly state his reasons for refusing to inquire into the alleged corruption, they appear to be an amalgam of the general impropriety of the inquiry, Fletcher's lack of "standing" to raise the issue, and the absence of an indispensable party, the state.[38] Whatever *Fletcher* held, however, it cannot be parlayed into a general pronouncement against judicial review of unconstitutional legislative motivation. First, of course, the constitutionality of the land grant was never in question. But more fundamentally, *Fletcher* dealt with a qualitatively different kind of "motivation" from that involved in *Palmer*, *O'Brien*, *Griffin*, and *Gomillion*. In *Fletcher* the question that the Court refused to ask was: what did the decisionmakers desire to achieve in terms of personal benefits (for example, lining their pockets) by the act of voting? The inquiry eschewed in *Palmer* and *O'Brien* bears closer resemblance to the traditional search for legislative purpose as an aid to statutory interpretation: what effects did the decisionmakers desire to achieve by the operation of their decision?[39] These inquiries differ functionally as well as formally, for the methods for proving corruption entail a judicial intrusion into the political processes that is largely absent in the latter inquiry.[40]

Finally, in *Palmer*, as in *O'Brien*, the Court failed to elucidate its functional arguments against judicial review of motivation, and failed entirely to consider the arguments that might favor such review. I will deal at length with these matters below, but some

---

[38] See 6 Cranch at 130–31.

[39] See Ely, at 1218; MacCallum, *Legislative Intent*, 75 Yale L.J. 754, 756–57 (1966).

[40] See text *infra*, at notes 126–44.

of the basic questions can be noted here. Even if legislative motivation is often difficult to ascertain,[41] is the inquiry inevitably so
problematic that it should never be undertaken? Why must the
inquiry be complicated by searching—as Mr. Justice Black assumed
one must search—for " 'sole' or 'dominant' motivation"?[42] Moreover, why is it "futile" to invalidate a law enacted for impermissible reasons just because it could be readopted for valid reasons?[43]
And, finally, what policies might support the invalidation of an
otherwise permissible law enacted for illicit reasons? So far as I
know, the Court has never squarely addressed the last question,
the answer to which would seem a prerequisite for any coherent
theory of judicial review of legislative motivation, and a precondi-
tion to *Palmer*'s flat assertion that "the closing of the Jackson
swimming pools to all its citizens [does not] constitute . . . a denial
of 'the equal protection of the laws.' "[44]

Legal scholars have offered the courts virtually no assistance
in handling the problem of judicial review of motivation. The
academic tradition of superficial treatment of the subject was essentially broken a year ago with the publication of Professor John
Ely's article, "Legislative and Administrative Motivation in Constitutional Law."[45] Ely raised and sharpened many important issues
that have long remained hidden, and he undertook a valuable
examination of legislative motivation in a number of substantive
areas of constitutional law.[46] Useful and important as his article is,
however, I believe that much of its analysis is incorrect and that it
failed in its effort to formulate a coherent doctrine to govern
judicial review of motivation.

---

[41] 403 U.S. at 224–25.

[42] *Ibid.*

[45] Note 33 *supra*.

[43] *Ibid.*; 391 U.S. at 384.

[44] 403 U.S. at 226.

[46] The extent to which a judicial determination of motivation is relevant to the
outcome of a case depends on the substantive doctrine in the particular area of law
involved. For example, if the courts become more willing to invalidate official acts
because they have undesirable effects, see Michelman, *On Protecting the Poor
through the Fourteenth Amendment*, 83 HARV. L. REV. 7 (1969)—if, for example,
school segregation is held unlawful simply because it is educationally harmful, see,
e.g., Fiss, *The Charlotte-Mecklenburg Case—Its Significance for Northern School
Desegregation*, 38 U. CHI. L. REV. 697 (1971)—the role of judicial review of legislative motivation will be diminished *pro tanto*. See Ely, at 1254–61, 1281–82. I do
not propose to enter into debate over these substantive issues. There are, and there
doubtless will remain, cases in which judicial review of legislative motivation can
have a determinative role. My central concern is what that role should be.

III. Some Basic Constitutional Concepts and Doctrines

Judicial review of motivation cannot be considered in isolation. The underlying concepts and policies are closely interdependent with those of constitutional review not concerned with legislative motive.

A. THE ANATOMY OF A LAW OR DECISION

1. *The paradigm case: the operative rule.* The paradigm law has three components or attributes: (*a*) an operative rule, (*b*) objectives (or purposes), and (*c*) effects (or consequences or impact).

The "operative[47] rule" is the "law" itself: a generalized prescription that certain persons shall act, or that certain persons or objects shall be treated, in a certain manner under certain circumstances, for example: "All trucks must be equipped with exhaust emission control devices."

An operative rule may be constitutionally "innocent," like the exhaust regulation, triggering only the demand for a rational justification;[48] or it may be "suspect," for example, "No person of Japanese ancestry may remain in the following area," triggering the demand for an extraordinary justification;[49] or it may simply be blatantly unconstitutional, for example, "Soldiers may, in time of peace, be quartered in houses without consent of the owners."[50] Once the Court has determined that a particular suspect rule, for example, one commanding racial segregation in public schools, cannot be justified, the rule effectively becomes illicit. (I use "illicit" to refer to suspect rules that have been held unjustified as well as rules that are unconstitutional per se.)[51]

An operative rule may be overt, "No Chinese may operate laundries," or may be covert, as where the official charged with issuing permits to operate laundries grants them to Caucasians and denies them to Chinese, and no variable other than nationality explains the pattern.[52]

---

[47] I use the adjective "operative" to distinguish the kind of rule described in the text from, *inter alia*, rules of a different level of generality that guide or constrain the formulation of operative rules or criteria.

[48] See text *infra*, at notes 62–69.

[49] See text *infra*, at notes 71–84.   [50] See note 70 *infra*.

[51] I employ the same usage with respect to suspect and unjustifiable motives.

[52] See Yick Wo v. Hopkins, 118 U.S. 356 (1886).

An "operative rule" has one or more "objectives" or "purposes" —the state of affairs or effects that the decisionmaker[53] seeks to establish or retain by promulgation of the rule.[54] For example, the objective of the exhaust emission regulation is to reduce exhaust emissions or, more generally, to reduce air pollution or, still more generally, to protect health or the environment.[55]

Every explicit or implicit distinction made by a law may have objectives. For example, the objective of limiting the exhaust regulation to trucks may be to impose the costs of emission control on those causing the most harm, on the assumption that trucks emit more, or more noxious, pollutants than automobiles, or on those best able to pay, on the assumption that those using trucks are better able to absorb the cost of an emission control device.

Objectives may be constitutionally innocent (reducing air pollution), or suspect (segregating by race), or impermissible (disadvantaging blacks or Catholics). To the extent that judicial review of legislative motivation is appropriate, characterizing an "objective" in one of these ways has effects analogous to characterizing an "operative rule" in the same way.[56]

"Operative rules" produce "effects"—changes in the state of affairs. The effects may or may not be prescribed by a rule itself. For example, the migration of indigents into a state may be deterred

---

[53] I use the term "decisionmaker" to refer to multimember governmental bodies—*e.g.*, administrative agencies and legislatures—as well as to individual government officials.

[54] An objective may also be described retrospectively, in terms of the mischief sought to be eliminated. Heydon's Case, 3 Co. Rep. 7a, 7b (1584). It is common, in the context of statutory construction, to talk of the law itself having an objective. This anthropomorphism is sometimes designed to buttress the assertion that the process of statutory construction is "not concerned with anything subjective," Frankfurter, *Some Reflections on the Reading of Statutes*, 47 COLUM. L. REV. 527, 539 (1947); see FULLER, THE MORALITY OF THE LAW 84–88 (1964), but it is sometimes merely a convenient ellipsis for the decisionmaker's purpose in adopting the rule. Only the latter use is apposite in the context of judicial review of legislative motivation, where the court's ultimate concern is the decisionmaker's state of mind.

[55] As the example in the text suggests, a rule's objectives can be described more or less immediately. The notion that a viable distinction can be drawn between "motive" and "purpose," based on the immediacy of the objective inquired into, has properly been put to rest by several recent commentators. See Ely, at 1217–21; Note, *Legislative Purpose and Federal Constitutional Adjudication*, 83 HARV. L. REV. 1887–88, n.1 (1970).

[56] See text *infra*, at notes 109–16.

by a law that provides, "No indigent may enter the state,"[57] or by a law that establishes a one-year period of residency for welfare eligibility.[58] Effects may or may not be objectives of the operative rule.[59] For example, the welfare residence requirement might be enacted for the purpose of deterring the immigration of indigents, or to serve administrative ends.[60] In some circumstances, the government cannot allow certain effects to occur, even though the operative rule and its objectives are themselves innocent.[61]

2. *Two nonparadigmatic cases: the operative criterion and the ad hoc decision.* Not all governmental action is conducted pursuant to operative rules. The factors entering into a decision may be numerous and nonquantifiable, making the formulation of a rule impracticable or impossible. For example, a park commissioner, in deciding where to locate a playground, may consider the costs of land acquisition and development, the proximity of a site to existing recreational facilities, traffic hazards, and numerous other factors. He even may have a checklist of "operative criteria" that he considers in each case, and he may consistently weigh some factors more heavily than others. But he has no formula—no rule—that, given each of the inputs, can generate a result.

For my purposes here, a fixed set of operative criteria to which the decisionmaker systematically resorts is equivalent to a rule. Like a rule, a criterion may itself be, and may have objectives that are, innocent, suspect, or impermissible.

Some governmental decisions are nonsystematic or ad hoc. These are not made according to any checklist or set of preexisting criteria, and the decisionmaker may give no thought to reconciling the action with past decisions or treating like cases alike in the future. For example, the park commissioner may not have developed guidelines for playground location, either because he seldom makes such decisions or simply because he operates unsystematically. To characterize a decision as ad hoc does not mean that it is

---

[57] See Edwards v. California, 314 U.S. 160 (1941).

[58] See Shapiro v. Thompson, 394 U.S. 618 (1969).

[59] This means that for purposes of judicial review of motivation a decisionmaker does not necessarily have as his objective all of the foreseen consequences of his decision. See PROSSER, LAW OF TORTS 31 (4th ed. 1971); A.L.I., RESTATEMENT (SECOND) OF TORTS, § 8A, comment *b* (1955).

[60] See Shapiro v. Thompson, 394 U.S. 618 (1969).

[61] See text *infra*, at notes 86–87.

arbitrary or irrational. The commissioner may be able to provide good reasons for choosing site X rather than sites Y or Z. Indeed, he may give the same reasons as the commissioner who follows criteria.

B. THE "RATIONAL RELATION" STANDARDS

The Due Process clauses require that an operative rule bear a rational relation to a constitutionally permissible objective.[62] This means that the rule must produce effects that advance, rather than retard or have no bearing on, the attainment of a permissible objective.[63]

Every governmental action imposes costs or confers benefits on some persons but not on others. The traditional equal protection standard requires that the differential treatment mandated by an operative rule bear a rational relation to a permissible objective.[64] Adjudication under the traditional due process and equal protection standards might seem to involve empirical questions. In practice it does not. The courts stand ready to assume any reasonably conceivable state of facts[65] that relates the regulation to any reasonably conceivable permissible objective.[66] The class of

[62] See Ferguson v. Skrupa, 372 U.S. 726, 733 (1963) (Harlan, J., concurring); Williamson v. Lee Optical Co., 348 U.S. 483 (1955); Nebbia v. New York, 291 U.S. 502 (1934).

[63] But cf. FREUND, ON UNDERSTANDING THE SUPREME COURT 88–89 (1949). Freund suggests that it is sufficient that reasonable legislators could believe that the rule would produce such effects.

[64] "[T]he classification must be reasonable, not arbitrary, and must rest upon some ground of difference having a fair and substantial relation to the object of the legislation, so that all persons similarly circumstanced shall be treated alike." Royster Guano Co. v. Virginia, 253 U.S. 412, 415 (1920). Despite the surface similarity of the due process and equal protection criteria, equal protection adjudication incorporates an element of subjectivity that is absent in adjudication under a Due Process Clause. For example, the chief equal protection vices are over- and under-inclusion, see Tussman & tenBroek, *The Equal Protection of the Laws*, 37 CALIF. L. REV. 341 (1949), but a classification "does not offend the Constitution simply because [it] 'is not made with mathematical nicety or because in practice it results in some inequality.'" Dandridge v. Williams, 397 U.S. 471, 485 (1970). The degree of permissible departure from strict congruence cannot be determined by any formula, but depends ultimately on an exercise of judgment.

[65] McGowan v. Maryland, 366 U.S. 420, 426 (1961).

[66] See, *e.g.*, Flemming v. Nestor, 363 U.S. 603 (1960); Williamson v. Lee Optical Co., 348 U.S. 483 (1955); Kotch v. Board of River Pilot Commissioners, 330 U.S. 552 (1947); Daniel v. Family Security Life Ins. Co., 336 U.S. 220 (1949); Railway

impermissible objectives is small,[67] and the class of permissible ones is as broad as "the general welfare." The decisionmaker has virtually plenary authority to choose which objectives to promote at the expense of which others, and to determine what costs shall be incurred to promote the objectives and on whom those costs shall be placed.[68]

With two possible exceptions,[69] every governmental decision must meet these minimal due process and equal protection standards of rationality. To trigger judicial review a complainant need only demonstrate that the regulation operates to his disadvantage (due process) or to his comparative disadvantage (equal protection). On this showing, the Court inquires whether the rule is rationally related to a plausible licit objective. The complainant wins or loses, depending on the answer.

C. THE DEMAND FOR AN EXTRAORDINARY JUSTIFICATION

The traditional due process and equal protection standards do not explain most constitutional doctrines developed under the Bill of Rights and the Fourteenth Amendment.

Some operative rules that are rationally related to legitimate objectives are simply forbidden by the Constitution.[70] Others are

---

Express Agency v. New York, 336 U.S. 106 (1949). This broad statement may have exceptions, see Ely, at 1225–26, but they are not germane to the approach to motivation developed here, cf. id. at 1227, n.75.

[67] See text infra, at note 109.

[68] Judgments allocating costs and benefits among the parties affected by a decision may not usually be subject to analysis under the due process or the equal protection rationality standards. See Ely, at 1246–49. Nonetheless, a decisionmaker's distributive judgment may be so far afield from shared notions of fairness or appropriate cost-benefit trade-offs that a court would invalidate the law, deeming it "irrational." Cf. BICKEL, note 2 supra, at 35–46; Butler v. Michigan, 352 U.S. 380 (1957). But "rationality" in this sense is value-dependent in a way that the minimal standard described in the text is not.

[69] See text infra, at notes 183–204.

[70] Whether a rule is forbidden or only "suspect" depends in large measure on the Court's methodology and on philosophical differences among the Justices. See, e.g., Note, Civil Disabilities and the First Amendment, 78 YALE L.J. 842 (1969) (comparing the "balancing" and "classificatory" approaches to First Amendment adjudication); LOCKHART, KAMISAR, & CHOPER, CONSTITUTIONAL LAW 883–93 (3d ed. 1970) (excerpting materials on "balancing" vs. "absolutism"). Nonetheless, there are some laws that all Justices would agree are flatly forbidden by the Constitution —for example, a law establishing and financing a government-operated church. See also text supra, at note 50.

not invalid on their face, but trigger the demand for more than a rational, *i.e.*, an extraordinary, justification. For example, a law classifying persons on the basis of race is "suspect." Even though it is "enacted pursuant to a valid state interest, [it] bears a heavy burden of justification . . . and will be upheld only if it is necessary, and not merely rationally related, to the accomplishment of a permissible state policy."[71] Laws that impose punishments or disabilities because of a person's political associations or the content of his speech trigger a similar demand.[72] To satisfy the demand for an extraordinary justification, the law must be narrowly drawn[73] to serve significant state interests,[74] and there must not exist "less onerous" means of serving those interests.[75] Review under these standards, of course, requires the court to reassess the legislative decision by balancing the benefits accruing to the government against the costs imposed on those adversely affected by the law.[76]

The extraordinary justification required in these and similar kinds of cases is not contingent upon a finding of illicit motivation,[77] nor is it triggered by the adverse impact of the rule upon a racial or political minority: the criterion itself initiates the demand for an extraordinary justification. Motivation and impact, however,

---

[71] McLaughlin v. Florida, 379 U.S. 184, 196 (1964). Although the Supreme Court has only once upheld a racial or ethnic classification, see Korematsu v. United States, 323 U.S. 214 (1944), the distinction between suspect and illicit criteria under the Equal Protection Clause is not entirely academic. Classifications based on alienage and sex—if sex becomes a suspect basis for classification, *compare* Sail'er Inn, Inc. v. Kirby, 5 Cal.3d 1 (1971), *with* Goesaert v. Cleary, 335 U.S. 464 (1948)—may sometimes survive judicial scrutiny. See also text *infra*, at notes 173–79; *cf.* Lee v. Washington, 390 U.S. 333, 334 (Black, Harlan, and Stewart, JJ., concurring) (prison segregation).

[72] See, *e.g.*, Thomas v. Collins, 323 U.S. 516, 530 (1945); United States v. Carolene Products Co., 304 U.S. 114, 152, n.4 (1938); cases cited in notes 73–76 *infra*.

[73] See, *e.g.*, United States v. Robel, 389 U.S. 258 (1967); Sei Fujii v. State, 38 Cal.2d 718, 732–33. *Cf.* Aptheker v. Secretary of State, 378 U.S. 500 (1964).

[74] See, *e.g.*, Shapiro v. Thompson, 394 U.S. 618, 658 (1969) (Harlan, J., dissenting); Bridges v. California, 314 U.S. 252, 262–63 (1941).

[75] See, *e.g.*, Shelton v. Tucker, 364 U.S. 479 (1960); Note, *Developments in the Law—Equal Protection*, 82 HARV. L. REV. 1065, 1102–03 (1969).

[76] See, *e.g.*, Konigsberg v. State Bar of California, 366 U.S. 36, 51 (1961); Dennis v. United States, 341 U.S. 494 (1951); Note, note 75 *supra*, at 1103–04.

[77] The Supreme Court engages in its usual search for conceivable legitimate purposes and attributes them to the legislature. *Cf.* United States v. O'Brien, 391 U.S. 367 (1968); Shapiro v. Thompson, 394 U.S. 618 (1969).

play an important role in the Court's decision to hold certain criteria "suspect." For example, it is highly probable that a racial classification reflects prejudice on the decisionmaker's part. Largely for this reason, minorities perceive racial classifications as insulting or stigmatic. Such classifications also have an anti-educative effect of legitimizing prejudice.[78] Moreover, the employment of racial classifications over the long run is likely to deprive members of the minority of their "fair share" of the benefits distributed by society, solely because of their race.[79]

These same considerations entail that a law which does not mandate racially disparate treatment may nonetheless trigger the demand for an extraordinary justification if race plays any operative role. For example, courts have invalidated state laws providing that the governor shall assume control over any school that becomes integrated,[80] that integrated schools shall or may be closed,[81] and that tuition grants shall be made available to any student (black or white) who otherwise would be required to attend an integrated school.[82] The cases assume that the state may structure the control of its schools as it deems fit, that it need not provide any public education at all,[83] and that the grants themselves are

---

[78] See Kaplan, *Equal Justice in an Unequal World: Equality for the Negro—the Problem of Special Treatment*, 61 Nw. U. L. Rev. 363, 379–80 (1966).

[79] *Cf.* United States v. Carolene Products Co., 304 U.S. 144, 152, n.4 (1938); Michelman, *Property, Utility and Fairness: Comments on the Ethical Foundations of "Just Compensation" Law*, 80 Harv. L. Rev. 1165, 1218–22 (1967).

The reasons for requiring an extraordinary justification for laws penalizing speech and association lie largely in the effect of such laws. Under our received political theory, deterring speech not only imposes direct costs on the speaker and his willing listener, but imposes external costs on society by depriving it of the full consideration of diverse viewpoints on different issues. See Mill, On Liberty, ch. 2 (1859). To allow government to interfere with speech, moreover, endangers the preconditions of a democratic polity.

[80] *E.g.*, James v. Almond, 170 F. Supp. 331 (E.D. Va. 1959), *appeal dismissed*, 359 U.S. 1006 (1959).

[81] *E.g.*, Bush v. Orleans Parish School Bd., 187 F. Supp. 42 (E.D. La. 1960), *aff'd*, 365 U.S. 569 (1961).

[82] Hawkins v. North Carolina State Bd. of Educ., Civ. No. 2067 (31 March 1966), 11 Race Rel. L. Rep. 745 (1966).

[83] Some of the cases and commentaries dealing with school closings focus on the comparison between the pupils in the district in which the schools are abandoned and pupils attending public schools in the remainder of the state, implying that this is the inequality that must be justified. See, *e.g.*, Griffin v. County School Bd., 377 U.S. 218 (1964); Horowitz & Neitring, *Equal Protection Aspects of Inequalities in*

constitutional.[84] But when implementation of these practices is explicitly triggered by integration, they—and the triggering itself—give rise to the dangers that make racial classifications "suspect."

D. THE ROLE OF "IMPACT"

The "impact" of a law generally has had little or no constitutional significance independent of a suspect operative rule. For example, although rules classifying persons on the basis of poverty and race are suspect, the demand for an extraordinary justification is not triggered by the adoption of a fixed license fee or sales tax, which falls more heavily on the poor, nor by the enactment and enforcement of criminal laws that may disproportionately burden particular ethnic minorities. It would be both impracticable and undesirable to require decisionmakers to assure that all decisions have an equal effect on rich and poor alike and on all races.[85]

In some circumstances, however, impact alone may trigger the demand for an extraordinary justification. This is the suggestion of some of the "new" equal protection cases which hold that, in the absence of a suspect classification—or of any classification at all[86]—governmental action that adversely affects a "fundamental interest" is permissible only if it serves "compelling" state interests.[87]

Public Education and Public Assistance Programs from Place to Place within a State, 15 U.C.L.A. L. REV. 787 (1968). But the policies that support holding an integration-triggered school closing "suspect" do not depend on interdistrict disparities. The same result should obtain if, under such a statute, every school district in the state was integrated and therefore closed. See Ely, at 1295.

[84] Whether and when tuition grants are unconstitutional simply because the state is supporting private segregated schools remain open questions. *Compare, e.g.,* Griffin v. State Bd. of Educ., 239 F. Supp. 560 (E.D. Va. 1965), *with* Coffey v. State Educational Finance Commission, 296 F. Supp. 1389 (S.D. Miss. 1969), *and* Green v. Kennedy, 309 F. Supp. 1127 (D.D.C. 1970), *appeal dismissed sub nom.* Cannon v. Green, 398 U.S. 956 (1970). See Poindexter v. Louisiana Financial Assistance Comm'n, 296 F. Supp. 686 (E.D. La. 1968), *aff'd*, 393 U.S. 17 (1968); Lee v. Macon Bd. of Educ., 267 F. Supp. 458 (M.D. Ala. 1967), *aff'd sub nom.* Wallace v. United States, 389 U.S. 215 (1967).

[85] See generally Ely, at 1254-61; Kaplan, *Segregation Litigation and the Schools—Part II: The General Northern Problem*, 58 Nw. U. L. REV. 157, 176-77 (1963).

[86] For example, although no law forbids indigent criminal defendants from retaining appellate counsel, the personal interest in freedom from the stigma of a conviction and the possibility of incarceration or fine compels the state to provide counsel to those who cannot afford it. See Douglas v. California, 372 U.S. 353 (1963).

[87] See Shapiro v. Thompson, 394 U.S. 618, 658 (1969) (Harlan, J., dissenting); Michelman, note 46 *supra;* Karst, *Invidious Discrimination: Justice Douglas and the*

IV. What Is "Motivation"?

Distinction should be made between two inquiries: (*a*) What (if any) operative rule is the decisionmaker systematically employing? (*b*) Why did the decisionmaker make a particular decision? Both of these sometimes have been subsumed under the inquiry into "motivation,"[88] and they do have some characteristics in common. They are analytically distinct, however, and I believe that the term "motivation" is most usefully reserved for the latter inquiry, which focuses on the process by which a rule was adopted rather than on the content of the rule itself.

A. WHAT OPERATIVE RULE IS THE DECISIONMAKER SYSTEMATICALLY EMPLOYING?

If a state college lists among its formal prerequisites for admission the requirement that an applicant be white, this would demand an extraordinary justification, which probably could not be forthcoming. But the college might be more circumspect, and not publish its rule. That the rule is made manifest only through systematic application does not make it less "real"—or less harmful[89] —than an overt regulation.[90]

Courts generally have been willing to inquire whether a decisionmaker systematically employs an illicit or suspect operative rule and to enjoin the decisionmaker from continuing to apply it.[91]

Return of the "Natural-Law-Due-Process Formula," 16 U.C.L.A. Rev. 716 (1969); Note, note 75 *supra,* at 1087–1132 (1969); Coons, Clune, & Sugarman, Private Wealth and Public Education, ch. 10 (1970). Impact may play a similar role in cases involving state burdens on interstate commerce, *e.g.,* Bibb v. Navajo Freight Lines, Inc., 359 U.S. 520 (1959); Southern Pacific Co. v. Arizona, 325 U.S. 761 (1945), and nonsubstantive burdens on the exercise of speech, *e.g.,* Martin v. Struthers, 319 U.S. 141 (1943); Schneider v. State, 308 U.S. 147 (1939).

[88] See, *e.g.,* Ely, at 1257–61; Bickel, note 2 *supra,* at 208–21; Note, note 75 *supra,* at 1091–1101.

[89] See text *supra,* at notes 77–79. If the rule is so well concealed that neither the public nor the rejected applicant knows of its existence, the anti-educative and stigmatic harms are eliminated, but this seldom happens, or at least such concealment when successful prevents the question from being raised.

[90] For this reason, a covert operative rule, once discovered, should trigger the same demand for a defense that would be triggered by an overt rule having the same content. *Cf.* Yick Wo v. Hopkins, 118 U.S. 356 (1886). But see Ely, at 1277 n.208, discussed in text *infra,* at notes 191–96.

[91] Relief of this nature, without relief with respect to any particular alleged application of the rule, sometimes is sought in civil actions brought by the Government

In *Yick Wo v. Hopkins*,[92] for example, the Supreme Court inferred from the San Francisco Board of Supervisors' pattern of granting and denying laundry permits that the board was systematically denying permits to Chinese applicants because of their nationality. Determinations of this sort are at the core of decisions finding unlawful patterns of discrimination in jury selection,[93] employment,[94] voter registration,[95] and pupil and teacher assignments.[96]

B. WHY DID THE DECISIONMAKER MAKE A PARTICULAR DECISION?

In contrast to the inquiry just described, a court may be asked to determine how the decisionmaker arrived at this particular decision. The decision in question may be one of specific applicability (for example, the state college's rejection of Smith's application), or it may consist of the adoption of a rule or criterion of general applicability (for example, the legislature's enactment of a law requiring one year's residence in the state for eligibility for welfare benefits). The decision may itself have been made either by reference to a rule of general applicability or by an ad hoc process.

1. *The rule-generated decision.* To say that a decisionmaker systematically follows an operative rule means that cases coming within the terms of the rule must be controlled by it.[97] But this does

---

and in private class actions. For example, most school desegregation actions do not request that the named plaintiffs be allowed to attend any particular school, but rather that the school system as a whole be desegregated. See also Turner v. Fouche, 396 U.S. 346 (1970) (affirmative action to end school board discrimination); Note, *Developments in the Law—Employment Discrimination and Title VII of the Civil Rights Act of 1964*, 84 HARV. L. REV. 1109, 1242 (1971).

[92] 118 U.S. 356 (1886). The ordinance made it unlawful to maintain a laundry in a wooden building without a license. The Court assumed that the law was fair on its face, but concluded that it was being discriminatorily administered: all 200 Chinese applicants were refused licenses; the applications of all but one of 80-odd Caucasian applicants were granted.

[93] See Finkelstein, *The Application of Statistical Decision Theory to the Jury Discrimination Cases*, 80 HARV. L. REV. 338 (1966), and cases discussed in *id.* at 340–49.

[94] See, *e.g.*, Parham v. Southwestern Bell Telephone Co., 433 F.2d 421 (8th Cir. 1970) (Title VII).

[95] See, *e.g.*, Turner v. Fouche, 396 U.S. 346 (1970); United States v. Duke, 332 F.2d 759 (5th Cir. 1964).

[96] See, *e.g.*, Davis v. Pontiac School District, 443 F.2d 573 (6th Cir. 1971); Hobson v. Hansen, 269 F. Supp. 401, 422–27 (D.D.C. 1967), *remanded sub nom.* Smuck v. Hobson, 408 F.2d 175 (D.C. Cir. 1969); *cf.* Swann v. Board of Education, 402 U.S. 1, 25–26 (1971).

[97] Of course, the rule may have exceptions. But, as Professor Ronald Dworkin has suggested in another context, "then it is inaccurate and incomplete to state the

not entail that any particular decision that could have been generated by the rule was generated by it: a rule is a sufficient, but often not a necessary, condition for a given result. If a state college adheres to the rule, "reject blacks," then the fact that Smith is black is a sufficient ground for rejecting his application. But the college may never have considered Jones's race (or even have known that he was black) before rejecting his application: Jones was taken out of the running because his grades or College Board scores were below the college's cut-off.

All other things being equal, the fact that a decisionmaker is known to follow a rule lends support to the inference that a particular decision consistent with the rule was generated by it. Courts have been willing to make this inference.[98] In the face of such a rule, the courts sometimes have shifted to the decisionmaker the burden of proving that a particular decision—for example, the rejection of an applicant for admission to college or for a job— was not an instance of the application of an impermissible rule.[99]

2. *The ad hoc (specific) decision.* Particular decisions often are not made pursuant to rules. A state college may have no racial criteria and, indeed, may have many black students. But the dean of admissions had an unpleasant encounter with a black student just before he considered Carter's application for admission. Temporarily entertaining some racial animus, the dean rejected Carter's application because Carter was black.

Courts sometimes have been willing to determine whether an ad hoc decision was based on the decisionmaker's consideration of an impermisible factor.[100] But sometimes, as in *Palmer v. Thomp-*

---

rule so simply, without enumerating the exceptions." Dworkin, *The Model of Rules*, 35 U. CHI. L. REV. 14, 25 (1967). The point made in the text applies to systematically applied operative criteria as well—for example, to the college's giving positive weight to the fact that an applicant is white or black.

[98] *E.g.*, Meredith v. Fair, 305 F.2d 343 (5th Cir. 1962); Alabama v. United States, 304 F.2d 583 (5th Cir.), *aff'd*, 371 U.S. 37 (1962); Lucy v. Adams, 134 F. Supp. 235 (N.D. Ala.), *aff'd*, 228 F.2d 619 (5th Cir. 1955).

[99] *E.g.*, Chambers v. Hendersonville Bd. of Educ., 364 F.2d 189, 192 (4th Cir. 1966); Williams v. Kimbrough, 295 F. Supp. 578 (W.D. La. 1969). *Cf.* Hawkins v. North Carolina Dental Society, 355 F.2d 718 (4th Cir. 1966).

[100] See, *e.g.*, Griffin v. County School Board, 377 U.S. 218 (1964); People v. Walker, 14 N.Y.2d 901 (1964) (discriminatory prosecution); People v. Gray, 254 Cal. App.2d 256 (1967) (same).

son, they have refused to undertake the inquiry on the ground that it would have constituted an (improper) inquiry into the decision-maker's motivation.

3. *The decision to adopt a rule of general applicability.* Rules themselves are seldom, if ever, generated by higher-level (rule-generating) rules. Rather they are adopted through an ad hoc process in which the decisionmaker considers and weighs a large variety of factors.[101] Just as someone making an ad hoc decision of specific applicability (deciding whether to admit Carter to college) can consider an impermissible factor (Carter's race), so too can a decisionmaker give weight to an impermissible factor in promulgating a general rule that is innocent on its face. For example, a state legislature may adopt a stringent voting literacy test for the purpose of excluding Negroes from the franchise.[102]

An inquiry to determine whether a decisionmaker considered constitutionally impermissible factors—or entertained constitutionally impermissible objectives—in adopting a rule of general applicability is the archetypal inquiry into "legislative motivation."[103]

C. CHARACTERISTICS OF THE TWO INQUIRIES

The two inquiries just described differ in several respects, one of which is analytically significant.[104] The first inquiry aims at

---

101 Of course, a decisionmaker may systematically measure a proposed rule against certain general principles—justice, constitutionality, efficiency, and the like. But these are not sufficiently precise or complete to determine the content of a particular rule. Many such principles are constraints rather than affirmative guidelines.

102 See cases cited in note 133 *infra*.

103 See, *e.g.*, United States v. O'Brien, note 26 *supra*.

104 The main operational difference lies in the methods of proof. The methodology for establishing that a decisionmaker is covertly employing an illicit operative rule or criterion has been basically that of statistical analysis. The court hypothesizes the illicit rule ("reject Blacks"), posits other factors (grades, test scores) that could conceivably explain the decisionmaker's pattern of conduct, and assesses the likelihood that one or another factor—or randomness—accounts for the decisionmaker's behavior. In testing a hypothesized operative rule one usually can identify a relevant datum (an application for admission and the college's disposition of it) quite precisely, and enough events often have occurred to allow control for other possible explanatory variables.

The determination that a particular decision was illicitly motivated—that it was generated by an illicit operative rule or that it was an ad hoc decision based on the consideration of illicit factors—typically depends on more intuitive and impression-

determining the content of a covert operative rule; and an impermissible operative rule, whether it is overtly promulgated or concealed, is substantively, and hence permanently, invalid. The second inquiry focuses on the process by which the rule or decision was made; it asks what criteria or objectives the decisionmaker took into account. The court does not hold the decision substantively invalid—it does not hold that an applicant excluded from college because of his race is entitled to attend the college, or that a state may not employ a difficult literacy test. It requires only that the college not exclude an applicant because he is black,[105] and that the state not adopt the literacy test in order to disfranchise blacks.[106] A legislative decision held invalid because it was impermissibly motivated may in theory be made again, in identical form, provided only that it is made for licit reasons.[107]

In general, the courts have reserved the characterization "motivation" for the subject of the second inquiry—the inquiry to determine whether impermissible criteria or objectives played a role in the decisionmaking process when the same result might have been achieved by the consideration of legitimate criteria or justified in terms of legitimate objectives. And it is this that is the subject of this article.

V. The Case for Judicial Review of Motivation

To my knowledge, no court or commentator has articulated the case for judicial review of legislative and administrative motivation.[108] The reasons supporting such review have, perhaps, seemed so obvious as not to call for elaboration. In fact, the full argument is moderately complex.

---

istic inferences. Statistical techniques generally are of less assistance in explaining the basis for a particular decision than in explaining the basis for a pattern of decisions. It often is not clear what events count as salient data for the inference, the sample is likely to be small, and the data are likely to consist of events so lacking in similarity as to preclude systematic analysis. Nonetheless, as I suggest below, see text *infra*, at notes 126–39, the determination of motivation often can be made with certitude sufficient to support a judgment invalidating the decision.

[105] See, *e.g.*, Lucy v. Adams, 134 F. Supp. 235 (N.D. Ala. 1955), *aff'd*, 228 F.2d 619 (5th Cir. 1955).

[106] See generally text *infra*, at notes 107–14.

[107] See generally text *infra*, at notes 145–57.

[108] But *cf.* text *infra*, at note 215.

A. ILLICIT MOTIVATION

The following four points set out what I believe to be the central argument for judicial invalidation of an illicitly motivated law.

1. Governments are constitutionally prohibited from pursuing certain objectives—for example, the disadvantaging of a racial group, the suppression of a religion, or the deterring of interstate migration.[109]

2. The fact that a decisionmaker gives weight to an illicit objective may determine the outcome of the decision. The decisionmaking process consists of weighing the foreseeable and desirable consequences of the proposed decision against its foreseeable costs. Considerations of distributive fairness play an important role. To the extent that the decisionmaker is illicitly motivated, he treats as a desirable consequence one to which the lawfully motivated decisionmaker would be indifferent or which he would view as undesirable.

3. Assuming that a person has no legitimate complaint against a particular decision merely because it affects him adversely, he does have a legitimate complaint if it would not have been adopted but for the decisionmaker's consideration of illicit objectives. If in fact the rule adopted is useful and fair, the adversely affected party might have no legitimate grievance, whatever considerations went into its adoption.[110] In our governmental system, however, only the

---

[109] See, e.g., Shapiro v. Thompson, 394 U.S. 618, 627–31 (1969). These particular objectives are proscribed because their pursuit is detrimental to society at large, or because it is unjust to disadvantage persons for possessing certain attributes, or for both reasons. A decision made for the purpose of disadvantaging a particular racial, ethnic, or religious minority, moreover, inflicts a stigmatic injury distinct from the operative consequences of the law: the act of adoption is itself an official insult to the minority.

The proposition in the text has operative consequences apart from judicial review of motivation. First, an illicit objective cannot be proffered in defense of a law subject to the requirement of a rational or extraordinary justification. See *id.* Second, the decisionmaker himself is obligated not to take account of illicit objectives. See U.S. Const. Art. VI, § 3; *cf.* Morgan, Congress and the Constitution (1966). In addition, Congress may enact legislation responsive to its own findings that state decisionmakers have acted out of impermissible motives. See, e.g., Oregon v. Mitchell, 400 U.S. 112 (1970); Katzenbach v. Morgan, 384 U.S. 641 (1966).

[110] A member of a minority group does have a complaint against being subjected to the opprobrium emanating from even a "good" decision adopted for discriminatory reasons.

political decisionmaker—and not the judiciary[111]—has general authority to assess the utility and fairness of a decision. And, since the decisionmaker has (by hypothesis) assigned an incorrect value to a relevant factor, the party has been deprived of his only opportunity for a full, proper assessment.[112]

4. If the decisionmaker gave weight to an illicit objective, the court should presume that his consideration of the objective determined the outcome of the decision and should invalidate the decision in the absence of clear proof to the contrary. Evidence sufficient to establish that the decisionmaker gave any weight to an illicit objective will also often establish that the decision would not have been made but for the pursuit of that objective.[113] A complainant may, however, prove clearly and convincingly that the decisionmaker gave weight to an illicit objective and yet fail to establish with equal certainty that this affected the outcome of the decision. It is conceivable—though seldom likely—that the same

[111] Where an extraordinary justification is required, text *supra*, at notes 70–84, the court undertakes a limited assessment of the law's utility and fairness. But, compared to the decisionmaker's authority, the scope of judicial review is very narrowly circumscribed. The Equal Protection Clause does not, for example, embody all principles of fairness, whatever they may be and however they are to be determined.

[112] This may seem to prove too much, for a person affected adversely by a decision has a grievance of sorts whenever the decisionmaker has not adequately considered its pros and cons. Since this grievance generally is not judicially cognizable, why should it become cognizable merely because the decisionmaker allegedly pursued constitutionally illicit objectives?

Although the decisionmaking process is sometimes constrained by formal procedural requirements designed to maximize the decisionmaker's consideration of relevant factors, see, *e.g.*, 1 DAVIS, ADMINISTRATIVE LAW TREATISE, ch. 6 (1958) (rulemaking), it is doubtful whether one could formulate workable standards for examining generally whether the decisionmaker really considered the matter adequately. It is doubtful in any case that the potential benefits from such review would outweigh the burden on the judiciary and the costs of judicial intrusion into the decisionmaking process.

The costs of judicial inquiry into constitutionally illicit motivation are likely to be smaller, and the benefits greater. By contrast to the open-ended question, "Has the decisionmaker adequately considered all points of view?" the inquiry into motivation is narrow: "Did the decisionmaker give weight to a particular illicit objective?" The chief methods for conducting the latter inquiry do not require judicial scrutiny of the internal workings of the decisionmaking process. Furthermore, illicitly motivated decisions are more likely than ill-considered decisions in general to be systematically unjust and injurious to those "discrete and insular" minorities, United States v. Carolene Products Co., 304 U.S. 144, 152–53, n.4 (1936), for whose protection certain objectives are constitutionally proscribed.

[113] See text *infra*, at notes 126–39.

decision would have been made even in the absence of illicit motivation. In this case, proof that the decisionmaker took account of an illicit objective rebuts whatever presumption of regularity otherwise attaches. For this reason, and because of the constitutional interests at stake, the court should place on the decisionmaker a heavy burden of proving that his illicit objective was not determinative of the outcome.[114]

B. SUSPECT MOTIVATION

A court may find that an operative rule innocent on its face was adopted with the objective of causing a result such that, had the operative rule in terms mandated that result, the rule would have been deemed constitutionally "suspect." For example, the court may find that an operative rule that does not classify by race has the purpose (and effect) of segregating by race.

It would be inappropriate to hold that the motivation as such invalidated the rule, for even if the rule explicitly classified by race it would not automatically fall, but would only trigger the demand for an extraordinary justification. It would be equally inappropriate to treat the motivation as innocent. For the same considerations that render an explicit racial classification suspect—the probability of an underlying prejudicial motivation, the anti-educative effects, and the dangers of systematic injury to minorities[115]—apply as well to the decisionmaker's objective of classifying on the basis of race.

The appropriate solution is to treat the objective itself as "suspect."[116] If an operative rule mandating segregation under the circumstances could be justified by a compelling state interest, the decisionmaker's motivation is licit. If the operative rule could not be justified, the decisionmaker's motivation should invalidate the decision—for the same reasons that his consideration of an objective that is illicit per se should invalidate it.

---

[114] The closest analogy is the test for harmless constitutional error in criminal cases. See Chapman v. California, 386 U.S. 18 (1967). The fact that the decisionmaker is known to have taken account of constitutionally illicit objectives, *cf.* 7 Moore, Federal Practice, § 61.07[3] (2d ed. 1970), together with the probability that the objectives were outcome-determinative, make the usual harmless error test, see, *e.g.*, Fed. R. Civ. Proc. 61, irrelevant.

[115] See text *supra*, at notes 78–79.

[116] See Hunter v. Erickson, 393 U.S. 385, 393 (1969) (Harlan, J., concurring). But see Ely, at 1300 n.282.

VI. The Arguments against Judicial Review

Palmer's and *O'Brien*'s objections to judicial review of motivation concern the difficulty of ascertaining motivation and the futility of invalidating an otherwise permissible law. Professors Tussman and tenBroek have suggested a third objection: the disutility of invalidating what may otherwise be a perfectly good law.[117] And one also can find in some of the commentaries a fourth objection, based on the general impropriety of the inquiry.[118]

A. ASCERTAINABILITY

Mr. Justice Black asserted in *Palmer* that it is generally "extremely difficult" to determine a decisionmaker's motivation and that it is especially difficult, or impossible, "to determine the 'sole' or 'dominant' motivation behind the choices of a group of legislators."[119] I shall consider these propositions in reverse order.

1. "*'Sole' or 'dominant' motivation.*" A complainant who can prove that, but for the decisionmaker's desire to promote an illicit objective, the decision would not have been made, should clearly have won his case.[120] But such rigorous proof is not essential. It should suffice to demonstrate that illicit motivation played a nontrivial part in the decisionmaking process, so that it might have affected the outcome.[121] Whichever of these ways one poses the inquiry, it is inappropriate to ask which of several possible objectives was "sole" or "dominant" in the decisionmaker's mind:[122] an illicit motive may have been "subordinate" and yet have determined the outcome of the decision.[123]

---

[117] Tussman & tenBroek, note 64 *supra*, at 360. Professor Ely suggests that the Court voices this objection in *O'Brien*, see note 158 *infra*, but if so, it does so only obliquely.

[118] See text *infra*, at notes 161–68.   [120] See text *supra*, at note 113.

[119] 403 U.S. at 224–25.   [121] *Ibid.*

[122] *Compare* Green Street Ass'n v. Daley, 373 F.2d 1 (7th Cir. 1967) (demanding proof of "sole" motivation), *with* Local 53 v. Vogler, 407 F.2d 1047, 1054 (5th Cir. 1969) (demanding, in a Title VII case, only that a union rule "arise at least in part from racial bases").

[123] Thus, it is incorrect to pose the question of motivation: did·the decisionmaker make this decision to serve legitimate or to serve illicit purposes—*e.g.*, did the superintendent adopt an ability grouping plan in order to promote educational achievement or to promote segregation? It is entirely possible that he had both objectives in mind, but the rule should be invalidated if the illicit objective played any material role in the decision.

Nothing in the nature of a multimember decisionmaking body makes the search for sole or dominant motivation more appropriate than in the case of a single decisionmaker.[124] Indeed, as the discussion below suggests, the main techniques for determining motivation treat the multimember body as a unit no different from the single decisionmaker.

2. *The general difficulty.* It is often impossible to establish that a decisionmaker entertained an illicit or suspect objective. But this does not justify a blanket refusal to undertake the inquiry if a decisionmaker's motivation can sometimes be determined with adequate certainty. And the Supreme Court and lower courts have rested judgments on findings of improper motivation—on records supporting those findings beyond serious dispute.[125] In view of the doubts that have been expressed over the possibility of ascertaining motivation, I shall identify some general recurrent bases for such findings.

a) Circumstantial evidence. The chief method of ascertaining a decisionmaker's motivation involves the drawing of inferences from his conduct, viewed in the context of antecedent and con-

---

[124] The observation of the preceding paragraph has, however, a corollary where the decisionmaker is a multimember body—for example, a legislature. If "legislative intent" is ever relevant for purposes of statutory construction, it is the intent of a majority of the legislators that counts. This has led Professor Ely to suggest that "the only motivations on the basis of which the Court would even consider . . . [invalidating a law] or, indeed, a litigant would have the temerity to suggest that it do so—are those which can confidently be said to have been shared by a majority of the decisionmakers." Ely, at 1219–20, 1268. But the matter is not so simple. The relevant question, again, is whether considerations of illicit motivation affected the outcome of the decisionmaking process. Thus, in theory, it should suffice to show that the decisions of those members whose votes were necessary for enactment of the challenged law were improperly motivated. (This should be qualified by the possibility that some legislators, who otherwise would support a measure for legitimate reasons, might vote against it because others were supporting it for avowedly illicit reasons.) The point is largely academic, however. Whether the relevant class is a majority of the legislators or only those legislators whose votes are necessary for the enactment, neither head-count usually is feasible—or necessary. See text *infra*, at notes 126–39.

[125] *E.g.,* Epperson v. Arkansas, 393 U.S. 97 (1968); Griffin v. Prince Edward County Board of Education, 377 U.S. 218 (1964); Gomillion v. Lightfoot, 364 U.S. 339 (1960); Poindexter v. Louisiana Financial Assistance Commission, 275 F. Supp. 833, 837–45 (E.D. La. 1967), *aff'd,* 389 U.S. 571 (1968), Lee v. Macon County Board of Education, 267 F. Supp. 458, 475–77 (M.D. Ala.), *aff'd sub nom.* Wallace v. United States, 389 U.S. 215 (1967); Bush v. Orleans Parish School Board, 187 F. Supp. 42 (E.D. La. 1960), *aff'd per curiam,* 365 U.S. 569 (1961); *id.,* 188 F. Supp. 916 (E.D. La. 1960), *aff'd per curiam,* 365 U.S. 569 (1961); *id.,* 190 F. Supp. 861 (E.D. La. 1960).

current events and situations. The process does not differ from that of inferring ultimate facts from basic facts in other areas of the law. It is grounded in an experiential, intuitive assessment of the likelihood that the decision was designed to further one or another objective.

The content of the operative rule may itself provide strong evidence of improper motivation. In *Gomillion v. Lightfoot*,[126] for example, the probability that a nonracially motivated delineation of Tuskegee's boundaries would have the effect it did is so minimal that, even without knowledge of the racial attitudes prevalent in Alabama,[127] one could not but conclude that the law was designed to exclude Negroes from the city.[128] Similarly, in *United States v. Kahriger*,[129] Mr. Justice Frankfurter—no partisan of inquiries into motivation—concluded from the "detailed scheme of administration [of the wagering tax laws] beyond the [government's] obvious fiscal needs," that "what was formally a means of raising revenue for the Federal Government was essentially an effort to check if not to stamp out professional gambling."[130]

Mr. Justice Frankfurter's analysis suggests that the merits—the desirability—of a law may constitute evidence of the motivation underlying it. The courts possess no general authority to invalidate a decision because it is "undesirable," and an allegation of illicit motivation does not enlarge their authority. A conscientious decisionmaker, however, considers the costs of a proposal, its conduciveness to the ends sought to be attained, and the availability of

---

[126] See text *supra*, at notes 34–35.

[127] But it would be proper for a court to take judicial notice of these attitudes. *Cf.* N.A.A.C.P. v. Button, 371 U.S. 415, 435–36 (1963); Johnson v. Branch, 364 F.2d 177, 182 (4th Cir. 1966). See generally 9 WIGMORE, EVIDENCE §§ 2580, 2583 (3d ed., 1940).

[128] See also Grosjean v. American Press Co., 297 U.S. 233 (1936), where a tax levied on Louisiana newspapers with circulations over 20,000 happened to fall on all publishers opposed to the Long regime, but on only one friendly publisher. See Ely, at 1330–34.

[129] 345 U.S. 22 (1953).

[130] *Id.* at 39 (dissenting opinion). The Court in *Kahriger*, as in other post-1937 decisions concerning the scope of national powers, *e.g.*, United States v. Darby, 312 U.S. 100, 115 (1941), eschewed the inquiry into motivation not (or not so much) because of functional difficulties with the inquiry, but because what was formerly deemed to be an impermissible purpose, see, *e.g.*, United States v. Constantine, 296 U.S. 287 (1935); Bailey v. Drexel Furniture Co., 259 U.S. 20 (1922), was now held legitimate. See Ely, at 1302–06.

alternatives less costly to the community as a whole or to a particular segment of the community. That a decision obviously fails to reflect these considerations with respect to any legitimate objective supports the inference that it was improperly motivated.

For example, a court would not question a city's decision to locate a park at site X rather, than site Y, merely because X seemed extremely costly, unattractive, and inaccessible, while Y seemed ideal. But this information, taken together with the fact that site X is the proposed location for a private interracial housing development strongly opposed by the white community, supports the inference that X was chosen to thwart construction of the project.[131] Similarly, the fact that a regulation, though minimally related to the promotion of health or educational achievement, is poorly or dubiously suited to its supposed legitimate objectives, would lend support to other evidence of illicit motivation.[132]

The juxtaposition of a decision with some prior event or sequence of events often bears on the inference of illicit motivation. The following chronological sequence, for example, is typical of a variety of cases: the decisionmaker enforces a discriminatory operative rule; a court enjoins this practice; the decisionmaker then adopts a constitutionally "innocent" rule that effectively maintains the *status quo ante*. For example, state voting officials are

---

[131] *Cf.* Progress Dev. Corp. v. Mitchell, 286 F.2d 222 (7th Cir. 1961); Deerfield Park District v. Progress Dev. Corp., 22 Ill. 2d 132 (1961).

Sometimes a court may be able to obtain more direct insight into the decision-making process. Courts normally do not inquire whether the decisionmaker considered, let alone considered adequately, the likely benefits and costs of a decision. See notes 111–12 *supra*. In the example in the text, however, the inference of illicit motivation would be supported by evidence that the city conducted only a short and perfunctory study before locating the new park (especially if in the past it had made such decisions only after lengthy and careful inquiry).

[132] See, *e.g.,* Ho Ah Kow v. Nunan, 12 F. Cas. 252 (No. 6546) (C.C.D. Cal. 1879) (ordinance requiring prisoners in San Francisco jail to be closely shorn); AMERICAN FRIENDS SERVICE COMMITTEE, THE STATUS OF SCHOOL DESEGREGATION IN THE SOUTH 1970, 35–37 (testing and tracking); *id.* at 86–88 (teacher testing); Baker v. Columbus Municipal Separate School Dist., No. EC-70-52-5 (N.D. Miss., 23 June, 1971) (teacher testing); Comment, *The Constitutionality of Sex Separation in School Desegregation Plans,* 37 U. CHI. L. REV. 296 (1970). Assessment of the utility of rules of this sort may thrust the court into unfamiliar substantive areas. But courts are required to make such determinations in other circumstances. See, *e.g.,* Griggs v. Duke Power Co., 401 U.S. 424 (1971); Cooper & Sobol, *Seniority and Testing under Fair Employment Laws: A General Approach to Objective Criteria of Hiring and Promotion,* 82 HARV. L. REV. 1598 (1969). And they can use expert witnesses to assist them. See, *e.g.,* Baker v. Columbus Municipal Separate School Dist., *supra*.

enjoined from refusing to register black applicants and the state then adopts difficult but apparently neutral registration requirements;[133] or, school districts are ordered to cease assigning students by race and the state then enacts a tuition grant law,[134] or abandons a public school system,[135] or engages in other practices that tend to maintain segregation.[136]

Each of these innovative practices serves conceivable permissible objectives. In considering the question, "Why did the decisionmaker adopt this practice?" the court, however, may properly consider the subquestion, "Why did the decisionmaker adopt this practice at this time?" The sequence of events may thus support the inference that the decisionmaker's objective was to do covertly that which he was forbidden to do overtly.[137] The strength of the inference will also be affected by the tenacity of the decisionmaker's past commitment to the forbidden rule, the extent to which the innovation marks a departure from traditionally established practices,[138] and the existence of other decisions that seem designed to serve the same illicit objective.[139]

b) Direct evidence of motivation. In theory, the decision-

---

133 *Cf., e.g.,* Davis v. Schnell, 81 F. Supp. 872 (S.D. Ala.), *aff'd per curiam,* 336 U.S. 933 (1949); United States v. Louisiana, 225 F. Supp. 353, 363–81 (E.D. La. 1963), *aff'd,* 380 U.S. 145 (1965).

134 See, *e.g.,* Poindexter v. Louisiana Financial Assistance Comm'n, 275 F. Supp. 833 (E.D. La. 1967), *aff'd,* 393 U.S. 17 (1968); Lee v. Macon County Board of Education, 267 F. Supp. 458 (M.D. Ala.), *aff'd sub nom.* Wallace v. United States, 389 U.S. 215 (1967).

135 See, *e.g.,* Griffin v. Prince Edward County Board of Education, 377 U.S. 218 (1964).

136 See AMERICAN FRIENDS SERVICE COMMITTEE, note 132 *supra,* at 35–37 (testing and tracking), 46–47 (abandonment or transfer of social activities), 47–48 (changes in student government election procedures), 50 (abandonment of athletic programs); Comment, note 132 *supra* (abandonment of coeducation); *cf.* Baker v. Columbus Municipal School Dist., No. EC-70-52-5 (N.D. Miss., 23 June 1971).

137 See, *e.g.,* Bush v. Orleans Parish Sch. Bd., 187 F. Supp. 42 (E.D. La. 1960), *aff'd,* 365 U.S. 569 (1961); *id.,* 188 F. Supp. 916 (E.D. La. 1960), *aff'd,* 365 U.S. 569 (1961); *id.,* 190 F. Supp. 861 (E.D. La. 1960); Hall v. St. Helena Parish School Board, 197 F. Supp. 649 (E.D. La. 1961), *aff'd,* 368 U.S. 515 (1962).

138 See, *e.g.,* the practices described in note 136 *supra.*

139 That is, the convergence of a number of decisions, each of which could be explained in terms of licit objectives or in terms of the same illicit objective (*e.g.,* thwarting school desegregation) may support the conclusion that each of the decisions is illicitly motivated.

maker's statements can provide the most reliable evidence of his actual objectives: usually no one knows a person's reasons for acting better than the actor himself. On occasion, a decisionmaker will concede his actual objectives in a judicial proceeding.[140] The utility of direct testimony, however, is seriously limited by the ease with which one can lie successfully about one's motives, by the costs of obtaining the testimony of the members of multimember decisionmaking bodies, and by legal doctrines that immunize legislators and high executive officials from having to account for their decisions.[141]

Of greater practical utility are statements made by decisionmakers in the course of the decisionmaking process—statements of the sort often used in statutory interpretation. Where the decisionmaker consists of a single person, such statements may be conclusive. But only a few members of a multimember body usually will have stated their objectives. Attribution of the statements of some members of the decisionmaking body to the others cannot properly be justified on a theory of adoption by silence or the fiction of delegated authority to speak.[142] Nonetheless, often the uncontested avowals of illicit motivation by the sponsors of a measure are in fact typical of the views of many others who vote for the measure. Such statements thus lend some support to an inference of illicit motivation, and have properly been used for this purpose,[143] though alone they would not provide a sufficient basis for invalidation.[144]

---

[140] See, *e.g.*, Palmer v. Thompson, 403 U.S. at 253–54; text *supra*, at note 15; United States v. Morehouse Parish, Civil No. 14429 (W.D. La. 1969) (abandonment of coeducation designed to prevent white flight); Banks v. St. James Parish, Civil No. 16173 (E.D. La. 1969) (abandonment of coeducation will retain public support for desegregation).

[141] See, *e.g.*, 8 WIGMORE, EVIDENCE §§ 2369–71 (McNaughton rev. 1961).

[142] *Cf.* MacCallum, note 39 *supra*, at 777–84. On rare occasions, the decisionmaking body as a whole may have announced its illicit or suspect objectives in the law's text or preamble. See, *e.g.*, Truax v. Raich, 239 U.S. 33 (1915); Hawkins v. North Carolina State Bd. of Educ., Civ. No. 2067 (W.D. N.C., 31 March 1966), 11 RACE REL. L. REP. 745 (1966). *Cf.* Parr v. Municipal Court, 3 Cal. 3d 861 (1971).

[143] *E.g.*, Poindexter v. Louisiana Financial Assistance Comm'n, 275 F. Supp. 833 (E.D. La. 1967), *aff'd*, 389 U.S. 571 (1968). *Cf.* Ely, at 1330–34.

[144] It is worth noting that the state's largest multimember decisionmaking body, the electorate, may make decisions of specific, see James v. Valtierra, 402 U.S. 137 (1971), or general, see Reitman v. Mulkey, 387 U.S. 369 (1967), applicability. The policies underlying judicial review of motivation, see text *supra*, at notes 107–16,

B. FUTILITY

> [T]here is an element of futility in a judicial attempt to in-
> validate a law because of the bad motives of its supporters. If
> the law is struck down for this reason, rather than because
> of its facial content or effect, it would presumably be valid
> as soon as the legislature or other relevant governing board
> repassed it for different reasons.[145]

If this means that the mere possibility of reenactment for proper
purposes necessarily makes futile the invalidation of an illicitly
motivated law, it misses the point of judicial review of motivation,
which assumes that the law as such is constitutional and that only
the process of its adoption—the decisionmaker's consideration of
improper objectives—is constitutionally impermissible.[146] Thus, in
theory the decisionmaker remains free to readopt a motive-in-
validated law at any time—provided that he does so solely for
legitimate reasons. Judicial review of motivation is no more "futile"
merely because reenactment is possible than appellate review is
futile because an appellee may prevail again on remand after a
trial court is reversed for giving weight to inadmissible evidence
or misapplying the law.

The "futility" argument, however, has two other, more substantial components. First, if courts engage in review of motivation,
decisionmakers may take greater care to conceal their illicit objectives.[147] The judicial practice will thus be self-defeating: once it is
engaged in, decisionmakers will cease providing the data on which
it depends.

The empirical assumptions underlying this argument are not
obviously correct. Determinations of motivation often do not
depend on manipulable data such as legislative history.[148] Moreover, decisionmakers may not take cognizance of the practice of

---

apply with no less force to decisions made by referendum; and opinion sampling
and other social science techniques might sometimes establish that the electorate
was seeking to promote illicit or suspect objectives. Whether such evidence should
be received, and when it should be deemed adequate, present interesting questions
for further exploration.

[145] 403 U.S. at 225. In United States v. O'Brien, 391 U.S. 367 (1968), the Court
declined to invalidate a law "which could be reenacted in its exact form if the same
or another legislator made a 'wiser' speech about it." *Id*. at 384.

[146] See text *supra*, at notes 107–16.

[147] BICKEL, note 2 *supra*, at 216.   [148] See text *supra*, at notes 126–39.

judicial inquiry into motivation and, in any case, may not take measures to conceal their actual purposes in enacting a law.

The second argument is that a particular decisionmaker whose law is once struck down because it was illicitly motivated will re-adopt the law, retaining his illicit motivation but taking care to conceal it. This has more force,[149] and it poses serious practical problems of formulating prospective relief. Since the law might be readopted for wholly licit reasons, a permanent injunction against its readoption could impose high costs on society without any countervailing justification in the policies supporting review of motivation.[150] On the other hand, to treat readoption as an entirely new matter, ignoring the decisionmaker's past motivation, would be unrealistic and would subvert those policies.

In general, the most satisfactory response to this dilemma will be to presume that the decisionmaker continues to entertain the motives that led to the original decision (and to its invalidation). In operational terms, the court should enjoin an administrative deci-sionmaker from making the same decision again unless he comes forward with persuasive evidence that this time it will be made only for legitimate reasons. Sometimes a material change of cir-cumstances,[151] or the passage of time accompanied by a change of community attitudes,[152] will be persuasive of the decisionmaker's good faith. In other circumstances the decisionmaker may be re-quired to demonstrate that the proposed decision is in fact desirable on the merits and that no practicable alternative is less burdensome to the class at whom the original decision was adversely aimed; and the court might require additionally that the decisionmaker take steps to protect that class.[153] If the court invalidates a legisla-

---

[149] If he did not previously take cognizance of, and respond to, the court's practice of reviewing motivation, he is likely to do so now: once burned, twice shy.

[150] The imposition of such costs would give some force to the "disutility" argu-ment. See text *infra*, at note 158.

[151] *Cf.* Note, *Developments in the Law—Injunctions*, 78 HARV. L. REV. 994, 1081–83 (1965).

[152] *Cf.* McGowan v. Maryland, 366 U.S. 420 (1961).

[153] Suppose, for example, that, upon being required to desegregate, a school dis-trict adopts an ability grouping system; the system has the effect of segregating by race and is invalidated on the ground that segregation was its objective. *Cf.* United States v. Sunflower County Sch. Dist., 430 F.2d 839 (5th Cir. 1970) (program in-validated on other grounds); Singleton v. Jackson Municipal Sep. School Dist., 419 F.2d 1211, 1219 (5th Cir. 1969) (same); AMERICAN FRIENDS SERVICE COMMITTEE,

tive enactment, it should similarly scrutinize reenactment of the identical or a similar law if it is challenged in a properly maintained action.

This degree of judicial intrusion into the decisionmaking process is extraordinary. The decisionmaker's past behavior, however, usually justifies the court's strong suspicion of his motives[154] and its concomitant scrutiny of the merits of a new decision and requirement of prophylactic measures. In some cases, the likelihood that a decision was readopted for legitimate reasons is so small that no inquiry into its merits is necessary.[155] The evaluation of many other decisions calls for little or no substantive expertise,[156] and when expertise is required the court can often gain sufficient information from documentary evidence and expert testimony.[157]

C. DISUTILITY

The invalidation of an unconstitutional rule is desirable: as a matter of law the rule is bad. But "it is altogether possible for a law which is the expression of a bad motive to be a good law . . . , [to make] a positive contribution to the public good."[158] As an argument against judicial review of motivation, this is misleading: it confuses the court's competence with that of the decisionmaker. It is beyond the court's normal authority to determine whether a law is "good."[159] This is the central task delegated to the decision-

---

note 132 *supra*, at 35–37. If the district wishes to readopt the plan—purportedly for educational reasons only—the court should require evidence that the particular plan is educationally sound, and should itself weigh the educational benefits against the probable harm to the black students. If the court approved readoption of the plan, it might properly require that the district employ procedural safeguards against discriminatory abuses of the system.

[154] Indeed, the core "futility" argument is itself based on the assumption of the decisionmaker's continuing bad faith.

[155] See, *e.g.*, Gomillion v. Lightfoot, 364 U.S. 339 (1960); Grosjean v. American Press Co., 297 U.S. 233 (1936), Bush v. Orleans Parish School Bd., 188 F. Supp. 916 (E.D. La. 1960), aff'd, 365 U.S. 569 (1961); *id.*, 190 F. Supp. 861 (E.D. La. 1960).

[156] *E.g.*, a school's termination of athletics or social activities. See note 136 *supra*.

[157] *Cf.* note 132 *supra*.

[158] Tussman & tenBroek, note 64 *supra*, at 360. Professor Ely suggests that the Court was getting at the same thing in *United States v. O'Brien*, where it expressed concern with voiding "a statute that is, under well-settled criteria, constitutional on its face . . . [and] which Congress had the undoubted power to enact." 391 U.S. at 383–84. Ely, at 1212, 1215–16, 1280–81.

[159] See note 111 *supra*.

maker. But when the decisionmaker has treated an illicit objective as desirable—as a benefit rather than as a cost or a neutral factor—he has not properly evaluated the "goodness" of the decision. The argument for judicial review of motivation is that it is the court's task to assure, to the limited extent of forbidding the decisionmaker to weigh improper objectives, that the decisionmaker himself determines that his decision is good.

Suppose, for example, that a school board adopts an ability-grouping system that has the effect of segregating black and white pupils.[160] This system might have been adopted to promote educational achievement, but the court finds that the board's objective was in fact to preserve segregation. Conceding, *arguendo*, that a child has no constitutional right to be assigned to classes with children of other races, he does have a right not to be segregated on the basis of race. It is no response that "reasonable men" might adopt the tracking system to serve legitimate objectives. The court is not authorized to make this educational decision. And the authorized decisionmaker, the school board, did not make the decision on proper grounds. The board may not even have considered the utility of the scheme as a means of promoting educational achievement; and if the board did, it might not have found enough utility to justify the rule's adoption absent the added, impermissible, benefit of segregation. The proper allocation of decision-making competence requires that the board make this decision on proper grounds—or that it not be made at all.

D. IMPROPRIETY

The argument against judicial review of motivation on the ground of its impropriety has focused largely on inquiries into the motives of legislative bodies and high executive officials.[161] By contrast, inquiry into the motivation of administrative officials is deemed permissible.[162] The argument has two components: first, the process of proving legislative motivation requires an undesirable intrusion into the political process; second, inquiry into motivation entails a lack of proper respect for a government's chief policy-making agencies.

---

[160] See note 153 *supra*.

[161] BICKEL, note 2 *supra*, at 208–21; Note, note 75 *supra*, at 1091–1101.

[162] *Ibid.*

The first point assumes that the inquiry into legislative motivation requires the "cross-examination of each individual legislator":[163]

> It is simply unthinkable that members of legislative majorities should from time to time be subject to cross-examination in various courts over the country regarding their states of mind when they voted. That is . . . [not] representative government. . . . [L]egislatures whose members were subject to call for testimony in this fashion would be hard put to it to find the time to legislate.

This argument is persuasive that legislators should not be subject to subpoena to explain their reasons for voting for a measure.[164] To the extent that proof of illicit motivation depends on such testimony, the case must fail. But proof of illicit motivation need not depend on such testimony.[165]

The second point involves "considerations of regard for 'the station,' so strong when the Court reviews the work of the legislature."[166] "[A] finding of impure motive sufficient to void an act of a legislature impugns the essential integrity of a coordinate branch of government."[167]

This argument has some force. To declare a law unconstitutional on its merits is to hold that the decisionmaker made an error. But a finding of illicit motivation often is tantamount to an accusation that the decisionmaker violated his constitutional oath of office.[168] Especially where the decisionmaker claims to have pur-

---

[163] BICKEL, note 2 *supra*, at 215.   [164] See also note 141 *supra*.

[165] See text *supra*, at notes 126–39. I have seen no cases inquiring into legislative motivation in which a legislator was called to testify in the judicial proceeding.

[166] BICKEL, note 2 *supra*, at 214.

[167] Note, note 75 *supra*, at 1093. The Note suggests that the argument applies, though less strongly, to state legislatures, "which, unlike Congress, are not co-equal with the federal judiciary." *Id*. at 1093–94 n.101. The Note further argues against inquiry into legislative motivation on the ground that it "involves a court in the give-and-take of politics and may compel the court to pass judgment on the legitimacy of political pressures and the responses to them." *Id*. at 1093–94. As an argument against subpoenaing legislators to account for their votes, this has merit. But if the argument suggests that illicit objectives are immunized because they are responsive to "political pressures," it is fundamentally at odds with the principle that constitutional interests cannot be subverted because of opposition to them. See, *e.g.*, Brown v. Board of Education, 349 U.S. 294, 300 (1955).

[168] U.S. Const., Art. VI, §3. This should not be confused with the accusation of bribery or corruption involved in Fletcher v. Peck, 6 Cranch 87 (1819), see text

sued only legitimate objectives, a judicial determination of illicit motivation carries an element of insult; it is an attack on the decisionmaker's honesty. These concerns apply to lower-echelon officials as well as to legislators and high executive officials. Our constitutional traditions, however, accord greater respect to the integrity of the higher agencies.

Nevertheless, legislators sometimes do act out of illicit motivations. And against the argument for nonintervention one must set the interests favoring judicial invalidation of an illicitly motivated legislative act—the injury and insult felt by those at whom it is aimed; the harm to the integrity of a system of government that pretends officially not to know what everyone knows is true. The critical commentators themselves have conceded the propriety of invalidation when the case is clear,[169] and the courts have so acted.[170] Herein lies the proper reconciliation of these competing interests: the courts should not refuse to inquire into the motivation of any governmental body, but they should not invalidate a decision on the ground that it was designed to serve illicit objectives unless that fact has been established by clear and convincing evidence.[171]

VII. SUMMARY OF AN APPROACH TO UNCONSTITUTIONAL MOTIVATION

I have arrived at the following position: A court should entertain an action challenging an otherwise constitutional decision—whether made by a legislature or an executive or administrative official—on the ground that it was designed in part to serve an illicit or suspect objective. The complainant must establish by clear and convincing evidence that such an objective played an affirmative role in the decisionmaking process. He need not, how-

---

supra, at notes 37–38, which, though not of constitutional magnitude, is probably regarded as considerably more damning.

[169] See BICKEL, note 2 *supra,* at 210–11.

[170] See, *e.g.,* cases cited in note 125 *supra.*

[171] Concededly the choice of this particular standard is arbitrary, but the "clear and convincing" standard seems properly to accommodate the competing interests involved. It would exceed the precision of the process to apply different standards to judicial review of administrative and legislative decisions unless one required proof beyond a reasonable doubt as to the latter. This seems too onerous a burden to place upon the complainant.

ever, establish that consideration of the objective was the sole, or dominant, or a "but-for" cause of the decision—only that its consideration may have affected the outcome of the process.

If the objective is illicit, the decision should simply be invalidated. If the objective is suspect, the court should treat it essentially as it treats a suspect operative rule, and invalidate the decision unless the defendant comes forward with an extraordinary justification.

The court should permit the decisionmaker to readopt the same decision only upon a showing that its readoption is designed to serve entirely legitimate objectives.

VIII. Palmer v. Thompson Revisited

On the record in *Palmer v. Thompson*, the Court could have concluded that respondents closed Jackson's municipal swimming pools either (1) simply to avoid integration, or (2) to avert interracial violence and the loss of revenues that might result if the pools were operated on an integrated basis.

The evidence heretofore outlined—the city's relentless opposition to desegregation, contemporary public statements by the mayor of Jackson, and respondents' failure to provide any factual basis for their predictions of violence and economic loss—supports the inference that the first objective played a significant role in the decision to close the pools. A finding to this effect should have invalidated the decision without further inquiry: the avoidance of integration is a suspect objective, requiring an extraordinary justification, and opposition to desegregation is no justification at all.[172]

If the Court was hesitant to find that respondents closed the Jackson pools simply out of opposition to integration, there could be no doubt that the pools were closed for the second reason: respondents conceded this.[173] A court normally would not seriously consider a constitutional challenge to the abandonment of a municipal activity,[174] and if the court did require a rational justification, the demand would be satisfied by the possibility, however small, that continuation of the activity would encourage violence or deplete the municipal fisc. In *Palmer*, however, respondents'

---

[172] See text *supra*, at note 33.   [173] See text *supra*, at note 15.

[174] *Cf.* Ely, at 1295–96. Ely would treat this as a "discretionary choice." See text *infra*, at notes 184–204.

only basis for this prediction was the imminent integration of the pools: however "neutral" respondents' ultimate objective, it was the prospect of integration that triggered the closing of the pools.

Mr. Justice White noted this in his dissent.[175] He found *Palmer* to be controlled by a series of cases holding that official speculations about violence cannot justify the continued maintenance of state-sponsored segregation.[176] These decisions certainly are relevant to *Palmer*, and in one important respect they are directly in point: by whatever means racial integration is avoided, and whatever reasons are proffered for avoiding it, there is a substantial likelihood that official racial prejudice played a determinative role.[177] Nonetheless, these cases arguably differ from *Palmer* in several respects:

1. The maintenance of segregated facilities is a continuous, open insult to the minority race, with concomitant anti-educative effects for the entire society. The closing of a facility to blacks and whites alike, when triggered by the prospect of integration, is also insulting and anti-educative, but it may be perceived as less notorious and continuous.

2. To allow the prospect of interracial violence as a defense for segregation encourages some white citizens to engage in violence and encourages sympathetic officials to promote or permit it: the segregationist has everything to gain and nothing to lose. Allowing the same defense for terminating the activity entirely may also have these effects, but the white community does have something to lose. (On the other hand, a policy of abandonment in response to integration may interpose "a major deterrent to seeking judicial or executive help in eliminating racial restrictions on the use of public facilities."[178] As Judge Wisdom stated in his dissent in the Fifth Circuit Court of Appeals, "[T]he price of protest is high. Negroes . . . now know that they risk losing even segregated public facilities if they dare to protest."[179])

3. Since separate facilities are rarely equal in fact, the exclusion

---

[175] 403 U.S. at 254.

[176] See, *e.g.*, Watson v. City of Memphis, 373 U.S. 526 (1963) (parks); Buchanan v. Warley, 245 U.S. 60 (1917) (residential areas). *Cf.* Cooper v. Aaron, 358 U.S. 1 (1958) (schools).

[177] See text *supra*, at notes 77–84.

[178] 403 U.S. at 269.   [179] 419 F.2d at 1236.

of Negroes from a white facility deprives them of benefits accorded whites. When the state abandons the facilities entirely, however, it provides no facilities to either race, and hence equal facilities to both.

These comparisons may imply that the aggregate harm caused by maintaining segregation to avoid violence and loss of revenues is greater than the harm caused by closing a facility to avoid desegregation for the same reasons. But there is substantial harm in the latter case as well—enough to treat the closing of the pools as "suspect" and to demand more than a rational justification for the decision. In *Palmer*, this should have been conclusive. Whatever sensitive balancing of interests might have been required had respondents demonstrated a serious likelihood of violence and economic loss, they provided the Court with nothing but conclusory assertions.

Had the Court reversed the judgment in *Palmer*, it would have been appropriate to order the city of Jackson to reopen at least the three pools it retained.[180] Of coure, the city might subsequently petition the court to allow it to close the pools again, either because the predicted adverse consequences do materialize or because of some other salient change of circumstances. One cannot easily generalize about the proof that the court should require under all possible future conditions. If respondents claim, however, that operation of the pools has resulted in interracial violence, the court should modify the decree only if the conflicts are serious and cannot be handled adequately by respondents' good-faith efforts.[181] If the claim is based on economic loss, the deficit should be substantial—as compared, for example, to that incurred before the pools were ordered desegregated.

IX. CONCLUSION

Judicial review of motivation is a troublesome enterprise. It poses difficulties concerning proof, appropriate relief, and re-

---

180 If necessary, the Court could properly have ordered respondents and others "to exercise the power that is theirs to levy taxes to raise funds adequate to reopen, operate and maintain [the facility] without racial discrimination." Griffin v. County School Board, 377 U.S. at 233.

181 Cf. Bachellar v. Maryland, 397 U.S. 564 (1970); Cox v. Louisiana, 379 U.S. 536 (1963); Blasi, *Prior Restraints on Demonstrations*, 68 MICH. L. REV. 1481, 1510–15 (1970).

spect for the political processes—difficulties that are quite different from, and often greater than, those inherent in the nonmotivational modes of review. Where a court can support a judgment invalidating a decision on grounds other than unconstitutional motivation, it usually should do so.[182] The main burden of my thesis is simply that a blanket refusal to inquire into legislative and administrative motivation is not justified. There will remain cases in which nonmotivational grounds for decision are not available, in which unconstitutional motivation can be established with adequate certainty, and in which, therefore, the courts should be willing to invalidate a decision because the decisionmaker sought thereby to promote constitutionally impermissible objectives.

X. THE ELY THEORY: A CRITICAL POSTSCRIPT

The fact that an operative rule or criterion works to someone's disadvantage is often sufficient to trigger the demand for a rational or an extraordinary justification.[183] The central thesis of Professor John Ely's article, "Legislative and Administrative Motivation in Constitutional Law," is that this nonmotivational "disadvantageous distinction" model, with its automatic demand for a "legitimate defense,"[184] does not apply where the decisionmaker has made either a "random" or a "discretionary" choice. He argues that judicial inquiry into motivation is appropriate only in those two situations.[185] Proof of illicit motivation serves merely to trigger the demand for a legitimate defense that would not otherwise be required because the disadvantageous distinction model is inapplicable.[186]

---

182 See, e.g., notes 46 and 84 supra. The Court's desire to avoid explicit determinations of improper motivation has influenced the development of doctrine in a number of other areas. See, e.g., N.A.A.C.P. v. Alabama, 377 U.S. 288 (1964) (inadequate state ground); Williams v. Georgia, 349 U.S. 375, 399 (1955) (Clark, J., dissenting) (same); Shelton v. Tucker, 364 U.S. 479 (1960) (freedom of association); Dean Milk Co. v. City of Madison, 340 U.S. 349 (1951) (interstate commerce).

183 See text supra, at notes 62–79.

184 Ely uses the phrase "legitimate defense" or "legitimately defensible difference" to refer to both a rational and an extraordinary justification. E.g., Ely, at 1223–24. But cf. text infra, at notes 191–96, 205.

185 Ely, at 1261–75, 1281–84.

186 Ibid.

A. THE TWO MOTIVATIONAL MODELS

1. *Random choice.* Governments sometimes choose persons at random for the imposition of burdens or conferring of benefits. The selection of jurors and of draftees under the national lottery are familiar examples. Nonrandom selection is made: jurors and recruits must meet certain physical and mental requirements pertinent to their duties.[187] But choices from this pool are random. The commissioner happened to select Jones's but not Smith's name from the jury wheel; and to demand a rational distinction between Smith and Jones is to deny that the government may select jurors randomly.

Ely argues that if, under the guise of making a random choice, a decisionmaker employs a nonrandom operative criterion, the criterion must meet the demand for a legitimate defense.[188] Certainly this is correct. Whether the court is asked to determine that the decisionmaker is systematically employing an illicit operative criterion (systematically excluding Negroes from the venire) or is asked to determine that he based a particular decision on an illicit criterion (excluding Smith because he is black),[189] judicial review is appropriate.[190]

When Ely comes to the nature of the legitimate defense required, however, he imposes an unjustified restriction on review under the "random choice" model.[191] Ely would hold that even when the covertly employed nonrandom criterion is illicit or suspect, it triggers only the demand for a rational justification.[192] As he explains elsewhere, "the concept of suspect classification should be reserved . . . for laws which *on their face* distinguish in terms of the 'suspect' characteristic."[193] Given the extreme leniency of the traditional equal protection standard, which tolerates a substantial

---

[187] See Carter v. Jury Commission, 396 U.S. 320, 332–35 (1970); Ely, at 1232.

[188] Ely, at 1261, 1269–79.

[189] Ely does not distinguish between these two inquiries and subsumes both under the random choice model.

[190] See text *supra*, at notes 89–99.

[191] The same restriction is imposed on review under the "discretionary choice" model. See text *infra*, at note 205.

[192] Ely, at 1269–71. An extraordinary justification would be required only if a "fundamental interest" were affected. See *id.* at 1269.

[193] *Id.* at 1277 n.208. (Emphasis added.)

lack of congruence between the classifying trait and its objective,[194] this position has startling and undesirable consequences. It would not be "irrational," for example, for a government employer who otherwise chooses at random among a surplus of qualified job applicants to prefer white applicants if, say, in his experience blacks as a class have a higher absentee rate than whites.[195] If this preference were promulgated as a regulation, it would be suspect; it would demand, and not receive an extraordinary justification.[196] I can see no reason why the decisionmaker's covert use of the same criterion should be treated any differently.

2. *Discretionary choice.* Ely argues that some official decisions are not random, yet cannot meaningfully be subjected to review under the disadvantageous distinction model. These cases appear to fall into two general categories, having in common the absence of judicially manageable standards of review.[197]

First,[198] an official may have authority to make nonrational choices concerning aesthetics, taste, or propriety. A court cannot determine whether a school board's prohibition of shorts but not blue jeans, or sneakers but not loafers, is "rationally related" to the promotion of taste or a "proper" school environment. Similarly, the aesthetic desirability of a particular site for a public park is not rationally assessable. At best, the court could substitute its own value preferences for those of the school board or park commissioner—something it is not ordinarily authorized to do.[199]

Second,[200] the decision may belong to a class of cases in which

---

[194] See text *supra*, at notes 64–68; Dandridge v. Williams, 397 U.S. 471 (1970); McGowan v. Maryland, 366 U.S. 420 (1961); Tussman & tenBroek, note 64 *supra*. at 368–72.

[195] *Cf.* Fiss, *A Theory of Fair Employment Laws*, 38 U. CHI. L. REV. 235, 239, 257 (1971); *cf.* also Note, note 91 *supra*, at 1172–76 (treatment of statistically based sex discrimination under Title VII).

[196] See text *supra*, at notes 78–79. The Equal Protection Clause protects against ethnic stereotypes even when they have some statistical validity. *Cf.* Fiss, note 195 *supra*, at 260–61.

[197] I do not think that Ely would reject a third category, encompassing cases where the decisionmaker is permitted to draw a quantitative line, the precise location of which is inevitably arbitrary—for example, a decision setting the time within which an appeal must be filed after judgment, or the minimum age for obtaining a driver's permit. *Cf.* Oregon v. Mitchell, 400 U.S. 112, 294–95 (1970) (Stewart, J.).

[198] See Ely, at 1239–43.

[199] But *cf.* text *infra*, at note 219, and notes 219–20.

[200] See Ely, at 1246–49.

"each choice will import its own goal, each goal will count as acceptable, and the requirement of a 'rational' choice-goal relation will be satisfied by the very making of the choice."[201] Decisions allocating costs and benefits—for example, determining the incidence of subsidies and tax burdens—are paradigm examples:[202] A subsidy usually can be related to the objective of promoting whatever activity is subsidized—farming, music, golfing, or aircraft construction. "To purport to require of all [such] choices a rational relation to some acceptable goal," Ely argues, would be a "charade": every politically imaginable decision relates to some plausible (sub)goal, and every choice "would duly be upheld on the ground that the government had carried its burden of rationally relating the choice to an acceptable goal."[203] Such "[a]n infinitely expandable 'set' of subgoals, one to fit every choice the political branches will make, is more realistically and economically viewed as one umbrella goal, the promotion of the general welfare."[204]

Under Ely's theory, proof that a discretionary choice (for example, an aesthetic regulation or a subsidy) was illicitly motivated neither automatically invalidates the choice nor triggers the demand for an extraordinary justification. As in the random choice case, its only effect "is to trigger the demand for a legitimate defense in situations where it would not otherwise attach."[205] Occasionally, an aesthetic rule (for example, a rule requiring students to wear shoes in school) can be related rationally to a legitimate objective (the promotion of health and safety), and thus survive this review; but otherwise an aesthetic choice is not rationally justifiable, and must fall. Usually, in an "umbrella" goal case (the subsidy), the only available "defense" is that the decision is related rationally to a discretionary "subgoal" (the promotion of the activity subsidized).[206] "[T]he very reason the disadvantageous distinction

201 *Id.* at 1247.

202 Other such "discretionary choices" include decisions determining school curricular offerings and what conduct to punish criminally. *Id.* at 1243–45.

203 *Id.* at 1247.

204 *Id.* at 1248. A decision in this area is essentially a value preference for one subgoal at the expense of others. *Id.* at 1240 n.110.

205 *Id.* at 1269. See *id.* at 1208, 1252–54, 1281–82, 1300 n.282.

206 Occasionally, Ely suggests, a legitimate defense is available. For example, although curriculum decisions usually can be related only to a "subgoal" such as "the development of the well-educated citizen," "the decision to exclude a certain

model is suspended . . . —the fact that explanations of the subgoal level . . . must be treated as nonrational in light of the amorphous nature of the ultimate acceptable goal—suggests with identical force that such explanations cannot be regarded as 'rational' for purposes of alternative justification either."[207] Such decisions must therefore be invalidated.

The following examples illustrate the operational consequences of Ely's thesis. If a complainant proves that a school district has prohibited the wearing of dashikis in order to disadvantage blacks, or that it has ceased sponsoring school social events in order to minimize contact between black and white pupils, those decisions must fall. These are discretionary choice cases. Proof of improper motivation triggers the demand for a legitimate defense. But decisions respecting taste and appropriate school activities are not "rationally" defensible;[208] so a legitimate defense cannot be forthcoming.

On the other hand, it would be fruitless to prove that a recently desegregated Mississippi school district, located in an area where most whites but few Negroes can afford overcoats, has adopted a regulation requiring all students to wear overcoats in the winter in order to decimate the black school population;[209] or to prove that a school district fired a teacher because of his race or political activities or associations; or to prove that the district has abandoned coeducation in order to reduce social contact between black boys and white girls. The first two decisions come within the disadvantageous distinction model: they demand, and would receive, a rational justification quite apart from proof of illicit motivation.[210]

---

subject from the curriculum . . . could rationally be justified on the ground that no teacher qualified to present it could be found." *Id*. at 1273.

[207] *Ibid*. Ely characterizes these explanations as mere "subgoal rationalizations." *Id*. at 1272.

[208] *Id*. at 1239–41, 1279, 1295–96.

[209] This is Ely's example, *id*. at 1279, except that I have placed it in the one state that has no compulsory attendance laws.

[210] The overcoat requirement "is legitimately defensible in terms of physical health." *Id*. at 1279. "Decisions to fire teachers . . . should be treated under the disadvantageous distinction model; a legitimate defense should be demanded simply because a choice has been made, and without a requirement of illicit motivation." *Id*. at 1294–95 n.268. The practical implications of the latter position are disastrous, especially, though not exclusively, in those southern states in which teachers do not have tenure and serve under one-year contracts. See, *e.g.*, AMERICAN FRIENDS SERVICE

Since the only function of such proof would be to trigger that same demand, it is simply irrelevant. If the abandonment of coeducation is a discretionary choice,[211] the district will nonetheless be able to justify the decision in terms of a "real" legitimate objective.[212]

The basis for the different treatment of disadvantageous distinction cases and discretionary choice cases is not self-evident. To understand how Ely arrives at it, one must first consider his basic argument for judicial review of motivation.

B. THE NEED FOR JUDICIAL REVIEW OF MOTIVATION IN DISCRETIONARY CHOICE CASES

Judicial review of motivation in discretionary choice cases "derives from the obvious need for some sort of review and the unacceptability of the alternatives—a disproportionate impact model and the ordinary disadvantageous distinction model."[213] Ely does not dwell at length on this need, but he develops the case for judicial review through the following example and argument: Suppose a legislature enacts a tax exemption for children, limited to the children of Caucasians. This must surely be unconstitutional,[214] Ely claims, but only judicial review of motivation can explain why:

> A distinction which disadvantages some persons relative to others has obviously been drawn, and no legitimate defense of the distinction can be postulated, for the only goals to which it can be rationally related are constitutionally impermissible.

COMMITTEE, note 132 *supra*, at 74–95. Ely's position does not represent the law in the courts. See, *e.g.*, Johnson v. Branch, 364 F.2d 177 (4th Cir. 1966); Chambers v. Hendersonville Board of Education, 364 F.2d 189 (4th Cir. 1966). Given the vast number of subjective criteria by which teachers are evaluated, a school district will almost always be able to manufacture some plausible legitimate basis for not renewing a particular teacher's contract. (This makes me doubt whether, under Ely's own criteria, he has properly placed the decision under the disadvantageous distinction model. *Cf.* Ely, at 1244 n.124. See generally note 217 *infra*.)

211 *Cf.* Ely, at 1245, 1273–74. But *cf.* Kirstein v. University of Virginia, 309 F. Supp. 184 (E.D. Va. 1970). See generally note 217 *infra*.

212 For example, there is some evidence that "[i]n separate education fewer discipline problems . . . arise because the tendency of boys to 'show-off' for girls does not exist." Comment, note 132 *supra*, at 325. *Cf.* Ely, at 1336–38 (implying that the maintenance of discipline or order is a legitimate objective).

213 Ely, at 1274.

214 Encouraging only Caucasians to propagate is suspect, and the state could produce no compelling interests sufficient to justify the classification.

But courts have recognized that it is senseless to hold decisions to encourage or discourage various sorts of activity by taxing or spending distinctions up to a requirement of rational connection with an acceptable goal and that, therefore, the disadvantageous distinction model as a whole is useless in such contexts. The offensiveness of the classification must therefore be taken account of by some mode of review other than an *ab initio* demand for a legitimate defense.

By hypothesis the law on its face distinguishes in terms of race, and that undoubtedly would be all the Court would point to. But explicit racial terminology cannot be the *sine qua non* of unconstitutionality; a law granting the exemption to "the children of . . . [listing the names of all Caucasians and no one else]" would be just as obviously unconstitutional.

Nor would the infirmity be cured by sprinkling into such a list the names of a few non-Caucasians. The law's susceptibility to judicial review must therefore rest on either the fact that its *impact* is to treat white persons better than others, or the fact that it was enacted with the *motivation* of distinguishing on the basis of race.

. . . The argument is, in brief, that measures like a tax exemption for only Caucasian children must be unconstitutional; disadvantageous distinction cannot sensibly trigger review in such situations; and a test conditioning judicial review upon impact *per se* would be inconsistent with the Court's resolution not to compel those designing tax codes, or drawing up dress codes or deciding whom to prosecute, to take into account and attempt to "balance" the races of the likely gainers and losers.

I make no apology for the form of this argument. Starting from a clearly unconstitutional course of action—and I have trouble seeing the unconstitutionality of a tax exemption for only Caucasian children as a controversial assumption—and attempting to explain why it is unconstitutional in terms of a theory capable of acceptable and consistent application to other areas, is a perfectly sensible way of developing constitutional doctrine. But the victory of the motivational model in areas of discretionary choice, it must be said, is by default, in the sense that nothing said so far supports it except the unacceptability of the alternatives.[215]

---

[215] Ely, at 1249–50, 1262. This is not a complete legal argument of the usual sort. Ely points out a potential dislocation in the law (the unacceptability of holding the "Caucasians only" rule constitutionally valid) and supports judicial review of motivation only because it removes the dislocation by producing the "needed" result (*i.e.*, invalidation). But he concededly provides no intrinsic justification for the

As I read this argument, it does not merely reiterate the assertion—made with respect to the random choice model—that the courts should be willing to determine whether a decisionmaker is employing a covert operative criterion ("Caucasians only") and should subject the criterion, once it is found, to the demand for a legitimate defense. This is certainly correct, but it is trivial. Ely seems to be making the far more significant statement that the nonmotivational models of review cannot properly invalidate even an overt statutory enactment of the "Caucasians only" law: Since subsidies are in the class of "discretionary choices," the argument goes, the disadvantageous distinction cannot itself trigger review (and a racially disproportionate impact does not suffice to invalidate).

This argument is incorrect for two independent reasons. Recall, first, Ely's basis for concluding that the disadvantageous distinction model is inapplicable to subsidies: every choice would be upheld as relating to some legitimate goal, so that review would be a meaningless gesture.[216] But Ely's "Caucasians only" case is a counter-example which demonstrates that it is not always futile—not inevitably a "charade"—to require that "discretionary choices" be rationally justified: every once in a while one will come across a discretionary choice that cannot be related rationally to any legitimate goal (or subgoal).[217]

---

review of motivation. *Cf.* text *supra*, at notes 107–14; WASSERSTROM, THE JUDICIAL DECISION 25–29 (1961), which contrasts the process by which a court intuitively arrives at its result in a case (essentially what Ely has provided in the quoted excerpt) with the process of justifying the result.

The form of Ely's case for judicial review of motivation best explains the restrictions he places on the scope of such review. Ely, at 1269, 1274. Ely has created review of motivation to fill a particular need—the need for some review where effect does not invalidate and the disadvantageous distinction model is inapplicable. See Ely, at 1241, 1245, 1249. He therefore has limited review to the scope necessary to satisfy that need. But legal doctrines have a Frankensteinian aspect: they take on an existence of their own which is determined, not by the dislocation that engendered their creation, but by the intrinsic policies justifying their existence. *Cf.* BICKEL, note 2 *supra*, at 49–50 (discussing Professor Wechsler's "neutral principles"). Limiting the application of a legal doctrine to the need that engendered it is like limiting the use of a drug to the disease for whose cure it was discovered, when it cures other diseases as well; or—to use a more familiar analogy—like limiting a case "to its facts."

[216] See text supra, at notes 200–04.

[217] This calls into question the viability of the distinction between the disadvantageous distinction and discretionary choice models, at least where the challenged decision purports to serve a social or economic policy (as distinguished from an

Second, even if discretionary choices could never be evaluated by a "rationality" standard, this does not entail that they cannot meaningfully be subjected to the demand for an extraordinary justification, triggered by use of a suspect criterion, such as "Caucasians only." A court presented with a suspect operative rule does not stop at, or necessarily even begin with, the determination that the rule is rational. Rather, the court inquires into the substantive merits—into the wisdom—of the decision, to determine whether the objectives served by the rule are so important, and are served so well, given available alternatives, as to outweigh the rule's potential harmful effects.[218]

This is true even with respect to nonrational, aesthetic choices.

---

aesthetic end). *Cf.* also Ely, at 1309–10 and n.313. Because this distinction is not germane to the analysis of motivation developed in this article, I shall not take it up at any length. But it raises interesting and complex problems with implications beyond the issue of motivation. Almost every politically conceivable decision would be upheld if it were reviewed under the rationality standard. But how do we know whether a decision would be upheld (*a*) because it is in fact rationally related to a legitimate purpose or (*b*) because it is a decision of the sort which inevitably will be upheld because it "import[s] its own acceptable goal," and which, therefore, should be placed in the category of "discretionary choices"? *Id.* at 1247. How in other words, can we tell whether the decisionmaker's proffered objective is a "real" objective, or merely a "subgoal rationalization"? See *id.* at 1272. Why, for example, are the promotion of safety, see Railway Express Agency v. New York, 336 U.S. 106 (1949), the protection of morals, see Goesaert v. Cleary, 335 U.S. 464 (1948), and the prevention of "commercialization" of a profession, see Williamson v. Lee Optical Co., 348 U.S. 483 (1955), real objectives rather than mere subgoal rationalizations that are better viewed "as one umbrella goal, the promotion of the general welfare"? Ely, at 1248. Ely has done an important service in pointing out that some sort of a distinction exists. But, perhaps because he has defined his models ostensibly and operationally rather than connotatively, and possibly because that is the only way they can be defined, further analysis is needed.

218 Almost immediately following the "Caucasians only" argument, Ely seems to make the same point that I have made in the text: "[A]n inability to evaluate the rationality of a criterion of choice imports no paralysis with regard to the Constitution's other limitations. If, therefore, the principle of selection employed by the decisionmakers can be identified, there is no reason why judges should refrain from measuring that principle, not in terms of rationality, but rather against the other commands of the Constitution. Political judgments concerning the promotion of the general welfare may not be amenable to rational evaluation by courts, but some such judgments—that the general welfare would be served by the separation of the races or by the conversion of everyone to Christianity—constitute constitutionally impermissible criteria of choice." Ely, at 1262–63. But see *id.* at 1236–37, 1252–54, 1281–82, 1300 n.282. Why then is an inquiry into motivation necessary to invalidate a statute providing a tax exemption for Caucasian children? Surely, the Equal Protection Clause renders "the propagation of the white race" as impermissible an objective as the First Amendment renders "the conversion of everyone to Christianity."

For example, if a high school principal seats black and white pupils on different sides of the graduation stage, for purely visual aesthetic reasons, the court is not put to the choice of determining the "rationality" of the decision or disputing his good intentions or abstaining. Rather, the court would, most probably, hold that whatever the aesthetic benefits gained, they cannot overcome the potential harm from purposive separation by race.[219] Similarly, perhaps *a fortiori*, a court would properly subject Ely's suspect "Caucasians only" tax exemption to the demand for extraordinary justification, which it could not meet.[220]

C. THE LIMITED SCOPE OF REVIEW

If the "Caucasians only" case is handled adequately by non-motivational modes of review, there nonetheless remain a variety of official decisions which should be and can only be invalidated by recourse to motivation. These include rationally justifiable decisions subject to the disadvantageous distinction model, as well as "discretionary choices."[221] Under Ely's doctrine, however, review of motivation is only appropriate in the latter cases; and a rational justification will protect an illicitly motivated decision from invalidation.

Why, however, should the Constitution be more solicitous of decisions that are subject to the disadvantageous distinction model and that meet the rationality requirement than of discretionary choices that are nonrational or are relatable only to an "umbrella" goal? Ely does not suggest that the harm to the complainant is any greater in one class of cases than the other. And if there is a noncircular answer,[222] it lies in differences with respect to ascertainability, futility, and disutility—matters to which Ely devotes some consideration.

1. *Ascertainability*. The fact that a rule is rationally related to a

---

[219] This is not to say that the court would necessarily strike down every racial classification based on an aesthetic judgment. Probably the court would permit the assignment of roles by race in a school play in which the race of particular characters was significant. *Cf.* Civil Rights Act of 1964, § 703(e).

[220] The point made in the text is not limited to race cases. For example, although matters of municipal economy and convenience may be beyond judicial evaluation under a "rationality" standard, a court would properly weigh these factors in reviewing a municipality's decision regulating the time, place, or duration of a large public assembly. See Blasi, note 181 *supra*, at 1489–92.

[221] See text *supra*, at notes 206–10.   [222] *Cf.* Ely, at 1274.

legitimate objective, Ely asserts, makes it virtually impossible to infer that it was designed to serve an illicit objective. By contrast, the inference of unconstitutional motivation "can sometimes be quite responsibly drawn" where the only available "justification" for the decision is in terms of a discretionary subgoal or an aesthetic preference.[223] By way of illustration, Ely provides two examples of disadvantageous distinction cases—a school district's adoption of the "overcoat" rule, and a state's adoption of a voting literacy test. "It would in all likelihood be impossible responsibly to conclude that a school principal's requirement of coats in winter was racially motivated," because the regulation is rationally related to the promotion of health.[224] Similarly, the literacy test could be invalidated only "on a record of a sort which will never exist or [by] a judge hell-bent on invalidation."[225]

These assertions do not seem obviously correct. Where the school district has not previously had health regulations of this sort, where the district has strenuously resisted desegregation and adopts the overcoat regulation soon after it is ordered to desegregate, and where the impact of the regulation is to exclude many black but few white children from the school system, it would seem quite responsible to conclude that the regulation was designed to have that impact. If it can be shown that the health benefits are marginal, the inference is, *pro tanto*, stronger.[226] And where a state has long tolerated the registration of white illiterates, and adopts a literacy test only after a court orders it to cease discriminating against black applicants, the inference of a racially discriminatory motivation seems equally proper.[227]

Of course, illicit motivation may often be difficult to prove with adequate certainty, and it may even be true (though it is not self-evident) that illicit motivation is more difficult to establish where a true rational justification is available than in other cases. But these are not reasons for refusing to act on a finding of improper motivation in those, albeit few, cases where it is adequately established.[228]

---

223 *Id*. at 1278–79.

224 *Id*. at 1279.

225 *Id*. at 1278.

226 See note 132 *supra*.

227 See cases cited note 133 *supra*.

228 "Of course, courts should 'eschew guesswork' in constitutional adjudication, as elsewhere. That resolution argues, however, for non-intervention when the proof

2. *Futility*. If a rationally defensible law is invalidated on the ground that it was illicitly motivated, the decisionmaker can fabricate a legislative history for reenactment, purporting to demonstrate that this time he considered only legitimate objectives. "When, however, the only articulable alternative explanation for an unconstitutionally motivated choice is . . . a judgment of taste, the likelihood of a futile judicial order, though it cannot be discounted, is substantially lessened."[229]

Reenactment of a law previously voided because of the decisionmaker's motivation does pose the problem to which Ely alludes. But it is not apparent that it poses a greater problem for one class of cases than the other. Readoption of a once-invalidated (discretionary choice) decision terminating school-sponsored social events, for example, is not inherently more, or less, suspicious than readoption of a once-voided (disadvantageous distinction) overcoat regulation.

3. *Disutility*

> Should proof of unconstitutional motivation be held either automatically to invalidate the choices it has produced, or to place on the state some burden of justification over and above the ordinary demand for a legitimately defensible difference, . . . [the Court's] fear of the invalidation of laws which measure up to the Constitution's usual test of legitimacy would be fulfilled. If, however, motivation is limited to the burden-triggering role implied by the considerations which support its cognizability, only those choices which are not supportable in terms of a legitimately defensible difference will fall. Proof of illegitimate motivation will function only to deny the government a privilege of non-justification which, owing to the peculiar nature of the area of choice involved, it would otherwise be able to invoke.[230]

The first point is largely correct. Judicial review of motivation may invalidate a rule that meets all other, nonmotivational, constitutional standards of review; that is what it is designed to do. The second point is misleading. Proof of illicit motivation in discretionary choice cases does not merely deny the government "a privilege of nonjustification." It prevents the government from

---

of motivation is less than clear and not necessarily for a total rejection of its relevance." Ely, at 1212.

[229] *Id.* at 1280.   [230] *Ibid.*

making rational—though perhaps not rationally reviewable—decisions which members of the community might desire for legitimate reasons and which might be conducive to the society's welfare. If the quotation implies that discretionary choices are less worthy of judicial respect than decisions subject to the disadvantageous distinction model, it is simply incorrect.[231]

---

[231] Many allocative decisions, for example, are as vital to the well-being of a society, and affect the behavior of individuals and enterprises as much as regulatory schemes that are subject to the disadvantageous distinction model. To approve a decision under the rationality standard, on the other hand, is to say nothing about its net utility or desirability. A regulation may impose great burdens on some persons with little benefits to others. But so long as it is positively (however weakly) related to a conceivable legitimate purpose (however trivial), it passes scrutiny. "[T]o call a statute constitutional is no more of a compliment than it is to say that it is not intolerable. In the eyes of the Court, constitutionality is as low a standard of legislative and political morals as we could have, and yet have any at all." Curtis, *A Modern Supreme Court in a Modern World*, 4 VAND. L. REV. 427, 433 (1951).